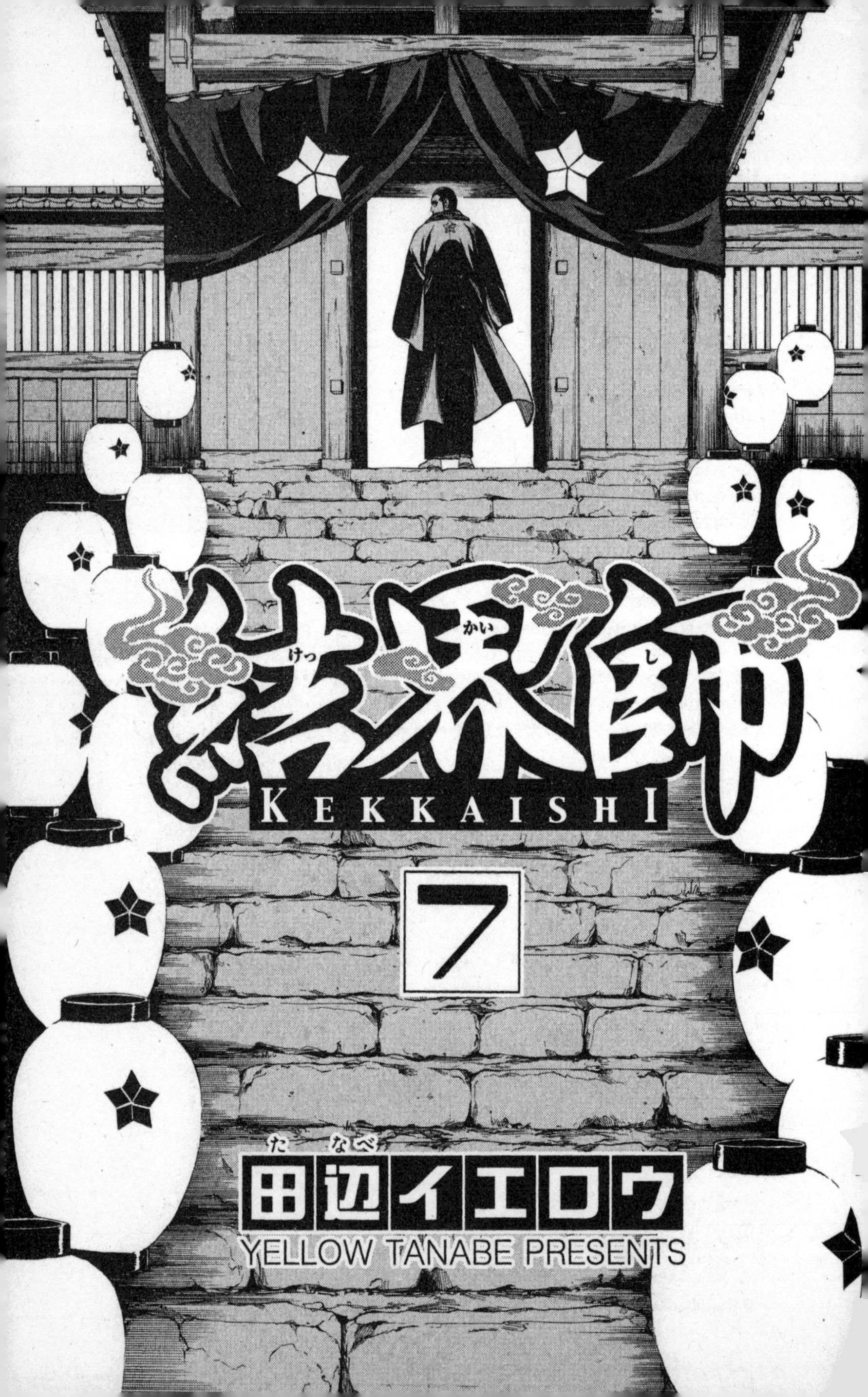
結界師
けっかいし
KEKKAISHI
7
田辺イエロウ
たなべ
YELLOW TANABE PRESENTS

The Story Thus Far

Yoshimori Sumimura and Tokine Yukimura have a special mission, passed down through their families for generations—to protect Karasumori forest from supernatural beings called *ayakashi*. People with this gift for terminating ayakashi are called *kekkaishi*, or barrier masters.

One day, an *ayakashi* perfectly disguised as a man enters the Karasumori site. After a violent encounter with him, Yoshimori and Tokine worry that more such *ayakashi* may soon begin intruding.

A few days later, a boy named Gen Shishio arrives; he has been sent by the mysterious "Shadow Organization" to assist the Karasumori kekkaishi. Gen, who possesses some ayakashi powers, is awkward around Masamori, Yoshimori's big brother, because he idolizes him.

Meanwhile, a secret organization with evil intentions awaits an opportunity to seize the Karasumori site...

KEKKAISHI VOL. 7
TABLE OF CONTENTS

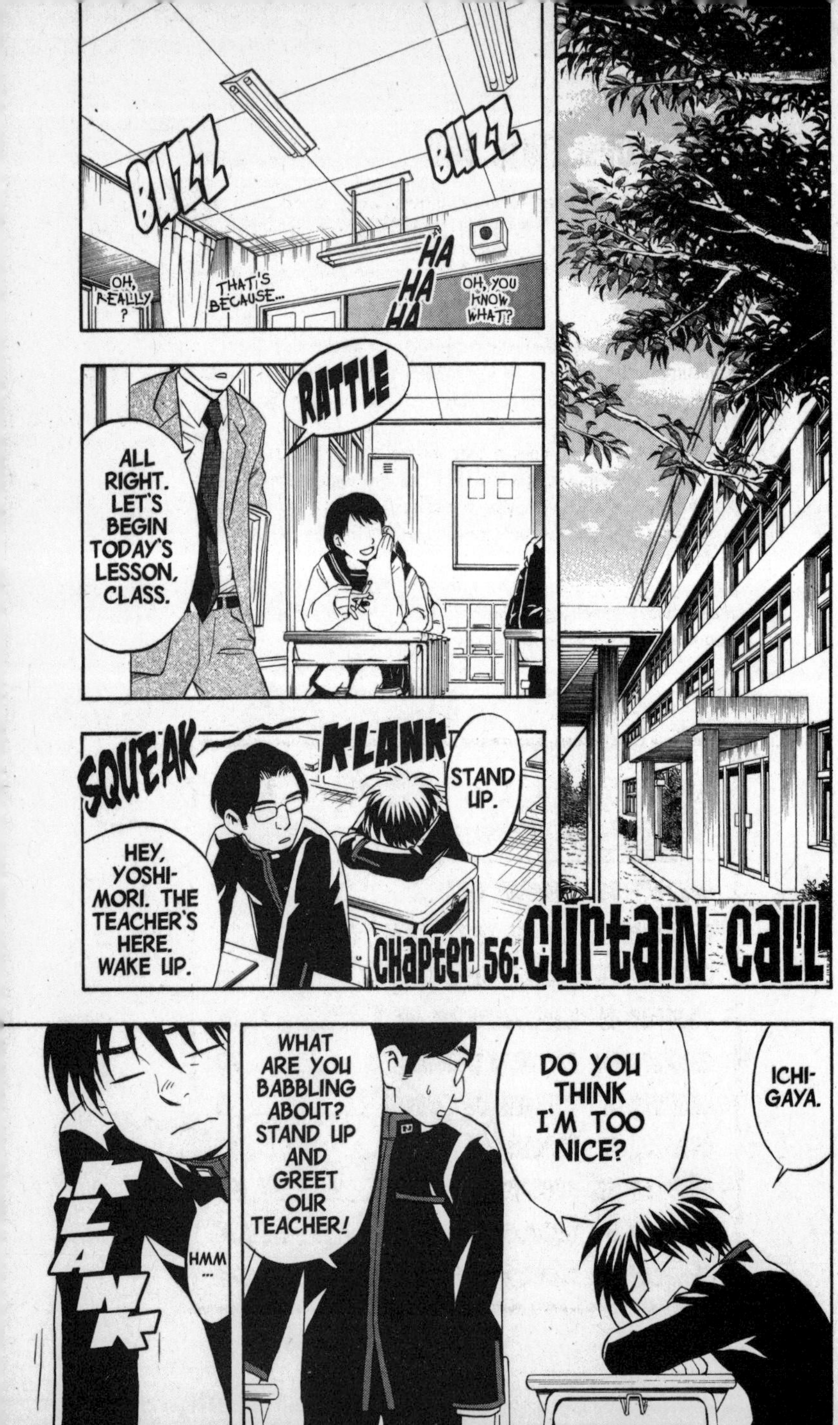

BUZZ
BUZZ
HA HA HA
OH, YOU KNOW WHAT?
THAT'S BECAUSE...
OH, REALLY?
RATTLE
ALL RIGHT. LET'S BEGIN TODAY'S LESSON, CLASS.
STAND UP.
KLANK
SQUEAK
HEY, YOSHIMORI. THE TEACHER'S HERE. WAKE UP.
Chapter 56: Curtain Call
ICHIGAYA.
DO YOU THINK I'M TOO NICE?
WHAT ARE YOU BABBLING ABOUT? STAND UP AND GREET OUR TEACHER!
HMM...
KLANK

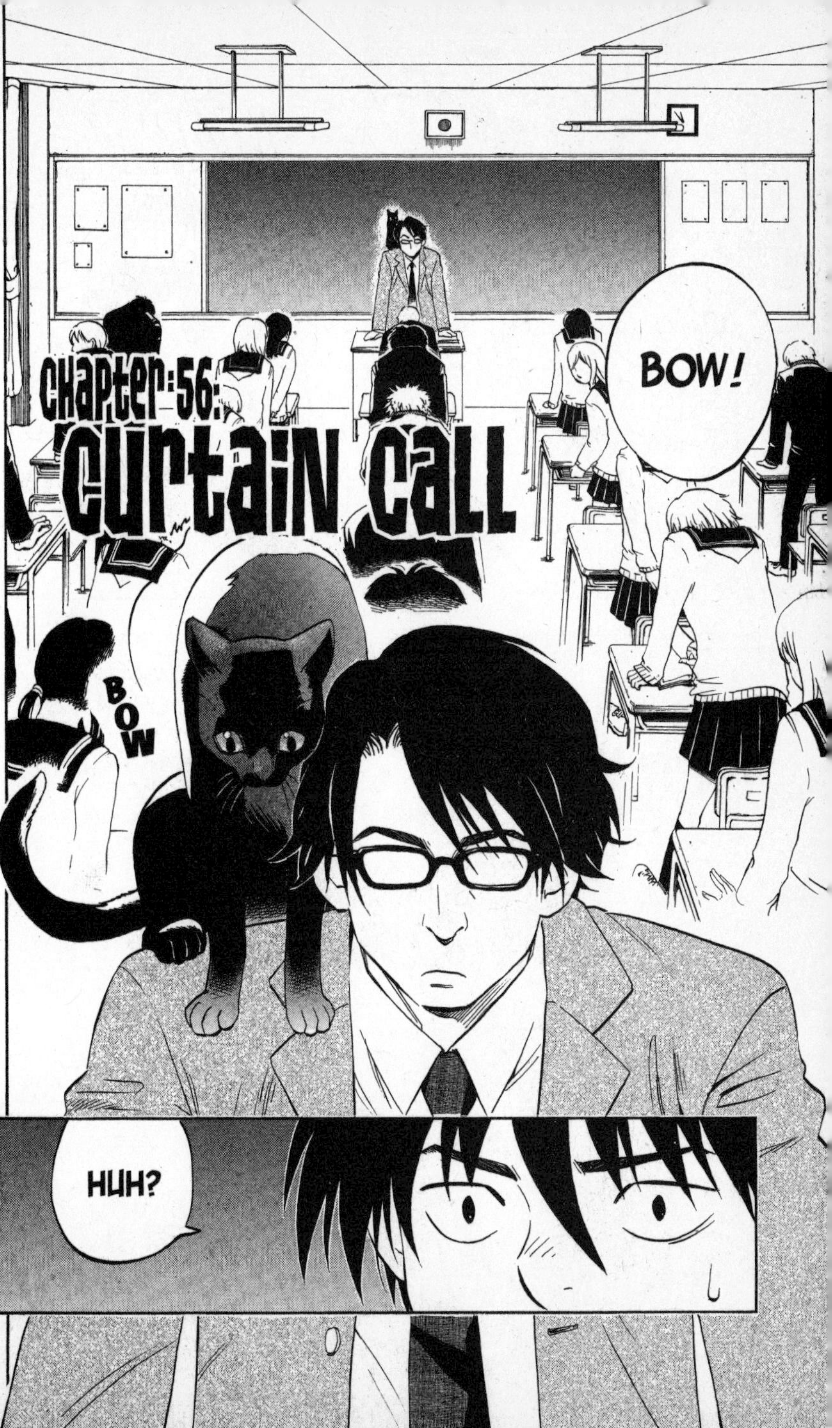
BOW!
CHAPTER 56: CURTAIN CALL
BOW
HUH?

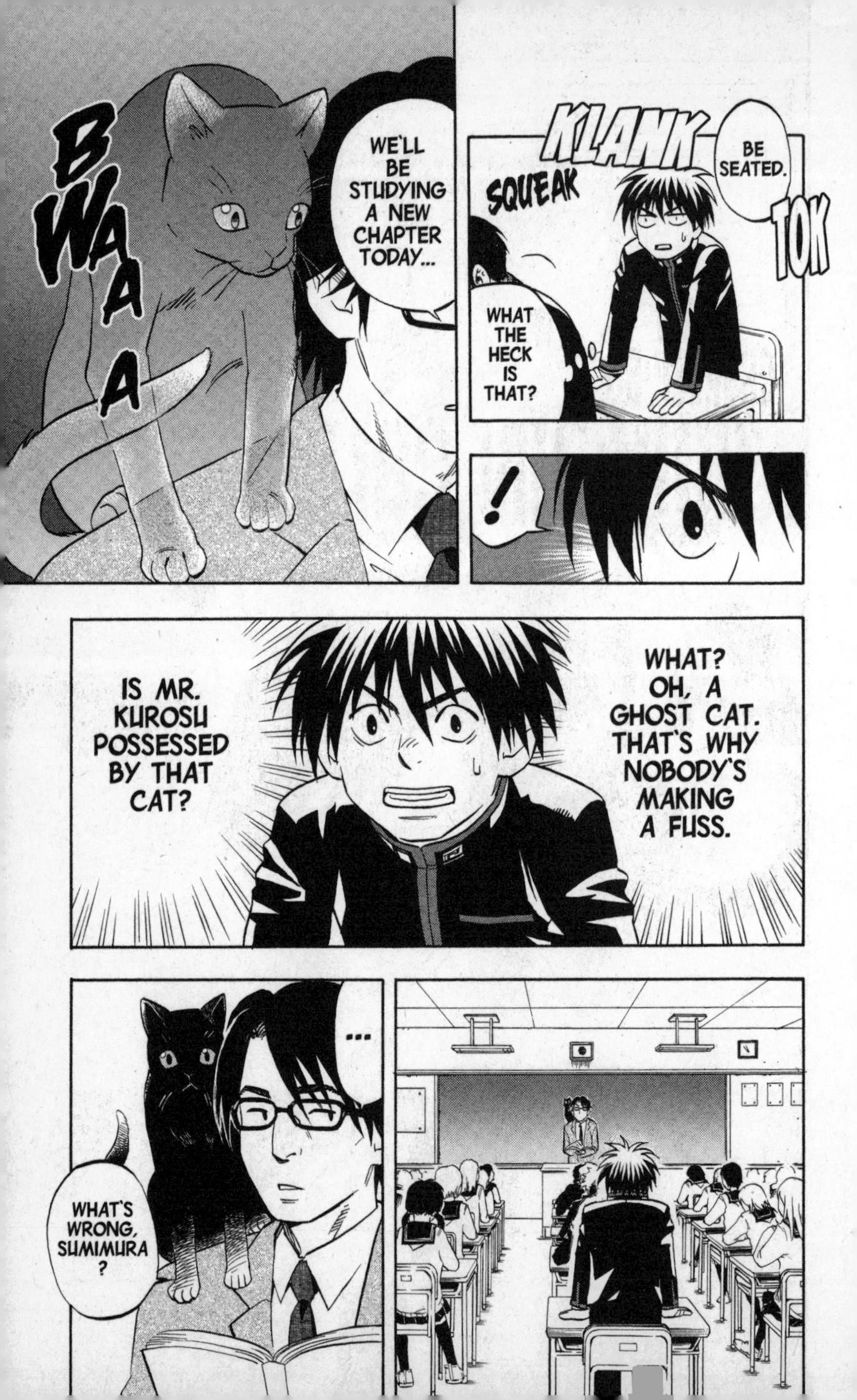
BE SEATED.
KLANK
TOK
SQUEAK
WHAT THE HECK IS THAT?
!
WE'LL BE STUDYING A NEW CHAPTER TODAY...
BWAAAA
WHAT? OH, A GHOST CAT. THAT'S WHY NOBODY'S MAKING A FUSS.
IS MR. KUROSU POSSESSED BY THAT CAT?
...
WHAT'S WRONG, SUMIMURA?

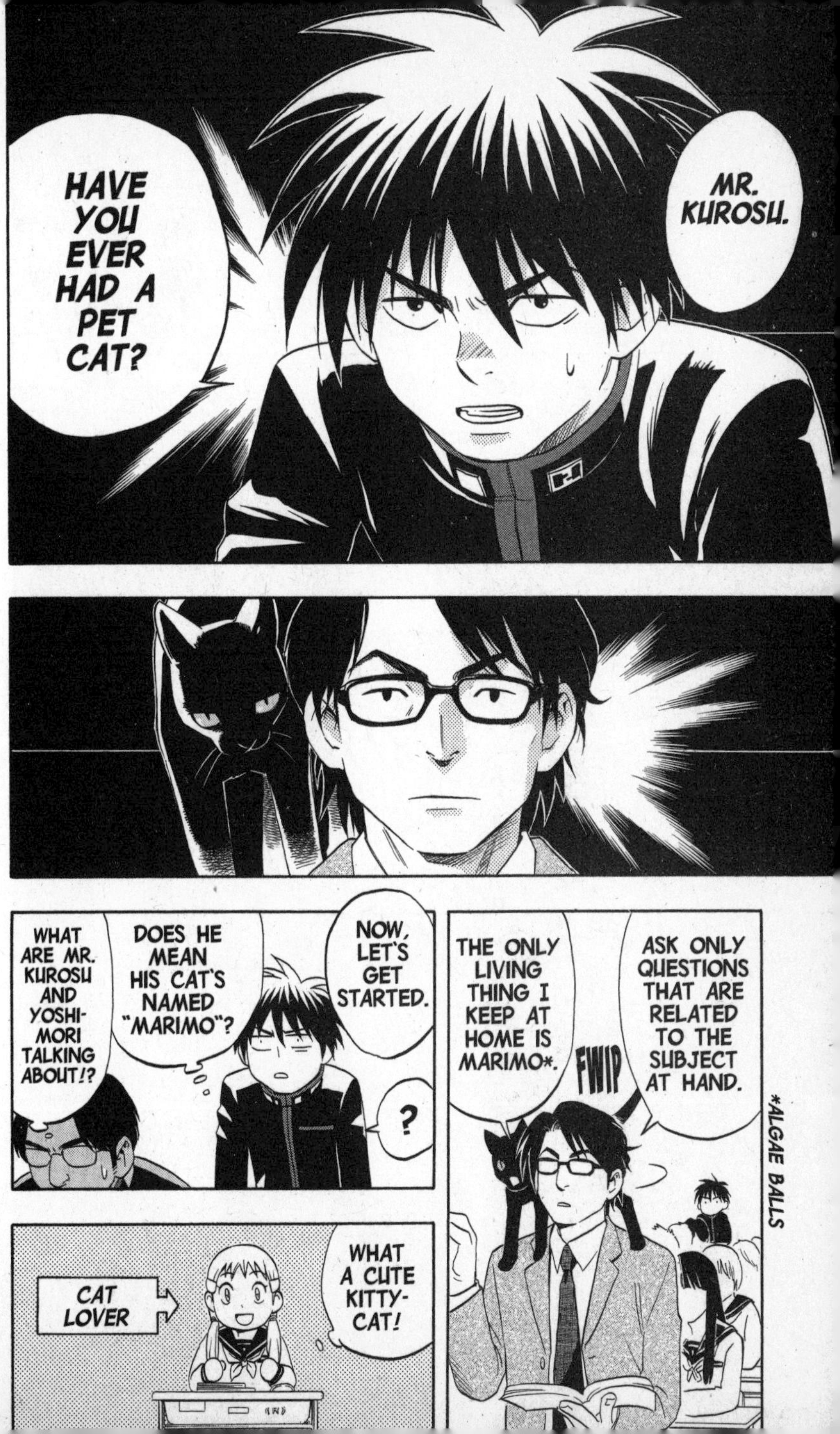
MR. KUROSU.
HAVE YOU EVER HAD A PET CAT?
ASK ONLY QUESTIONS THAT ARE RELATED TO THE SUBJECT AT HAND.
FWIP
THE ONLY LIVING THING I KEEP AT HOME IS MARIMO*.
NOW, LET'S GET STARTED.
?
DOES HE MEAN HIS CAT'S NAMED "MARIMO"?
WHAT ARE MR. KUROSU AND YOSHIMORI TALKING ABOUT!?
WHAT A CUTE KITTY-CAT!
CAT LOVER

*ALGAE BALLS

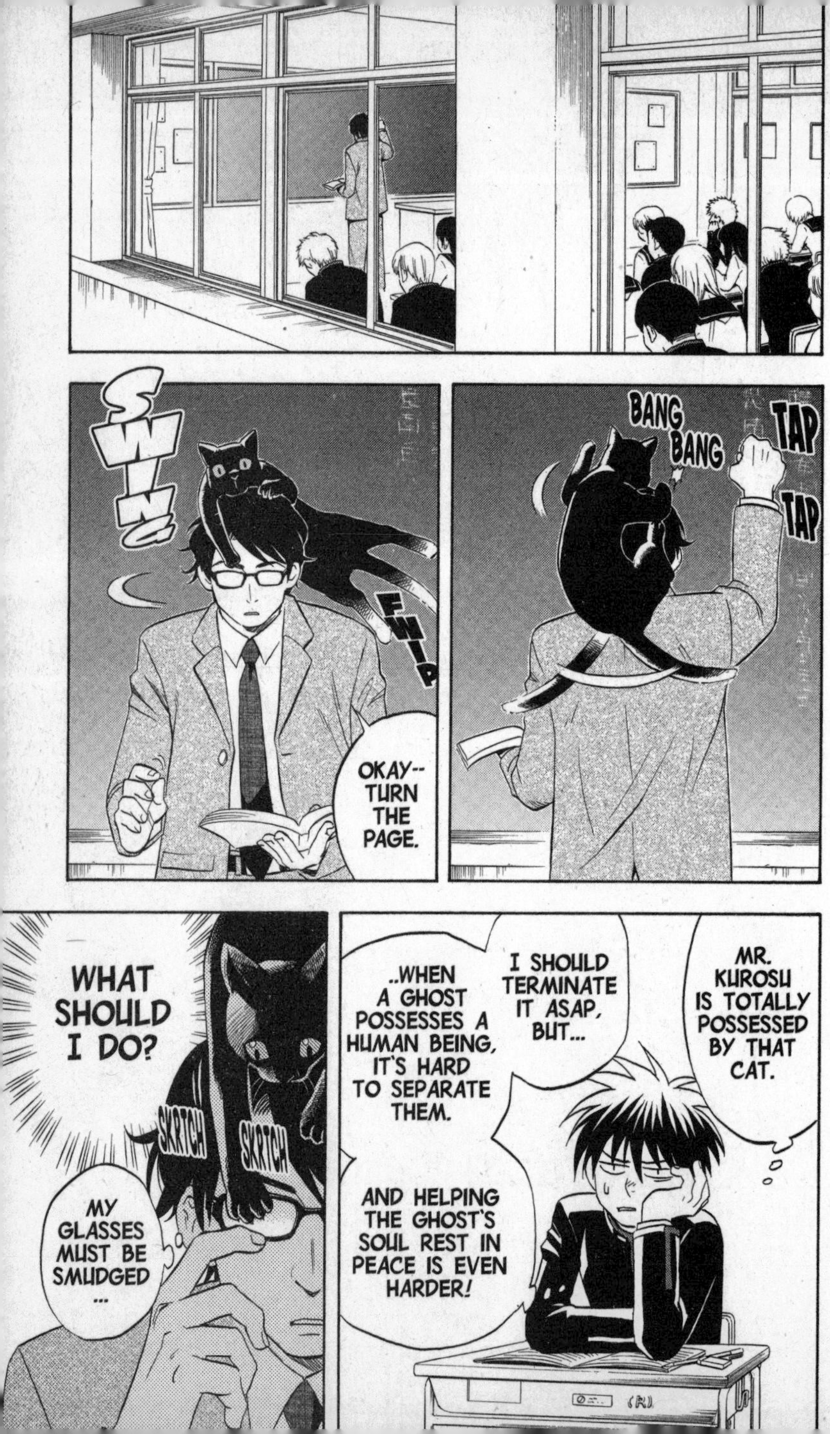
BANG
BANG
TAP
TAP
SWING
FWIP
OKAY-- TURN THE PAGE.
MR. KUROSU IS TOTALLY POSSESSED BY THAT CAT.
I SHOULD TERMINATE IT ASAP, BUT...
..WHEN A GHOST POSSESSES A HUMAN BEING, IT'S HARD TO SEPARATE THEM.
AND HELPING THE GHOST'S SOUL REST IN PEACE IS EVEN HARDER!
WHAT SHOULD I DO?
SKRTCH
SKRTCH
MY GLASSES MUST BE SMUDGED ...

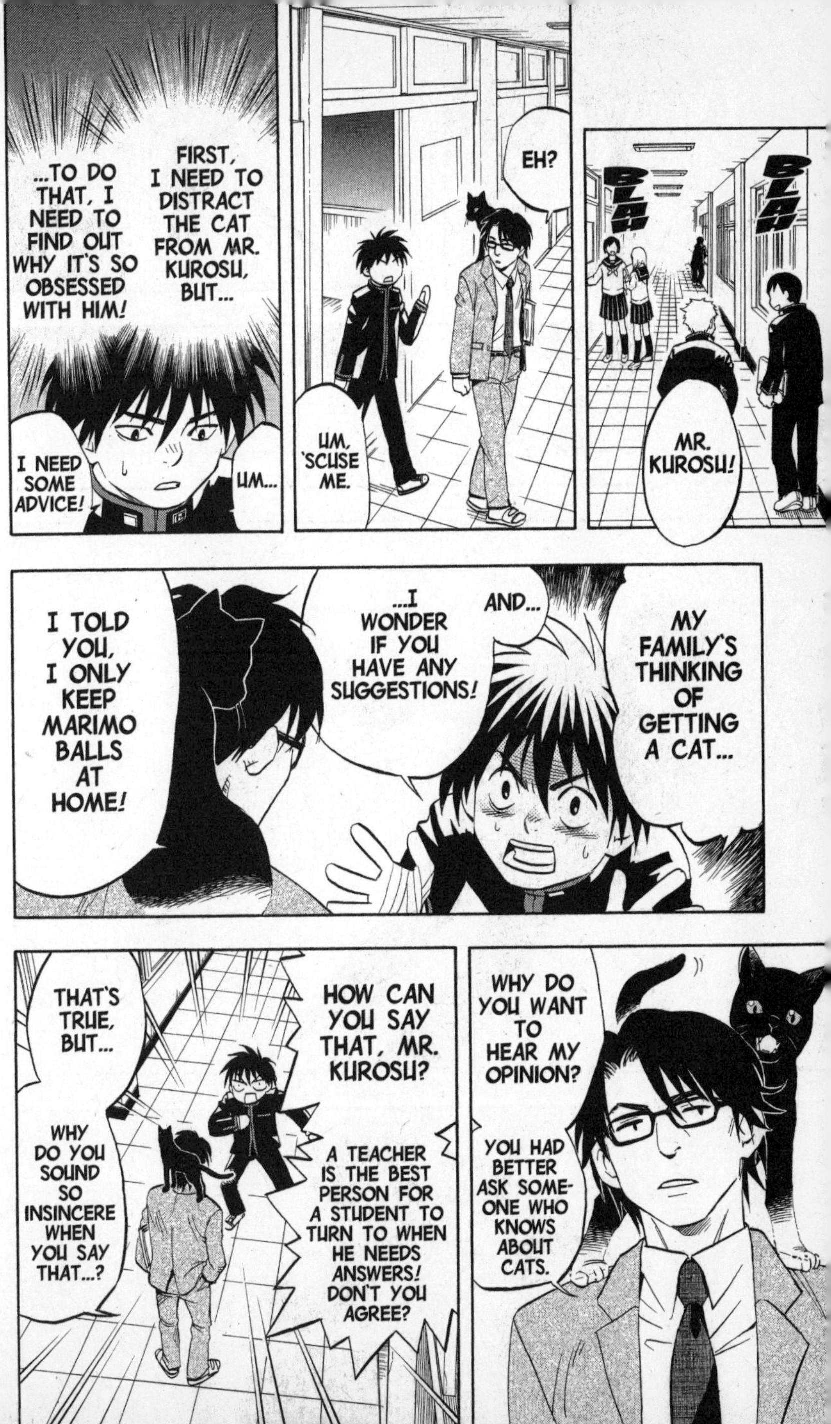
BLA BLA
MR. KUROSU!
EH?
UM, 'SCUSE ME.
FIRST, I NEED TO DISTRACT THE CAT FROM MR. KUROSU, BUT...
...TO DO THAT, I NEED TO FIND OUT WHY IT'S SO OBSESSED WITH HIM!
UM...
I NEED SOME ADVICE!
MY FAMILY'S THINKING OF GETTING A CAT...
AND...
...I WONDER IF YOU HAVE ANY SUGGESTIONS!
I TOLD YOU, I ONLY KEEP MARIMO BALLS AT HOME!
WHY DO YOU WANT TO HEAR MY OPINION?
YOU HAD BETTER ASK SOME-ONE WHO KNOWS ABOUT CATS.
HOW CAN YOU SAY THAT, MR. KUROSU?
THAT'S TRUE, BUT...
A TEACHER IS THE BEST PERSON FOR A STUDENT TO TURN TO WHEN HE NEEDS ANSWERS! DON'T YOU AGREE?
WHY DO YOU SOUND SO INSINCERE WHEN YOU SAY THAT...?

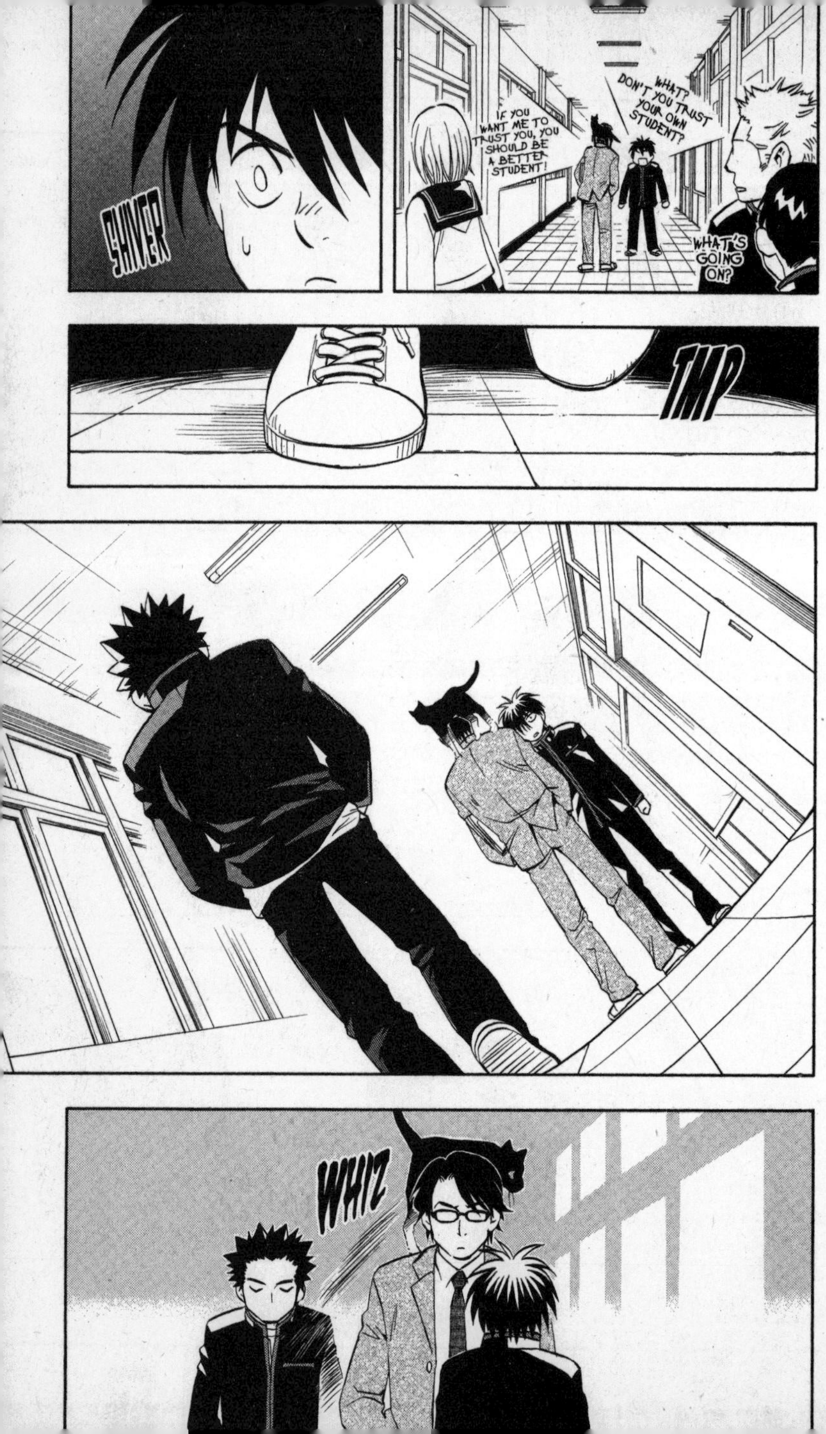
WHAT? DON'T YOU TRUST YOUR OWN STUDENT?
IF YOU WANT ME TO TRUST YOU, YOU SHOULD BE A BETTER STUDENT!
WHAT'S GOING ON?
SHIVER
TMP
WHIZ

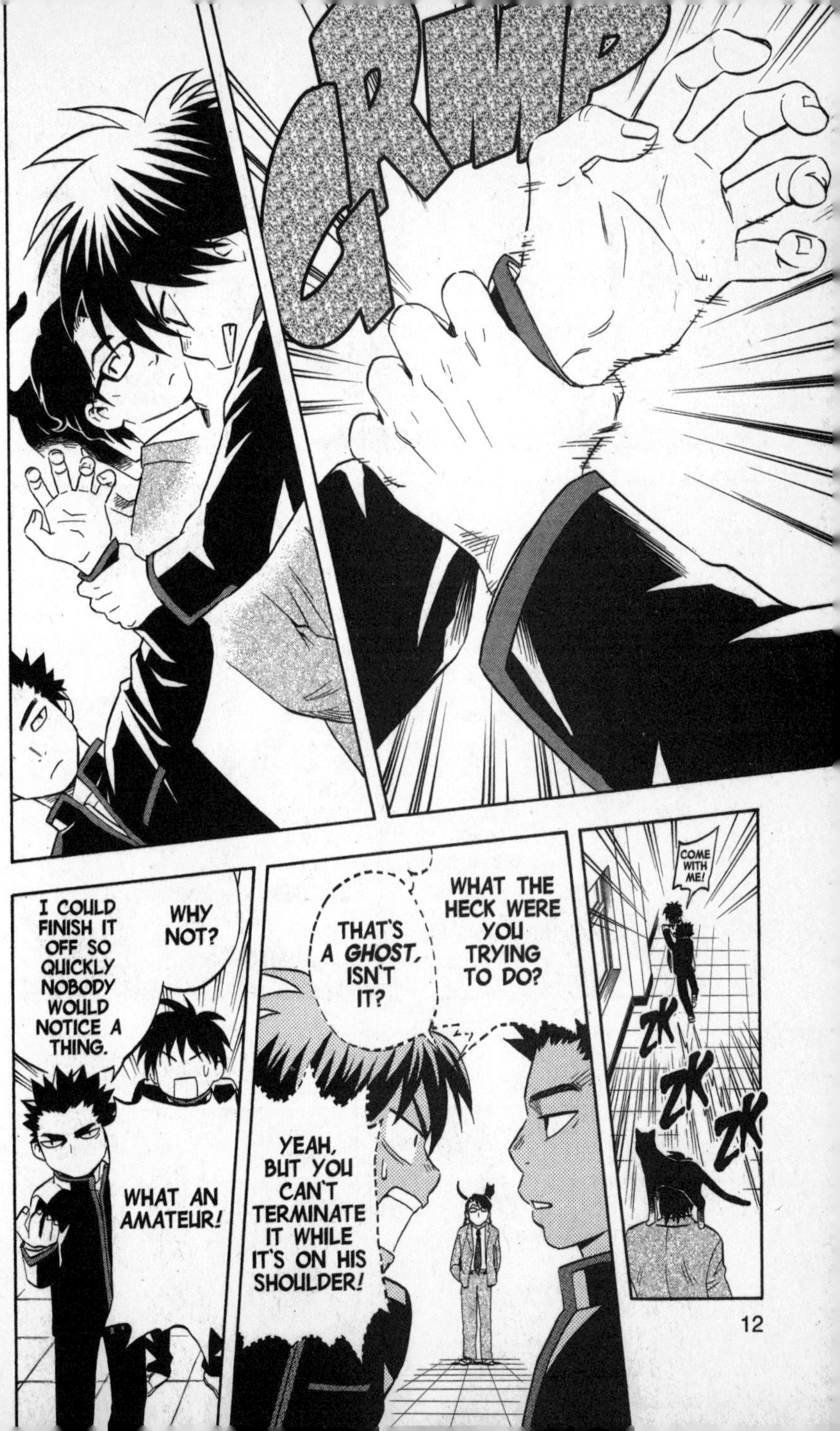
CRUMP
COME WITH ME!
ZK
ZK
ZK
WHAT THE HECK WERE YOU TRYING TO DO?
THAT'S A *GHOST*, ISN'T IT?
YEAH, BUT YOU CAN'T TERMINATE IT WHILE IT'S ON HIS SHOULDER!
WHY NOT?
I COULD FINISH IT OFF SO QUICKLY NOBODY WOULD NOTICE A THING.
WHAT AN AMATEUR!

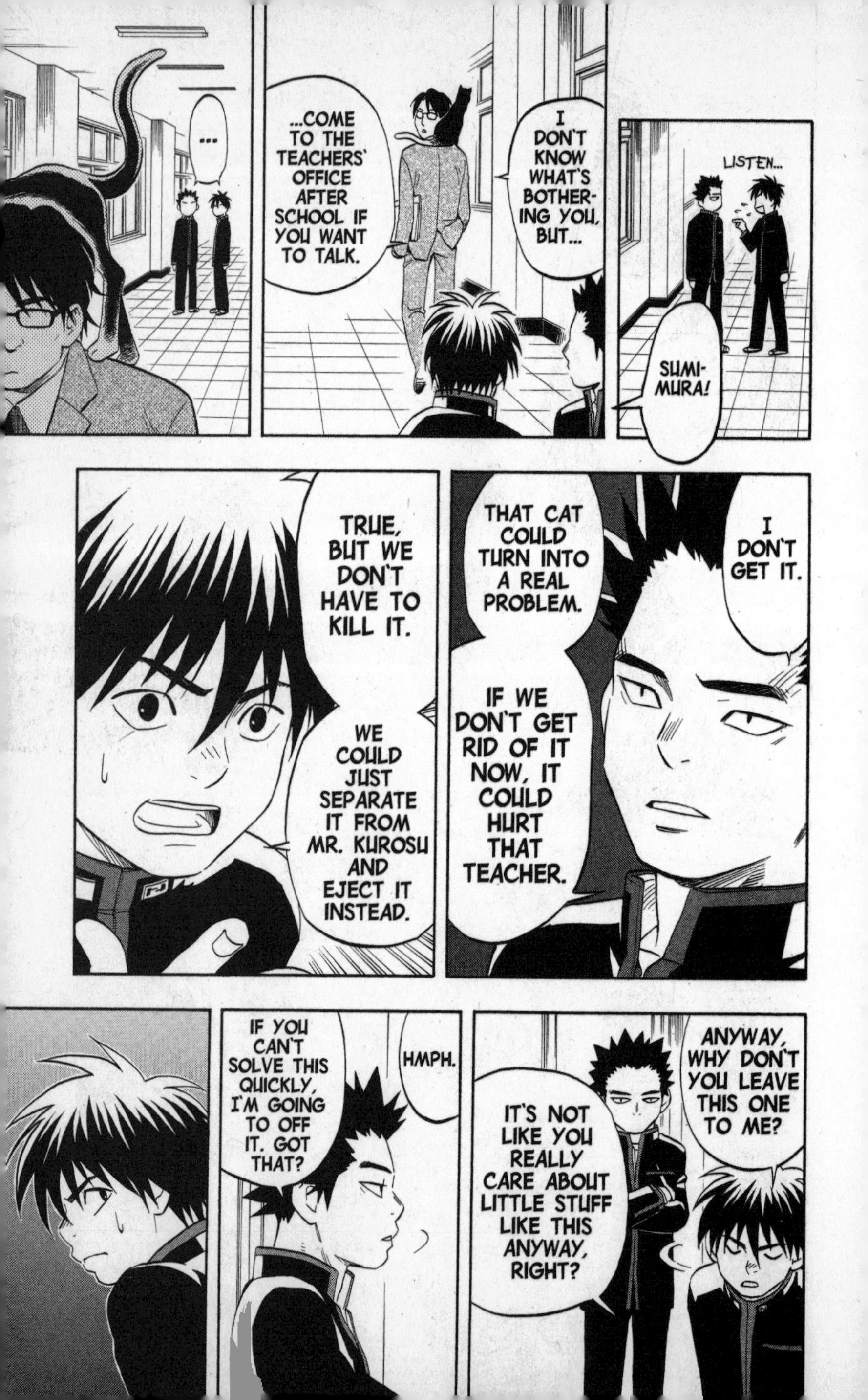
LISTEN...
SUMIMURA!
I DON'T KNOW WHAT'S BOTHERING YOU, BUT...
...COME TO THE TEACHERS' OFFICE AFTER SCHOOL IF YOU WANT TO TALK.
...
I DON'T GET IT.
THAT CAT COULD TURN INTO A REAL PROBLEM.
IF WE DON'T GET RID OF IT NOW, IT COULD HURT THAT TEACHER.
TRUE, BUT WE DON'T HAVE TO KILL IT.
WE COULD JUST SEPARATE IT FROM MR. KUROSU AND EJECT IT INSTEAD.
ANYWAY, WHY DON'T YOU LEAVE THIS ONE TO ME?
IT'S NOT LIKE YOU REALLY CARE ABOUT LITTLE STUFF LIKE THIS ANYWAY, RIGHT?
HMPH.
IF YOU CAN'T SOLVE THIS QUICKLY, I'M GOING TO OFF IT. GOT THAT?

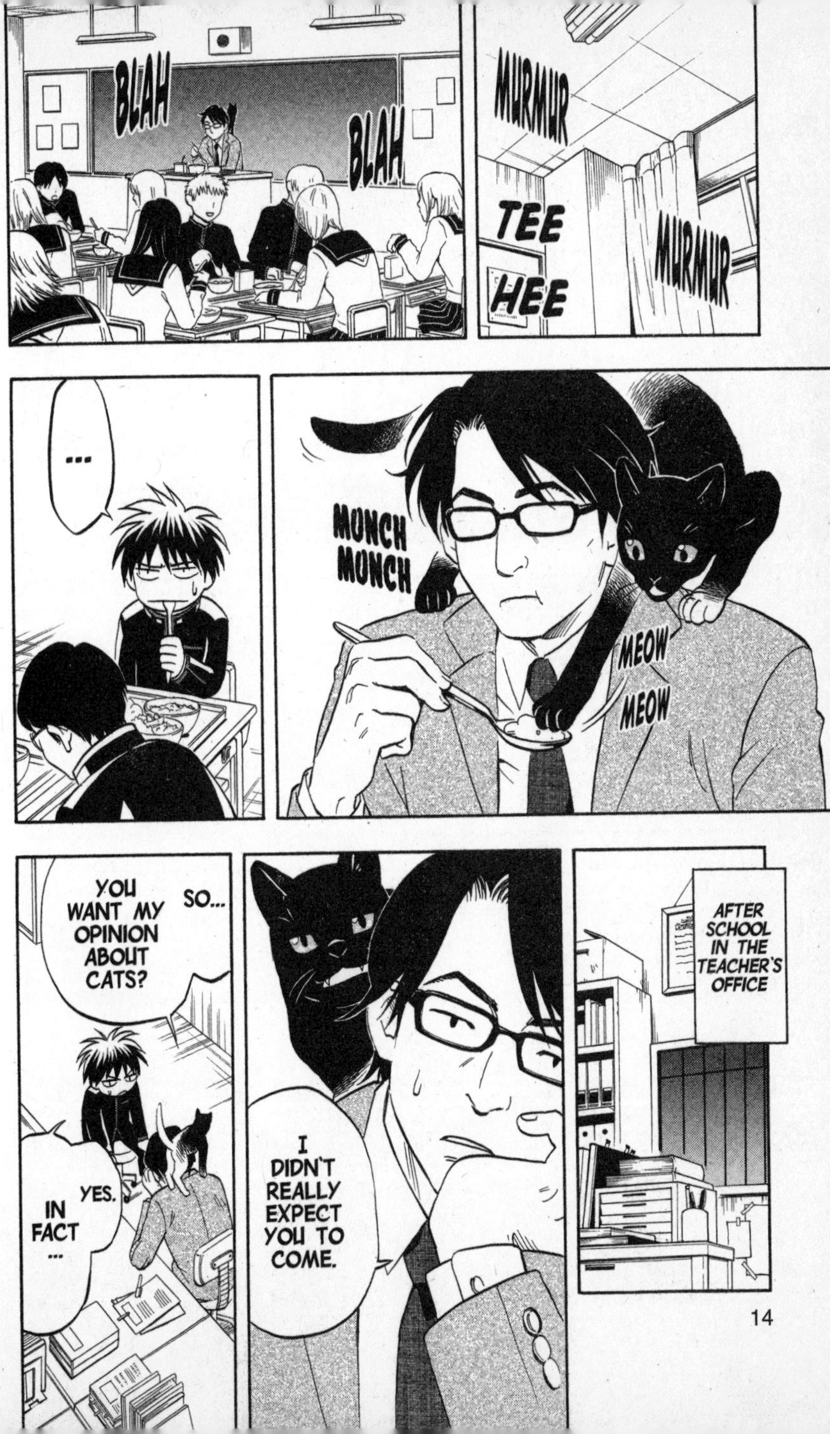
MURMUR
TEE HEE
MURMUR
BLAH
BLAH
MUNCH MUNCH
MEOW MEOW
...
AFTER SCHOOL IN THE TEACHER'S OFFICE
I DIDN'T REALLY EXPECT YOU TO COME.
SO...
YOU WANT MY OPINION ABOUT CATS?
YES.
IN FACT ...

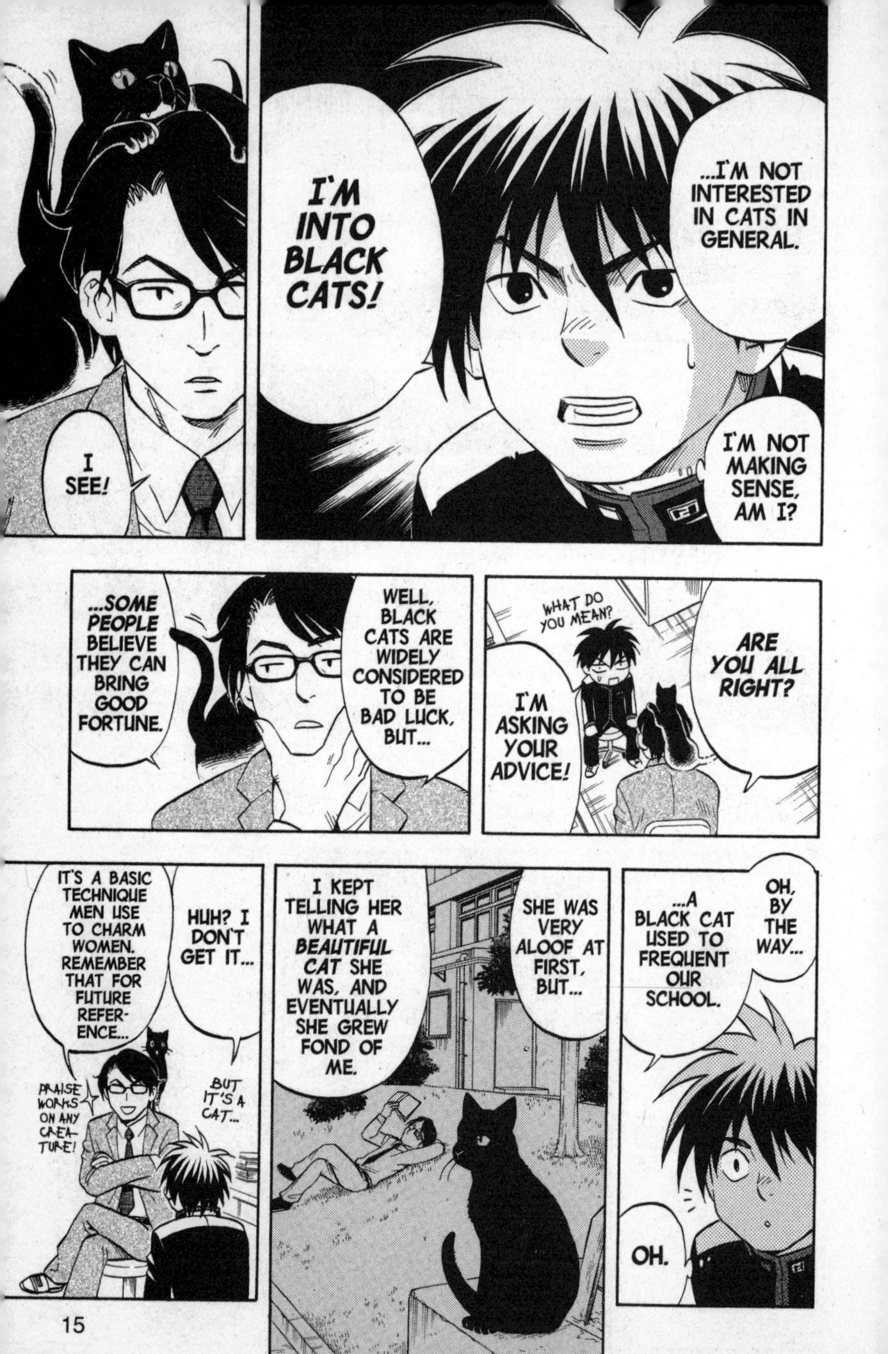

...I'M NOT INTERESTED IN CATS IN GENERAL.
I'M INTO BLACK CATS!
I'M NOT MAKING SENSE, AM I?
I SEE!
ARE YOU ALL RIGHT?
WHAT DO YOU MEAN?
I'M ASKING YOUR ADVICE!
WELL, BLACK CATS ARE WIDELY CONSIDERED TO BE BAD LUCK, BUT...
...SOME PEOPLE BELIEVE THEY CAN BRING GOOD FORTUNE.
OH, BY THE WAY...
...A BLACK CAT USED TO FREQUENT OUR SCHOOL.
OH.
SHE WAS VERY ALOOF AT FIRST, BUT...
I KEPT TELLING HER WHAT A BEAUTIFUL CAT SHE WAS, AND EVENTUALLY SHE GREW FOND OF ME.
HUH? I DON'T GET IT...
IT'S A BASIC TECHNIQUE MEN USE TO CHARM WOMEN. REMEMBER THAT FOR FUTURE REFERENCE...
BUT IT'S A CAT...
PRAISE WORKS ON ANY CREATURE!

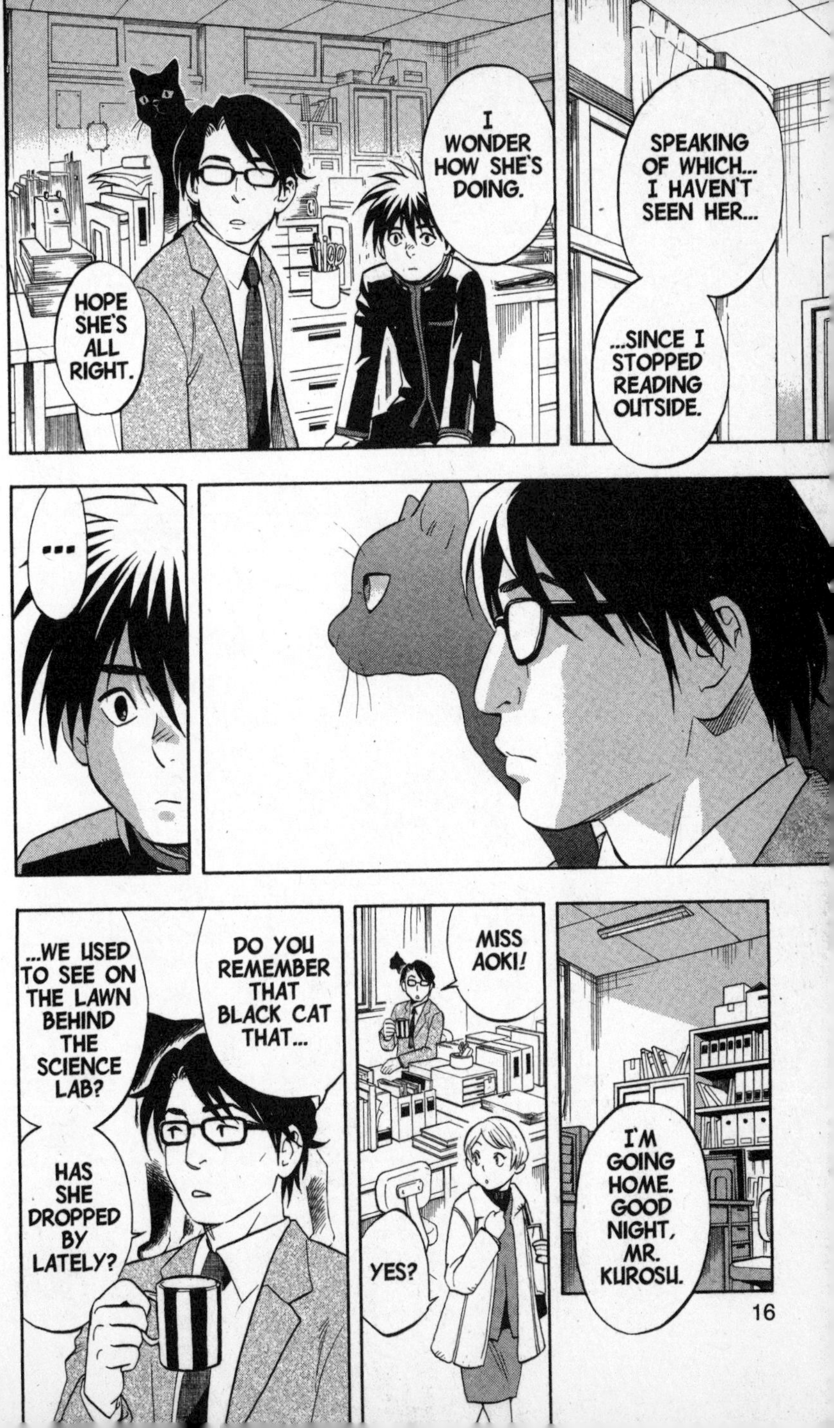
SPEAKING OF WHICH... I HAVEN'T SEEN HER...
...SINCE I STOPPED READING OUTSIDE.
I WONDER HOW SHE'S DOING.
HOPE SHE'S ALL RIGHT.
...
I'M GOING HOME. GOOD NIGHT, MR. KUROSU.
MISS AOKI!
YES?
DO YOU REMEMBER THAT BLACK CAT THAT...
...WE USED TO SEE ON THE LAWN BEHIND THE SCIENCE LAB?
HAS SHE DROPPED BY LATELY?

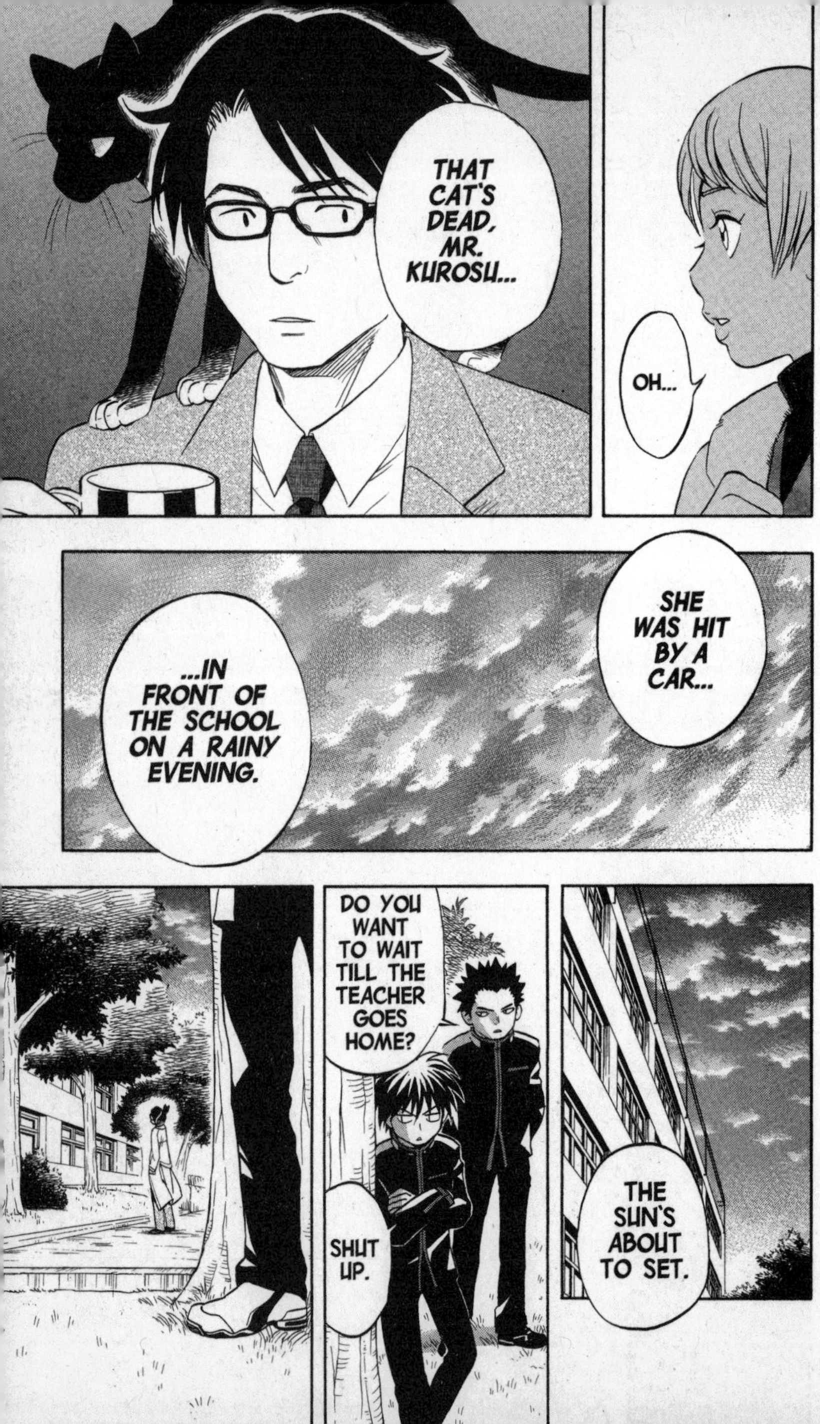
OH...
THAT CAT'S DEAD, MR. KUROSU...
SHE WAS HIT BY A CAR...
...IN FRONT OF THE SCHOOL ON A RAINY EVENING.
THE SUN'S ABOUT TO SET.
DO YOU WANT TO WAIT TILL THE TEACHER GOES HOME?
SHUT UP.

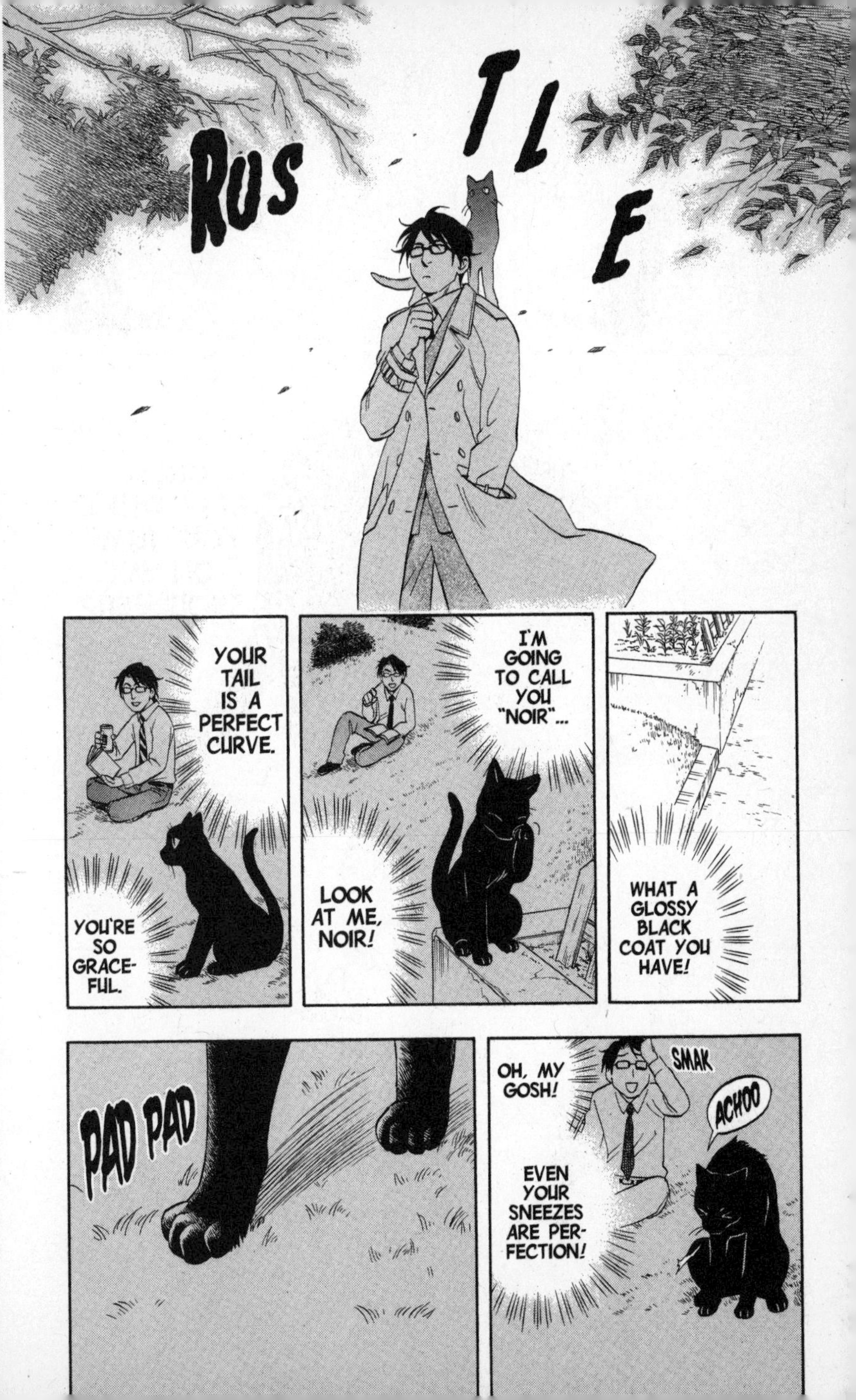
RUSTLE
WHAT A GLOSSY BLACK COAT YOU HAVE!
I'M GOING TO CALL YOU "NOIR"...
LOOK AT ME, NOIR!
YOUR TAIL IS A PERFECT CURVE.
YOU'RE SO GRACE-FUL.
OH, MY GOSH!
SMAK
ACHOO
EVEN YOUR SNEEZES ARE PER-FECTION!
PAD PAD

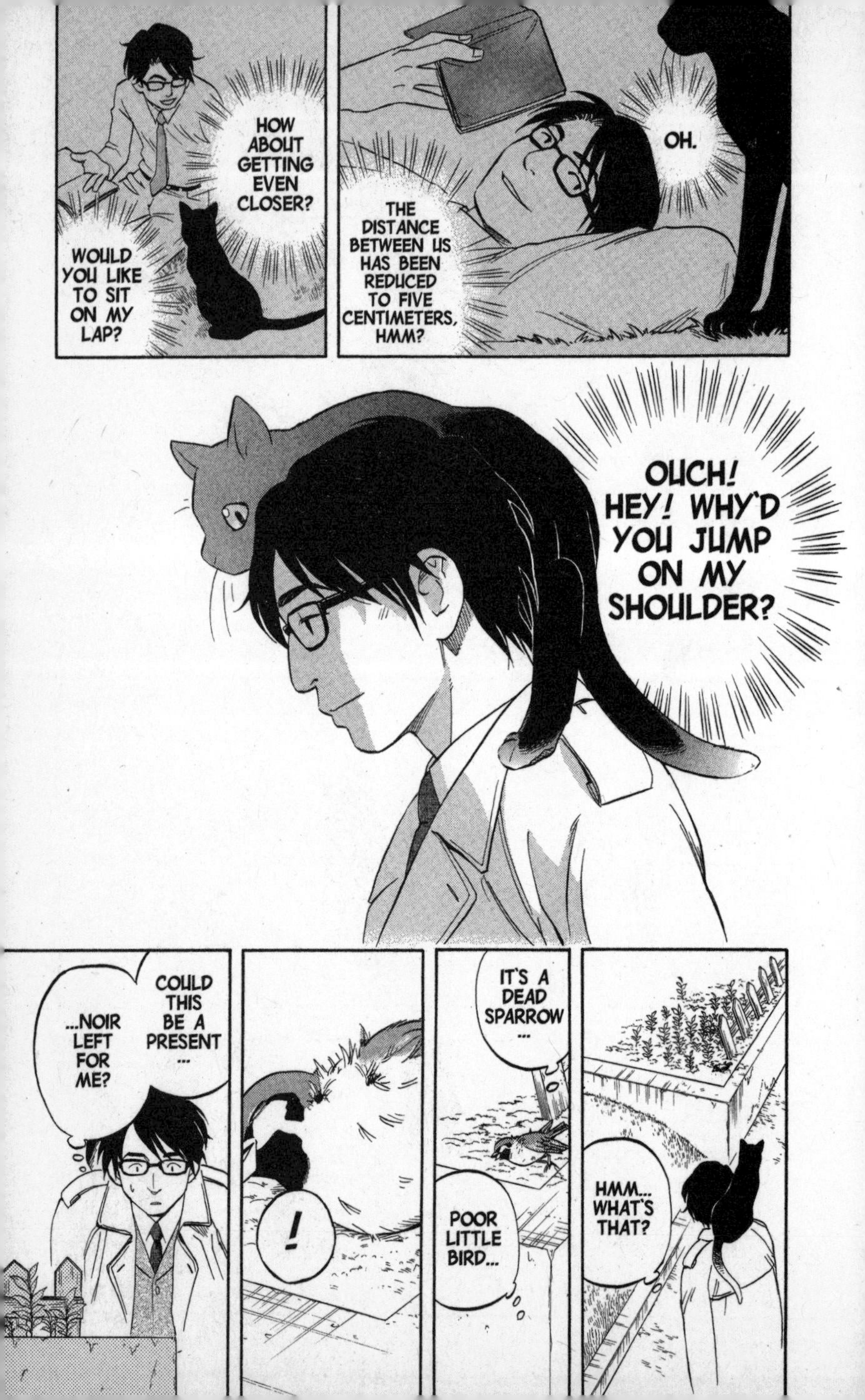
OH.
THE DISTANCE BETWEEN US HAS BEEN REDUCED TO FIVE CENTIMETERS, HMM?
HOW ABOUT GETTING EVEN CLOSER?
WOULD YOU LIKE TO SIT ON MY LAP?
OUCH! HEY! WHY'D YOU JUMP ON MY SHOULDER?
HMM... WHAT'S THAT?
IT'S A DEAD SPARROW ...
POOR LITTLE BIRD...
!
COULD THIS BE A PRESENT ...
...NOIR LEFT FOR ME?

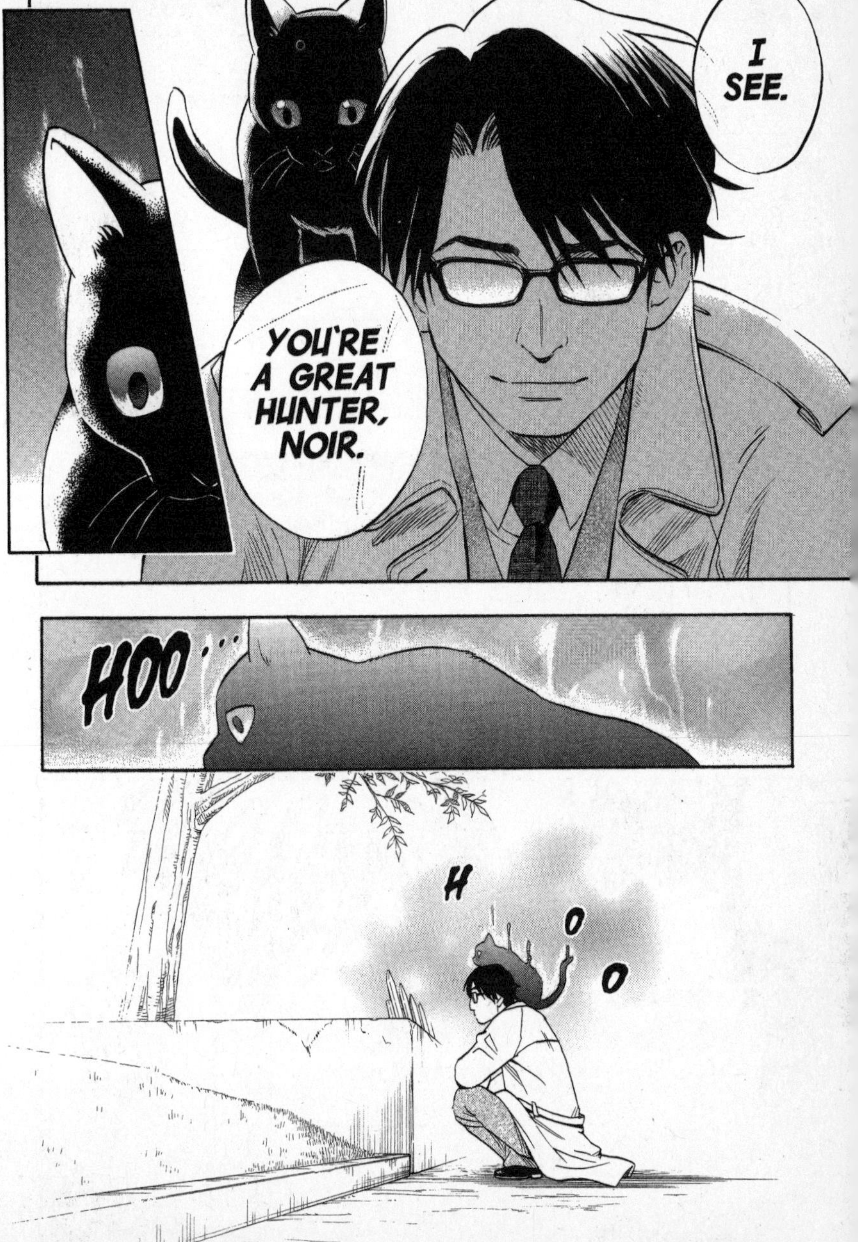
I SEE.
YOU'RE A GREAT HUNTER, NOIR.
HOO...
H O O

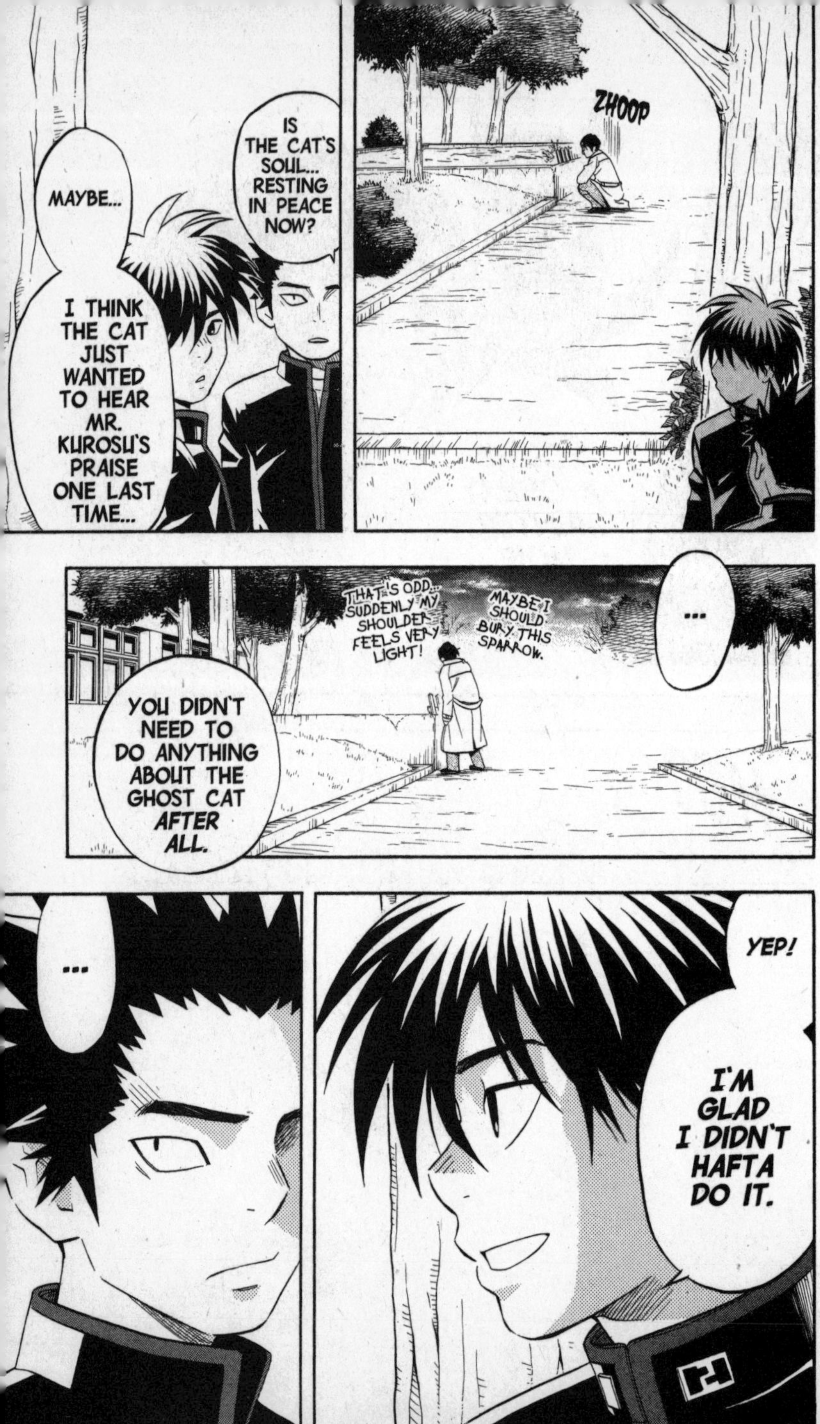
ZHOOP
IS THE CAT'S SOUL... RESTING IN PEACE NOW?
MAYBE...
I THINK THE CAT JUST WANTED TO HEAR MR. KUROSU'S PRAISE ONE LAST TIME...
...
MAYBE I SHOULD BURY THIS SPARROW.
THAT'S ODD... SUDDENLY MY SHOULDER FEELS VERY LIGHT!
YOU DIDN'T NEED TO DO ANYTHING ABOUT THE GHOST CAT AFTER ALL.
YEP!
I'M GLAD I DIDN'T HAFTA DO IT.
...

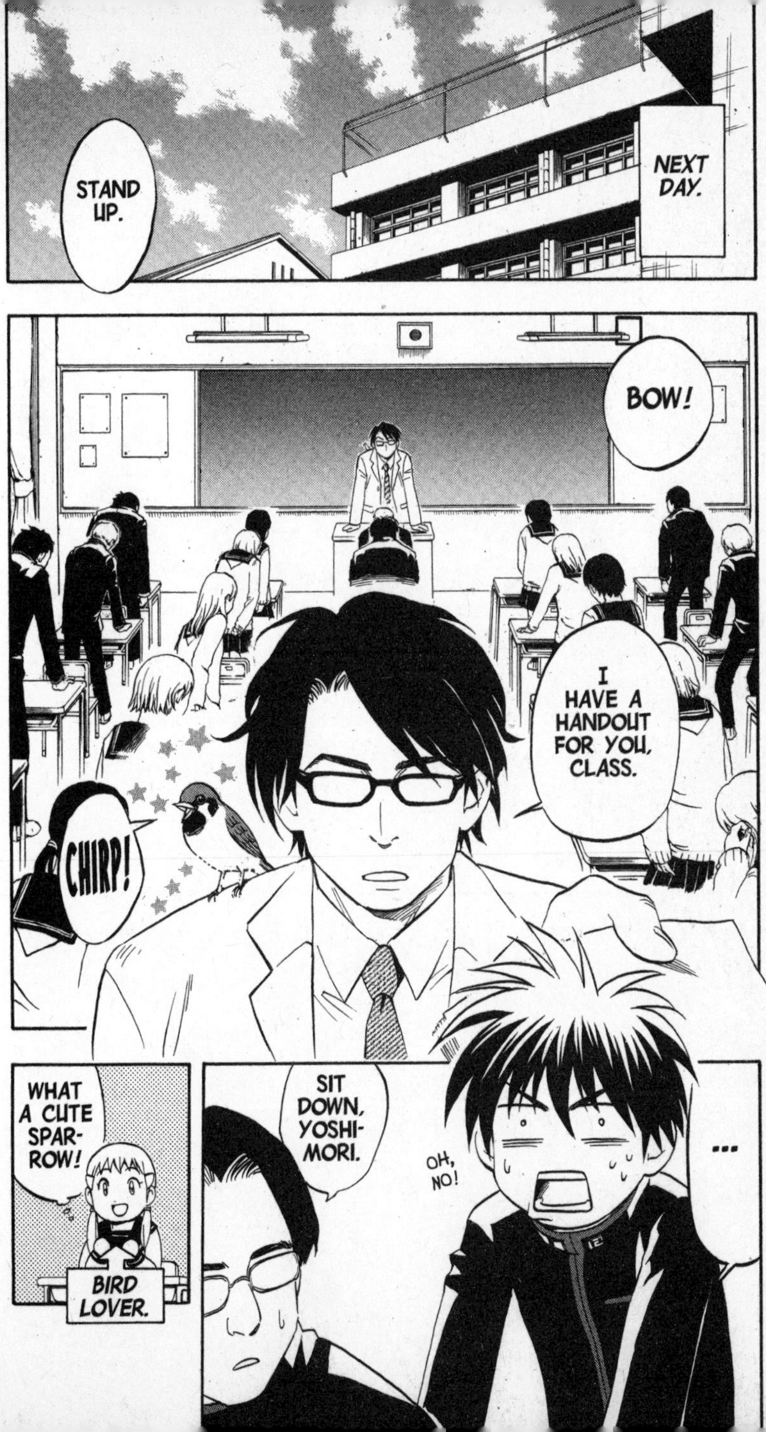
NEXT DAY.
STAND UP.
BOW!
I HAVE A HANDOUT FOR YOU, CLASS.
CHIRP!
...
OH, NO!
SIT DOWN, YOSHIMORI.
WHAT A CUTE SPARROW!
BIRD LOVER.

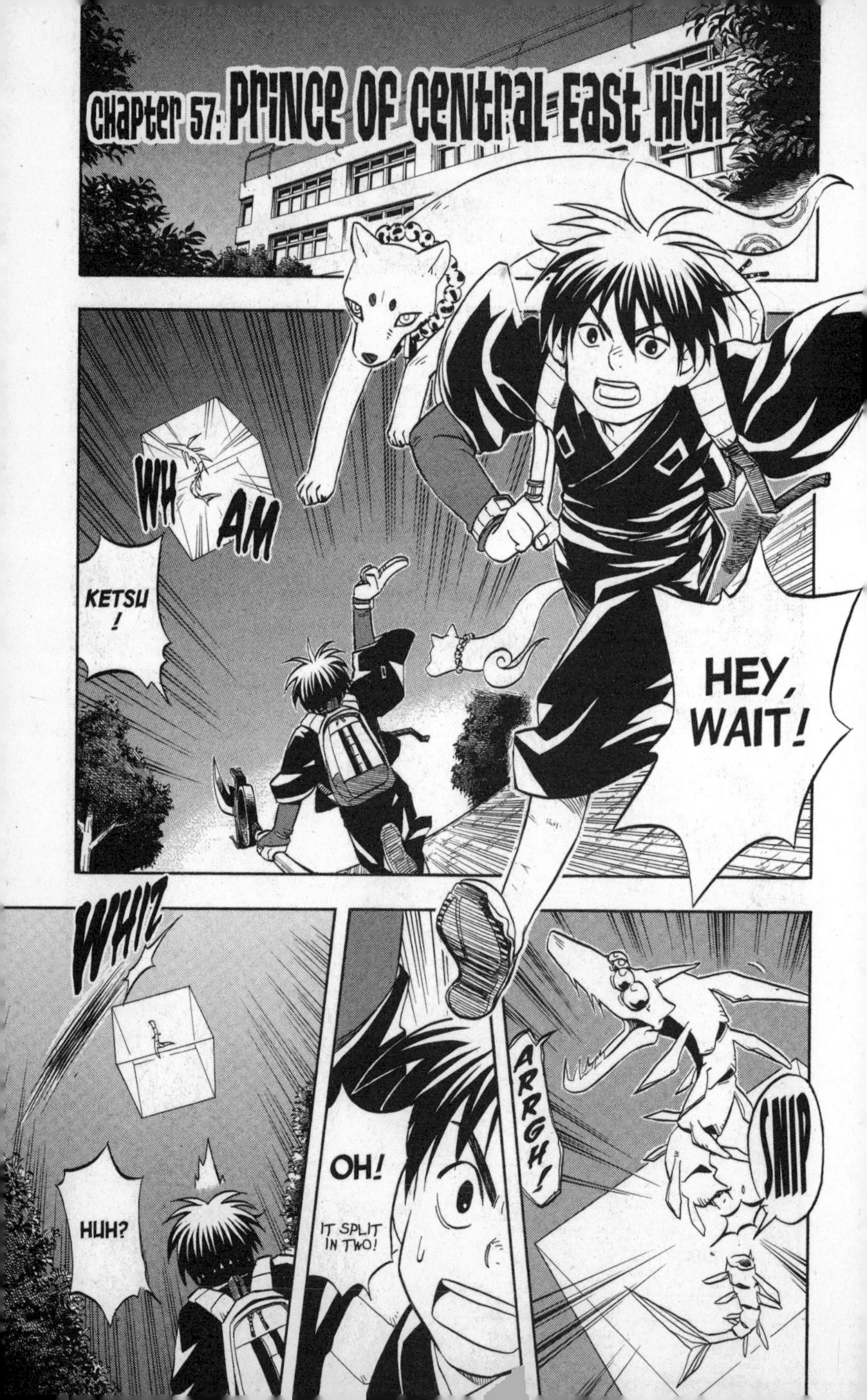
Chapter 57: Prince of Central East High
HEY, WAIT!
WH AM
KETSU!
SNIP
ARRGH!
OH!
IT SPLIT IN TWO!
WHIZ
HUH?

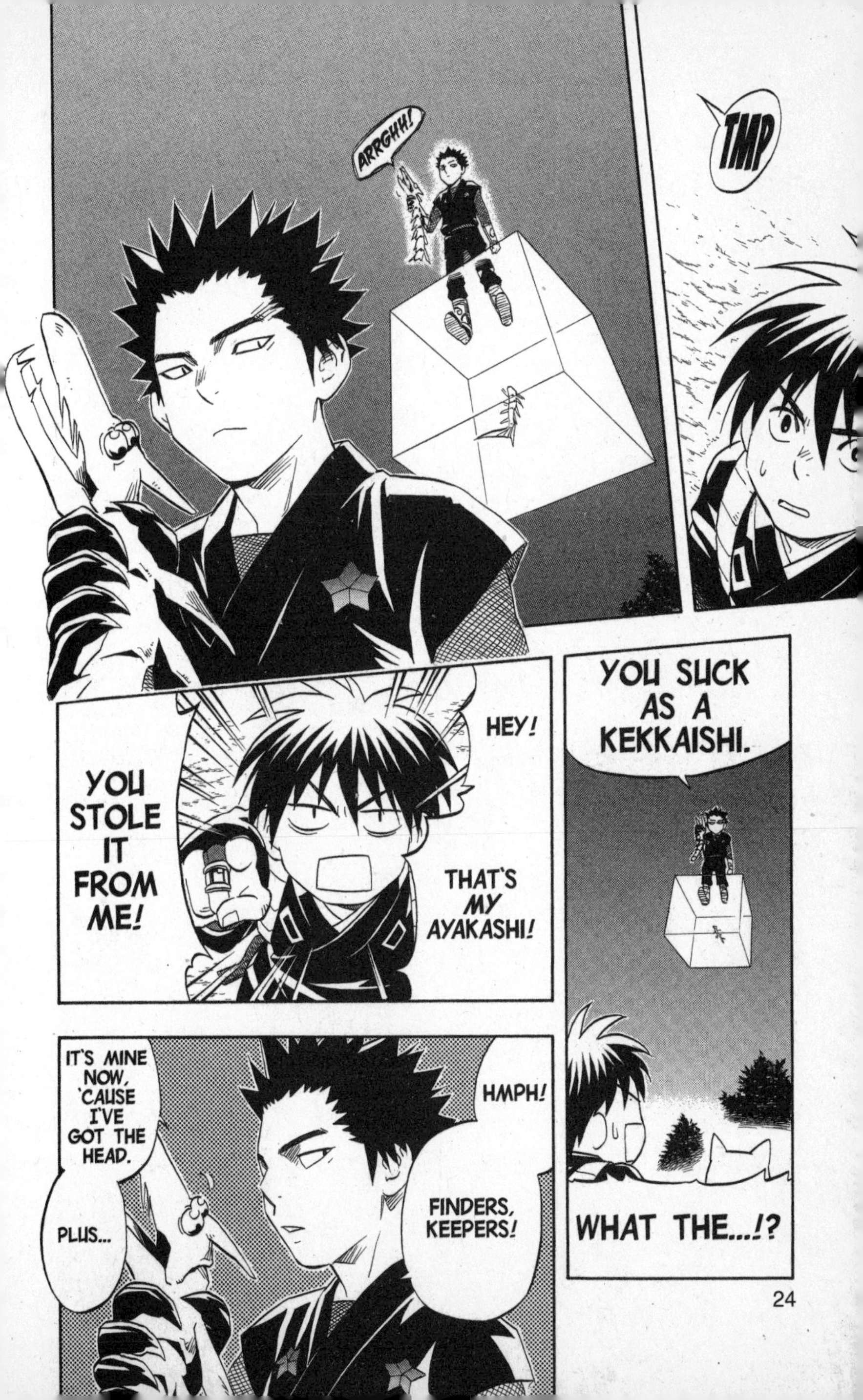
TMP
ARRGHH!
YOU SUCK AS A KEKKAISHI.
WHAT THE...!?
HEY!
THAT'S MY AYAKASHI!
YOU STOLE IT FROM ME!
HMPH!
FINDERS, KEEPERS!
IT'S MINE NOW, 'CAUSE I'VE GOT THE HEAD.
PLUS...

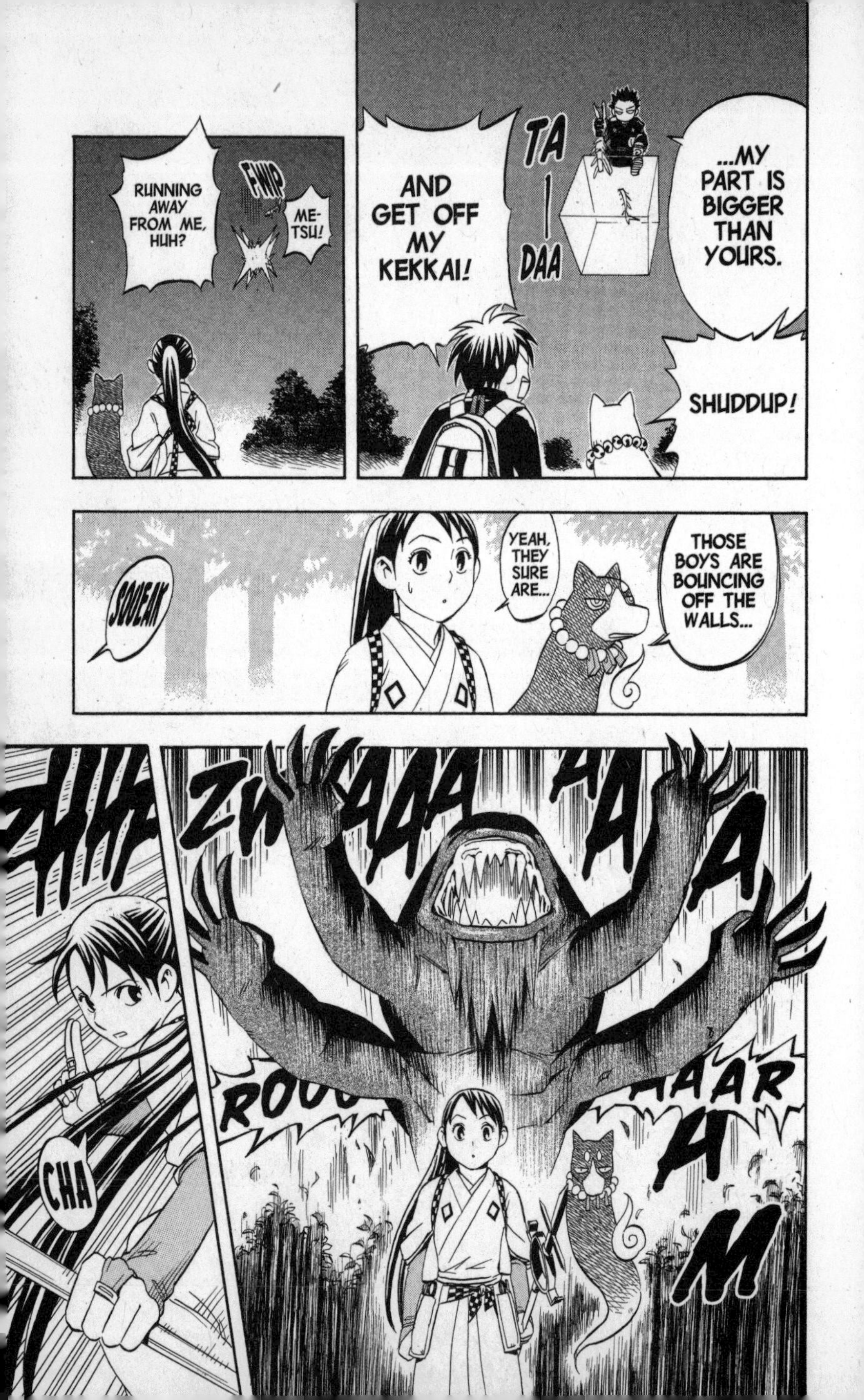
...MY PART IS BIGGER THAN YOURS.
TA-DAA
AND GET OFF MY KEKKAI!
SHUDDUP!
FWIP
METSU!
RUNNING AWAY FROM ME, HUH?
THOSE BOYS ARE BOUNCING OFF THE WALLS...
YEAH, THEY SURE ARE...
SQUEAK
ZW AAAA AA A A
ROOU AAAR A M
CHA

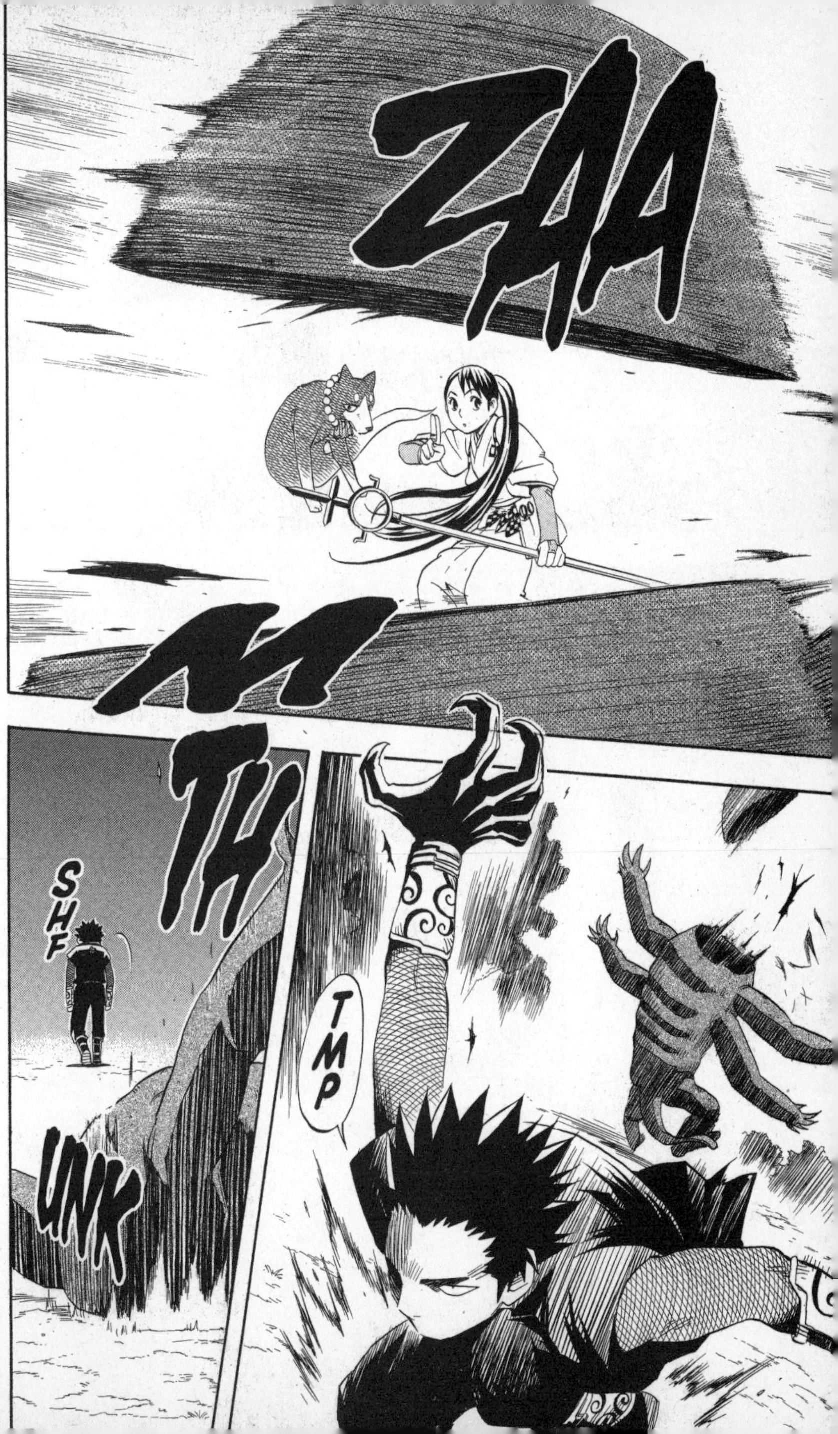
ZAAAM
TMP
SHF
THUNK

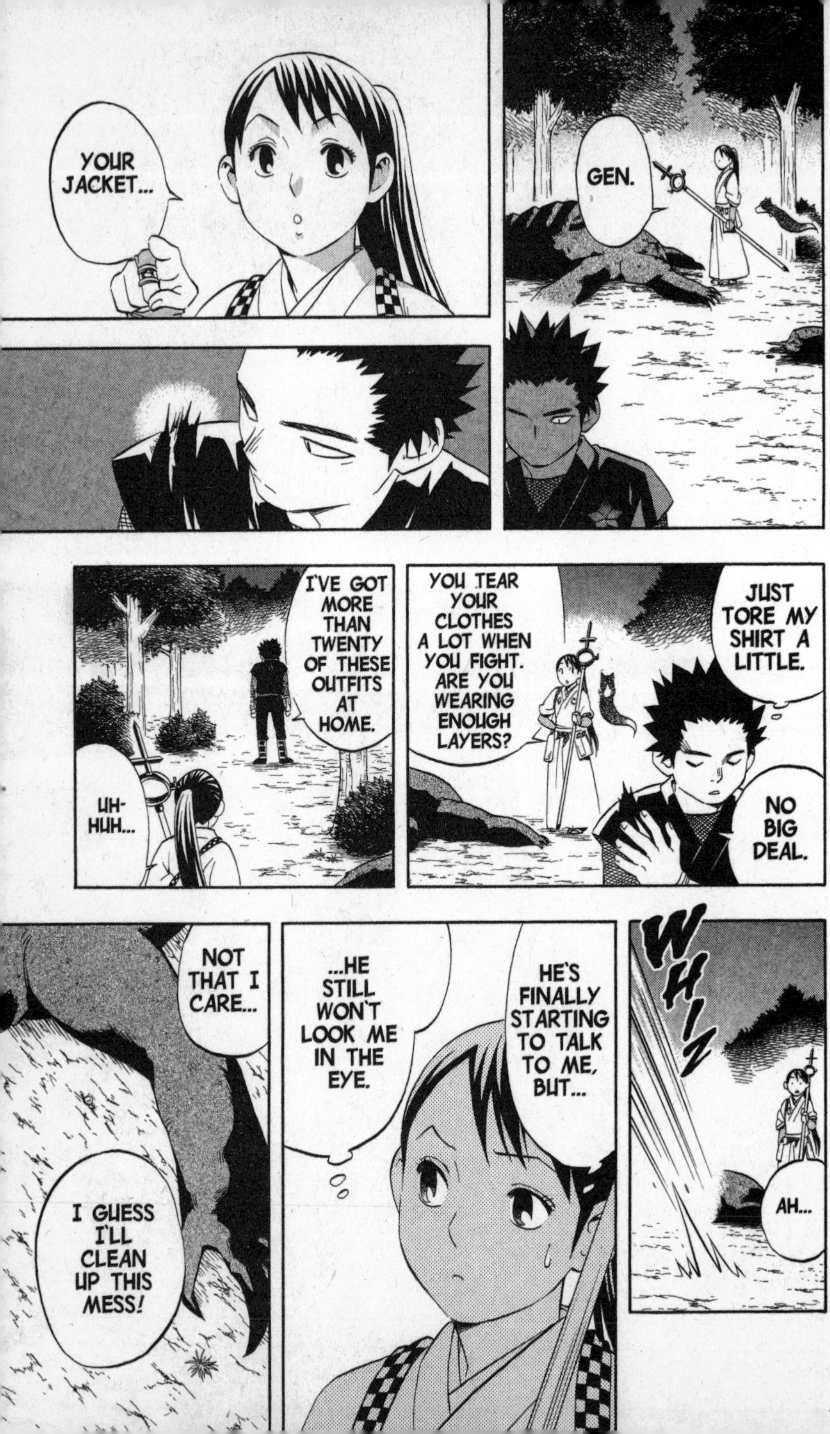
GEN.
YOUR JACKET...
JUST TORE MY SHIRT A LITTLE.
NO BIG DEAL.
YOU TEAR YOUR CLOTHES A LOT WHEN YOU FIGHT. ARE YOU WEARING ENOUGH LAYERS?
I'VE GOT MORE THAN TWENTY OF THESE OUTFITS AT HOME.
UH-HUH...
WHIZ
AH...
HE'S FINALLY STARTING TO TALK TO ME, BUT...
...HE STILL WON'T LOOK ME IN THE EYE.
NOT THAT I CARE...
I GUESS I'LL CLEAN UP THIS MESS!

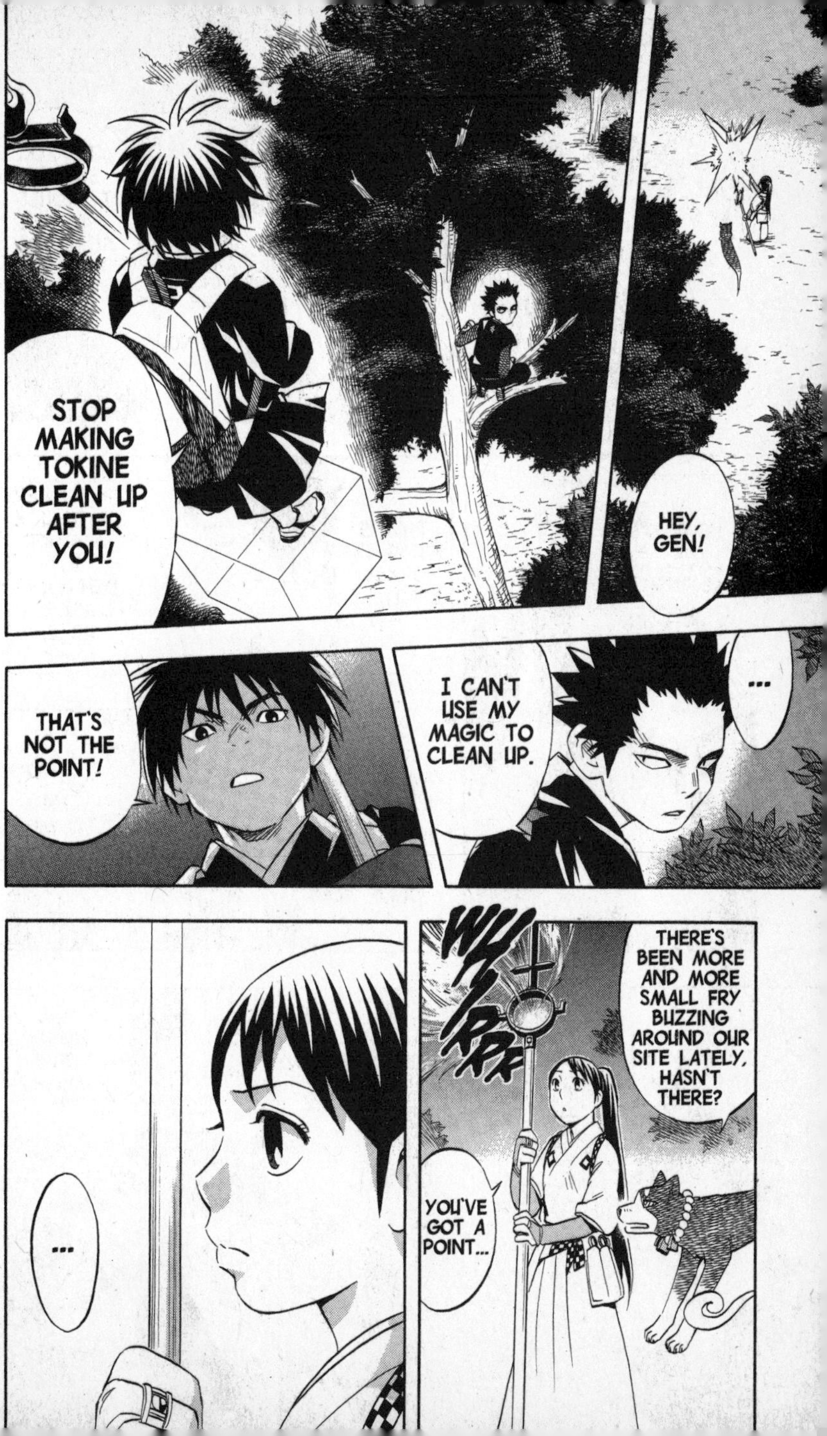
HEY, GEN!
STOP MAKING TOKINE CLEAN UP AFTER YOU!
...
I CAN'T USE MY MAGIC TO CLEAN UP.
THAT'S NOT THE POINT!
WHIRRR
THERE'S BEEN MORE AND MORE SMALL FRY BUZZING AROUND OUR SITE LATELY, HASN'T THERE?
YOU'VE GOT A POINT...
...

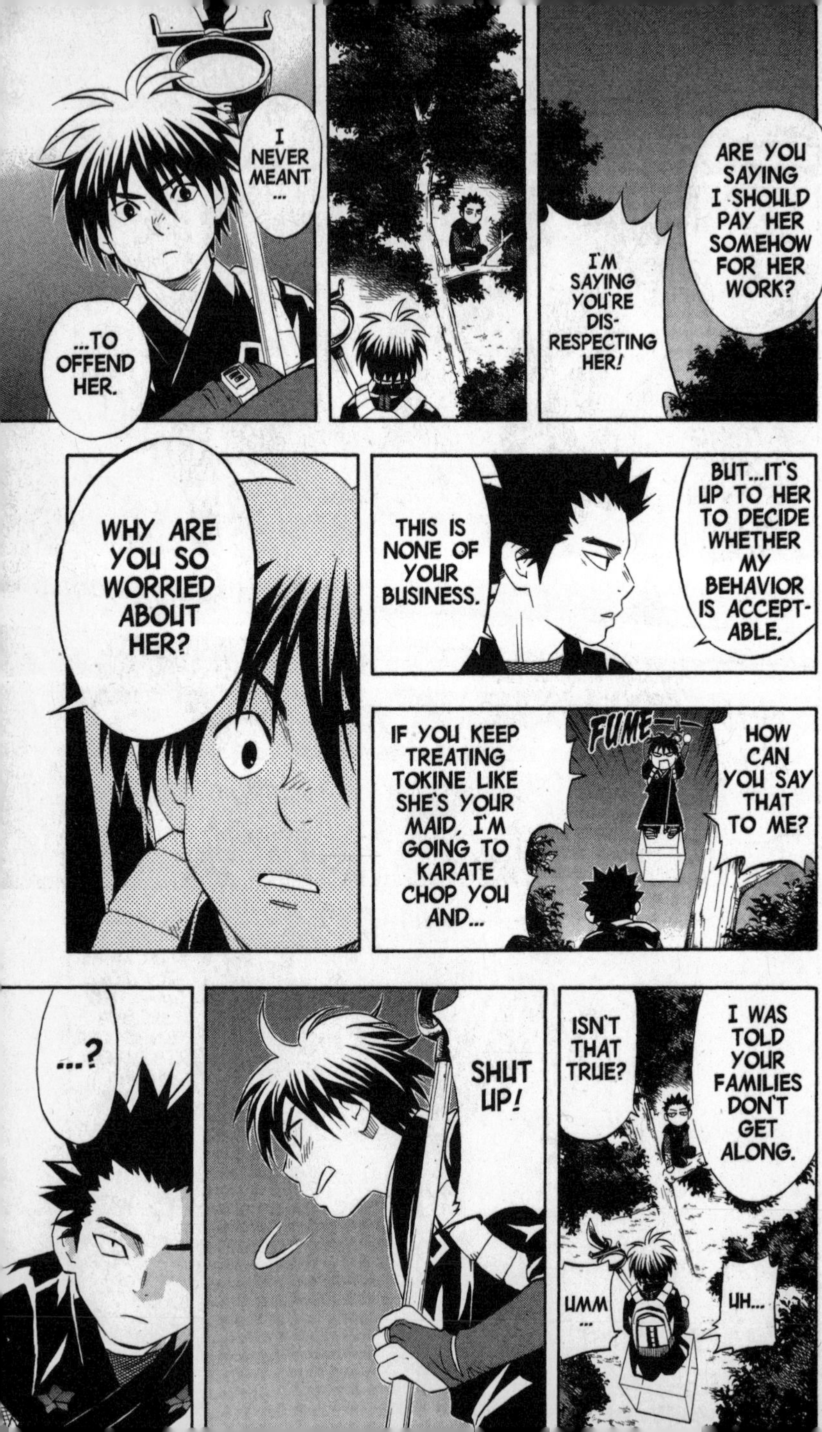
ARE YOU SAYING I SHOULD PAY HER SOMEHOW FOR HER WORK?
I'M SAYING YOU'RE DIS-RESPECTING HER!
I NEVER MEANT ...
...TO OFFEND HER.
BUT...IT'S UP TO HER TO DECIDE WHETHER MY BEHAVIOR IS ACCEPT-ABLE.
THIS IS NONE OF YOUR BUSINESS.
HOW CAN YOU SAY THAT TO ME?
FUME
IF YOU KEEP TREATING TOKINE LIKE SHE'S YOUR MAID, I'M GOING TO KARATE CHOP YOU AND...
WHY ARE YOU SO WORRIED ABOUT HER?
I WAS TOLD YOUR FAMILIES DON'T GET ALONG.
ISN'T THAT TRUE?
UH...
UMM ...
SHUT UP!
...?

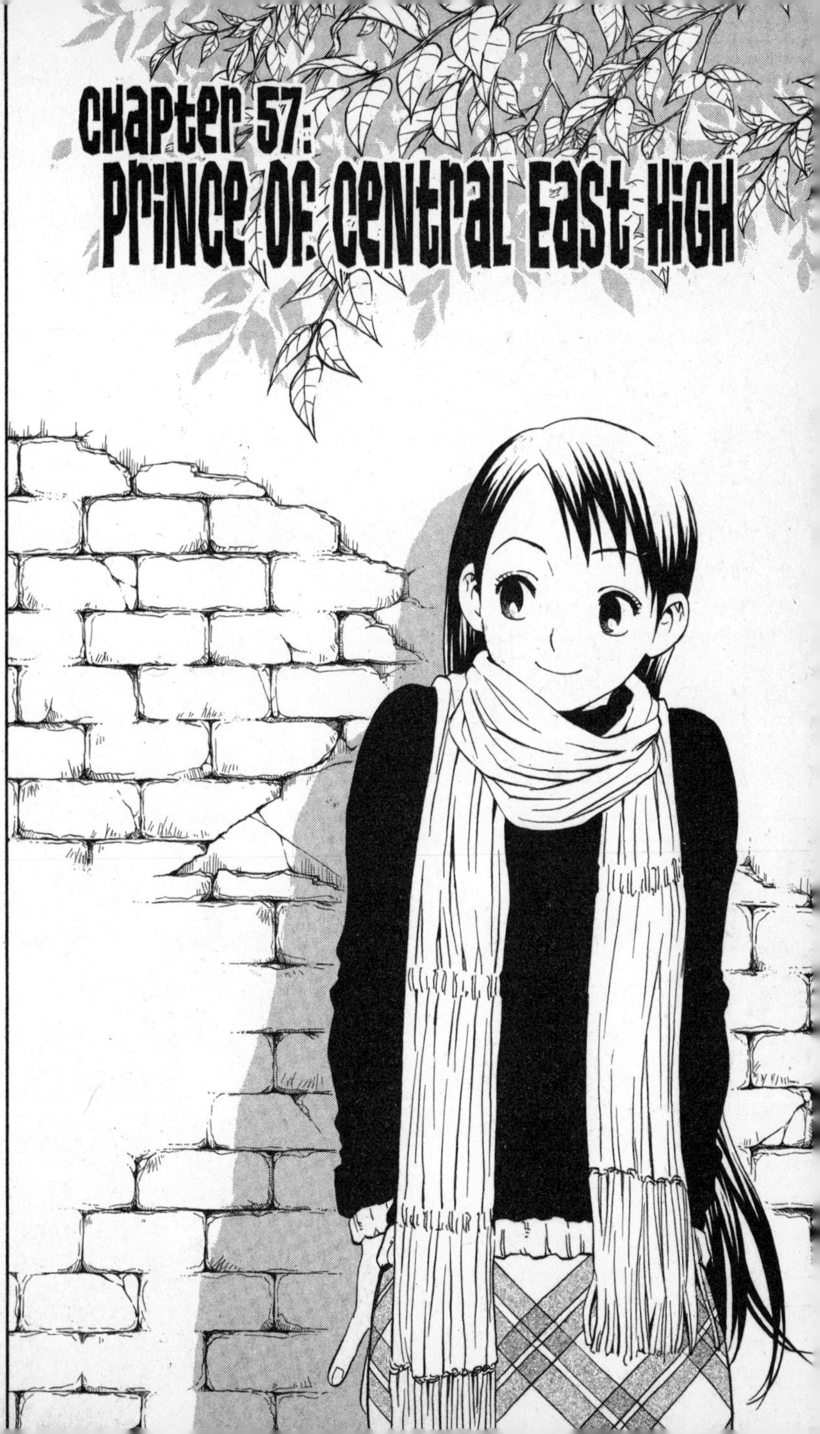
Chapter 57:
Prince of Central East High

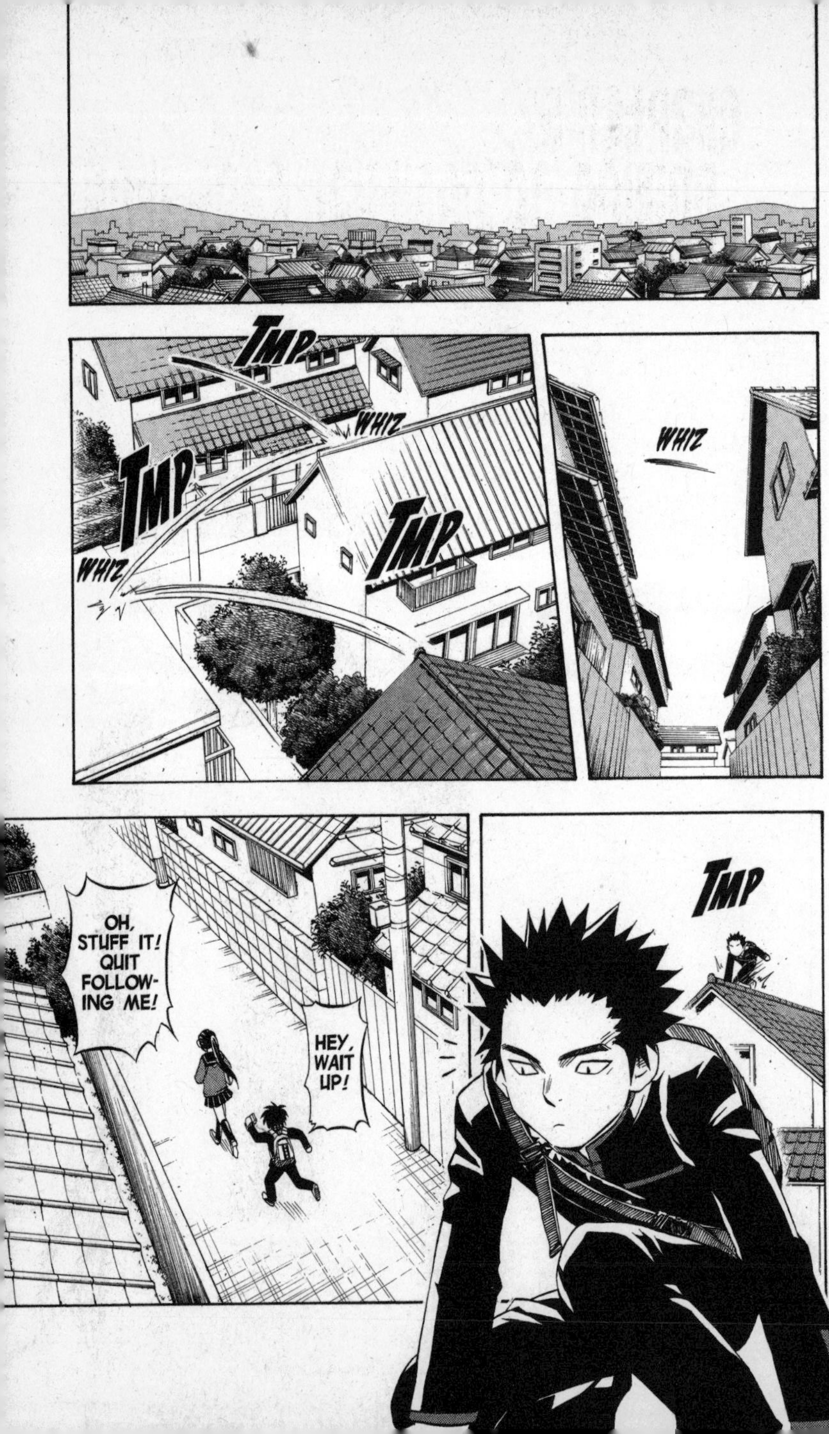
WHIZ
TMP
WHIZ
TMP
TMP
WHIZ
TMP
HEY, WAIT UP!
OH, STUFF IT! QUIT FOLLOW-ING ME!

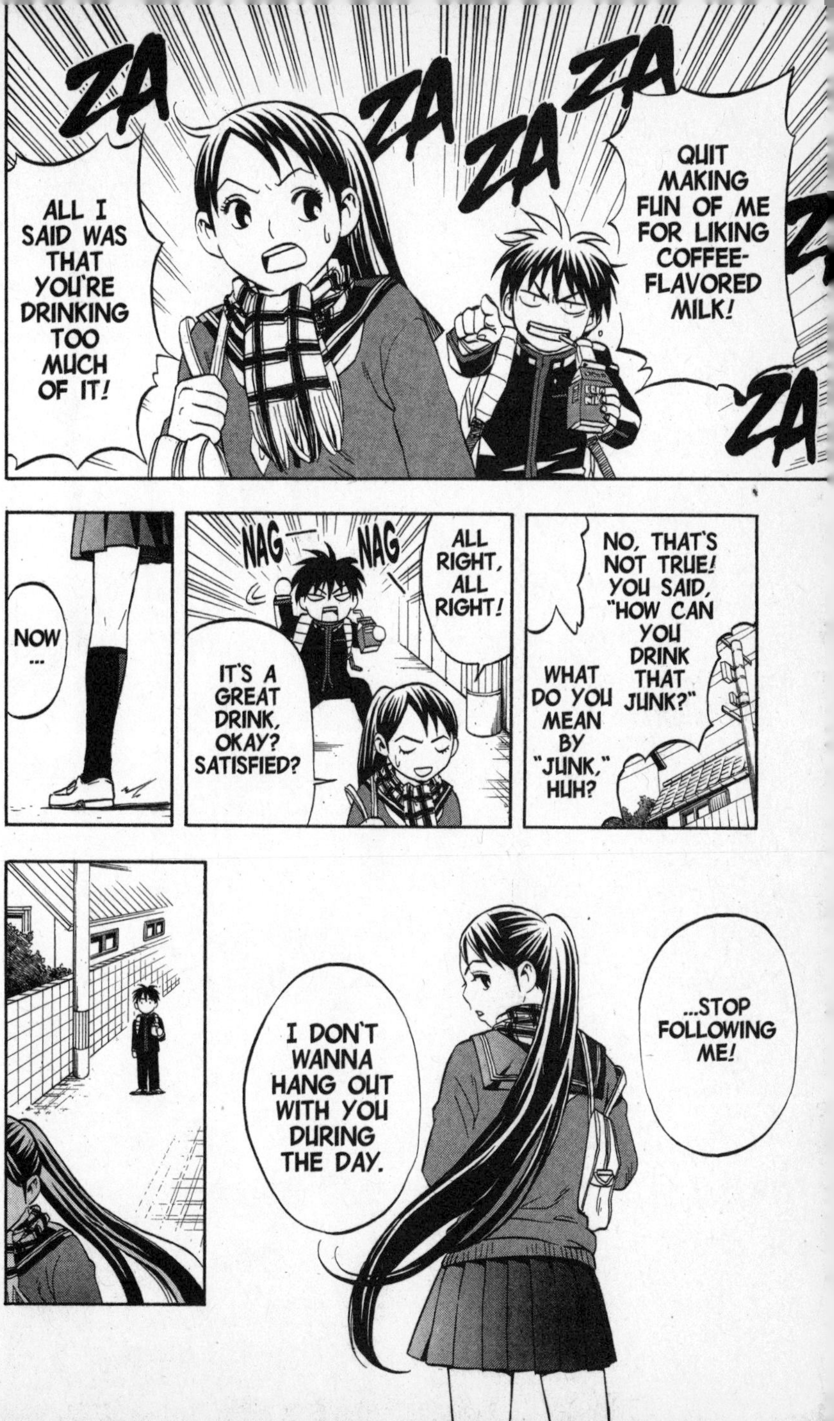
ZA
ZA
ZA
ZA
QUIT MAKING FUN OF ME FOR LIKING COFFEE-FLAVORED MILK!
ZA
ZA
ALL I SAID WAS THAT YOU'RE DRINKING TOO MUCH OF IT!
NO, THAT'S NOT TRUE! YOU SAID, "HOW CAN YOU DRINK THAT JUNK?"
WHAT DO YOU MEAN BY "JUNK," HUH?
NAG— NAG
ALL RIGHT, ALL RIGHT!
IT'S A GREAT DRINK, OKAY? SATISFIED?
NOW ...
...STOP FOLLOWING ME!
I DON'T WANNA HANG OUT WITH YOU DURING THE DAY.

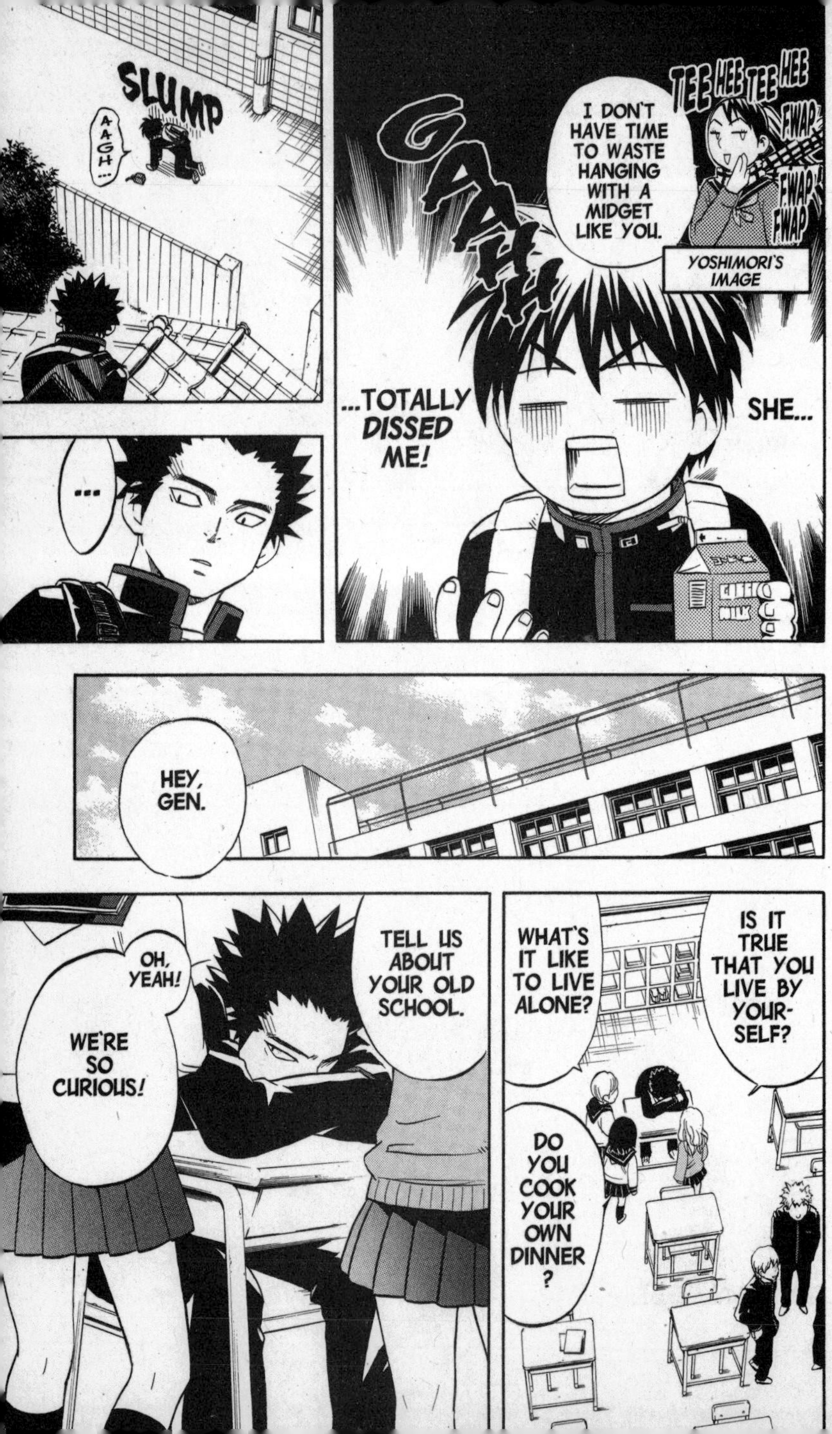
TEE HEE TEE HEE
FWAP FWAP FWAP
I DON'T HAVE TIME TO WASTE HANGING WITH A MIDGET LIKE YOU.
YOSHIMORI'S IMAGE
GAAAH
SHE...
...TOTALLY DISSED ME!
SLUMP
AAGH...
...
HEY, GEN.
IS IT TRUE THAT YOU LIVE BY YOUR-SELF?
WHAT'S IT LIKE TO LIVE ALONE?
DO YOU COOK YOUR OWN DINNER?
TELL US ABOUT YOUR OLD SCHOOL.
OH, YEAH!
WE'RE SO CURIOUS!

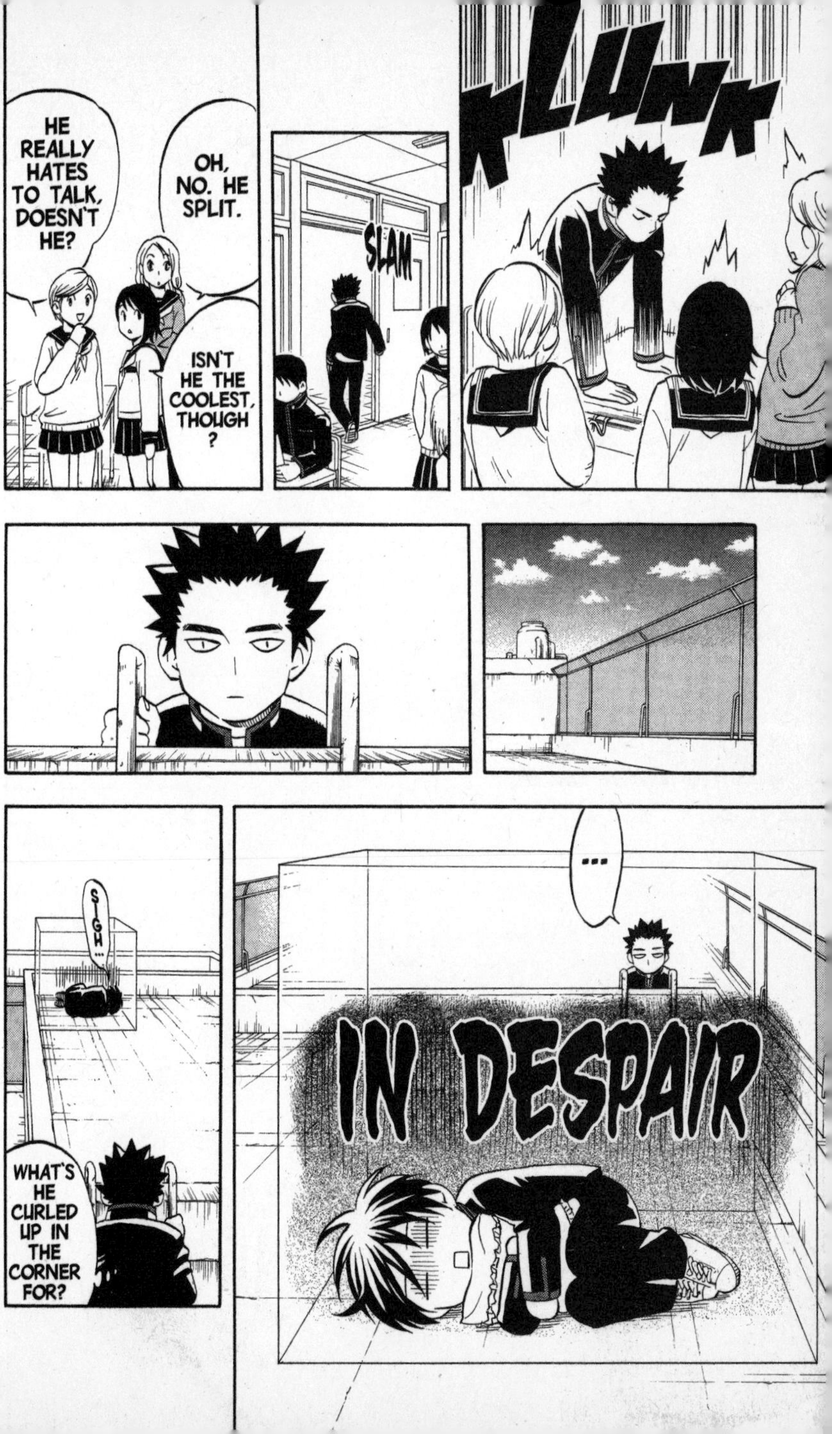
KLUNK
SLAM
OH, NO. HE SPLIT.
HE REALLY HATES TO TALK, DOESN'T HE?
ISN'T HE THE COOLEST, THOUGH?
...
IN DESPAIR
SIGH...
WHAT'S HE CURLED UP IN THE CORNER FOR?

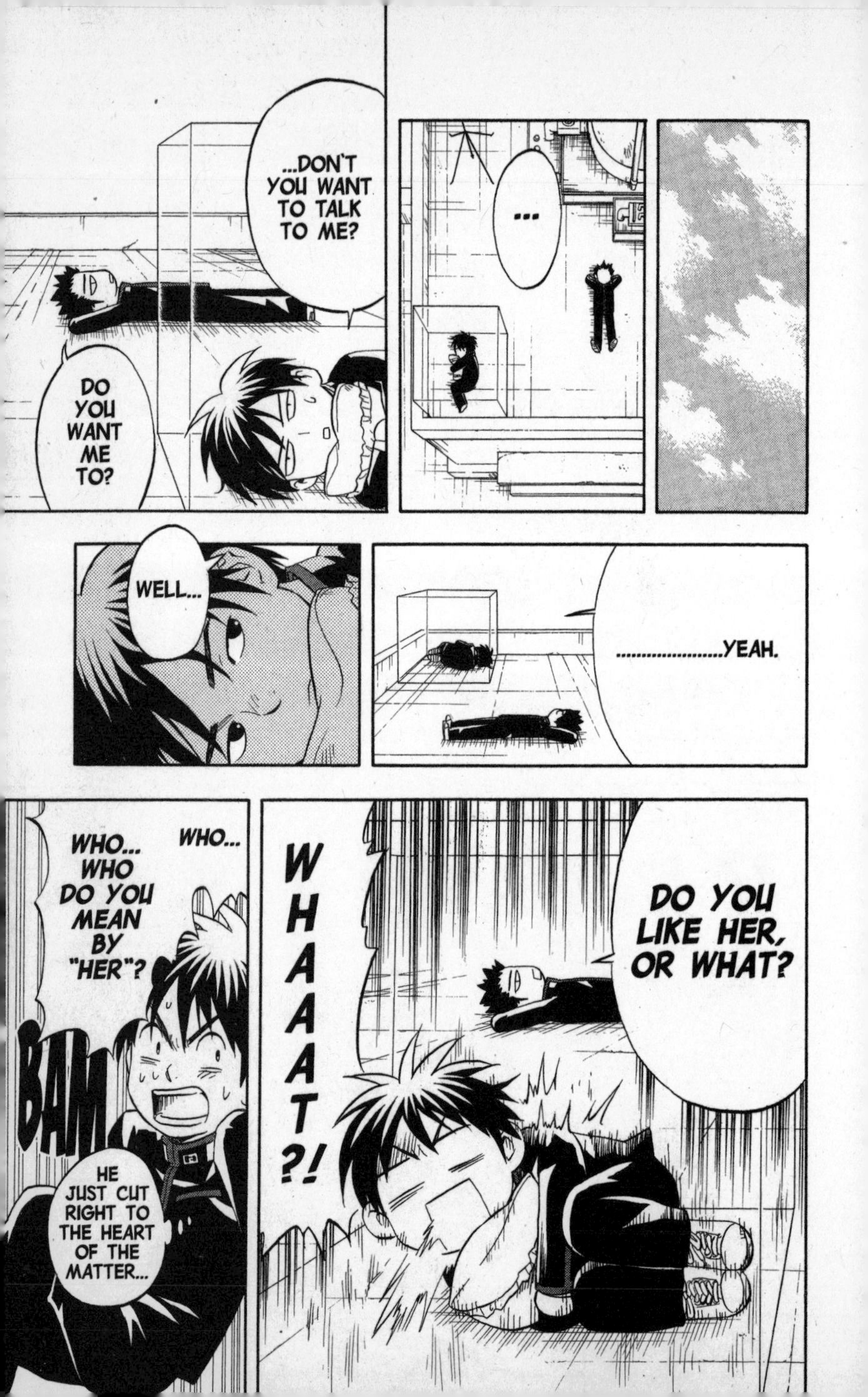
...
...DON'T YOU WANT TO TALK TO ME?
DO YOU WANT ME TO?
......................YEAH.
WELL...
DO YOU LIKE HER, OR WHAT?
WHAAAAT?!
WHO...
WHO... WHO DO YOU MEAN BY "HER"?
BAM
HE JUST CUT RIGHT TO THE HEART OF THE MATTER...

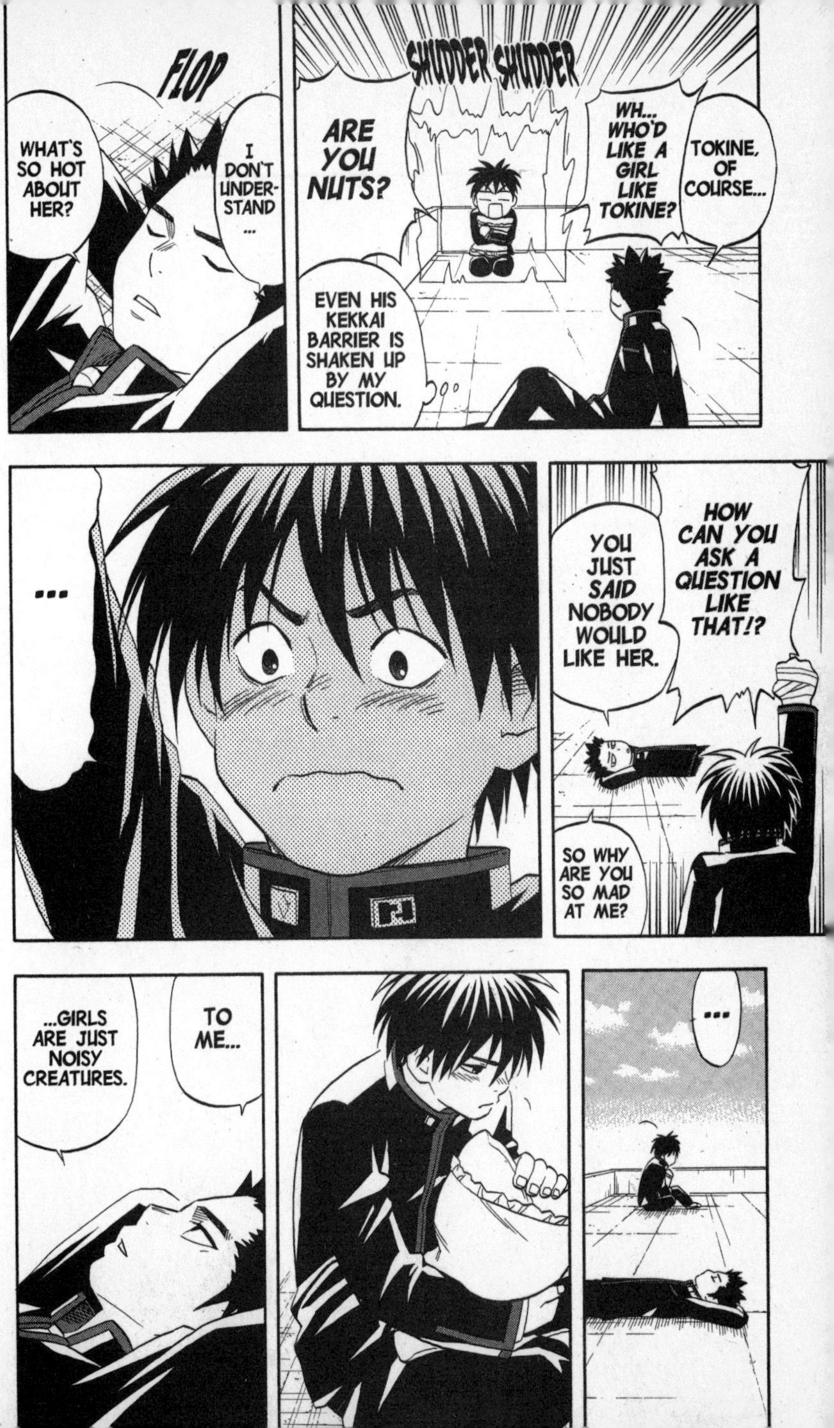
SHUDDER SHUDDER
TOKINE, OF COURSE...
WH... WHO'D LIKE A GIRL LIKE TOKINE?
ARE YOU NUTS?
EVEN HIS KEKKAI BARRIER IS SHAKEN UP BY MY QUESTION.
FLOP
I DON'T UNDERSTAND...
WHAT'S SO HOT ABOUT HER?
HOW CAN YOU ASK A QUESTION LIKE THAT!?
YOU JUST SAID NOBODY WOULD LIKE HER.
SO WHY ARE YOU SO MAD AT ME?
...
...
TO ME...
...GIRLS ARE JUST NOISY CREATURES.

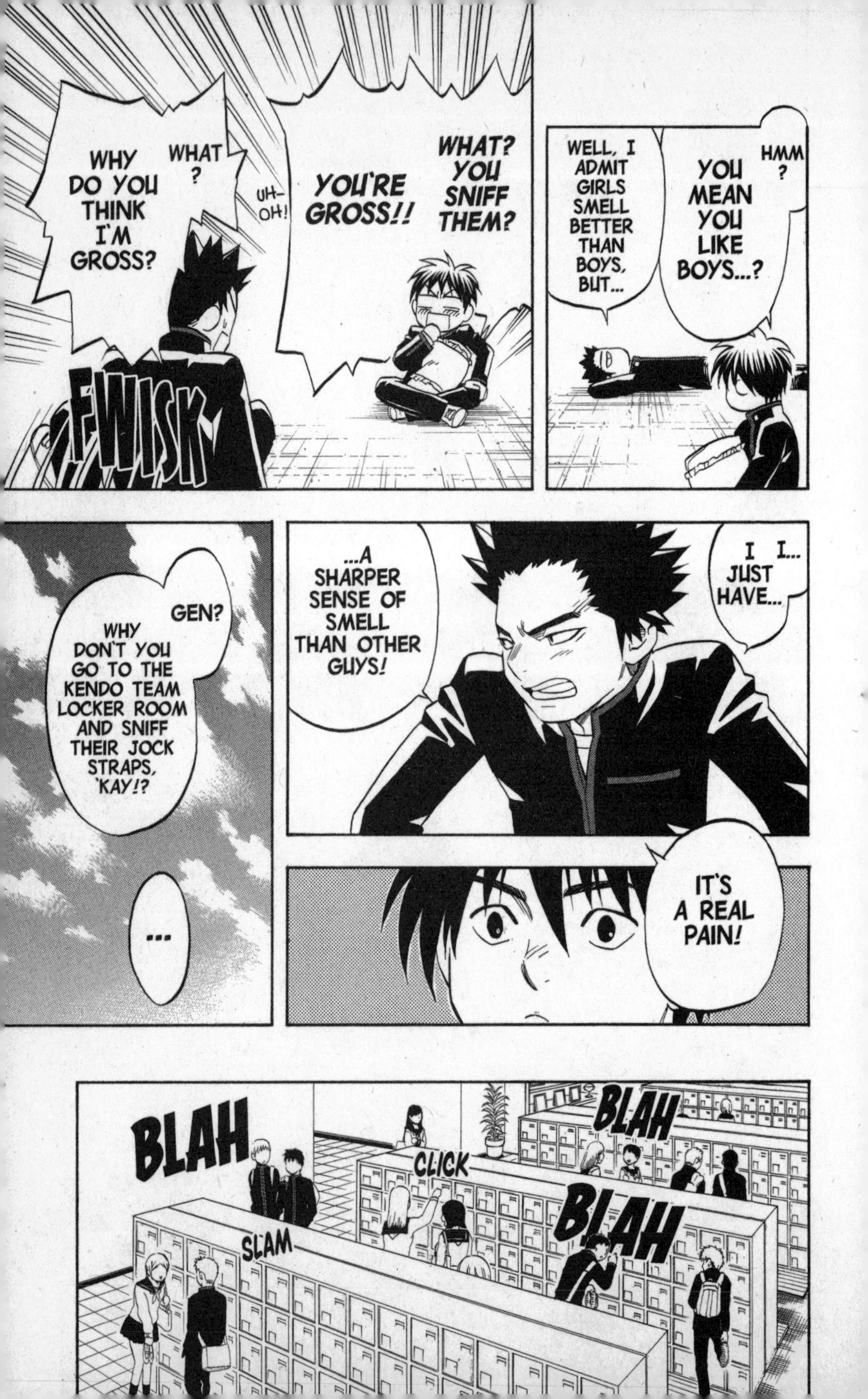
HMM ?
YOU MEAN YOU LIKE BOYS...?
WELL, I ADMIT GIRLS SMELL BETTER THAN BOYS, BUT...
WHAT? YOU SNIFF THEM?
YOU'RE GROSS!!
UH-OH!
WHAT ?
WHY DO YOU THINK I'M GROSS?
FWISK
I I... JUST HAVE...
...A SHARPER SENSE OF SMELL THAN OTHER GUYS!
IT'S A REAL PAIN!
GEN?
WHY DON'T YOU GO TO THE KENDO TEAM LOCKER ROOM AND SNIFF THEIR JOCK STRAPS, 'KAY!?
...
BLAH
BLAH
CLICK
BLAH
SLAM

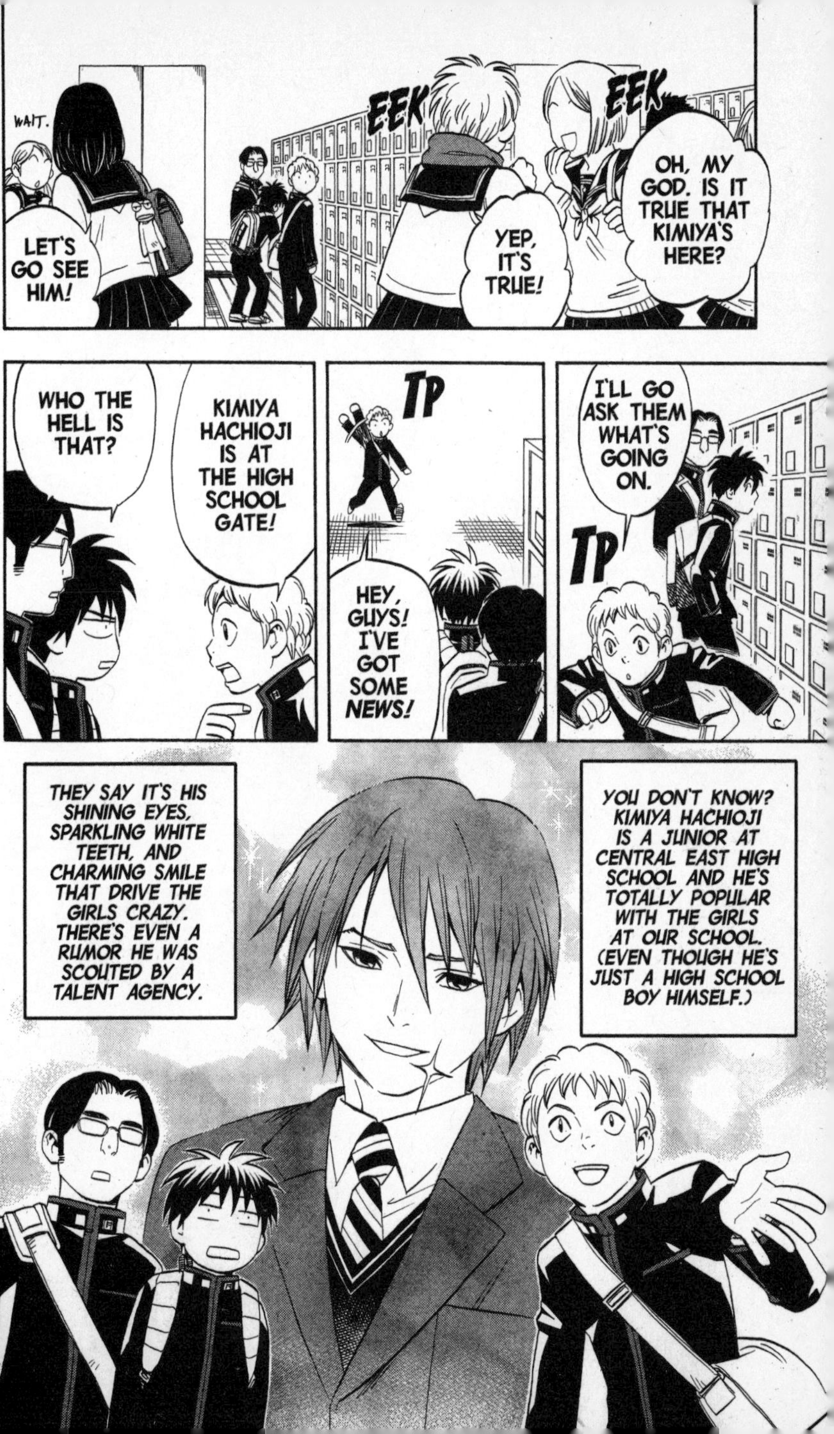
EEK
EEK
OH, MY GOD. IS IT TRUE THAT KIMIYA'S HERE?
YEP, IT'S TRUE!
WAIT.
LET'S GO SEE HIM!
I'LL GO ASK THEM WHAT'S GOING ON.
TP
TP
HEY, GUYS! I'VE GOT SOME NEWS!
KIMIYA HACHIOJI IS AT THE HIGH SCHOOL GATE!
WHO THE HELL IS THAT?
YOU DON'T KNOW? KIMIYA HACHIOJI IS A JUNIOR AT CENTRAL EAST HIGH SCHOOL AND HE'S TOTALLY POPULAR WITH THE GIRLS AT OUR SCHOOL. (EVEN THOUGH HE'S JUST A HIGH SCHOOL BOY HIMSELF.)
THEY SAY IT'S HIS SHINING EYES, SPARKLING WHITE TEETH, AND CHARMING SMILE THAT DRIVE THE GIRLS CRAZY. THERE'S EVEN A RUMOR HE WAS SCOUTED BY A TALENT AGENCY.

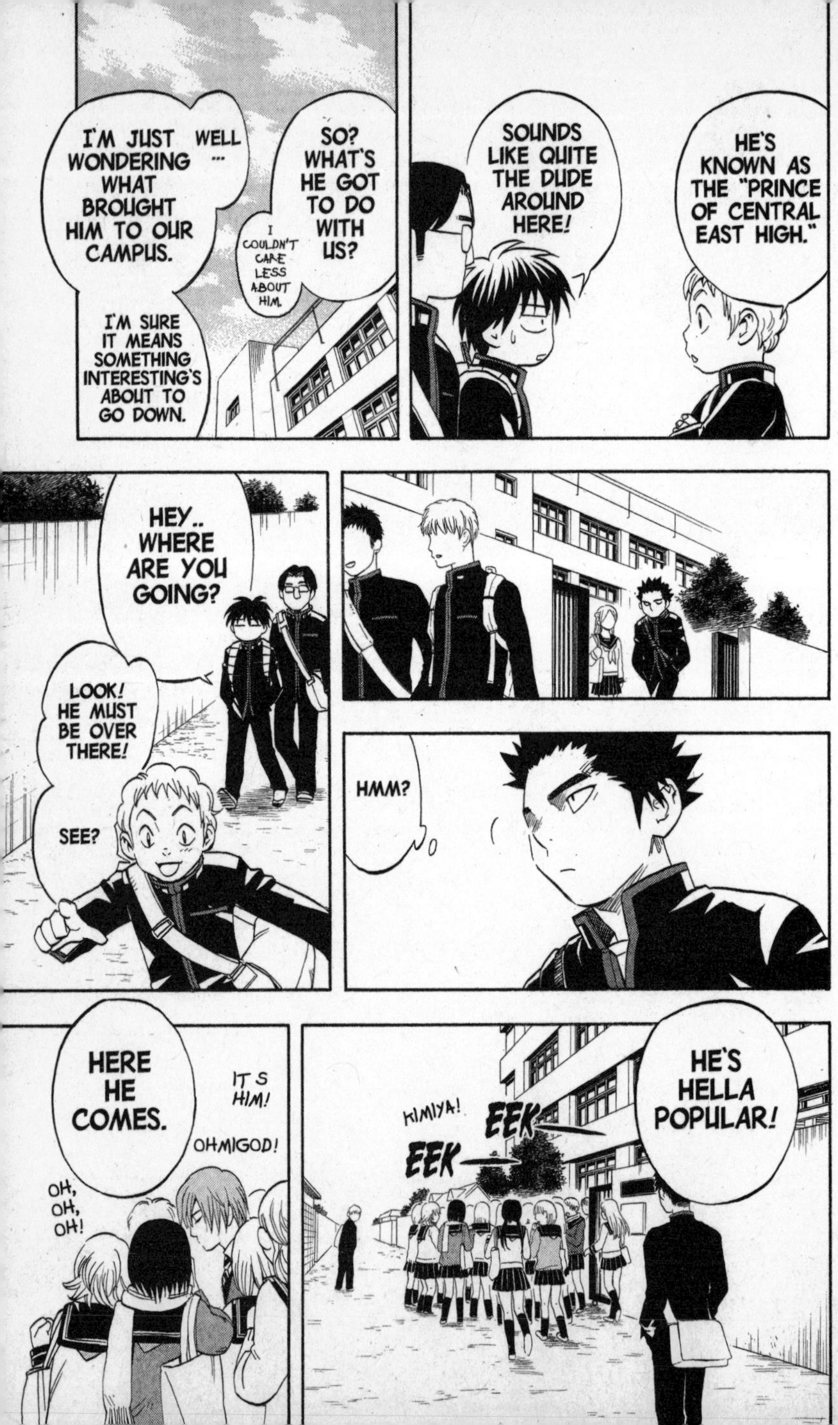
HE'S KNOWN AS THE "PRINCE OF CENTRAL EAST HIGH."
SOUNDS LIKE QUITE THE DUDE AROUND HERE!
SO? WHAT'S HE GOT TO DO WITH US?
I COULDN'T CARE LESS ABOUT HIM.
WELL ...
I'M JUST WONDERING WHAT BROUGHT HIM TO OUR CAMPUS.
I'M SURE IT MEANS SOMETHING INTERESTING'S ABOUT TO GO DOWN.
HMM?
HEY.. WHERE ARE YOU GOING?
LOOK! HE MUST BE OVER THERE!
SEE?
HE'S HELLA POPULAR!
EEK
KIMIYA!
EEK
IT S HIM!
HERE HE COMES.
OHMIGOD!
OH, OH, OH!

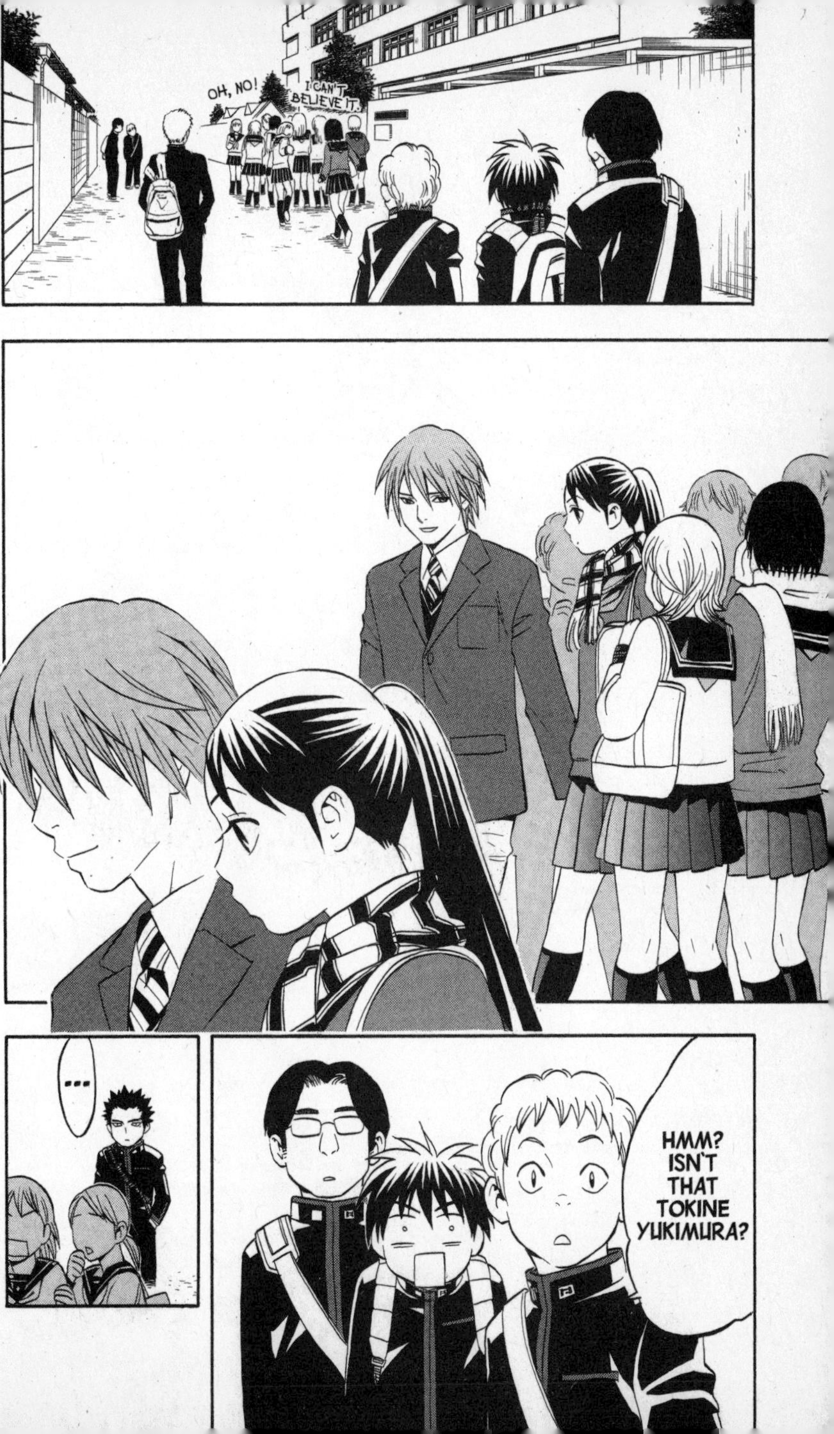
I CAN'T BELIEVE IT.
OH, NO!
HMM? ISN'T THAT TOKINE YUKIMURA?
...

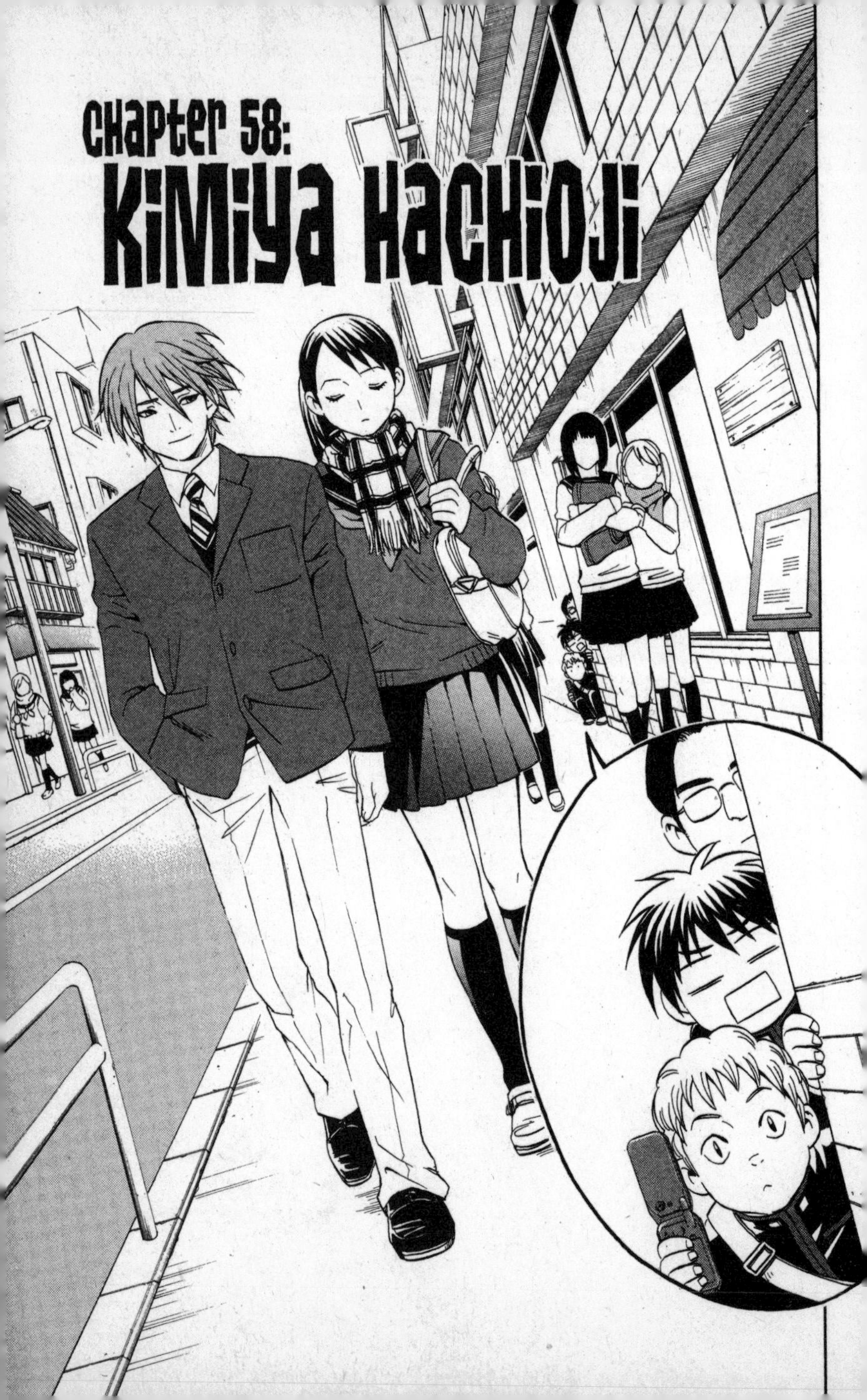
Chapter 58:
Kimiya Hachioji

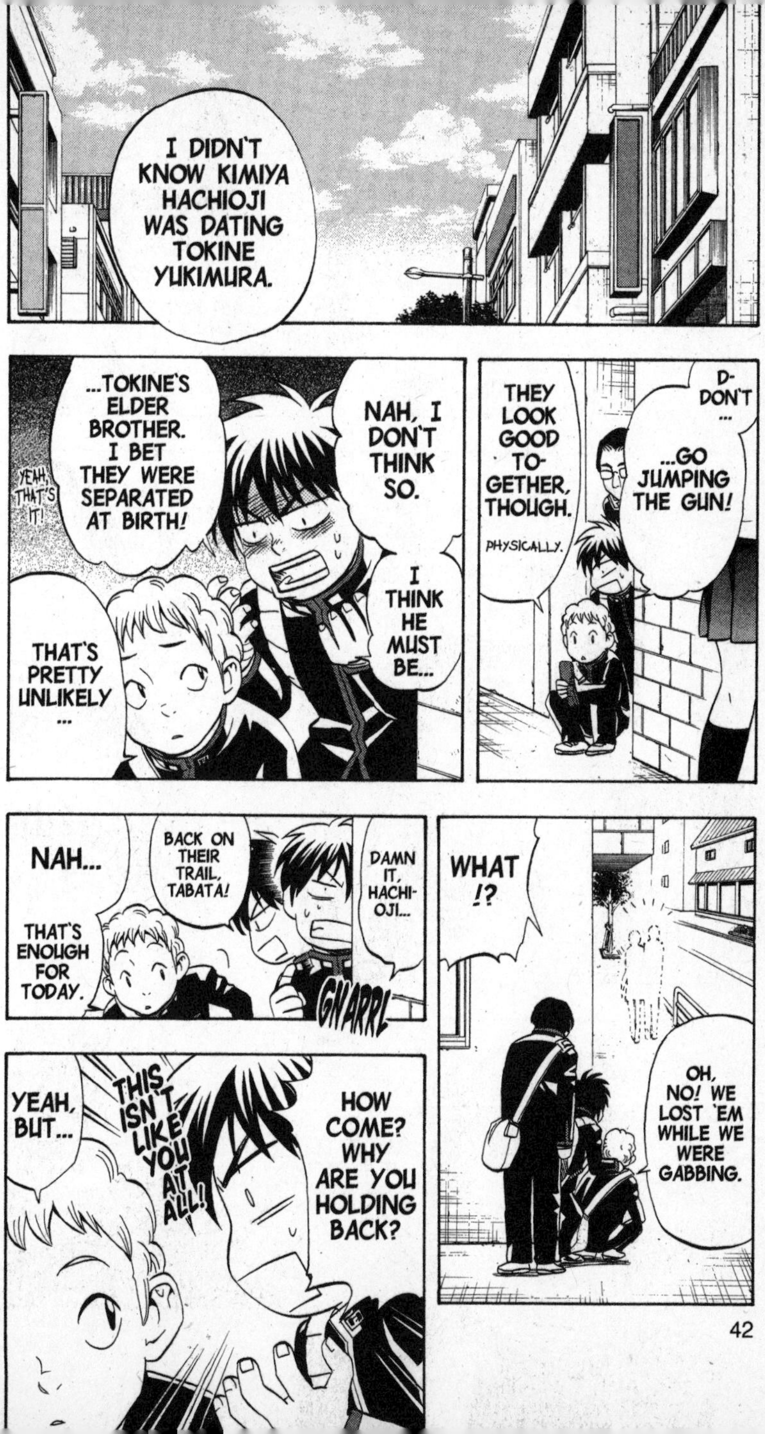
I DIDN'T KNOW KIMIYA HACHIOJI WAS DATING TOKINE YUKIMURA.
D-DON'T ...
...GO JUMPING THE GUN!
THEY LOOK GOOD TOGETHER, THOUGH.
PHYSICALLY.
NAH, I DON'T THINK SO.
I THINK HE MUST BE...
...TOKINE'S ELDER BROTHER. I BET THEY WERE SEPARATED AT BIRTH!
YEAH, THAT'S IT!
THAT'S PRETTY UNLIKELY ...
WHAT !?
OH, NO! WE LOST 'EM WHILE WE WERE GABBING.
DAMN IT, HACHIOJI...
BACK ON THEIR TRAIL, TABATA!
GNARRL
NAH...
THAT'S ENOUGH FOR TODAY.
HOW COME? WHY ARE YOU HOLDING BACK?
THIS ISN'T LIKE YOU AT ALL!
YEAH, BUT...

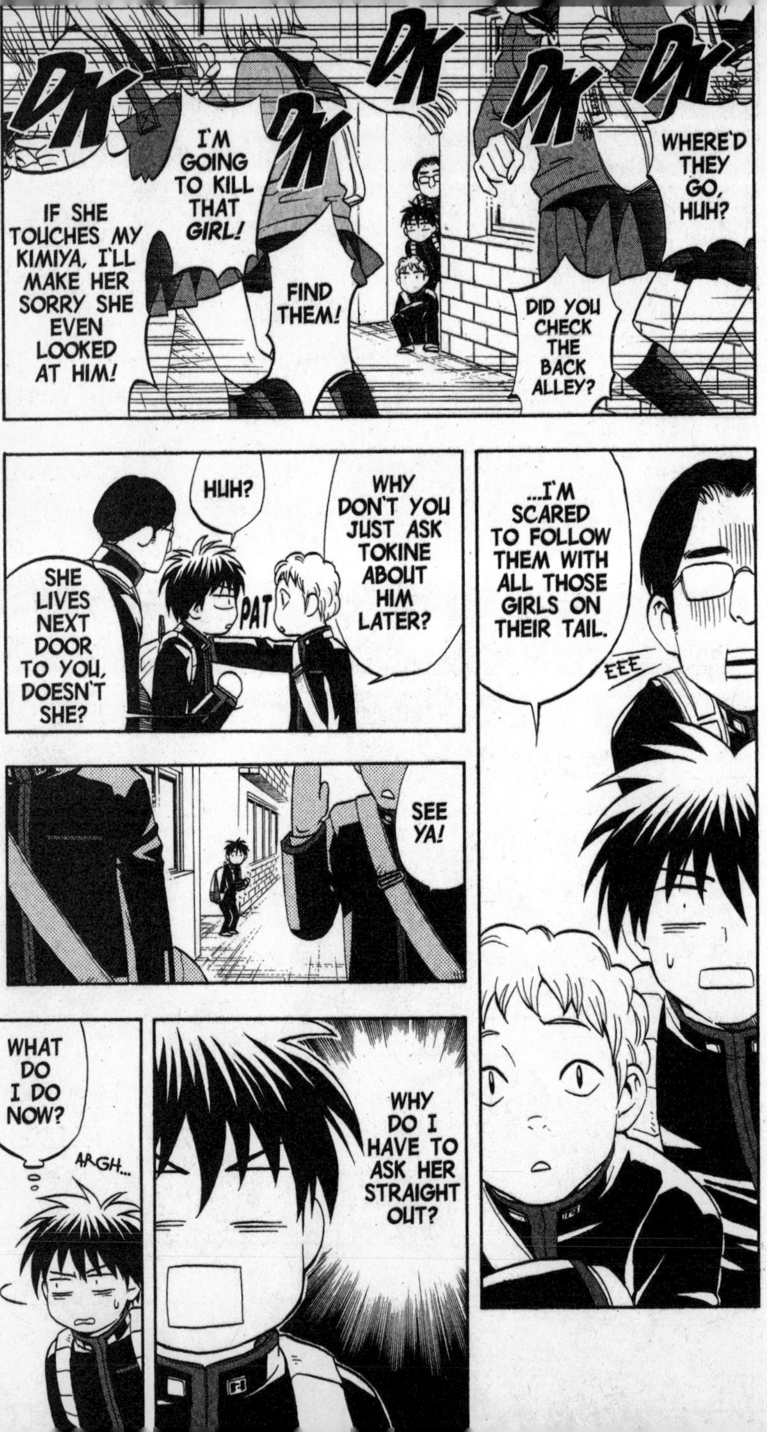
DK
DK
DK
WHERE'D THEY GO, HUH?
DID YOU CHECK THE BACK ALLEY?
DK
DK
I'M GOING TO KILL THAT GIRL!
FIND THEM!
DK
IF SHE TOUCHES MY KIMIYA, I'LL MAKE HER SORRY SHE EVEN LOOKED AT HIM!
...I'M SCARED TO FOLLOW THEM WITH ALL THOSE GIRLS ON THEIR TAIL.
EEE
WHY DON'T YOU JUST ASK TOKINE ABOUT HIM LATER?
HUH?
PAT
SHE LIVES NEXT DOOR TO YOU, DOESN'T SHE?
SEE YA!
WHY DO I HAVE TO ASK HER STRAIGHT OUT?
WHAT DO I DO NOW?
ARGH...

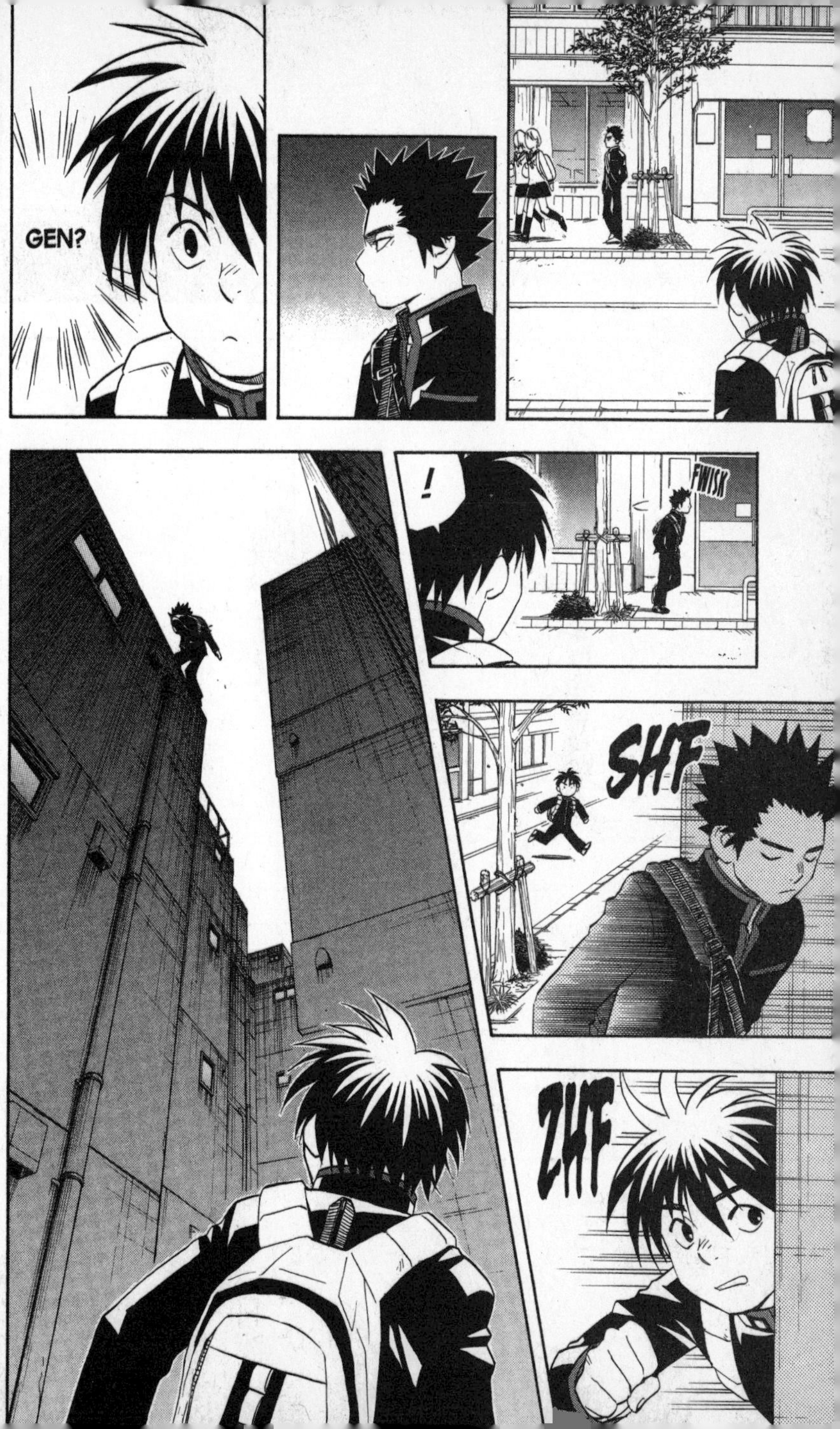
GEN?
!
FWISK
SHF
ZHF

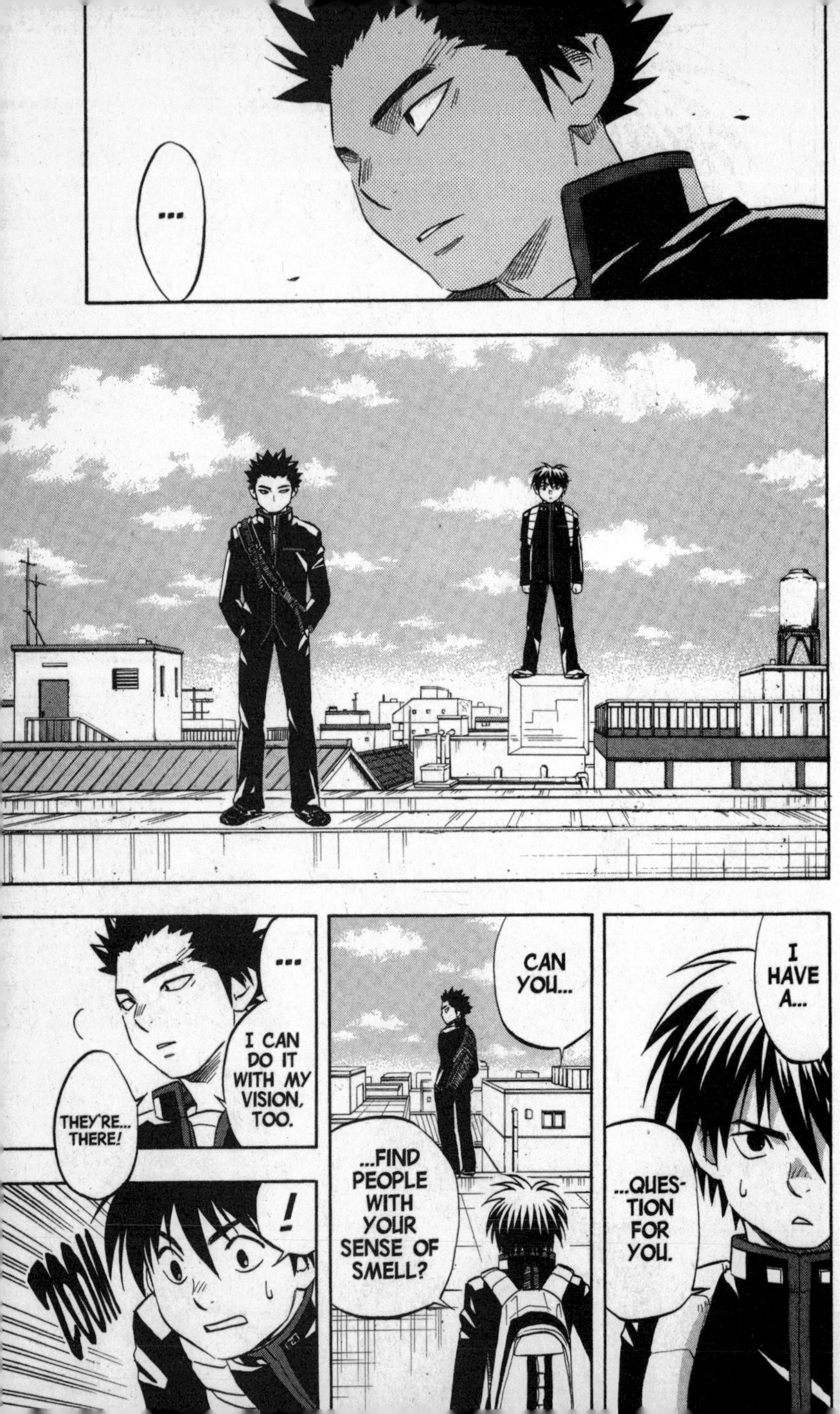
...
I HAVE A...
...QUES-TION FOR YOU.
CAN YOU...
...FIND PEOPLE WITH YOUR SENSE OF SMELL?
...
I CAN DO IT WITH MY VISION, TOO.
THEY'RE... THERE!
!
ZOOM

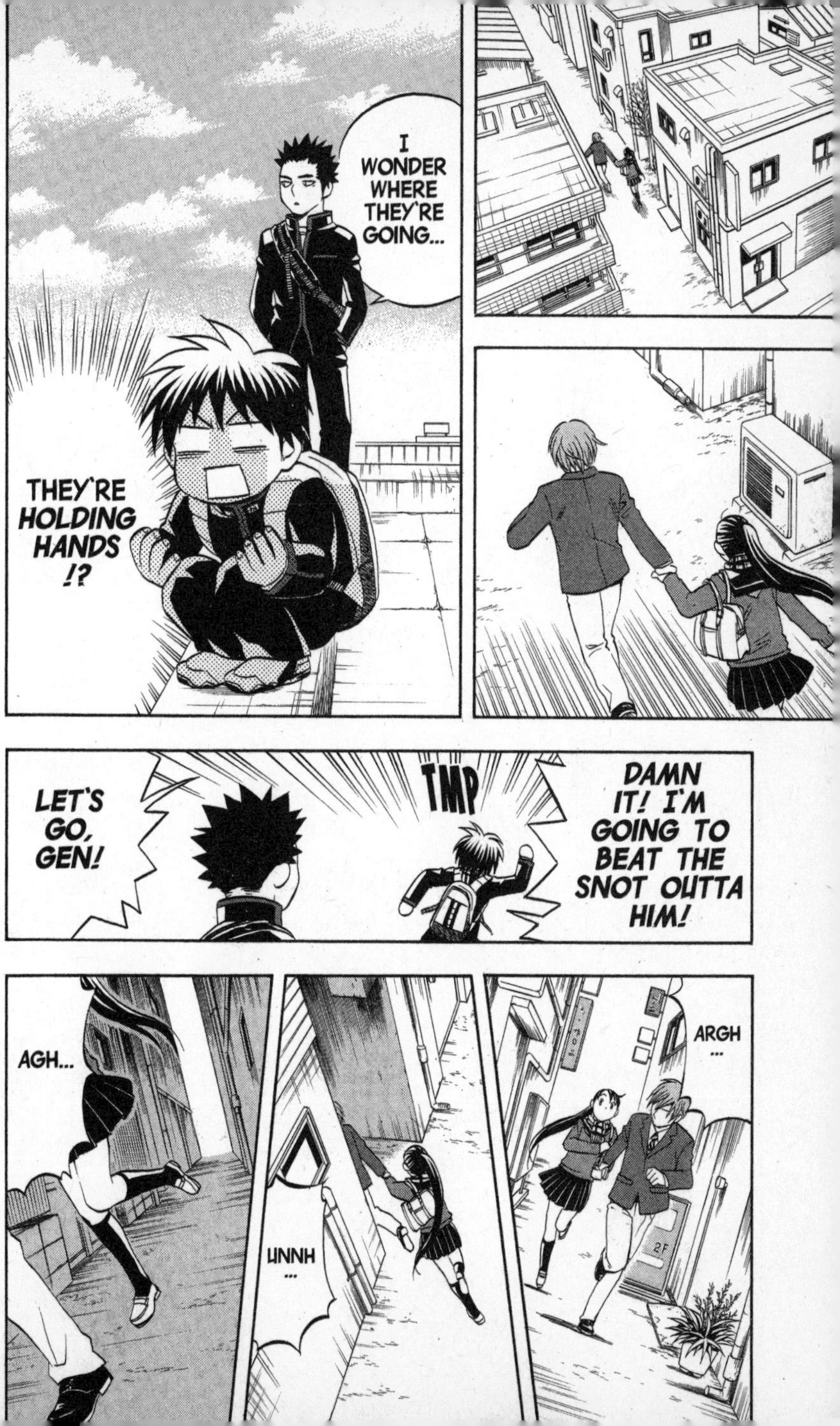
I WONDER WHERE THEY'RE GOING...
THEY'RE HOLDING HANDS !?
DAMN IT! I'M GOING TO BEAT THE SNOT OUTTA HIM!
TMP
LET'S GO, GEN!
ARGH ...
UNNH ...
AGH...

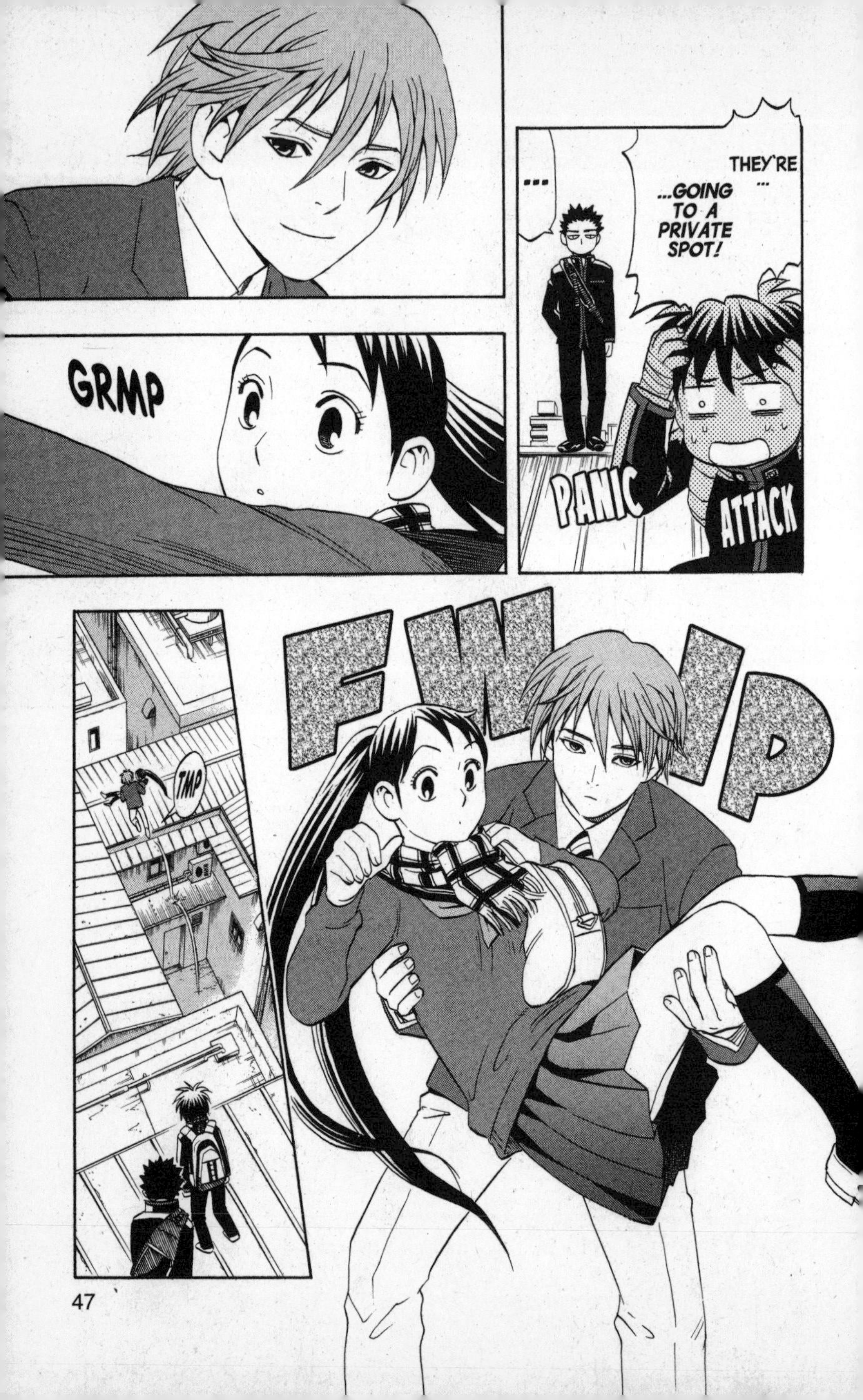
...
THEY'RE ...
...GOING TO A PRIVATE SPOT!
PANIC
ATTACK
GRMP
FWIP
TMP

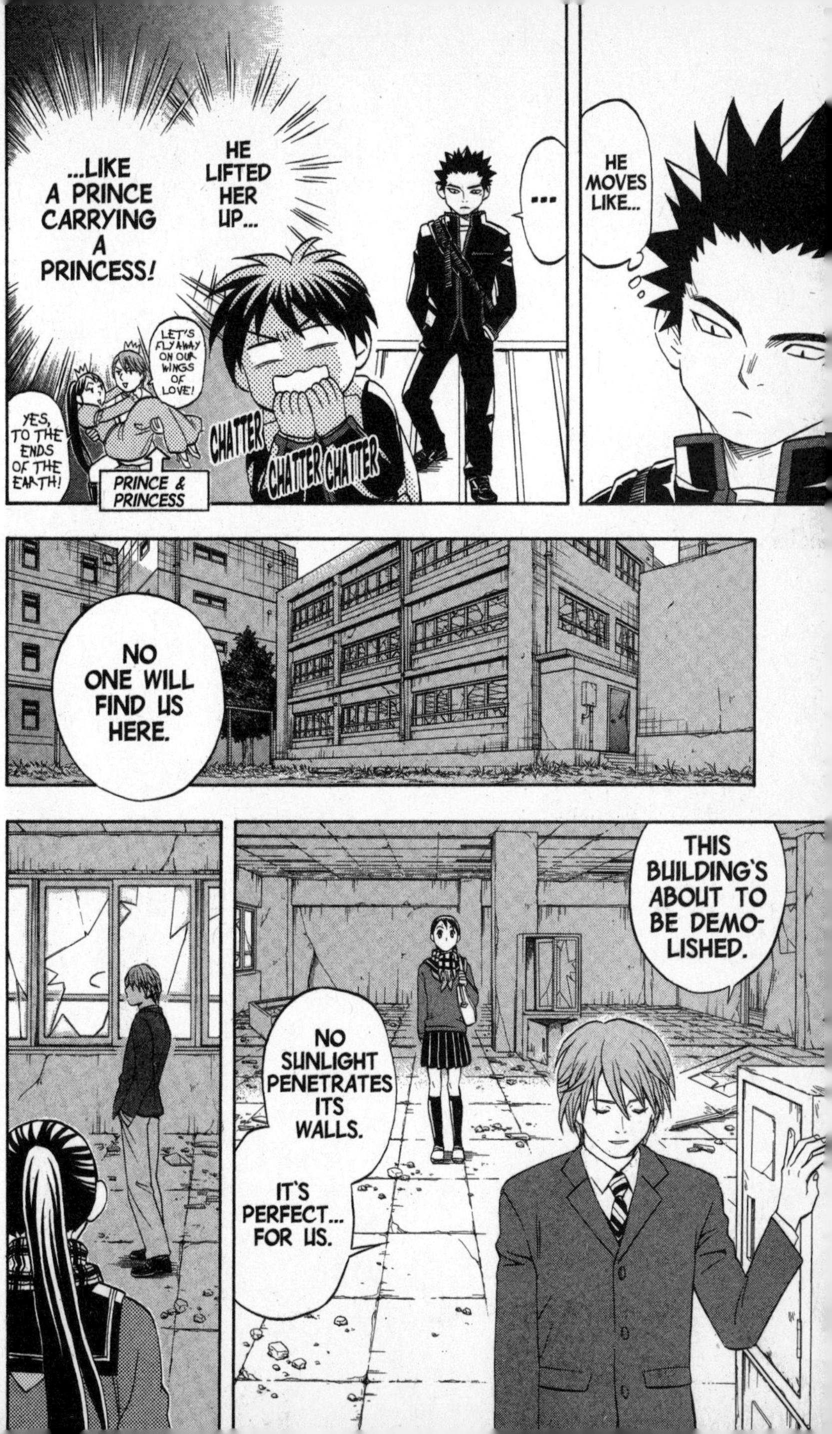
HE MOVES LIKE...
...
HE LIFTED HER UP...
...LIKE A PRINCE CARRYING A PRINCESS!
LET'S FLY AWAY ON OUR WINGS OF LOVE!
YES, TO THE ENDS OF THE EARTH!
PRINCE & PRINCESS
CHATTER CHATTER CHATTER
NO ONE WILL FIND US HERE.
THIS BUILDING'S ABOUT TO BE DEMO-LISHED.
NO SUNLIGHT PENETRATES ITS WALLS.
IT'S PERFECT... FOR US.

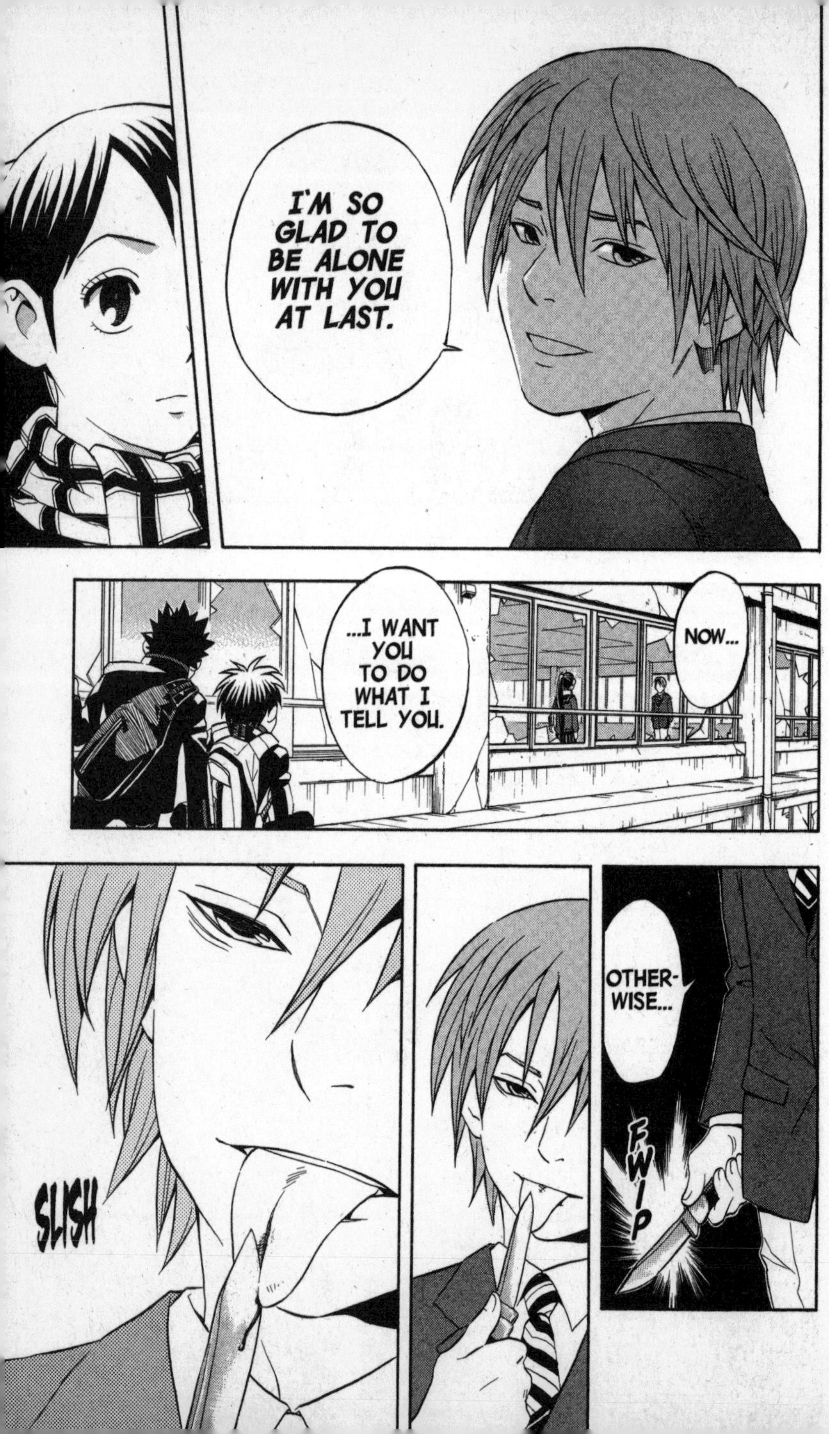
I'M SO GLAD TO BE ALONE WITH YOU AT LAST.
NOW...
...I WANT YOU TO DO WHAT I TELL YOU.
OTHER-WISE...
FWIP
SLISH

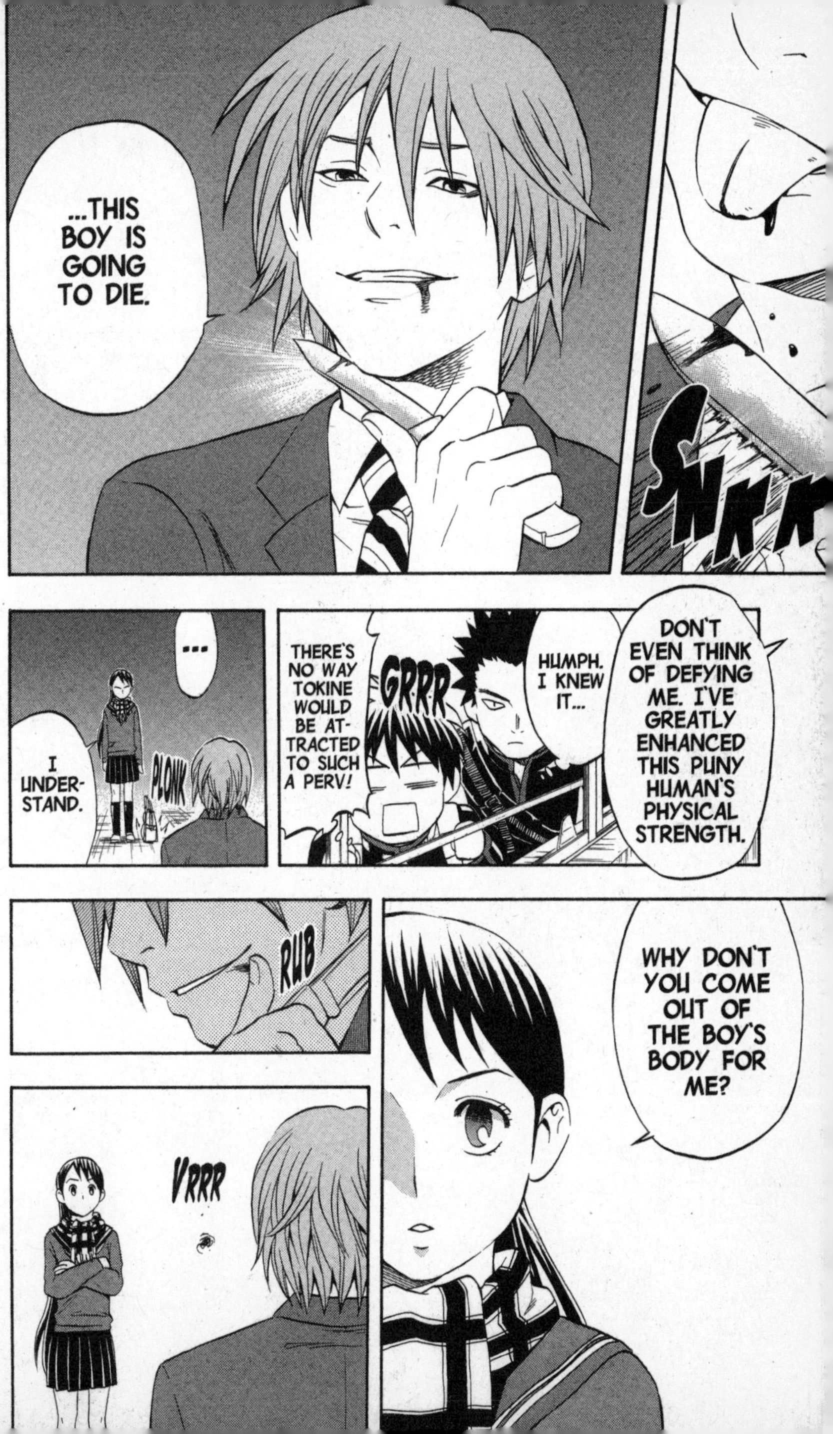
SNKK
...THIS BOY IS GOING TO DIE.
DON'T EVEN THINK OF DEFYING ME. I'VE GREATLY ENHANCED THIS PUNY HUMAN'S PHYSICAL STRENGTH.
HUMPH. I KNEW IT...
GRRR
THERE'S NO WAY TOKINE WOULD BE AT-TRACTED TO SUCH A PERV!
...
I UNDER-STAND.
PLONK
WHY DON'T YOU COME OUT OF THE BOY'S BODY FOR ME?
RUB
VRRR

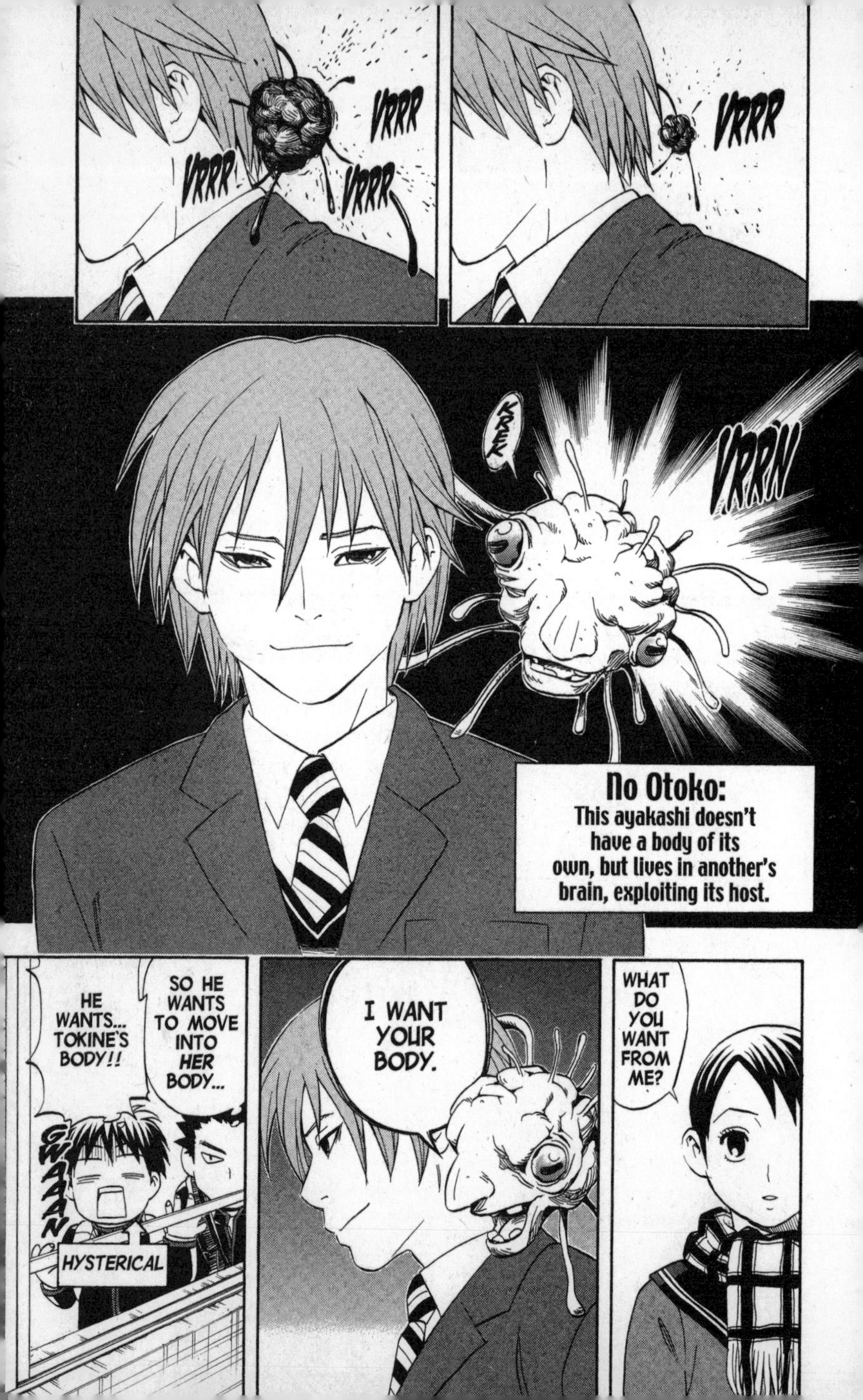
VRRR
VRRR
VRRR
VRRR
VRRN
KREK
No Otoko:
This ayakashi doesn't have a body of its own, but lives in another's brain, exploiting its host.
WHAT DO YOU WANT FROM ME?
I WANT YOUR BODY.
SO HE WANTS TO MOVE INTO HER BODY...
HE WANTS... TOKINE'S BODY!!
GWAAAN
HYSTERICAL

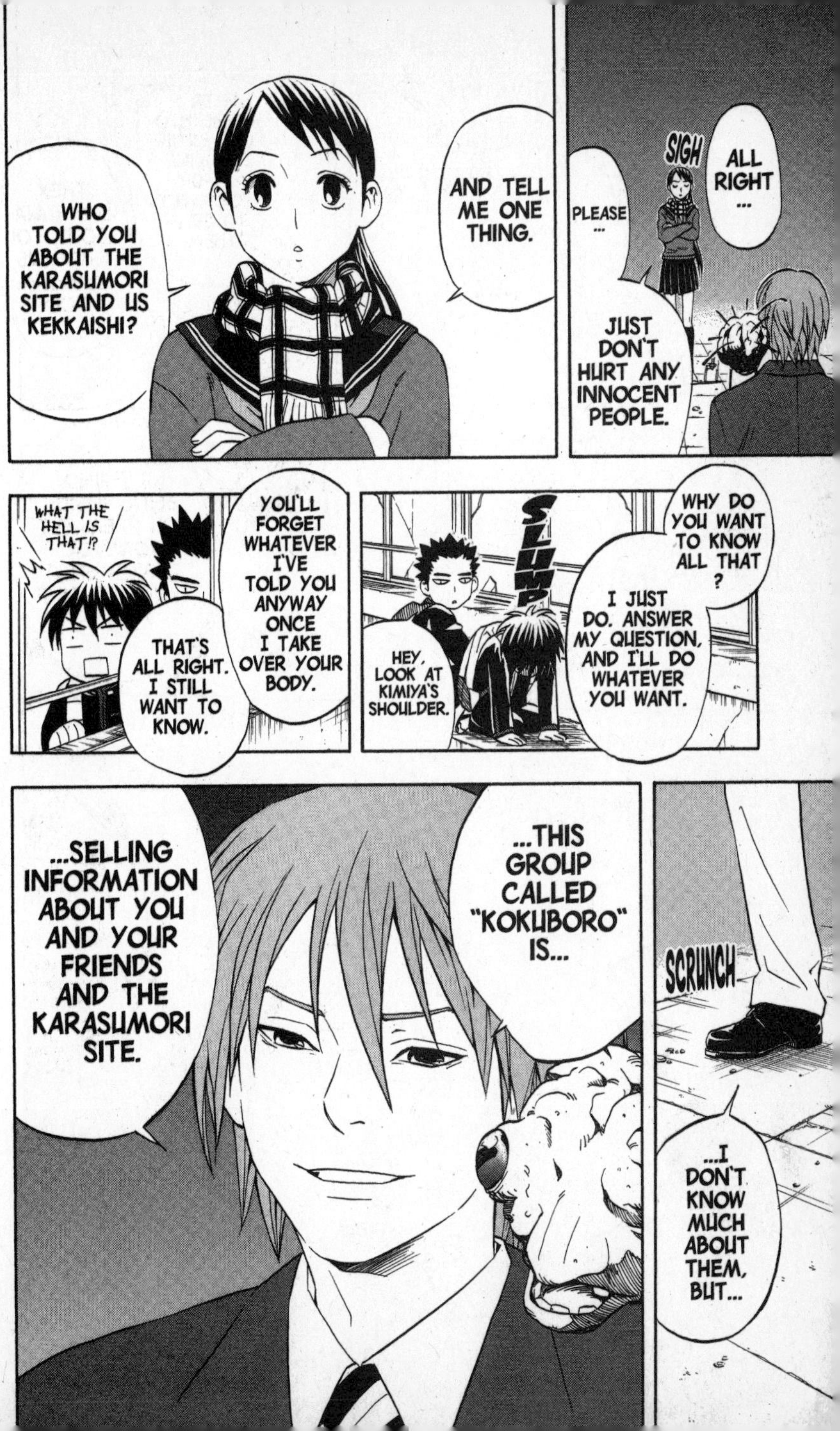
SIGH
ALL RIGHT ...
PLEASE ...
JUST DON'T HURT ANY INNOCENT PEOPLE.
AND TELL ME ONE THING.
WHO TOLD YOU ABOUT THE KARASUMORI SITE AND US KEKKAISHI?
WHY DO YOU WANT TO KNOW ALL THAT?
I JUST DO. ANSWER MY QUESTION, AND I'LL DO WHATEVER YOU WANT.
SLUMP
HEY, LOOK AT KIMIYA'S SHOULDER.
YOU'LL FORGET WHATEVER I'VE TOLD YOU ANYWAY ONCE I TAKE OVER YOUR BODY.
THAT'S ALL RIGHT. I STILL WANT TO KNOW.
WHAT THE HELL IS THAT!?
SCRUNCH
...I DON'T KNOW MUCH ABOUT THEM, BUT...
...THIS GROUP CALLED "KOKUBORO" IS...
...SELLING INFORMATION ABOUT YOU AND YOUR FRIENDS AND THE KARASUMORI SITE.

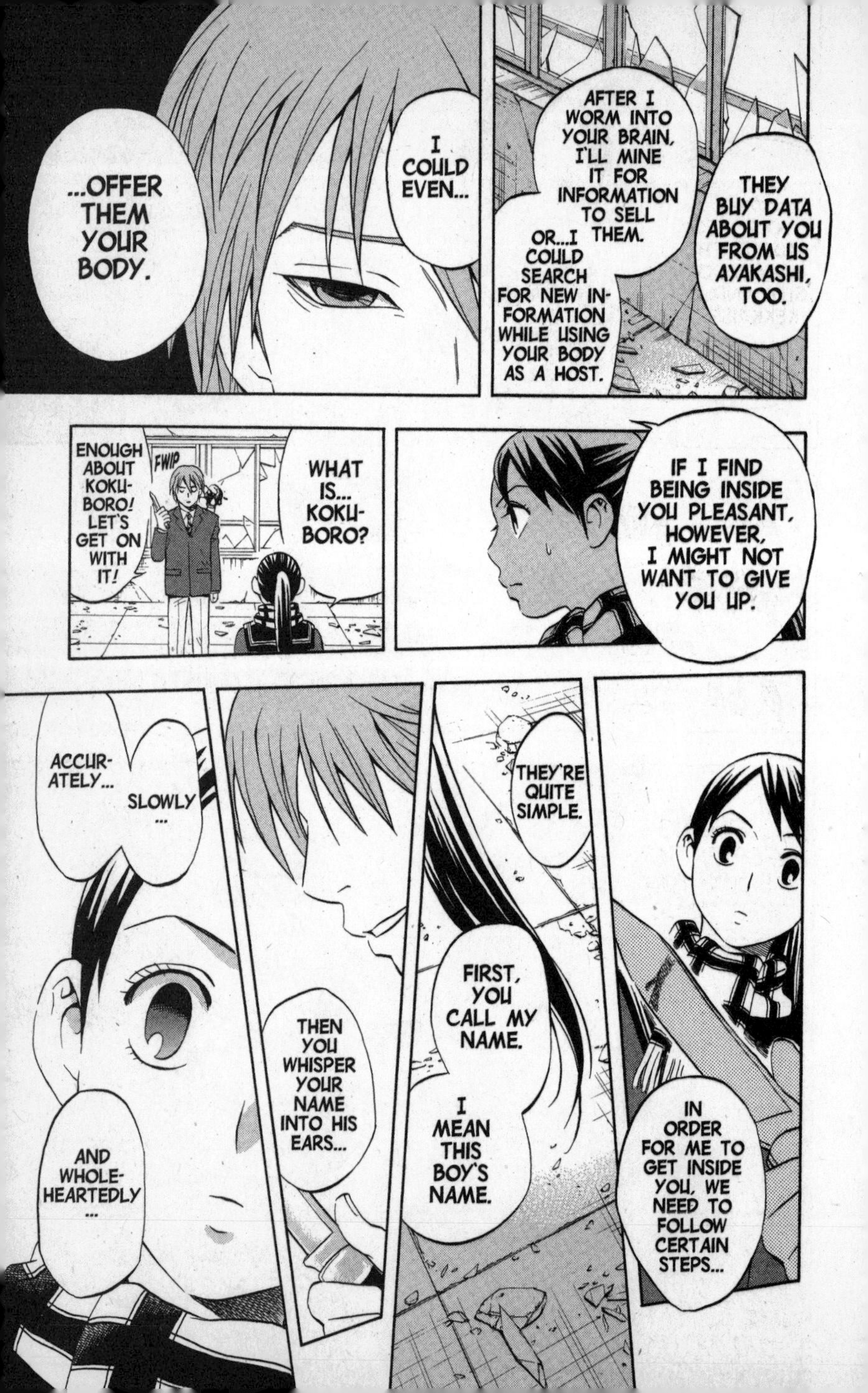
THEY BUY DATA ABOUT YOU FROM US AYAKASHI, TOO.
AFTER I WORM INTO YOUR BRAIN, I'LL MINE IT FOR INFORMATION TO SELL THEM.
OR...I COULD SEARCH FOR NEW INFORMATION WHILE USING YOUR BODY AS A HOST.
I COULD EVEN...
...OFFER THEM YOUR BODY.
IF I FIND BEING INSIDE YOU PLEASANT, HOWEVER, I MIGHT NOT WANT TO GIVE YOU UP.
WHAT IS... KOKU-BORO?
ENOUGH ABOUT KOKU-BORO! LET'S GET ON WITH IT!
FWIP
IN ORDER FOR ME TO GET INSIDE YOU, WE NEED TO FOLLOW CERTAIN STEPS...
THEY'RE QUITE SIMPLE.
FIRST, YOU CALL MY NAME.
I MEAN THIS BOY'S NAME.
THEN YOU WHISPER YOUR NAME INTO HIS EARS...
ACCUR-ATELY...
SLOWLY...
AND WHOLE-HEARTEDLY...

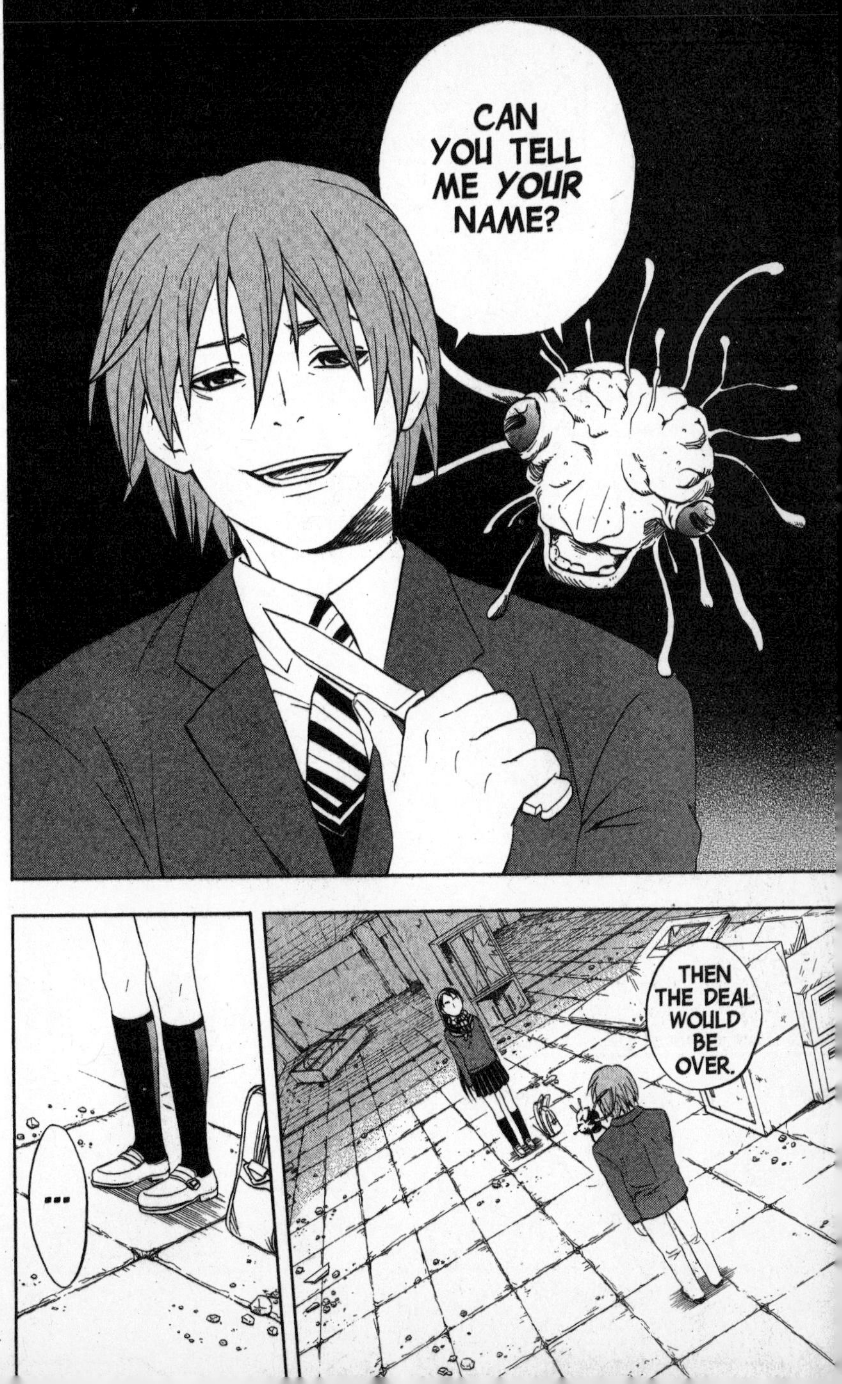
CAN YOU TELL ME *YOUR* NAME?
THEN THE DEAL WOULD BE OVER.
...

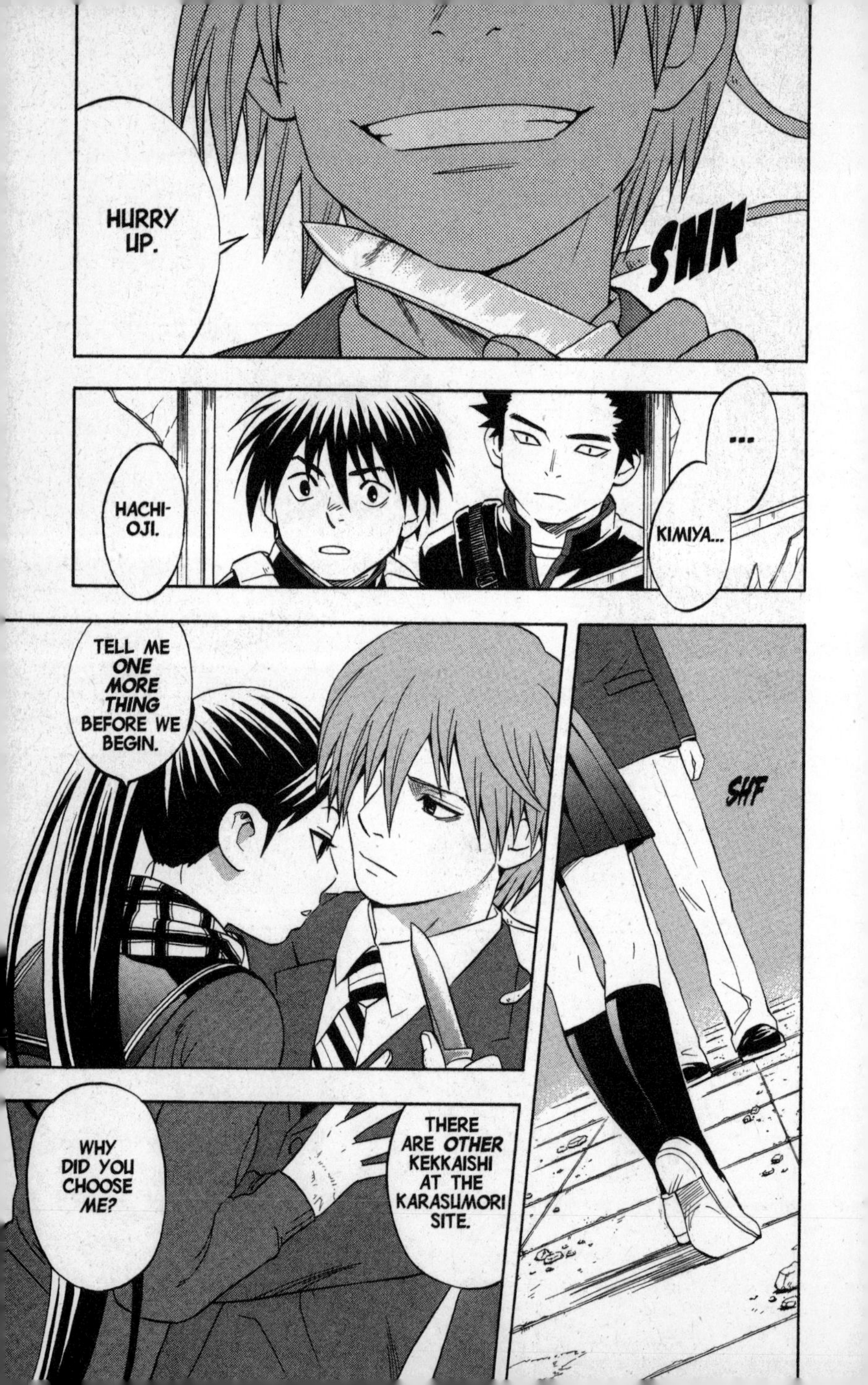
SNK
HURRY UP.
...
KIMIYA...
HACHI-OJI.
SHF
TELL ME *ONE MORE THING* BEFORE WE BEGIN.
THERE ARE *OTHER* KEKKAISHI AT THE KARASUMORI SITE.
WHY DID YOU CHOOSE *ME*?

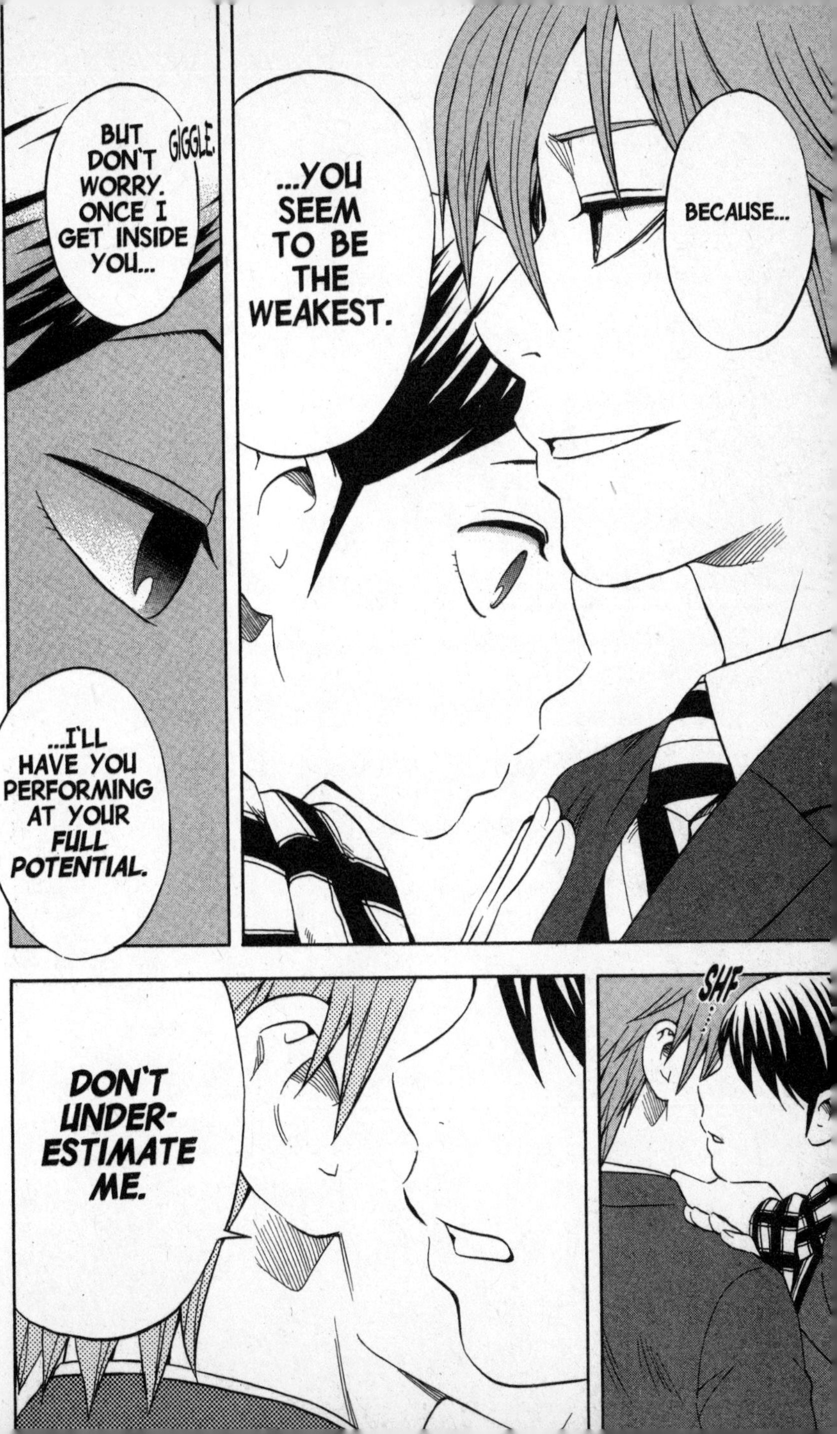
BECAUSE...
...YOU SEEM TO BE THE WEAKEST.
GIGGLE.
BUT DON'T WORRY. ONCE I GET INSIDE YOU...
...I'LL HAVE YOU PERFORMING AT YOUR FULL POTENTIAL.
SHF
DON'T UNDER-ESTIMATE ME.

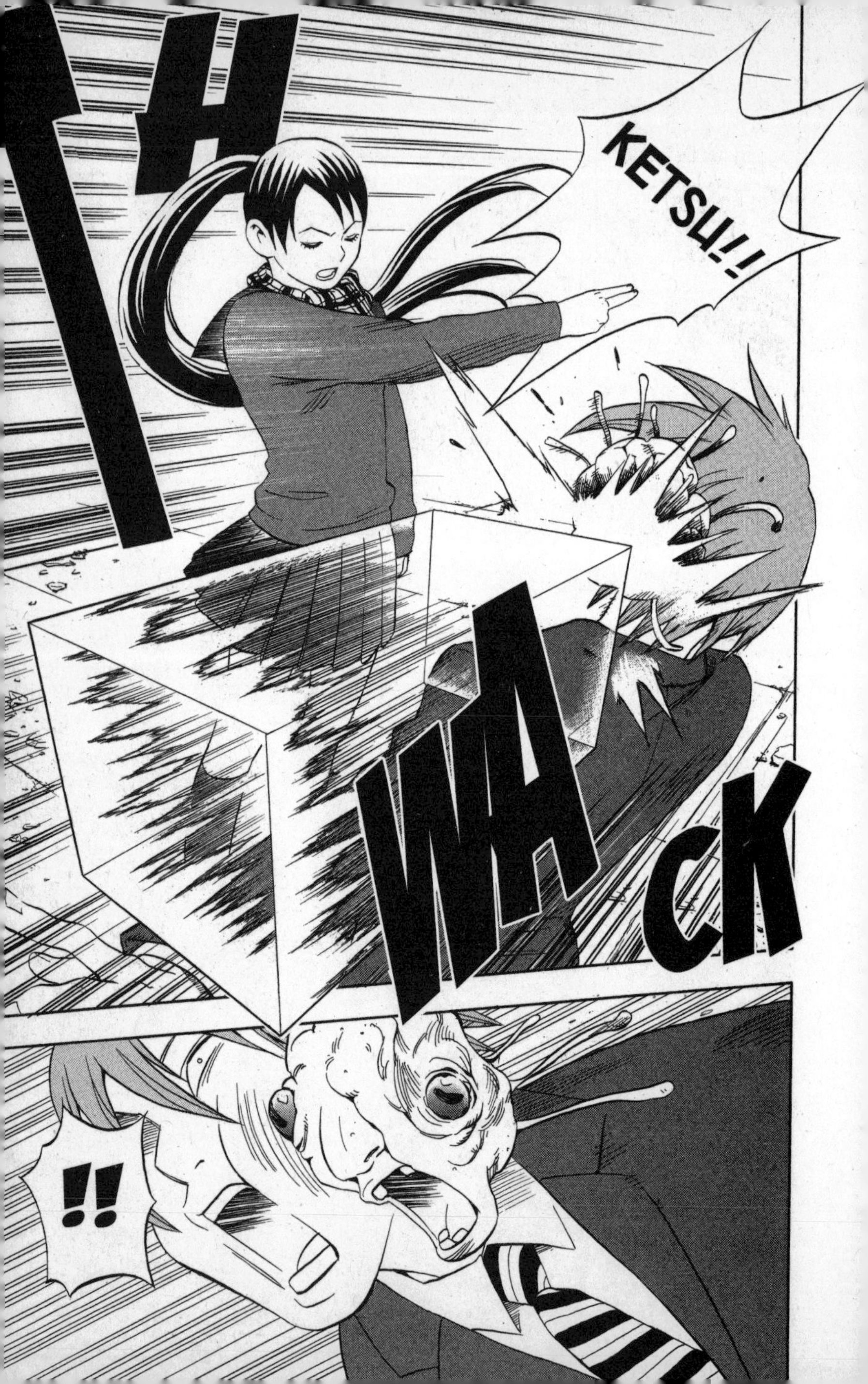
KETSU!!
THWACK
!!

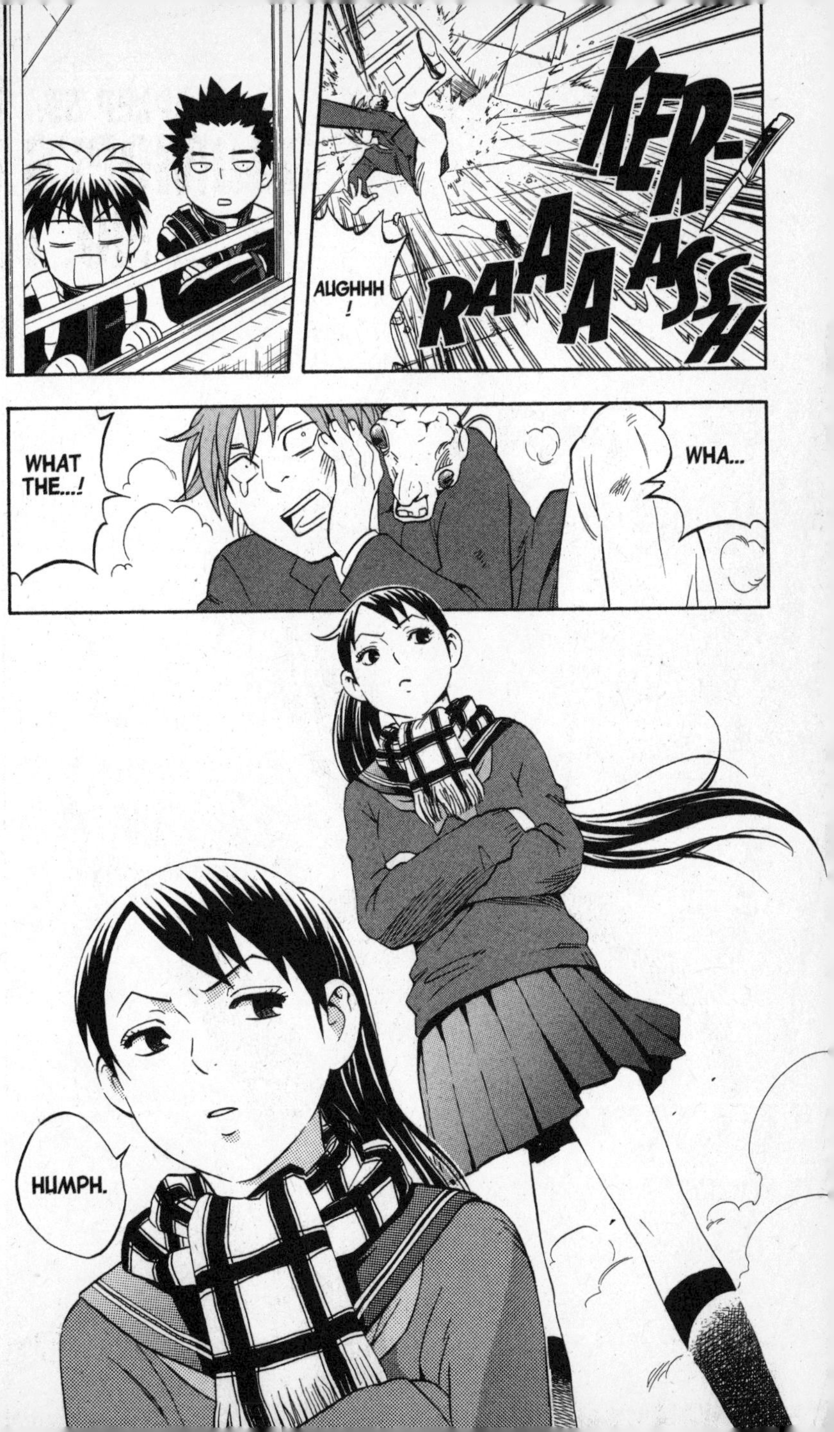
KER-RAAAAASH
AUGHHH!
WHA...
WHAT THE...!
HUMPH.

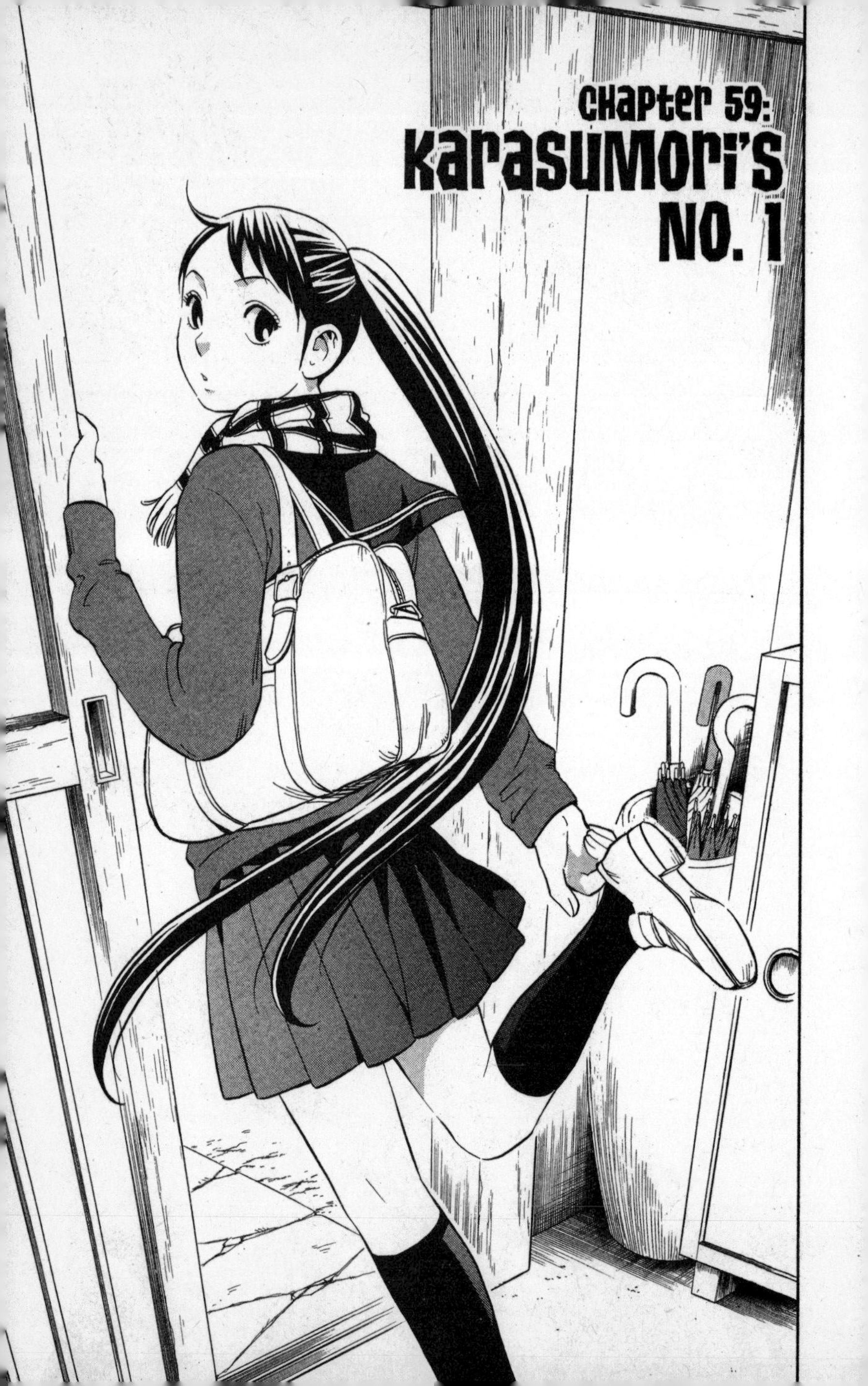
Chapter 59:
Karasumori's
No. 1

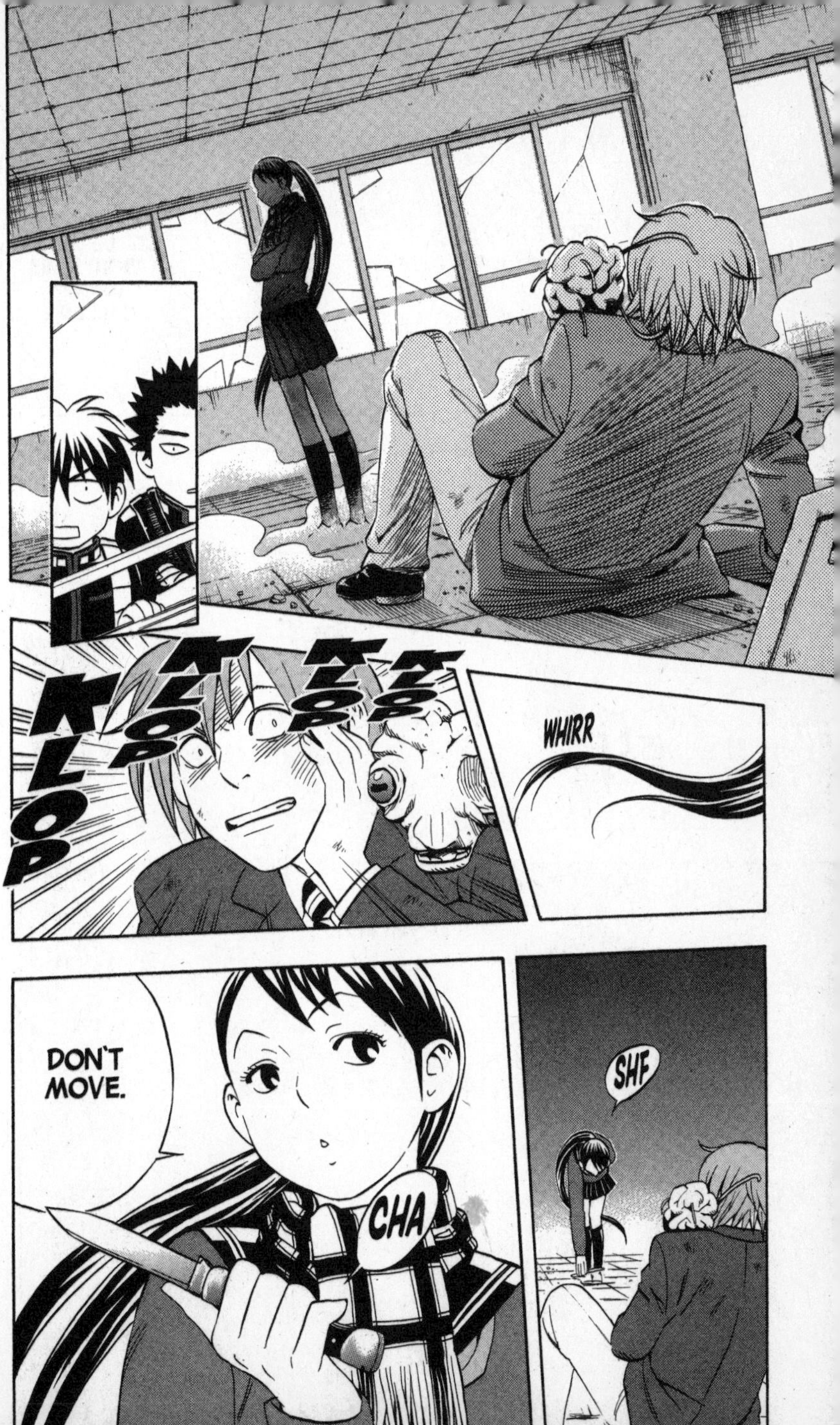
WHIRR
KLOP
KLOP
KLOP
KLOP
SHF
DON'T MOVE.
CHA

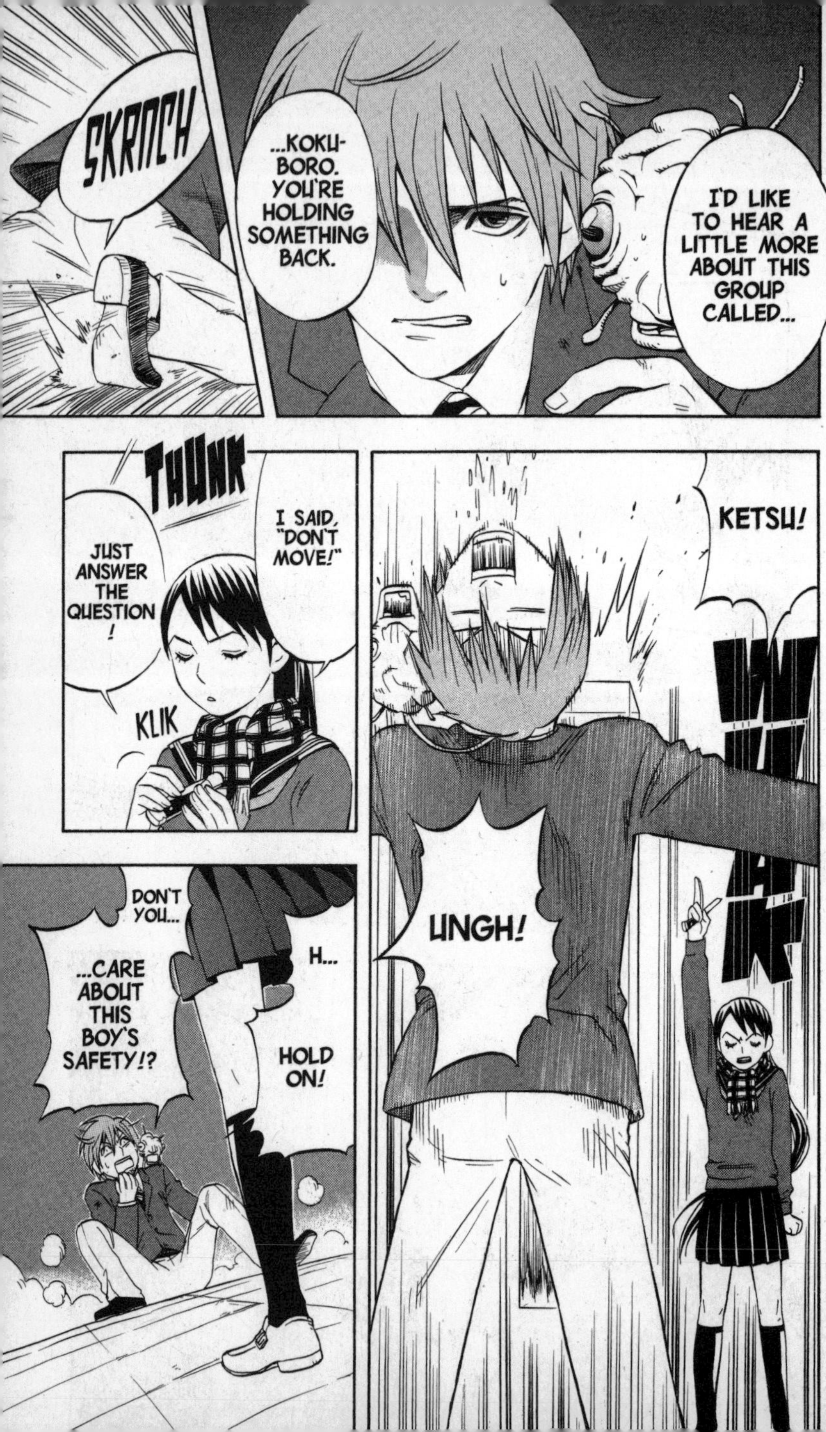
I'D LIKE TO HEAR A LITTLE MORE ABOUT THIS GROUP CALLED...
...KOKU-BORO. YOU'RE HOLDING SOMETHING BACK.
SKRNCH
KETSU!
WHAK
UNGH!
I SAID, "DON'T MOVE!"
THUNK
JUST ANSWER THE QUESTION!
KLIK
H...
HOLD ON!
DON'T YOU...
...CARE ABOUT THIS BOY'S SAFETY!?

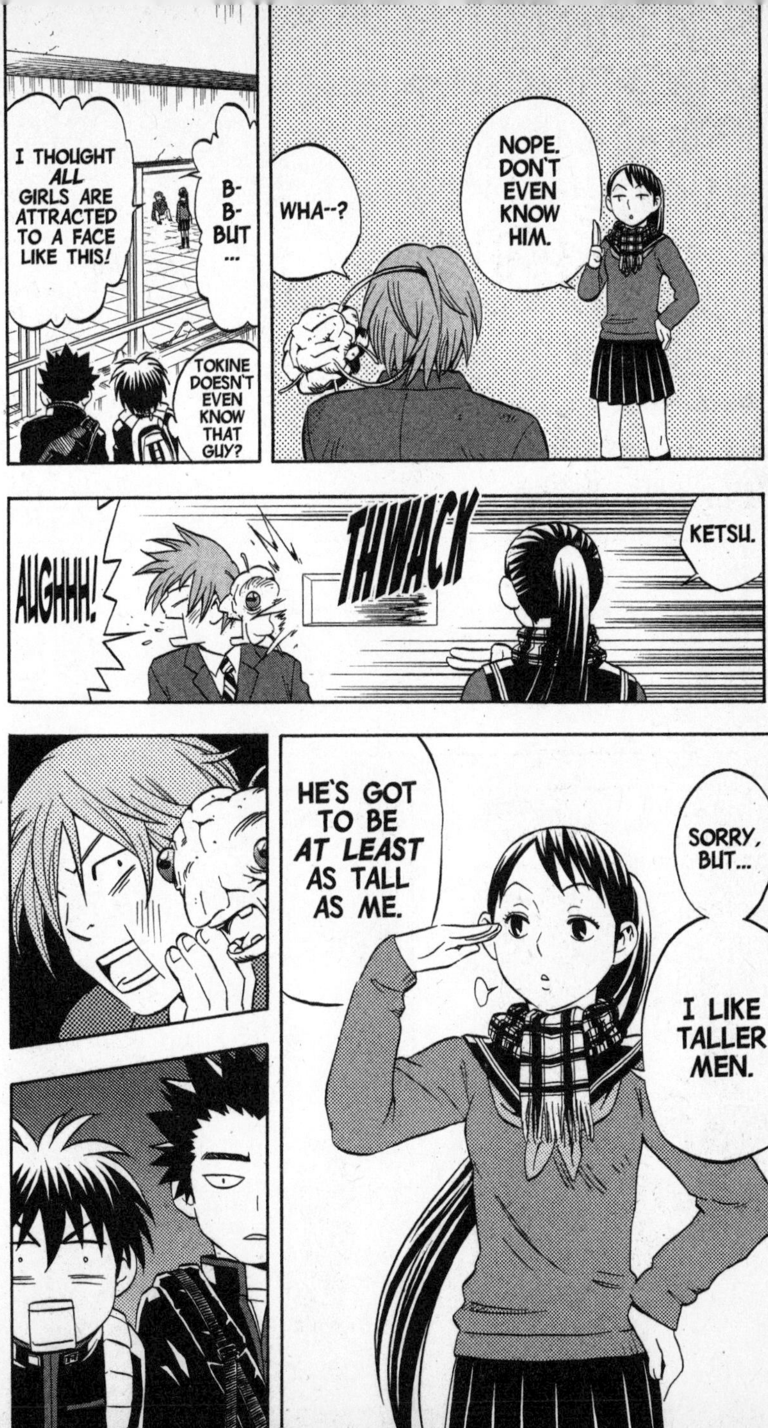
NOPE. DON'T EVEN KNOW HIM.
WHA--?
B-B-BUT...
I THOUGHT ALL GIRLS ARE ATTRACTED TO A FACE LIKE THIS!
TOKINE DOESN'T EVEN KNOW THAT GUY?
KETSU.
THWACK
AUGHHH!
SORRY, BUT...
I LIKE TALLER MEN.
HE'S GOT TO BE AT LEAST AS TALL AS ME.

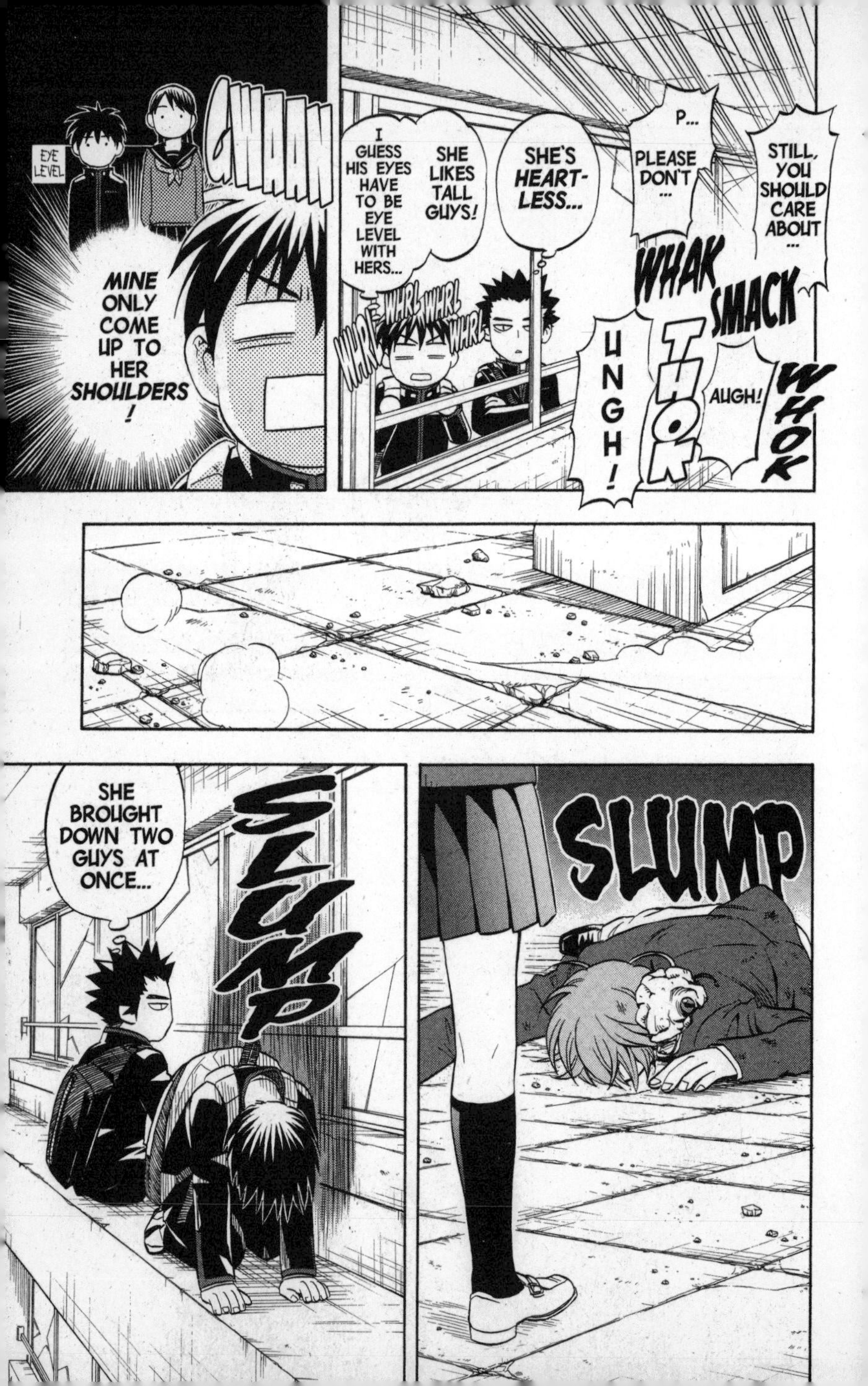
STILL, YOU SHOULD CARE ABOUT ...
P... PLEASE DON'T ...
WHAK
SMACK
WHOK
AUGH!
THOK
UNGH!
SHE'S HEARTLESS...
SHE LIKES TALL GUYS!
I GUESS HIS EYES HAVE TO BE EYE LEVEL WITH HERS...
WHRL WHRL WHRL WHRL
GWAAN
EYE LEVEL
MINE ONLY COME UP TO HER SHOULDERS!
SLUMP
SLUMP
SHE BROUGHT DOWN TWO GUYS AT ONCE...

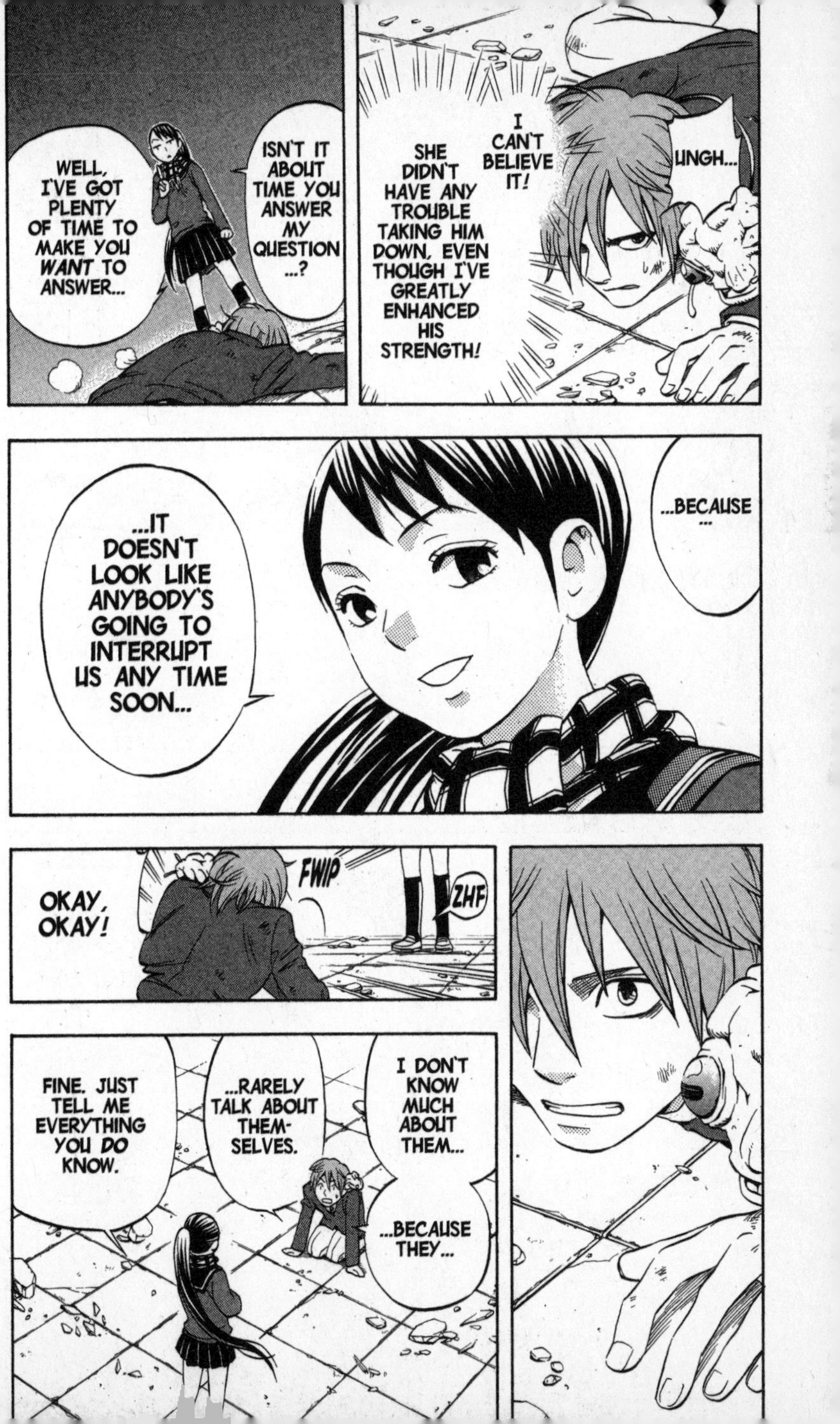
UNGH...
I CAN'T BELIEVE IT!
SHE DIDN'T HAVE ANY TROUBLE TAKING HIM DOWN, EVEN THOUGH I'VE GREATLY ENHANCED HIS STRENGTH!
ISN'T IT ABOUT TIME YOU ANSWER MY QUESTION ...?
WELL, I'VE GOT PLENTY OF TIME TO MAKE YOU *WANT* TO ANSWER...
...BECAUSE ...
...IT DOESN'T LOOK LIKE ANYBODY'S GOING TO INTERRUPT US ANY TIME SOON...
FWIP
ZHF
OKAY, OKAY!
I DON'T KNOW MUCH ABOUT THEM...
...BECAUSE THEY...
...RARELY TALK ABOUT THEM-SELVES.
FINE. JUST TELL ME EVERYTHING YOU *DO* KNOW.

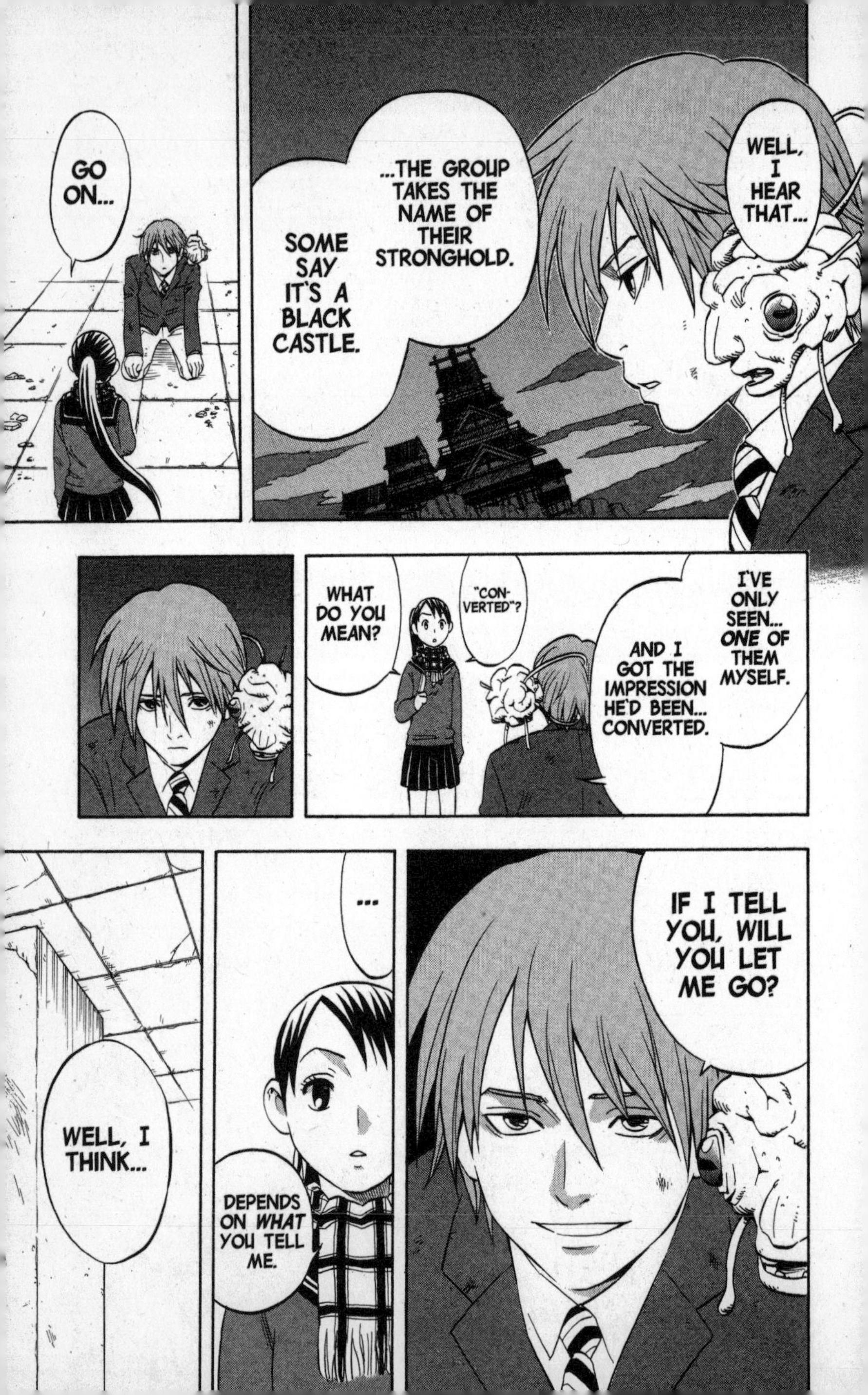
WELL, I HEAR THAT...
...THE GROUP TAKES THE NAME OF THEIR STRONGHOLD.
SOME SAY IT'S A BLACK CASTLE.
GO ON...
I'VE ONLY SEEN... *ONE* OF THEM MYSELF.
AND I GOT THE IMPRESSION HE'D BEEN... CONVERTED.
"CONVERTED"?
WHAT DO YOU MEAN?
IF I TELL YOU, WILL YOU LET ME GO?
...
DEPENDS ON *WHAT* YOU TELL ME.
WELL, I THINK...

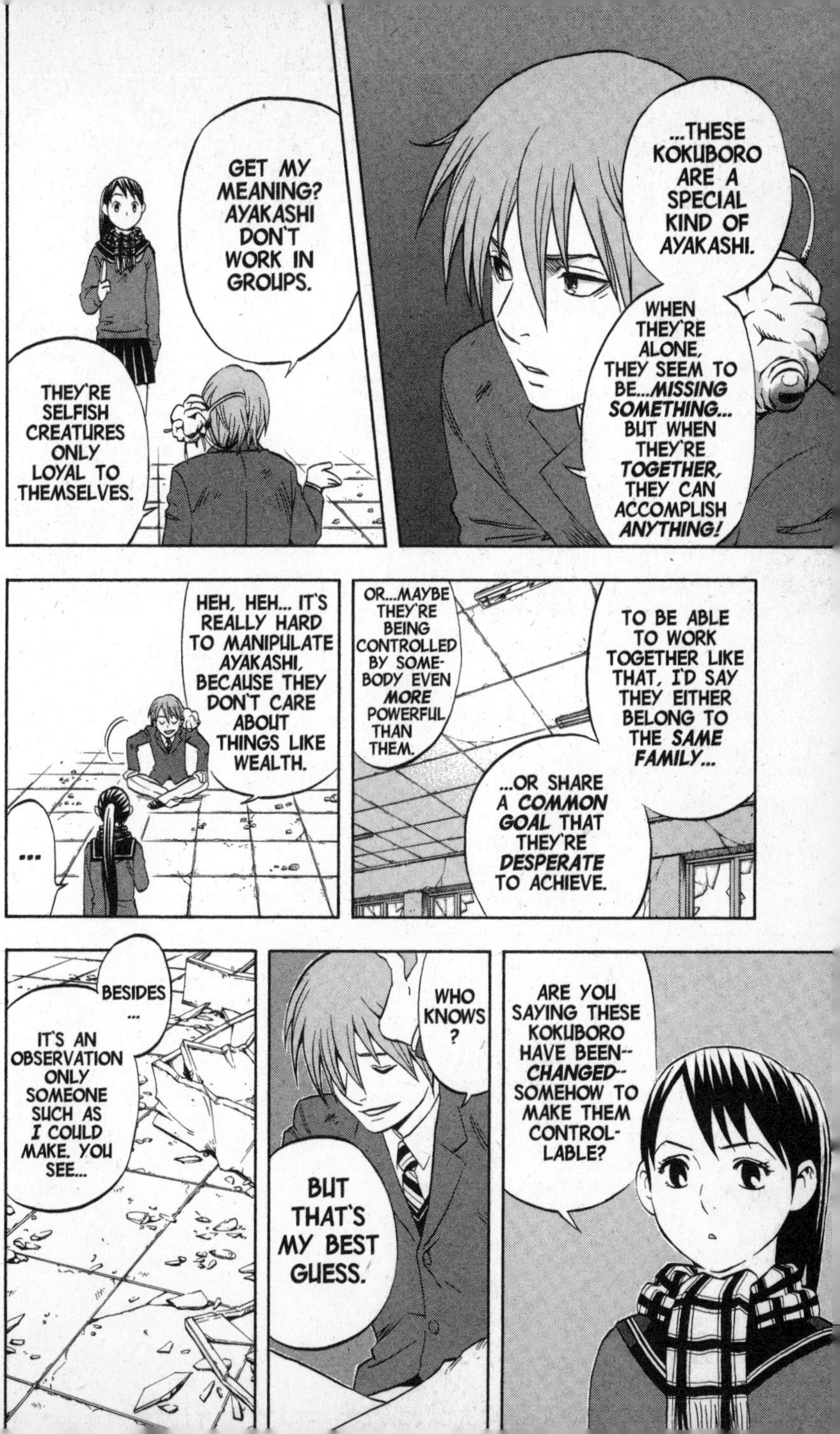
...THESE KOKUBORO ARE A SPECIAL KIND OF AYAKASHI.
WHEN THEY'RE ALONE, THEY SEEM TO BE...*MISSING SOMETHING*... BUT WHEN THEY'RE *TOGETHER*, THEY CAN ACCOMPLISH *ANYTHING!*
GET MY MEANING? AYAKASHI DON'T WORK IN GROUPS.
THEY'RE SELFISH CREATURES ONLY LOYAL TO THEMSELVES.
TO BE ABLE TO WORK TOGETHER LIKE THAT, I'D SAY THEY EITHER BELONG TO THE *SAME FAMILY*...
...OR SHARE A ***COMMON GOAL*** THAT THEY'RE ***DESPERATE*** TO ACHIEVE.
OR...MAYBE THEY'RE BEING CONTROLLED BY SOME-BODY EVEN *MORE* POWERFUL THAN THEM.
HEH, HEH... IT'S REALLY HARD TO MANIPULATE AYAKASHI, BECAUSE THEY DON'T CARE ABOUT THINGS LIKE WEALTH.
...
ARE YOU SAYING THESE KOKUBORO HAVE BEEN-- *CHANGED*-- SOMEHOW TO MAKE THEM CONTROL-LABLE?
WHO KNOWS?
BUT THAT'S MY BEST GUESS.
BESIDES...
IT'S AN OBSERVATION ONLY SOMEONE SUCH AS *I* COULD MAKE. YOU SEE...

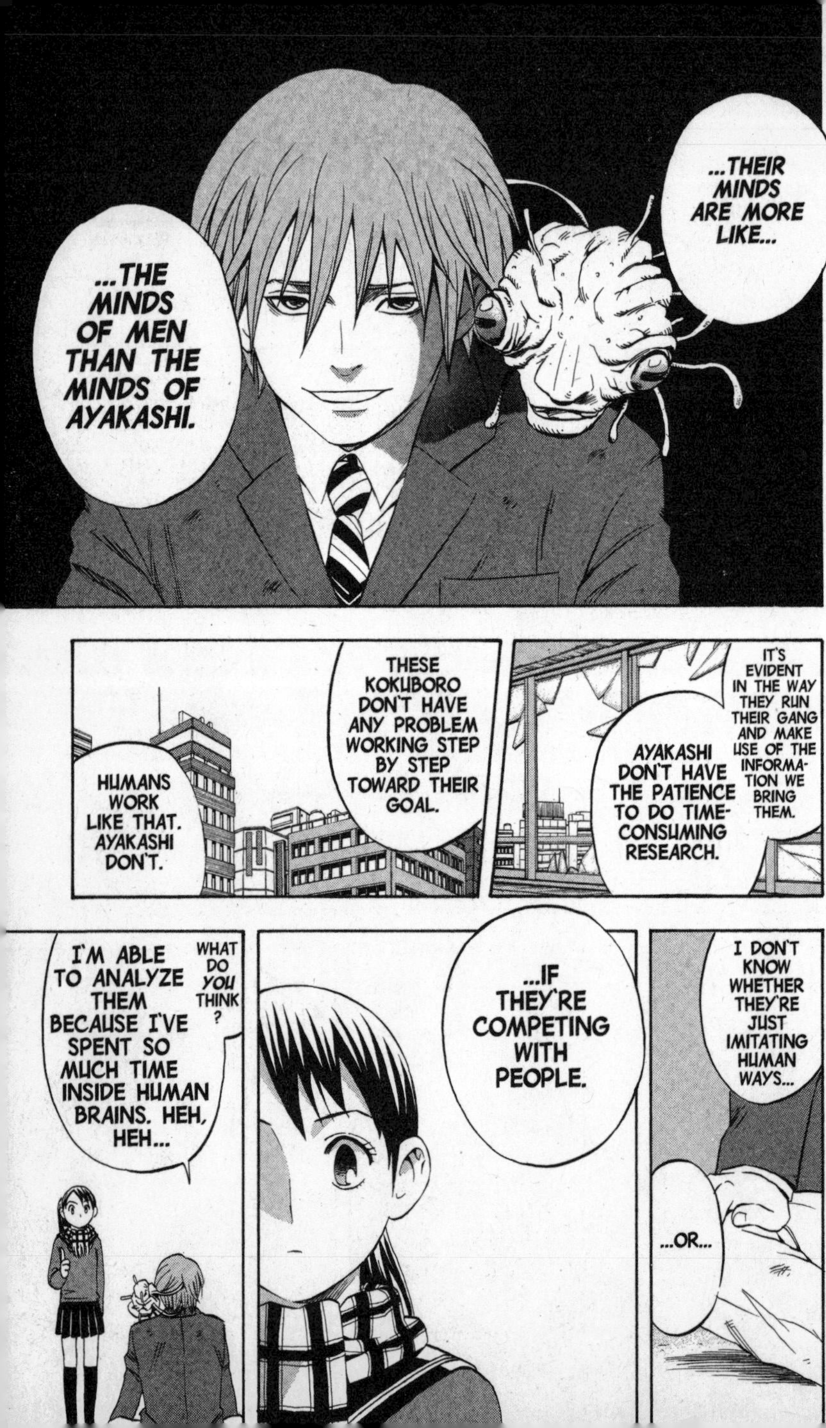
...THEIR MINDS ARE MORE LIKE...
...THE MINDS OF MEN THAN THE MINDS OF AYAKASHI.
IT'S EVIDENT IN THE WAY THEY RUN THEIR GANG AND MAKE USE OF THE INFORMATION WE BRING THEM.
AYAKASHI DON'T HAVE THE PATIENCE TO DO TIME-CONSUMING RESEARCH.
THESE KOKUBORO DON'T HAVE ANY PROBLEM WORKING STEP BY STEP TOWARD THEIR GOAL.
HUMANS WORK LIKE THAT. AYAKASHI DON'T.
I DON'T KNOW WHETHER THEY'RE JUST IMITATING HUMAN WAYS...
...OR...
...IF THEY'RE COMPETING WITH PEOPLE.
WHAT DO *YOU* THINK?
I'M ABLE TO ANALYZE THEM BECAUSE I'VE SPENT SO MUCH TIME INSIDE HUMAN BRAINS. HEH, HEH...

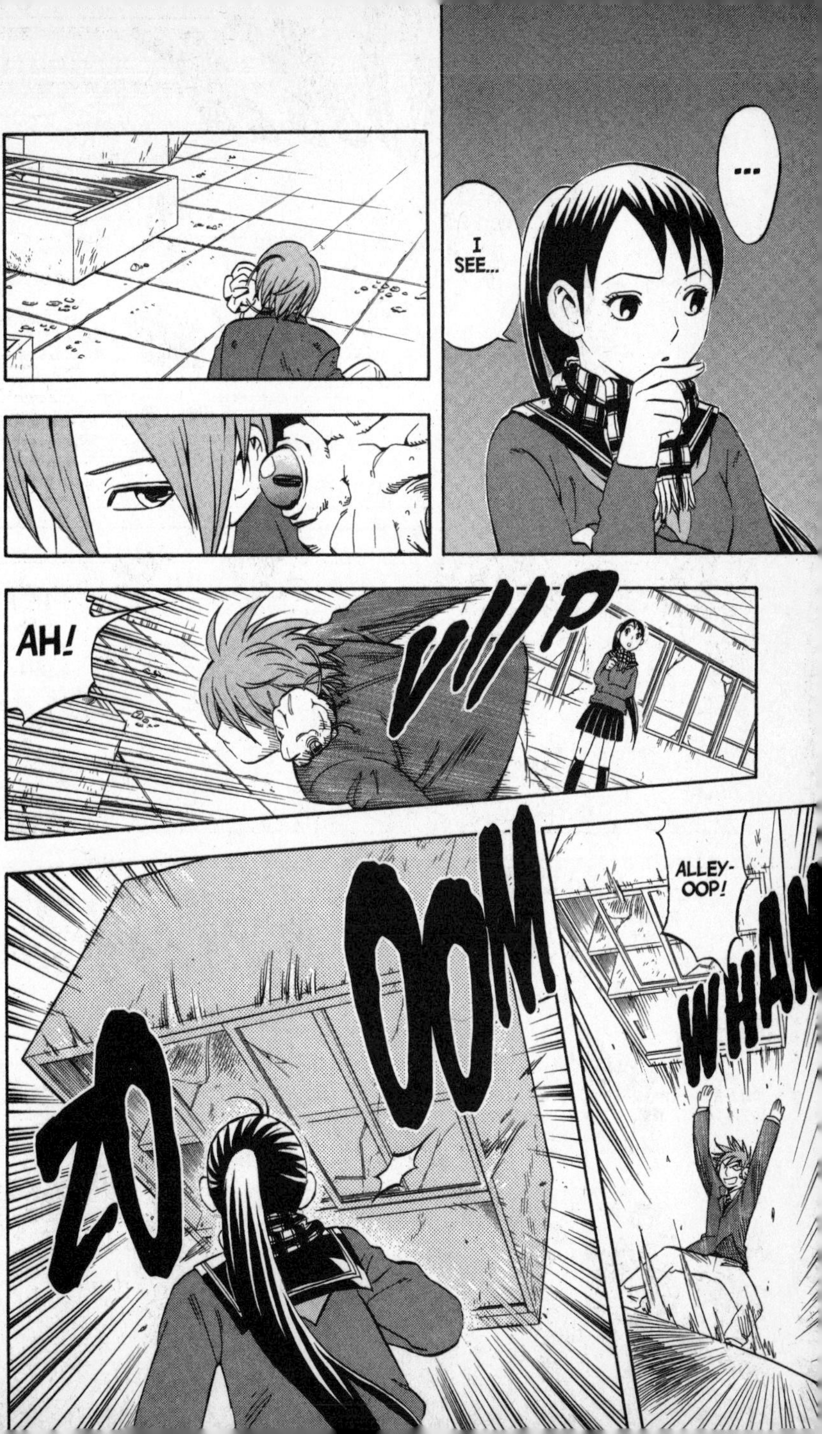
...
I SEE...
AH!
VUP
ALLEY-OOP!
WHAM
ZOOM

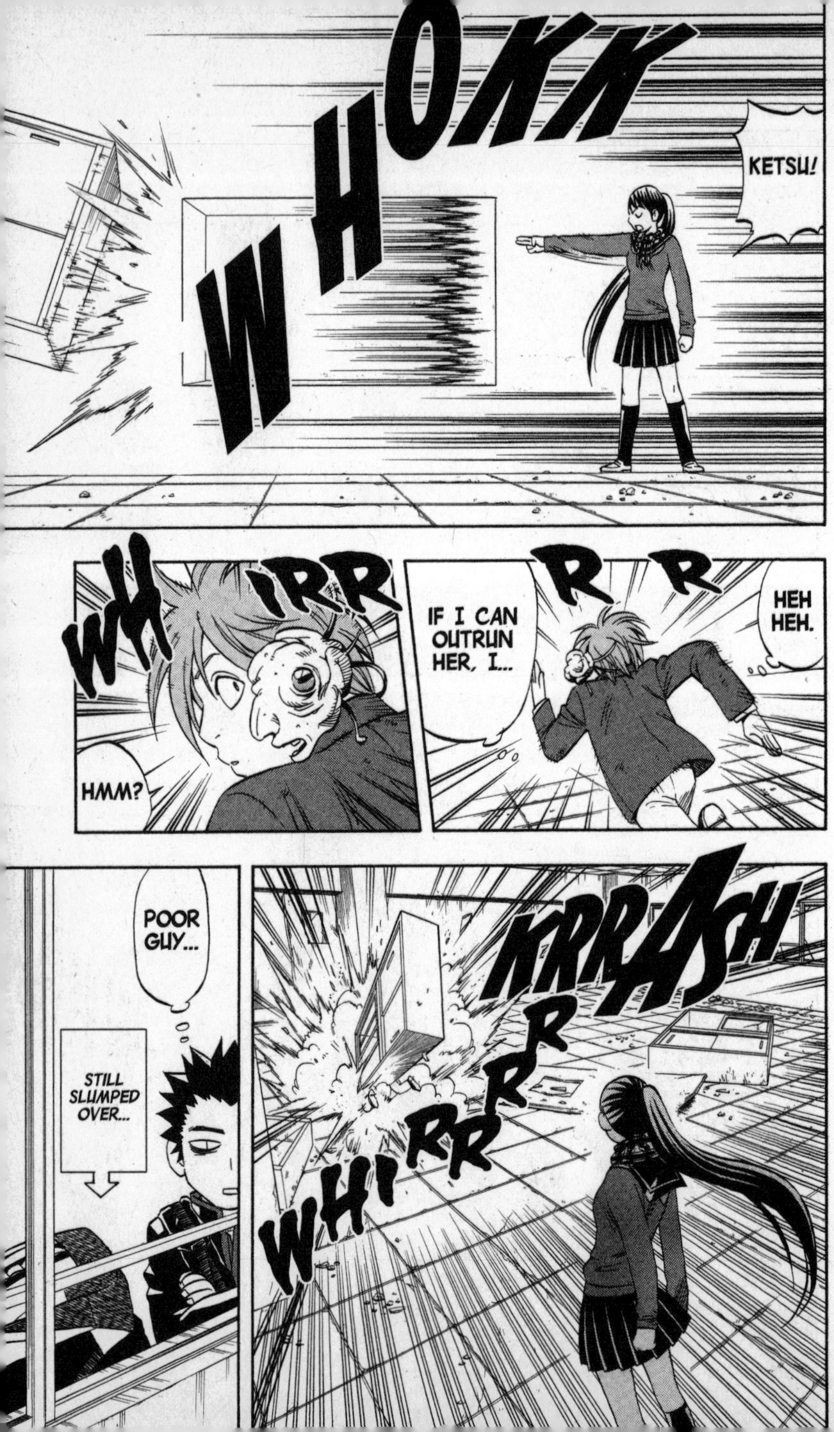
KETSU!
WHOKK
HEH HEH.
R R
IF I CAN OUTRUN HER, I...
WH IRR
HMM?
KRRASH
WHIRRRR
POOR GUY...
STILL SLUMPED OVER...

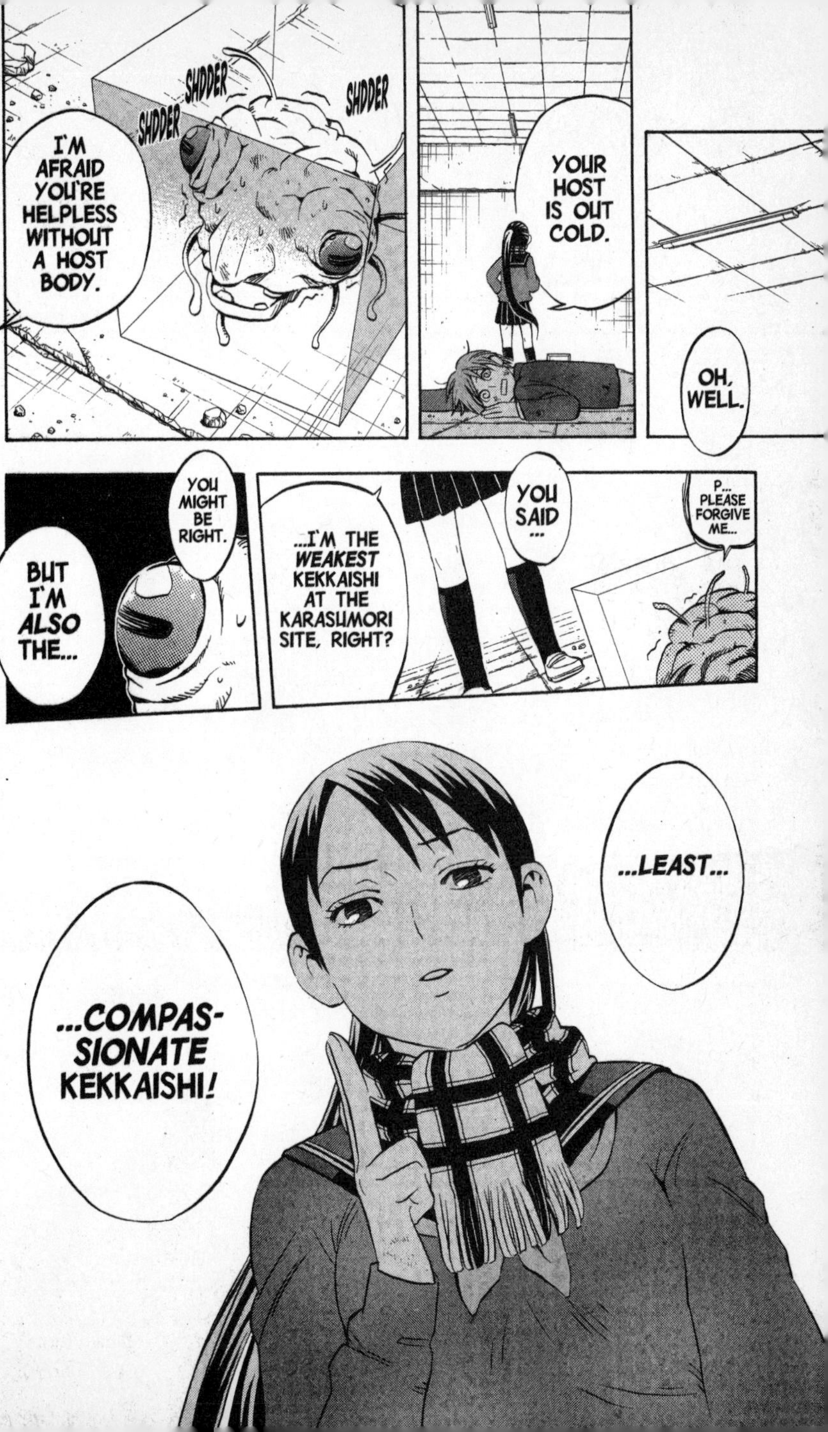
OH, WELL.
YOUR HOST IS OUT COLD.
SHDDER
SHDDER
SHDDER
I'M AFRAID YOU'RE HELPLESS WITHOUT A HOST BODY.
P... PLEASE FORGIVE ME...
YOU SAID...
...I'M THE *WEAKEST* KEKKAISHI AT THE KARASUMORI SITE, RIGHT?
YOU MIGHT BE RIGHT.
BUT I'M *ALSO* THE...
...LEAST...
...COMPAS-SIONATE KEKKAISHI!

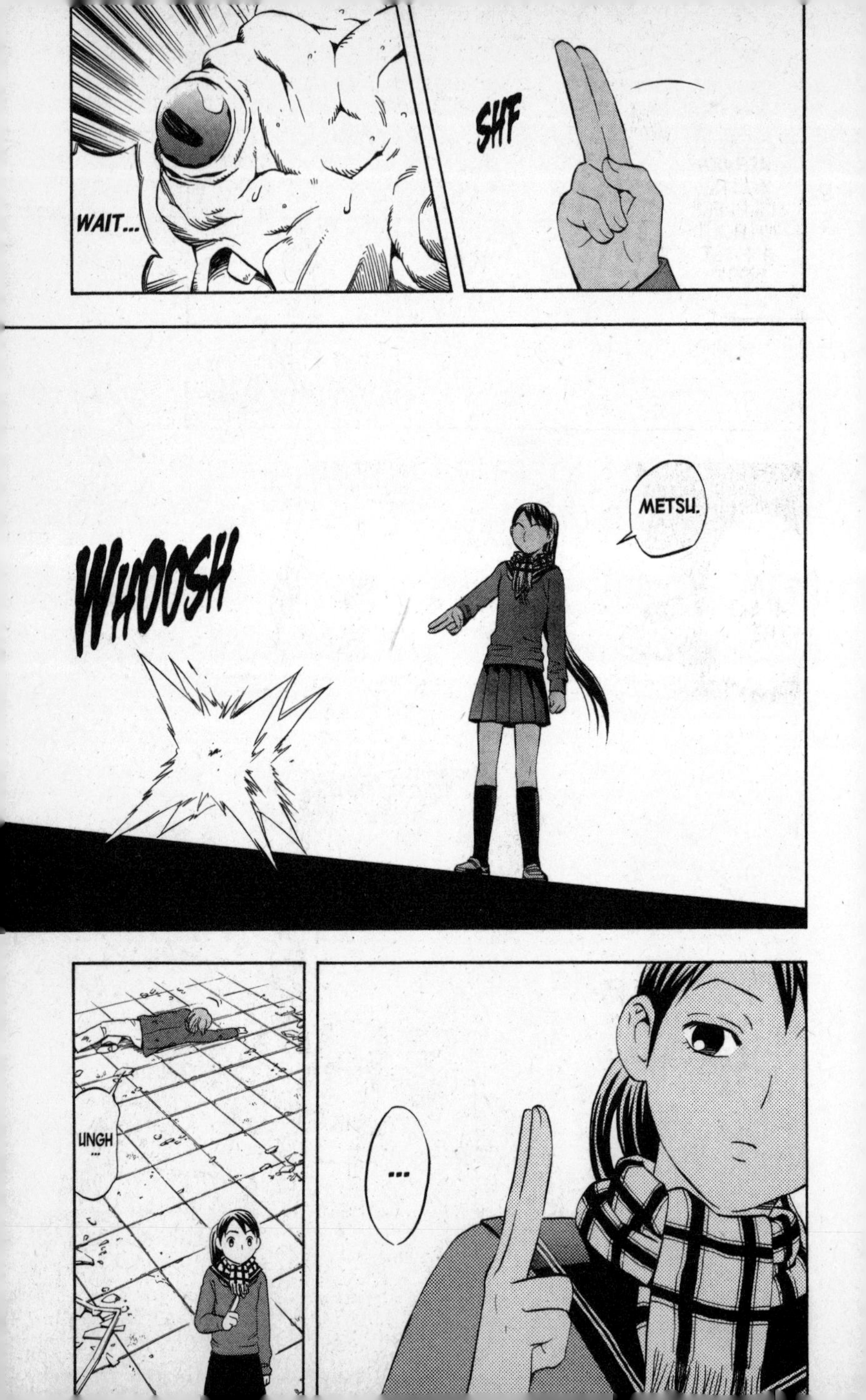
SHF
WAIT...
METSU.
WHOOSH
...
UNGH...

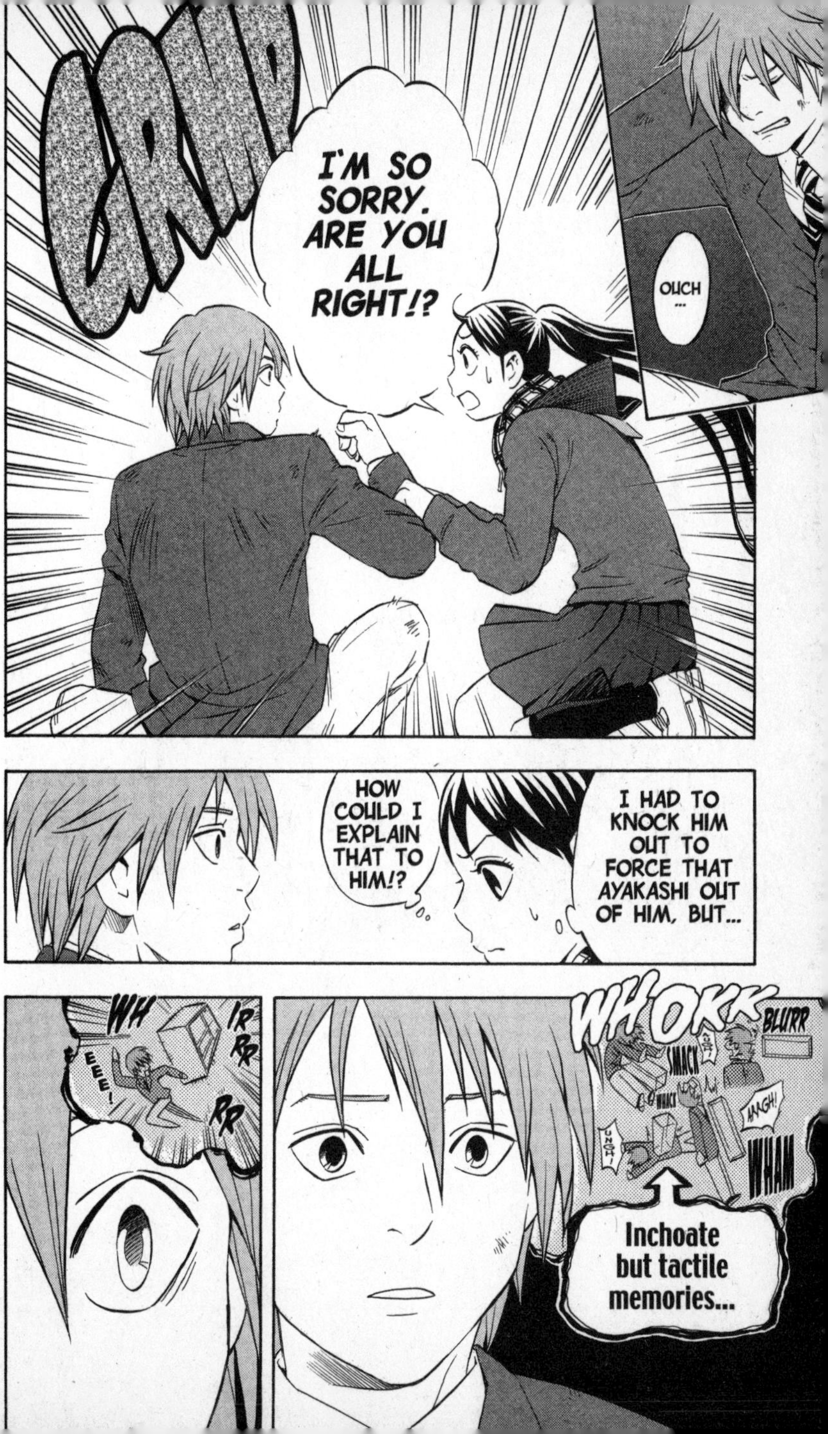
OUCH...
CRAMP
I'M SO SORRY. ARE YOU ALL RIGHT!?
I HAD TO KNOCK HIM OUT TO FORCE THAT AYAKASHI OUT OF HIM, BUT...
HOW COULD I EXPLAIN THAT TO HIM!?
WHOKK
BLURR
SMACK
WHACK
AARGH!
UNGH!
WHAM
Inchoate but tactile memories...
WH
IRR
RR
RR
EEE!

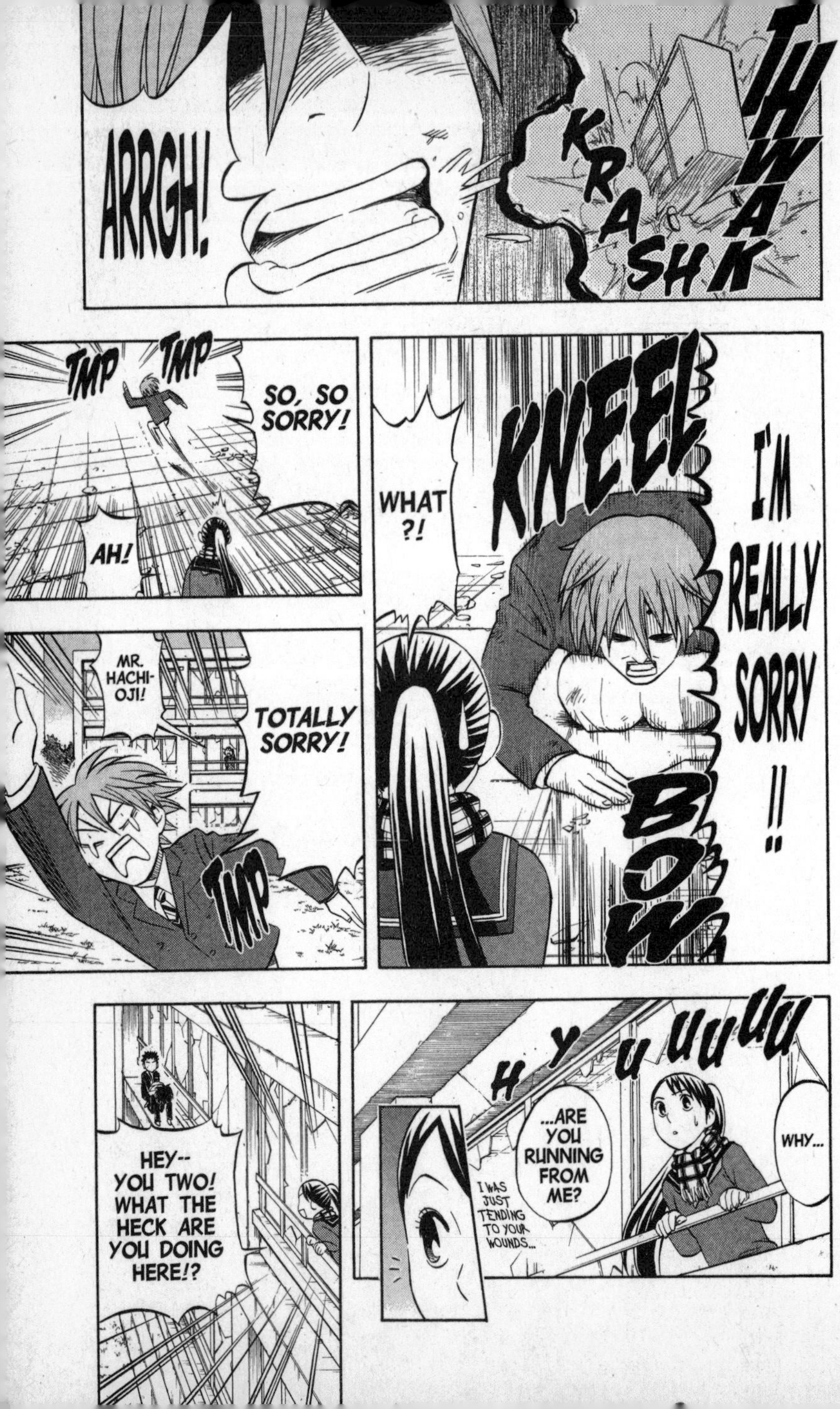
THWAK
KRASH
ARRGH!
I'M REALLY SORRY!!
KNEEL
WHAT?!
BOW
TMP TMP
SO, SO SORRY!
AH!
TOTALLY SORRY!
MR. HACHIOJI!
TMP
HYUUUUUU
WHY...
...ARE YOU RUNNING FROM ME?
I WAS JUST TENDING TO YOUR WOUNDS...
HEY-- YOU TWO! WHAT THE HECK ARE YOU DOING HERE!?

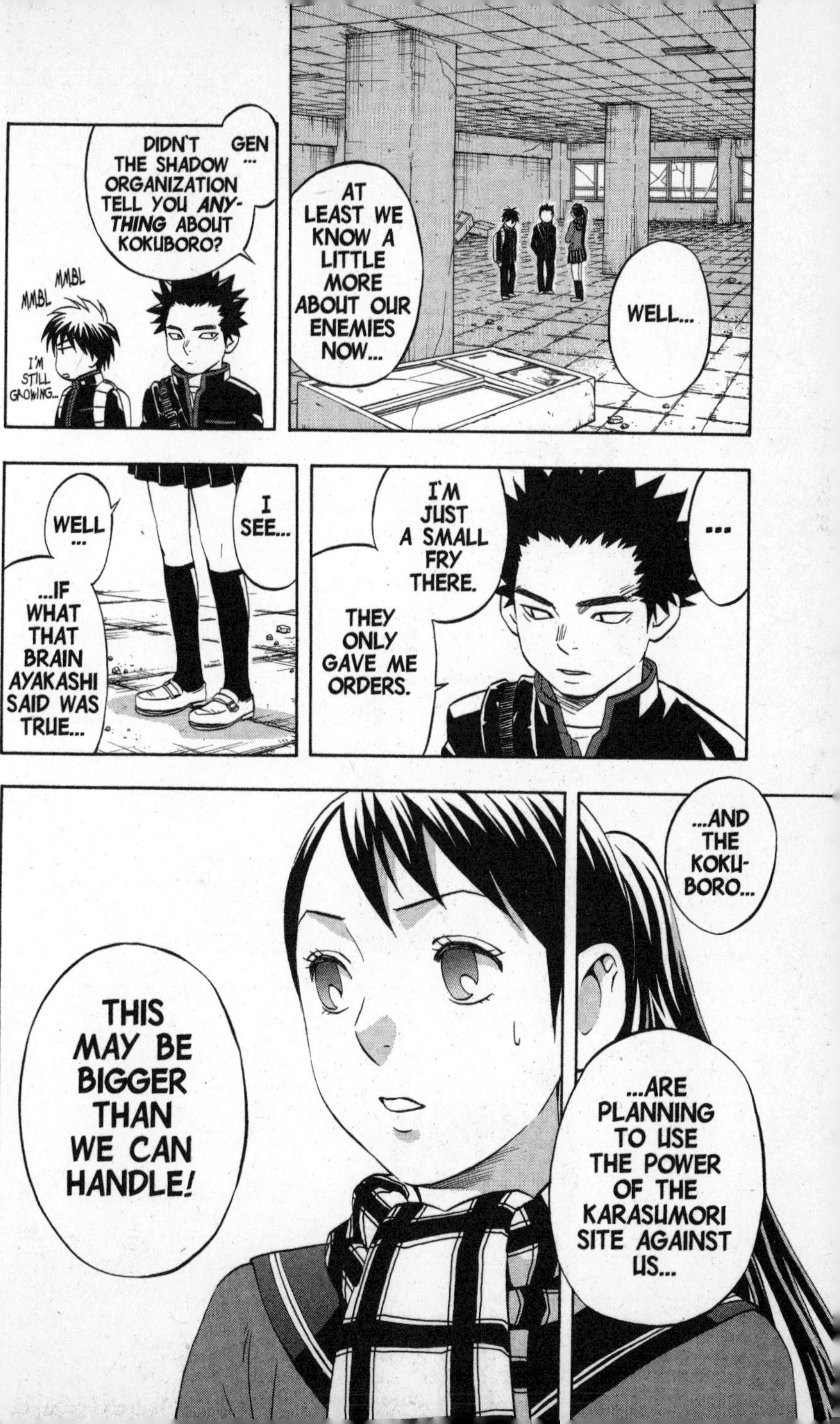
AT LEAST WE KNOW A LITTLE MORE ABOUT OUR ENEMIES NOW...
WELL...
GEN...
DIDN'T THE SHADOW ORGANIZATION TELL YOU *ANYTHING* ABOUT KOKUBORO?
MMBL MMBL
I'M STILL GROWING...
...
I'M JUST A SMALL FRY THERE.
THEY ONLY GAVE ME ORDERS.
I SEE...
WELL...
...IF WHAT THAT BRAIN AYAKASHI SAID WAS TRUE...
...AND THE KOKUBORO...
...ARE PLANNING TO USE THE POWER OF THE KARASUMORI SITE AGAINST US...
THIS MAY BE BIGGER THAN WE CAN HANDLE!

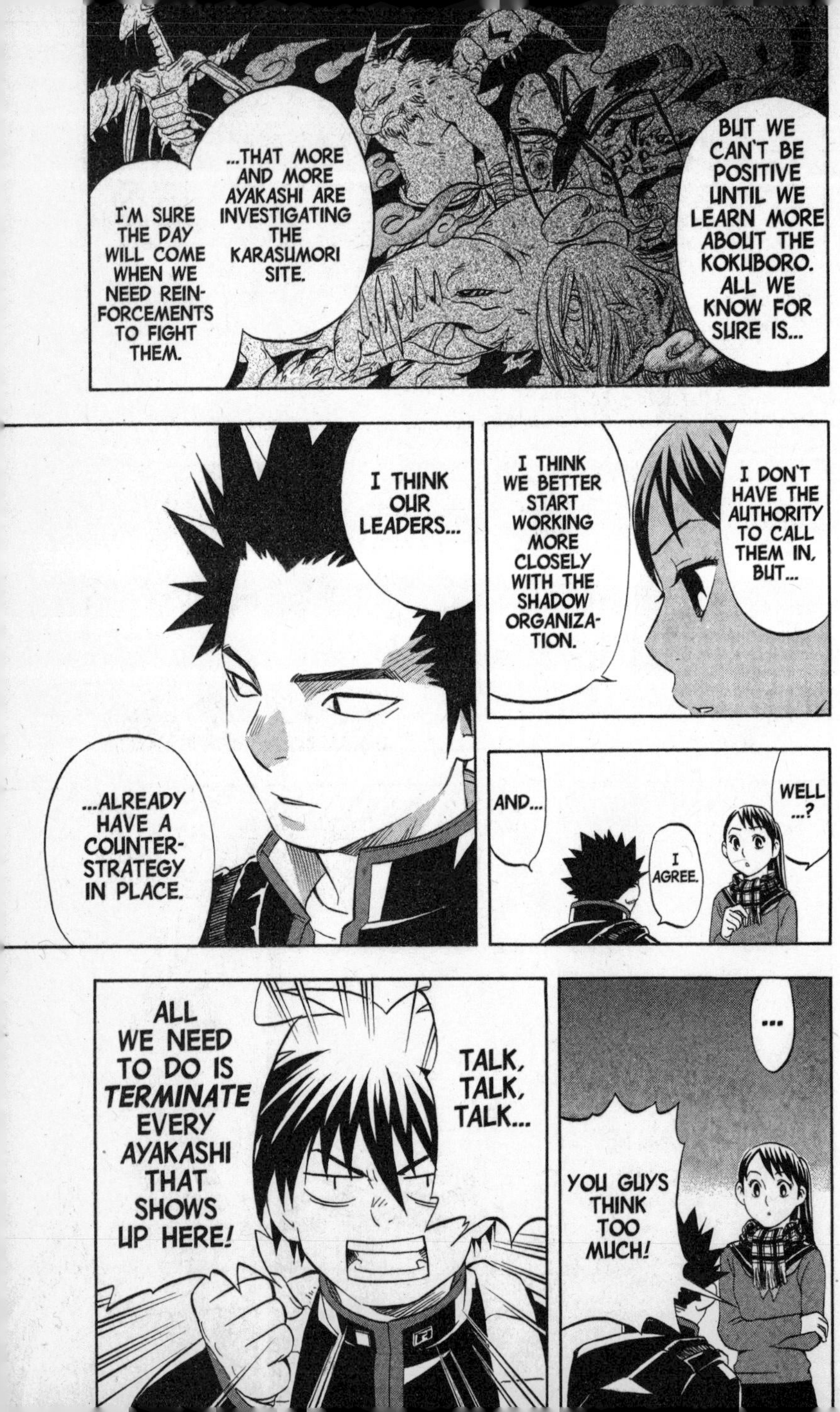
BUT WE CAN'T BE POSITIVE UNTIL WE LEARN MORE ABOUT THE KOKUBORO. ALL WE KNOW FOR SURE IS...
...THAT MORE AND MORE AYAKASHI ARE INVESTIGATING THE KARASUMORI SITE.
I'M SURE THE DAY WILL COME WHEN WE NEED REIN-FORCEMENTS TO FIGHT THEM.
I DON'T HAVE THE AUTHORITY TO CALL THEM IN, BUT...
I THINK WE BETTER START WORKING MORE CLOSELY WITH THE SHADOW ORGANIZA-TION.
WELL ...?
I AGREE.
AND...
I THINK OUR LEADERS...
...ALREADY HAVE A COUNTER-STRATEGY IN PLACE.
...
YOU GUYS THINK TOO MUCH!
TALK, TALK, TALK...
ALL WE NEED TO DO IS *TERMINATE* EVERY AYAKASHI THAT SHOWS UP HERE!

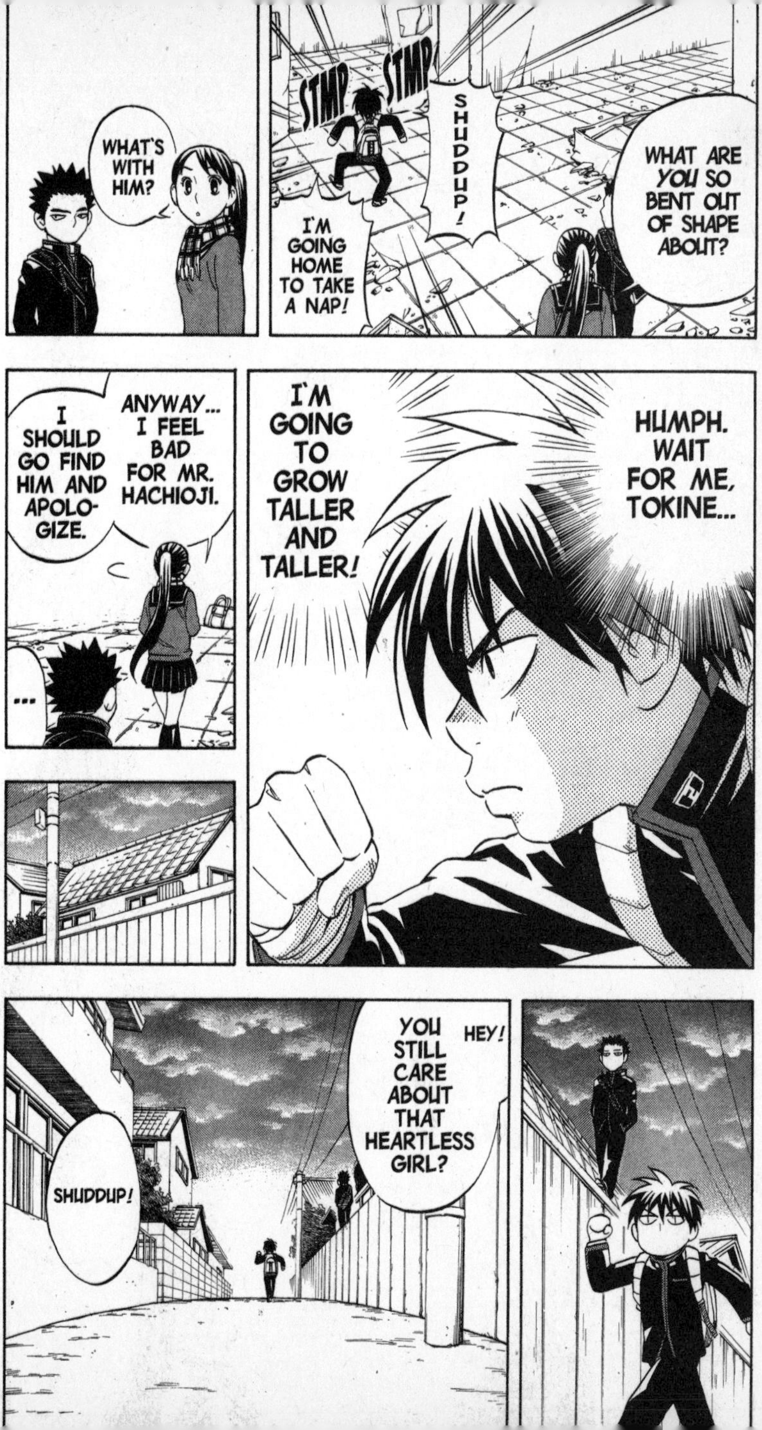
WHAT ARE YOU SO BENT OUT OF SHAPE ABOUT?
SHUDDUP!
STMP STMP
I'M GOING HOME TO TAKE A NAP!
WHAT'S WITH HIM?
HUMPH. WAIT FOR ME, TOKINE...
I'M GOING TO GROW TALLER AND TALLER!
ANYWAY... I FEEL BAD FOR MR. HACHIOJI.
I SHOULD GO FIND HIM AND APOLOGIZE.
...
HEY!
YOU STILL CARE ABOUT THAT HEARTLESS GIRL?
SHUDDUP!

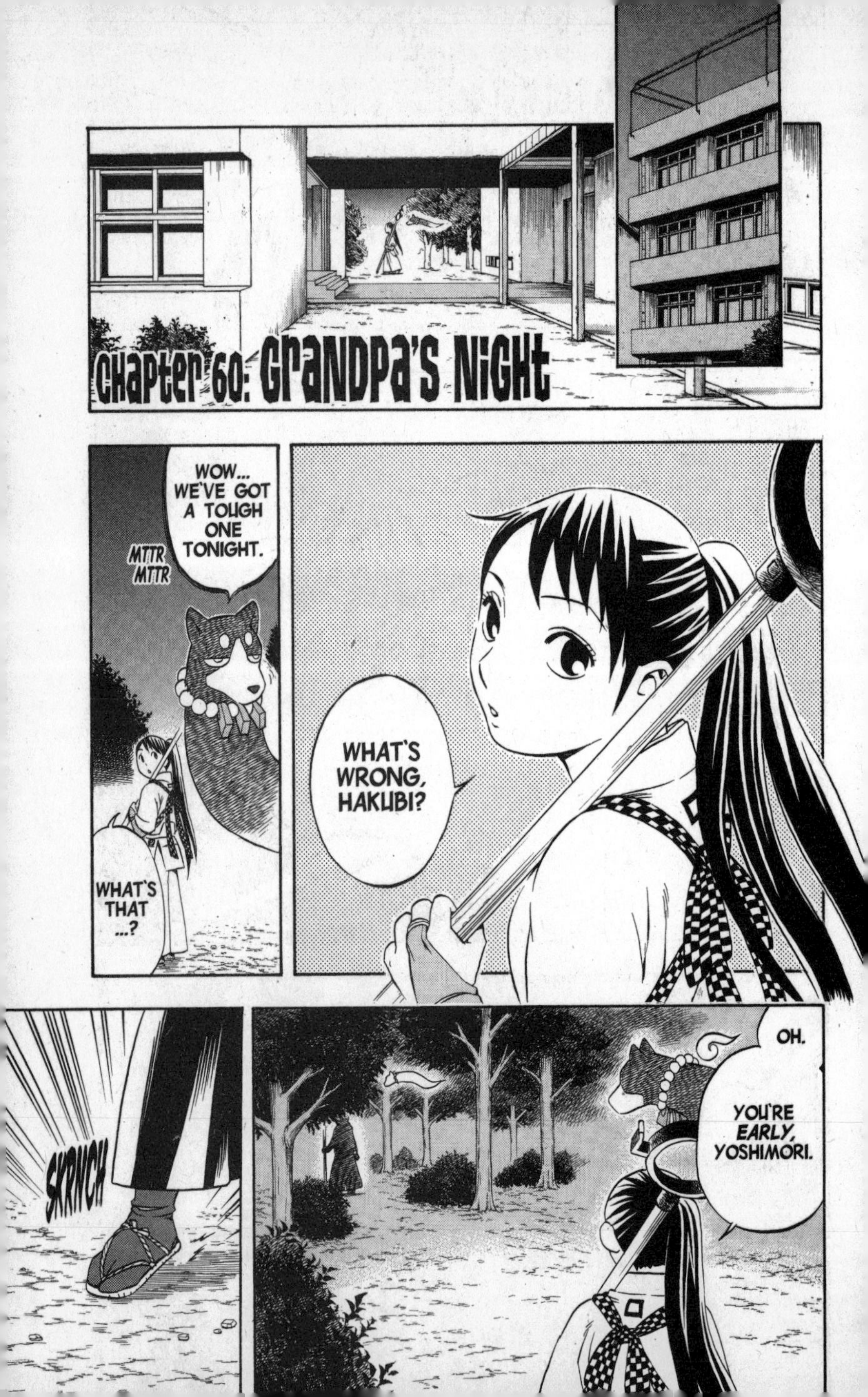
Chapter 60: Grandpa's Night
WHAT'S WRONG, HAKUBI?
WOW... WE'VE GOT A TOUGH ONE TONIGHT.
MTTR MTTR
WHAT'S THAT ...?
OH.
YOU'RE EARLY, YOSHIMORI.
SKRNCH

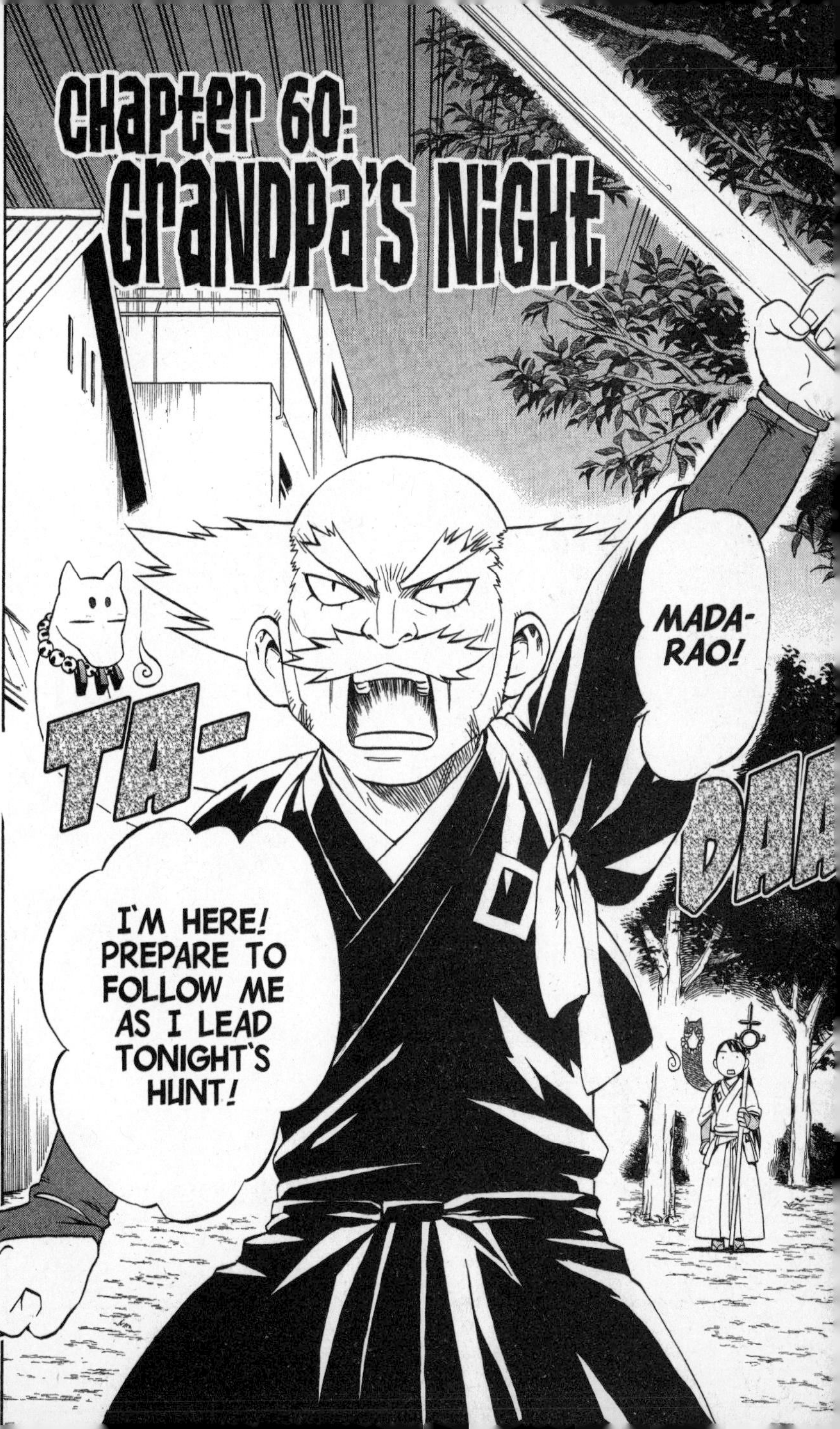
CHAPTER 60:
GRANDPA'S NIGHT
MADA-RAO!
TA-
DAA
I'M HERE! PREPARE TO FOLLOW ME AS I LEAD TONIGHT'S HUNT!

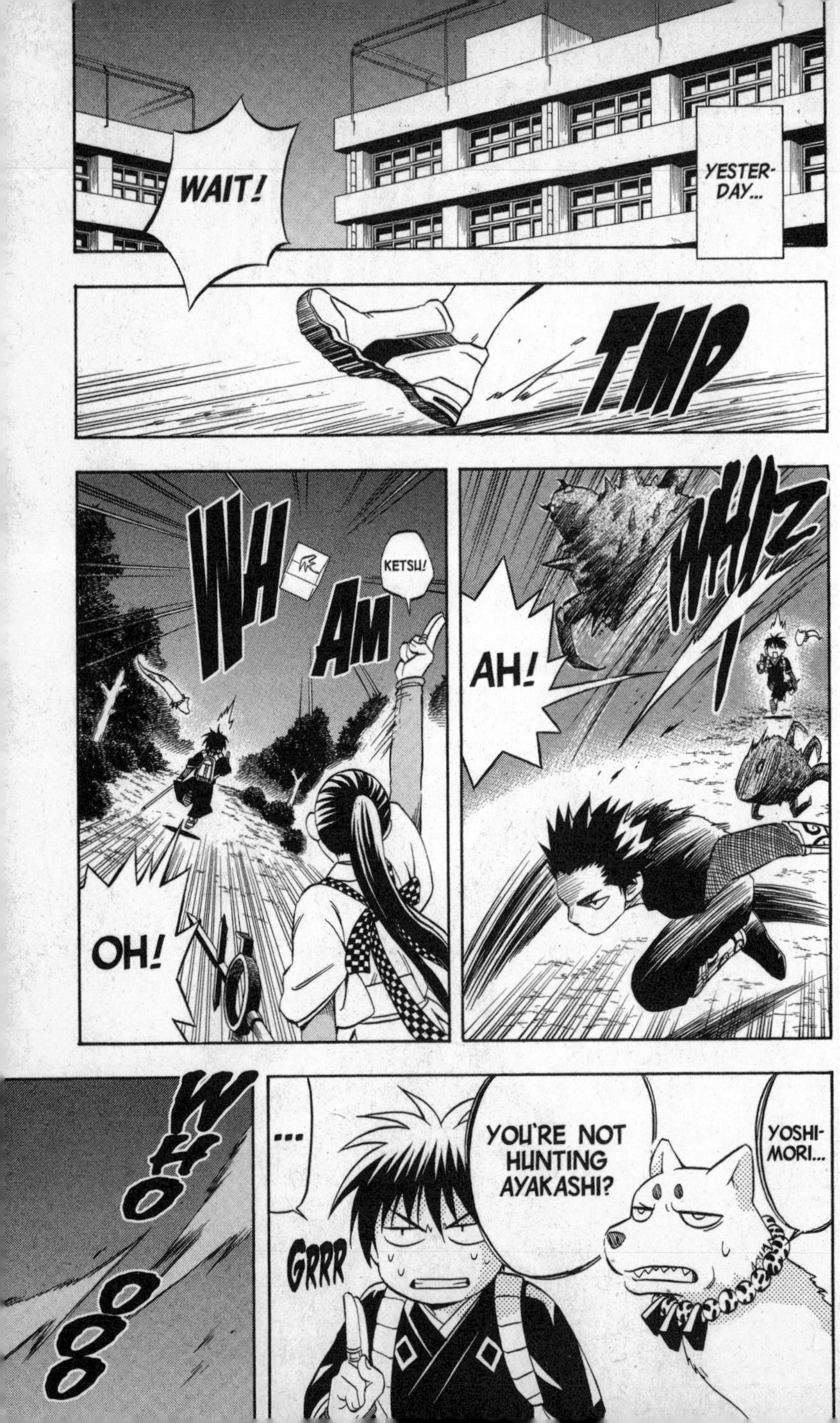
YESTER-DAY...
WAIT!
TMP
WHIZ
AH!
KETSU!
WHAM
OH!
YOSHI-MORI...
YOU'RE NOT HUNTING AYAKASHI?
...
GRRR
WHOOOO

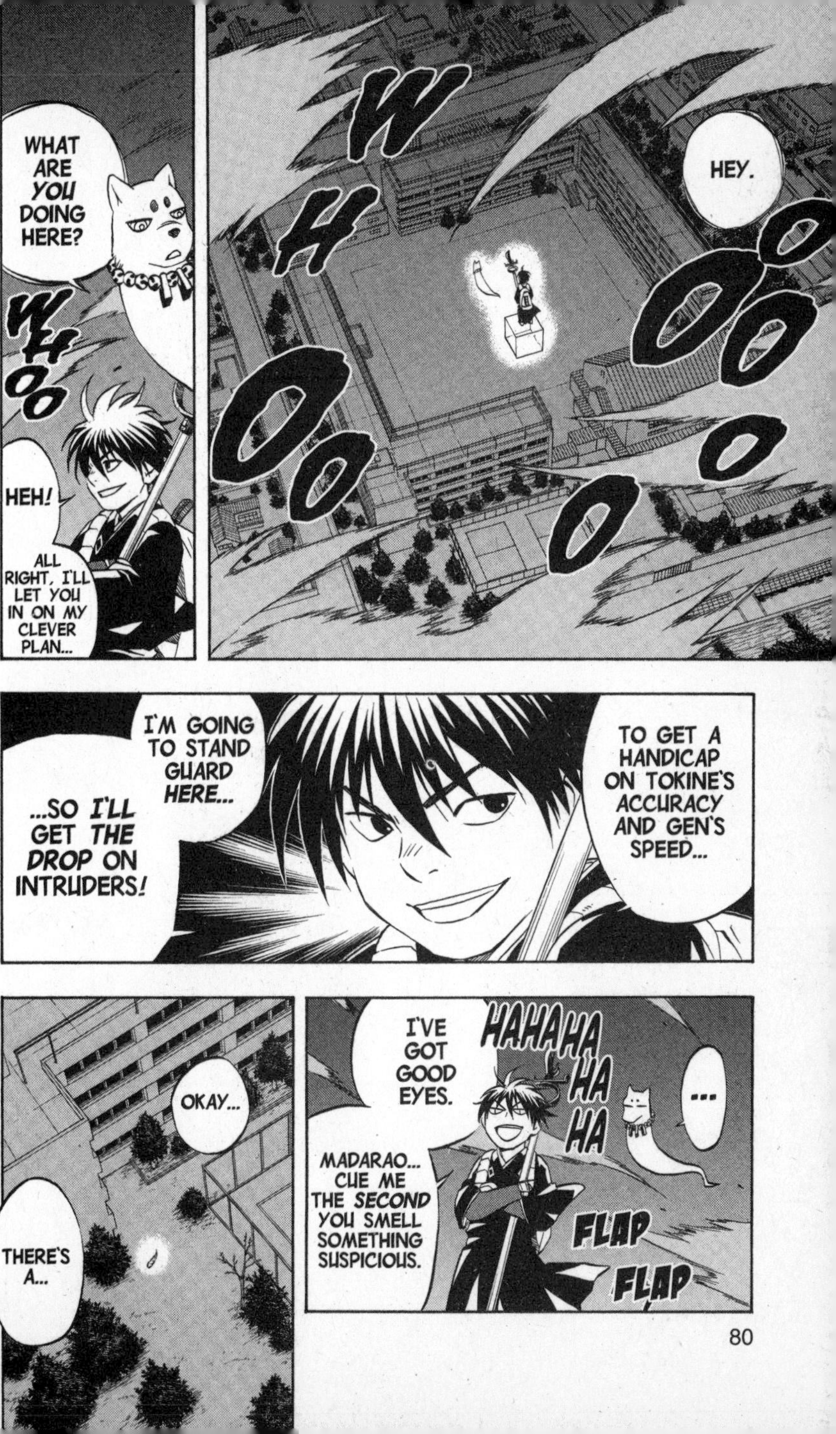
HEY.
WHOOOOOOOOO
WHAT ARE YOU DOING HERE?
WHOO
HEH!
ALL RIGHT, I'LL LET YOU IN ON MY CLEVER PLAN...
TO GET A HANDICAP ON TOKINE'S ACCURACY AND GEN'S SPEED...
I'M GOING TO STAND GUARD HERE...
...SO I'LL GET THE DROP ON INTRUDERS!
...
HAHAHA HA HA
I'VE GOT GOOD EYES.
MADARAO... CUE ME THE SECOND YOU SMELL SOMETHING SUSPICIOUS.
FLAP
FLAP
OKAY...
THERE'S A...

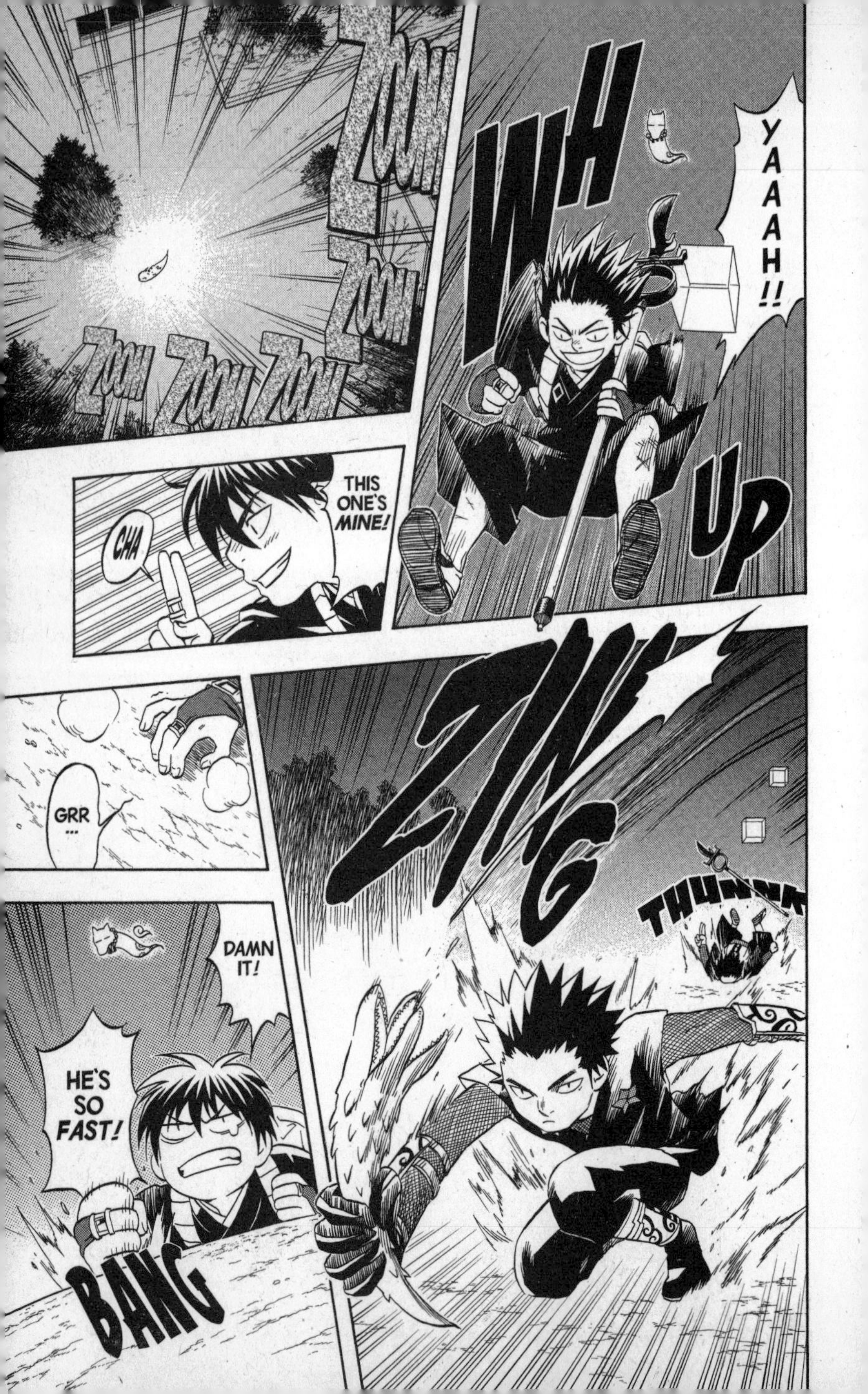
YAAAAH!!
WHH
UP
ZOOM
ZOOM
ZOOM ZOOM ZOOM
THIS ONE'S *MINE!*
CHA
ZING
THUNNK
GRR...
DAMN IT!
HE'S SO *FAST!*
BANG

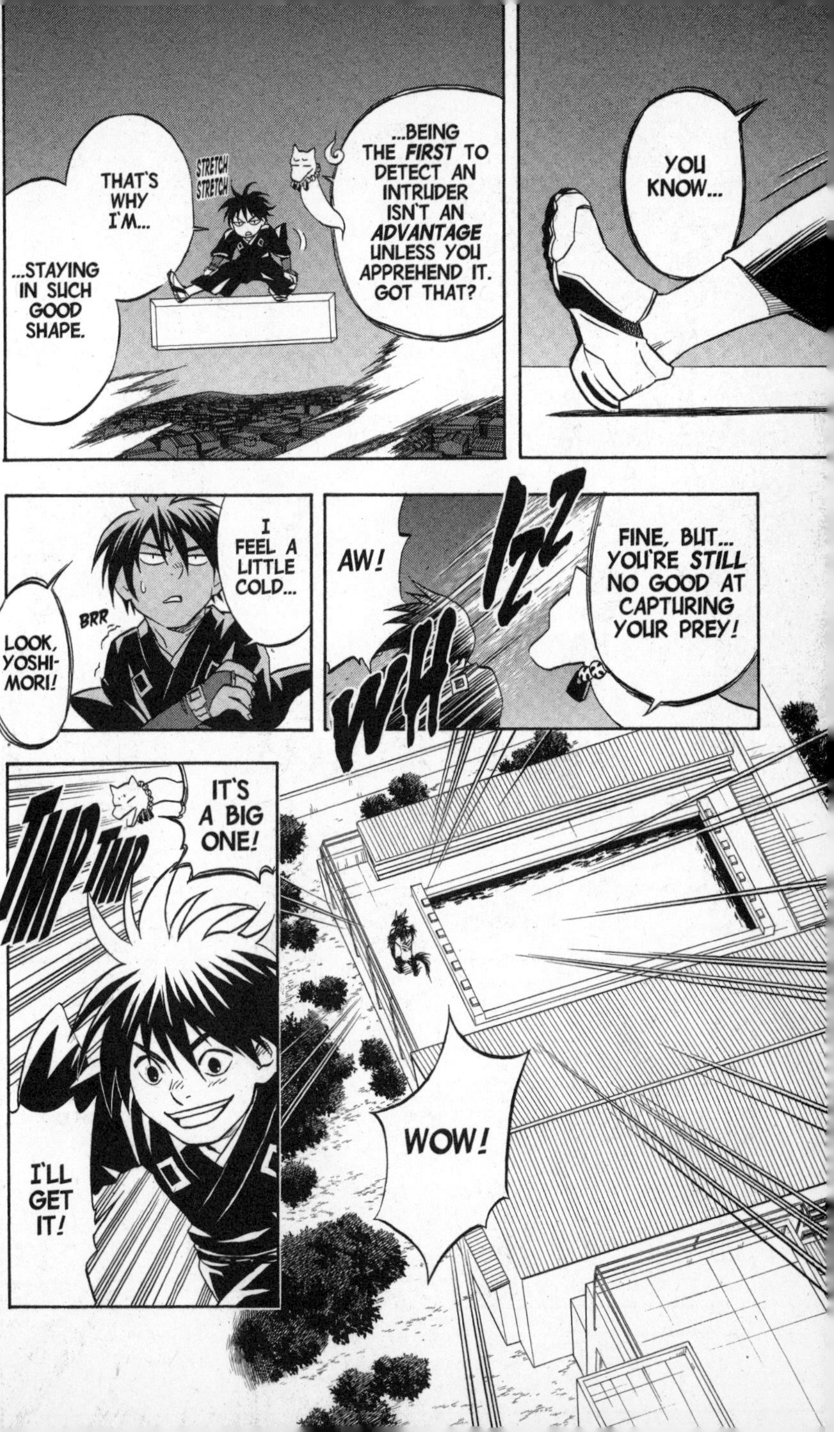
YOU KNOW...
...BEING THE FIRST TO DETECT AN INTRUDER ISN'T AN ADVANTAGE UNLESS YOU APPREHEND IT. GOT THAT?
STRETCH STRETCH
THAT'S WHY I'M...
...STAYING IN SUCH GOOD SHAPE.
FINE, BUT... YOU'RE STILL NO GOOD AT CAPTURING YOUR PREY!
WHIZZ
AW!
I FEEL A LITTLE COLD...
BRR
LOOK, YOSHIMORI!
WOW!
IT'S A BIG ONE!
THP THP
I'LL GET IT!

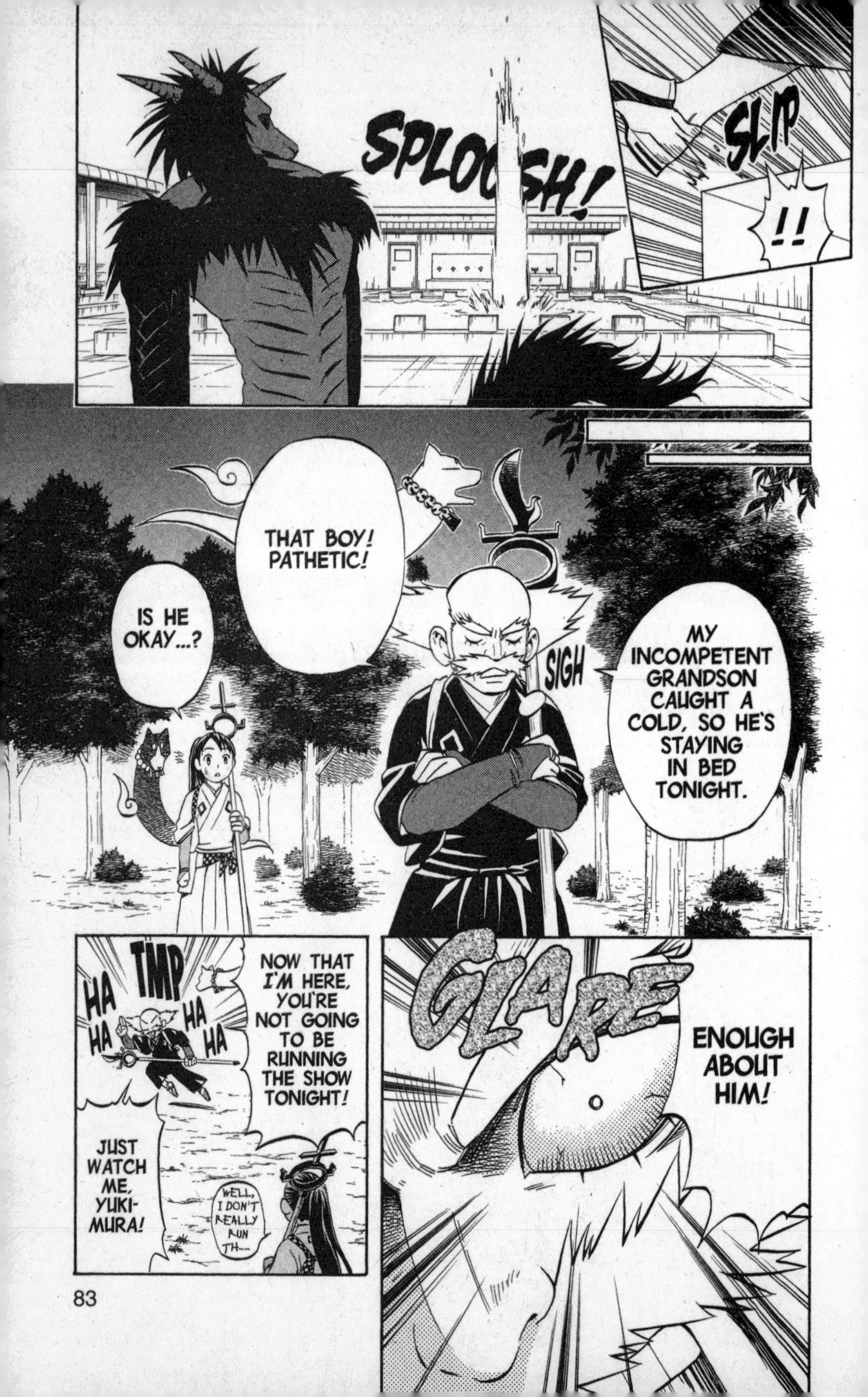
SLIP
!!
SPLOOSH!
MY INCOMPETENT GRANDSON CAUGHT A COLD, SO HE'S STAYING IN BED TONIGHT.
SIGH
THAT BOY! PATHETIC!
IS HE OKAY...?
GLARE
ENOUGH ABOUT HIM!
NOW THAT I'M HERE, YOU'RE NOT GOING TO BE RUNNING THE SHOW TONIGHT!
TMP
HA HA HA HA
JUST WATCH ME, YUKI-MURA!
WELL, I DON'T REALLY RUN TH—

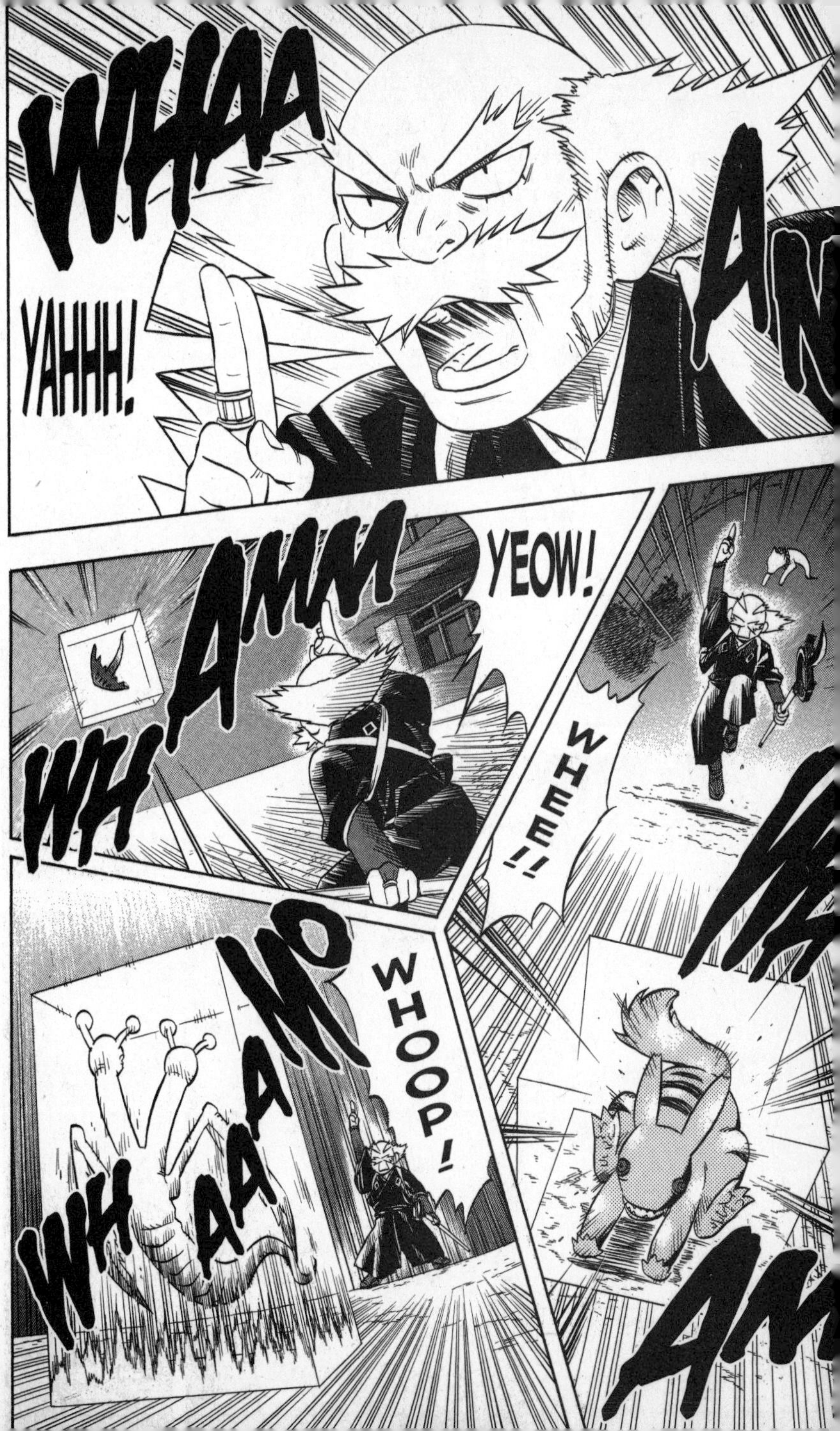
WHAAA
AN
YAHHH!
WHEE!!
YEOW!
WHAMM
WHOOP!
WHAAM!

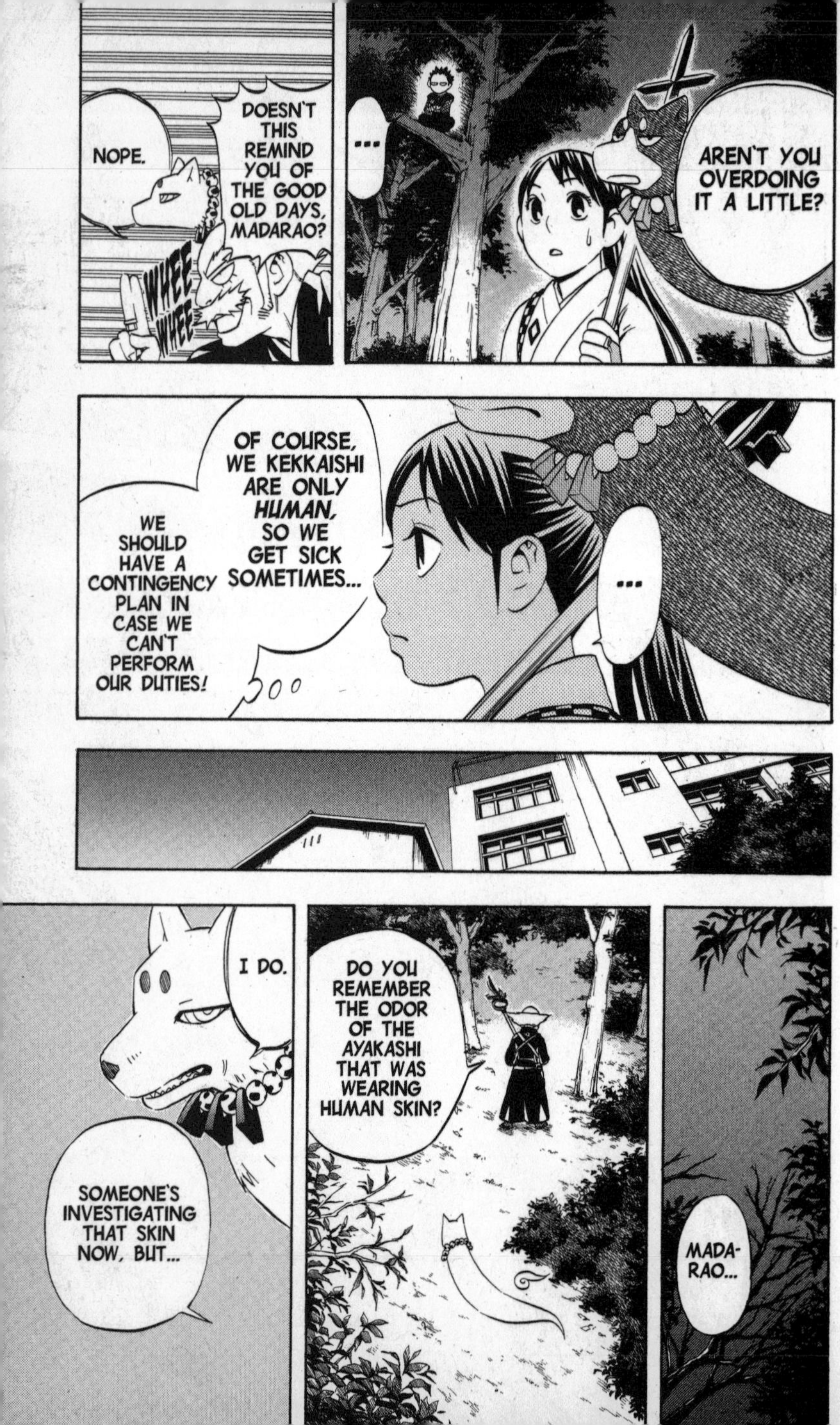

AREN'T YOU OVERDOING IT A LITTLE?
...
DOESN'T THIS REMIND YOU OF THE GOOD OLD DAYS, MADARAO?
NOPE.
WHEE WHEE
OF COURSE, WE KEKKAISHI ARE ONLY *HUMAN,* SO WE GET SICK SOMETIMES...
WE SHOULD HAVE A CONTINGENCY PLAN IN CASE WE CAN'T PERFORM OUR DUTIES!
...
MADA-RAO...
DO YOU REMEMBER THE ODOR OF THE AYAKASHI THAT WAS WEARING HUMAN SKIN?
I DO.
SOMEONE'S INVESTIGATING THAT SKIN NOW, BUT...

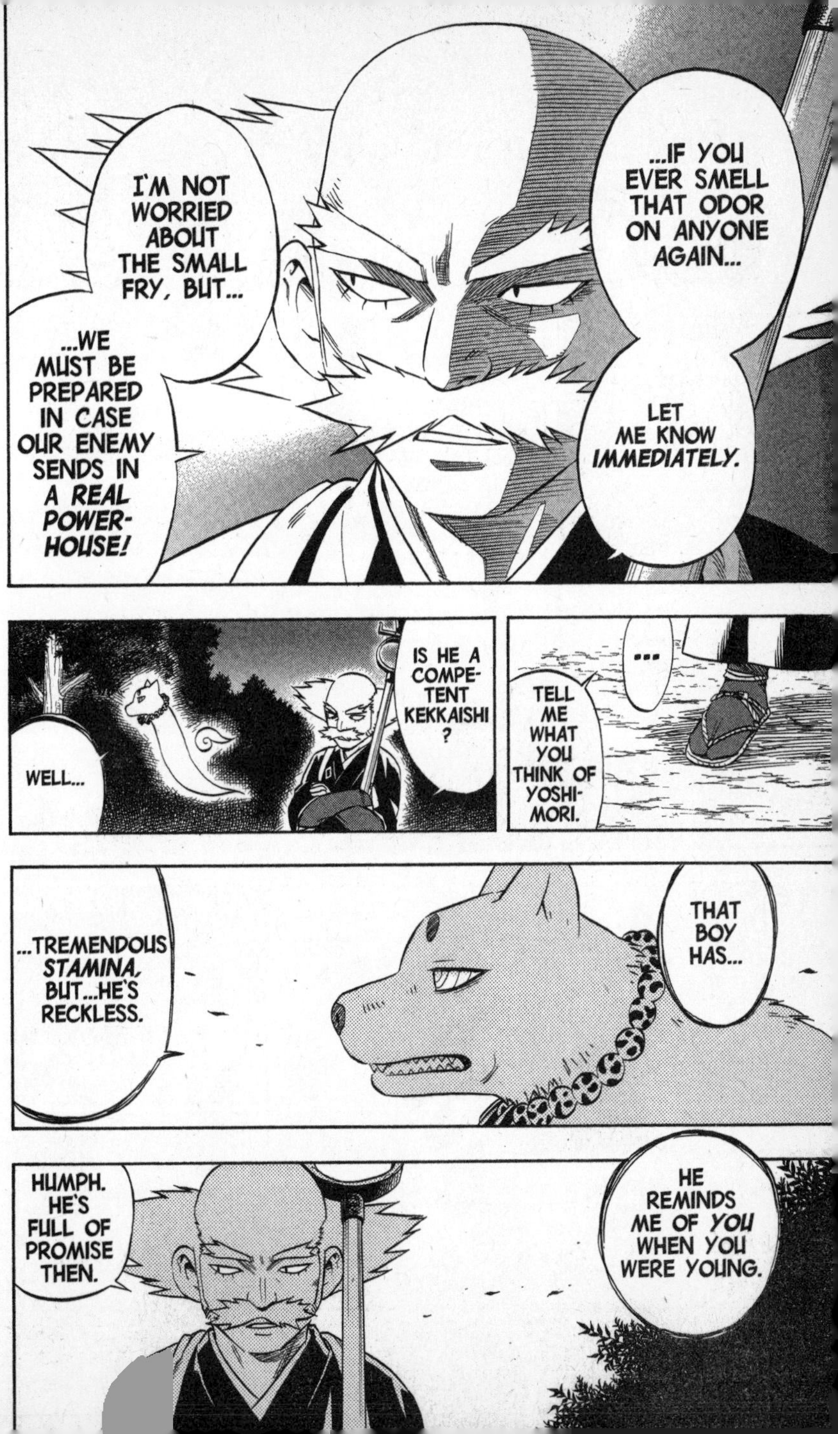
I'M NOT WORRIED ABOUT THE SMALL FRY, BUT...
...WE MUST BE PREPARED IN CASE OUR ENEMY SENDS IN A *REAL POWER-HOUSE!*
...IF YOU EVER SMELL THAT ODOR ON ANYONE AGAIN...
LET ME KNOW *IMMEDIATELY.*
...
TELL ME WHAT YOU THINK OF YOSHI-MORI.
IS HE A COMPE-TENT KEKKAISHI?
WELL...
THAT BOY HAS...
...TREMENDOUS *STAMINA,* BUT...HE'S RECKLESS.
HE REMINDS ME OF *YOU* WHEN YOU WERE YOUNG.
HUMPH. HE'S FULL OF PROMISE THEN.

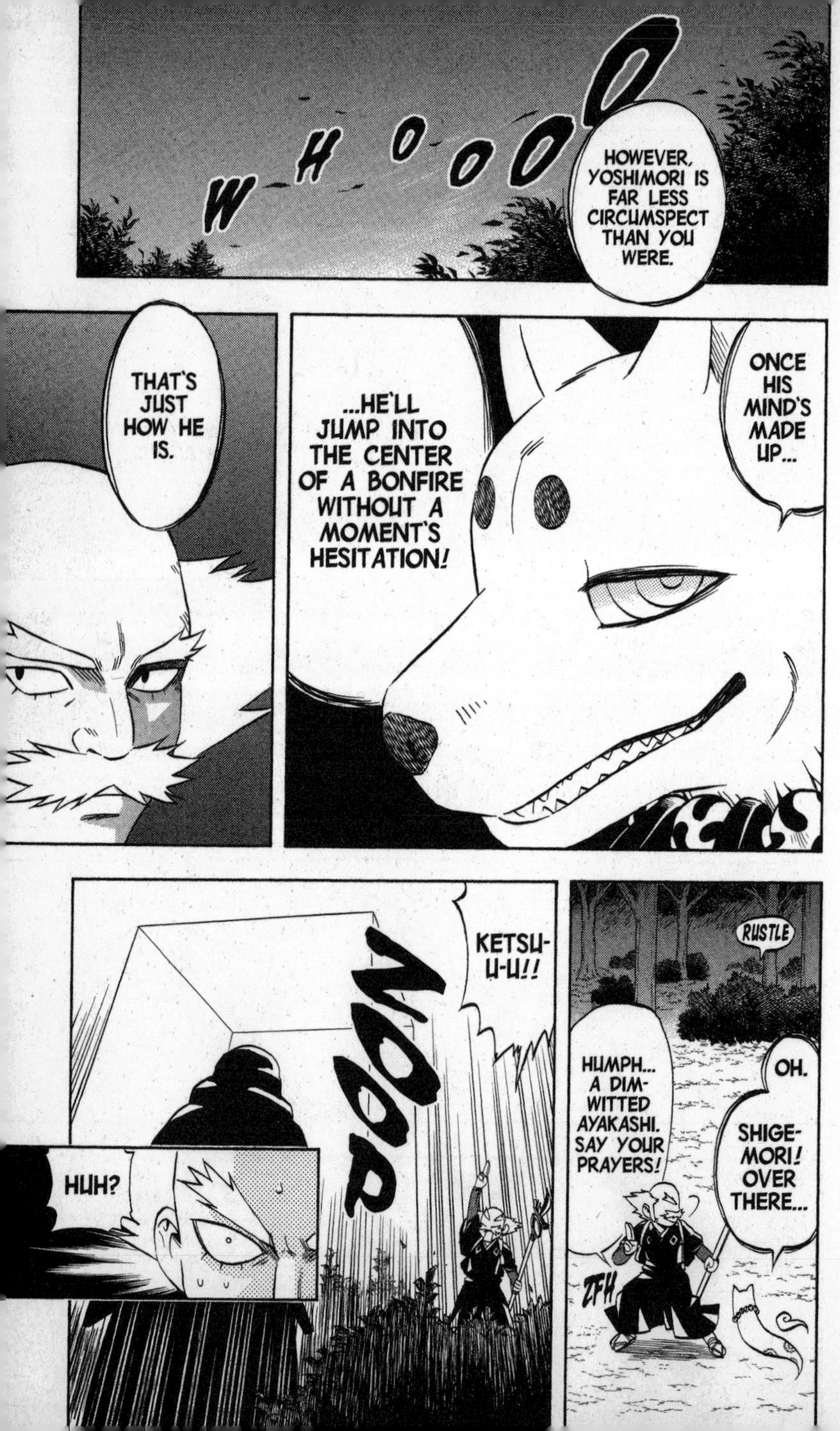
WHOOOO
HOWEVER, YOSHIMORI IS FAR LESS CIRCUMSPECT THAN YOU WERE.
ONCE HIS MIND'S MADE UP...
...HE'LL JUMP INTO THE CENTER OF A BONFIRE WITHOUT A MOMENT'S HESITATION!
THAT'S JUST HOW HE IS.
RUSTLE
OH.
SHIGE-MORI! OVER THERE...
HUMPH... A DIM-WITTED AYAKASHI. SAY YOUR PRAYERS!
ZFH
KETSU-U-U!!
VOOP
HUH?

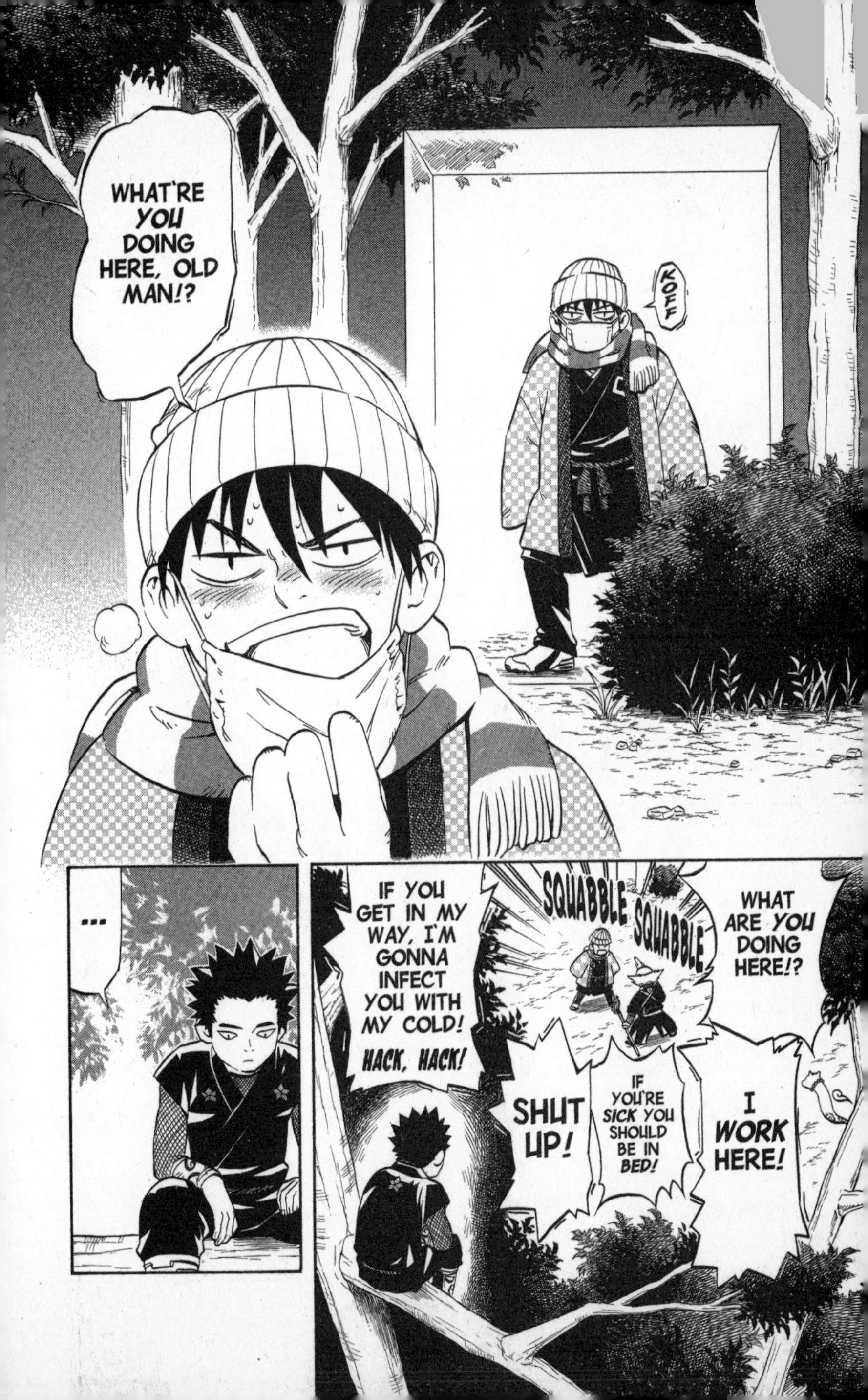
WHAT'RE *YOU* DOING HERE, OLD MAN!?
KOFF
WHAT ARE *YOU* DOING HERE!?
SQUABBLE SQUABBLE
IF YOU GET IN MY WAY, I'M GONNA INFECT YOU WITH MY COLD! HACK, HACK!
I *WORK* HERE!
IF YOU'RE *SICK* YOU SHOULD BE IN *BED!*
SHUT UP!
...

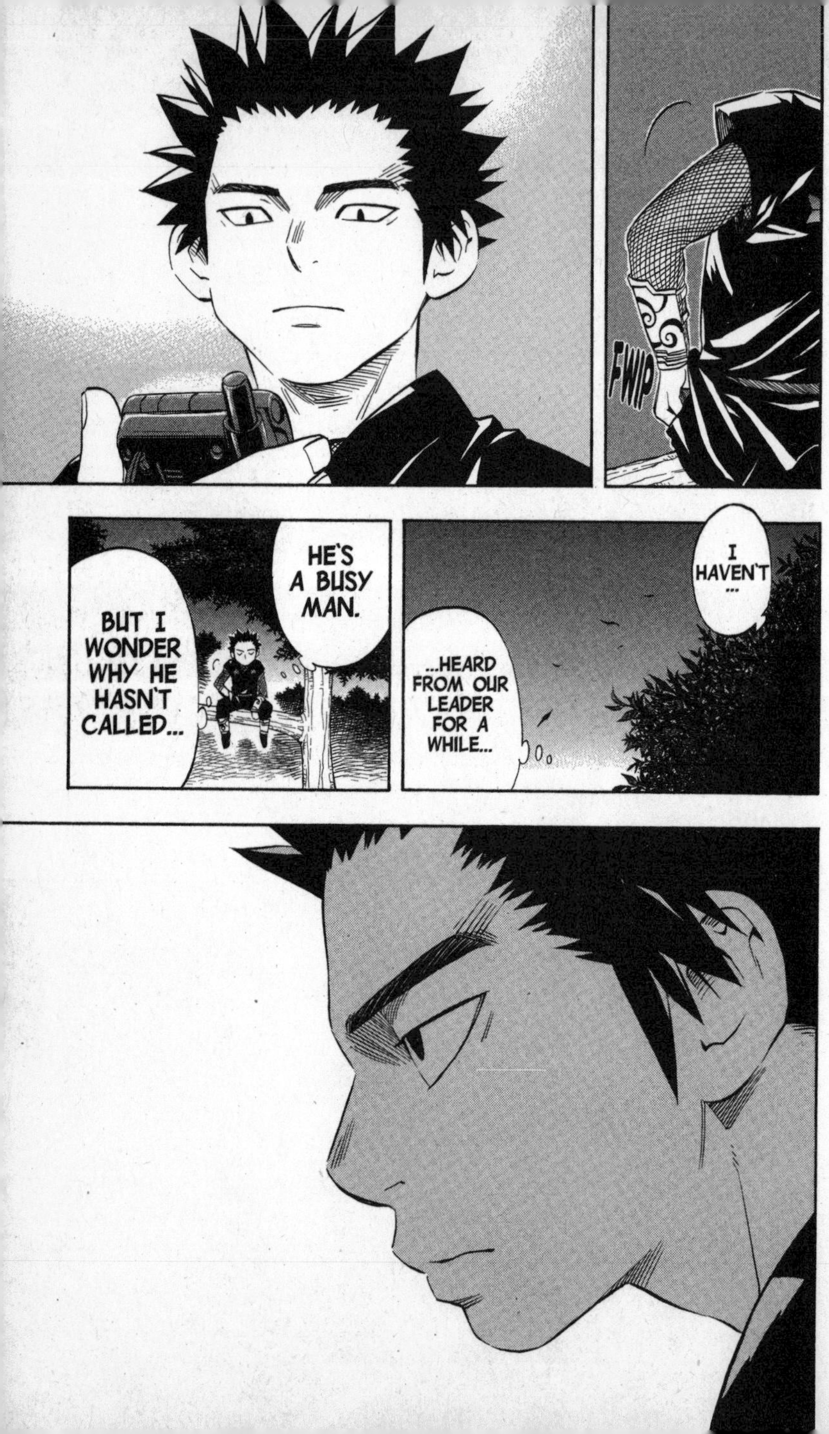
FWIP
I HAVEN'T ...
...HEARD FROM OUR LEADER FOR A WHILE...
HE'S A BUSY MAN.
BUT I WONDER WHY HE HASN'T CALLED...

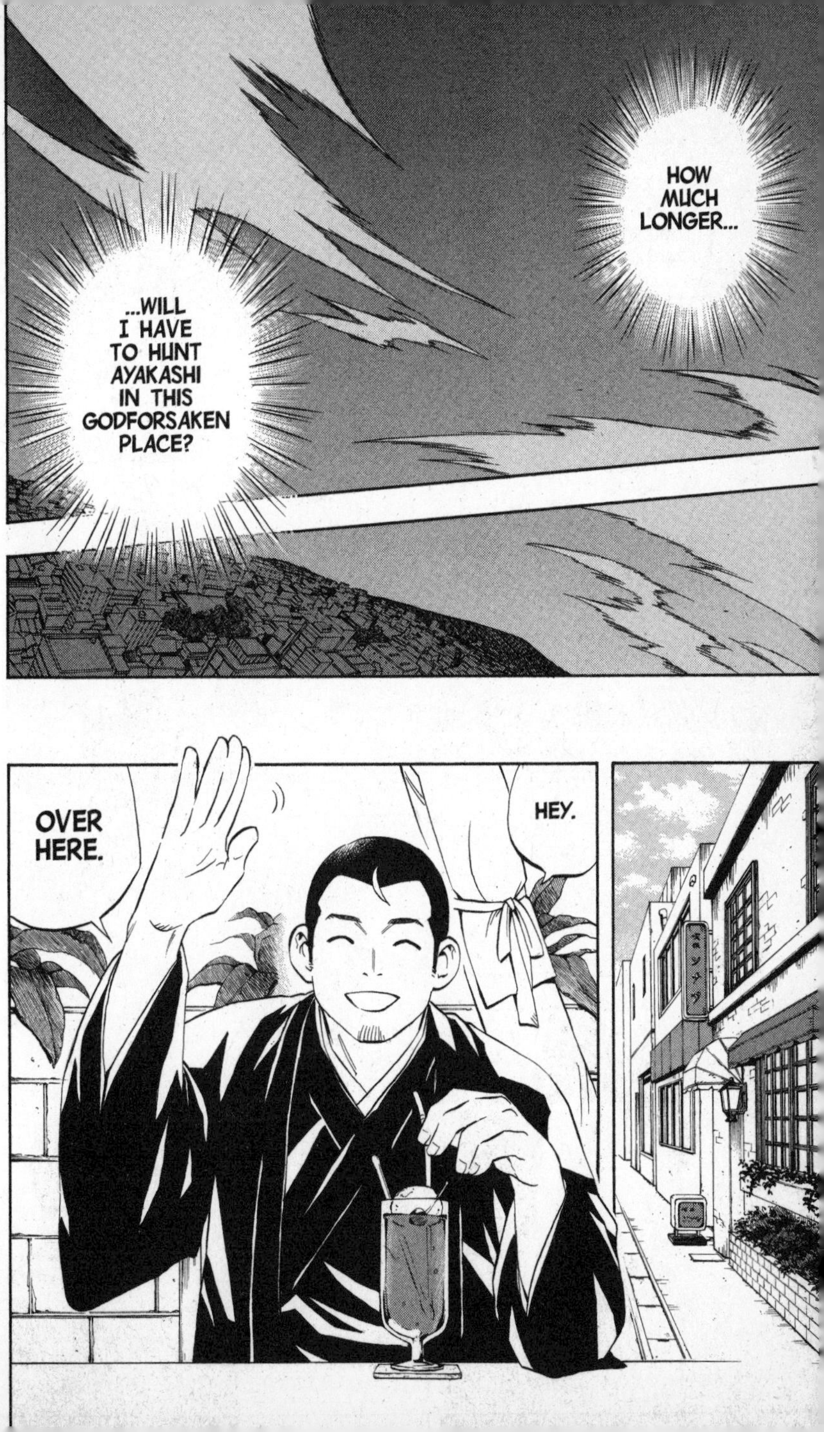
HOW MUCH LONGER...
...WILL I HAVE TO HUNT AYAKASHI IN THIS GODFORSAKEN PLACE?
HEY.
OVER HERE.

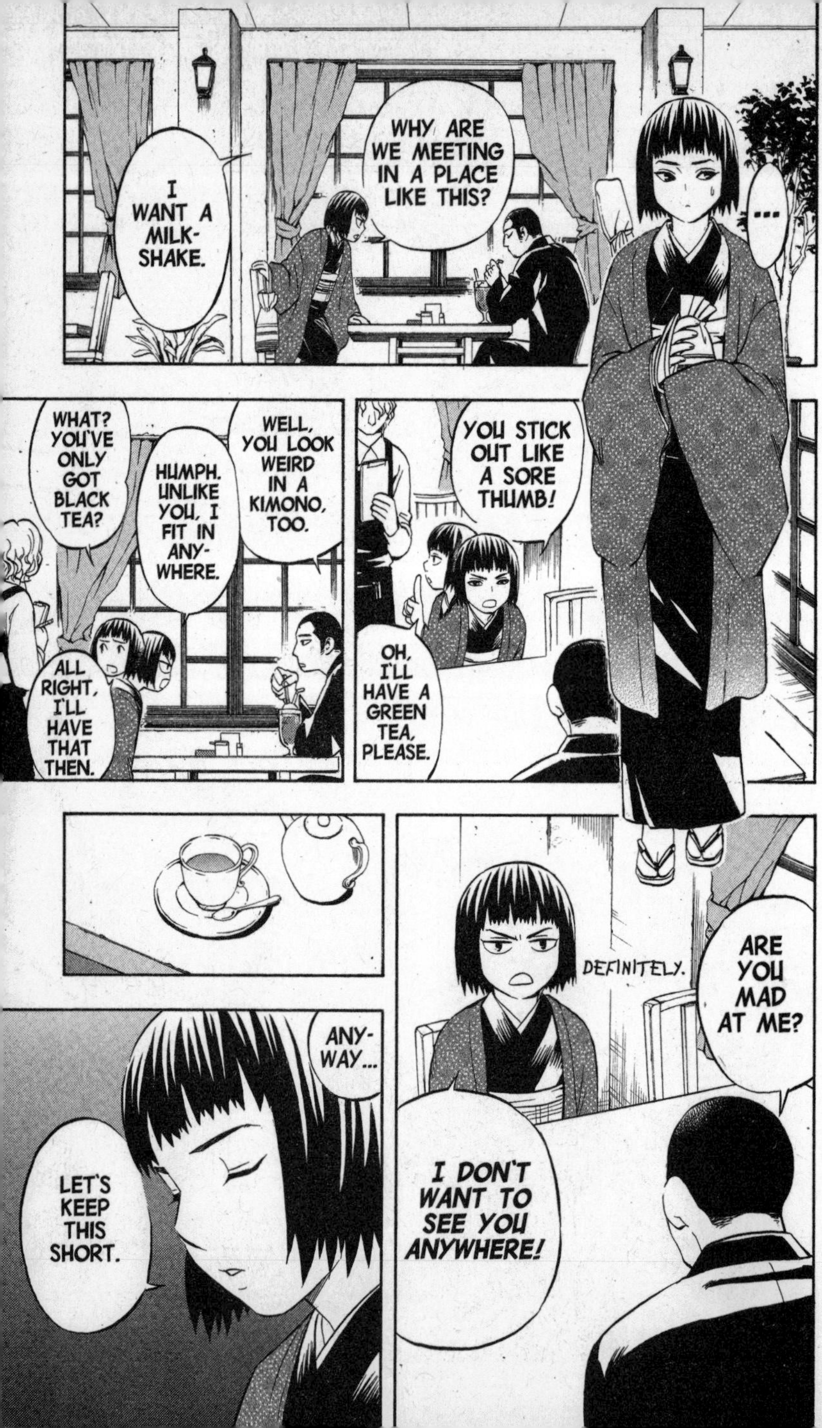
...
WHY ARE WE MEETING IN A PLACE LIKE THIS?
I WANT A MILK-SHAKE.
YOU STICK OUT LIKE A SORE THUMB!
OH, I'LL HAVE A GREEN TEA, PLEASE.
WELL, YOU LOOK WEIRD IN A KIMONO, TOO.
HUMPH. UNLIKE YOU, I FIT IN ANY-WHERE.
WHAT? YOU'VE ONLY GOT BLACK TEA?
ALL RIGHT, I'LL HAVE THAT THEN.
ARE YOU MAD AT ME?
DEFINITELY.
I DON'T WANT TO SEE YOU ANYWHERE!
ANY-WAY...
LET'S KEEP THIS SHORT.

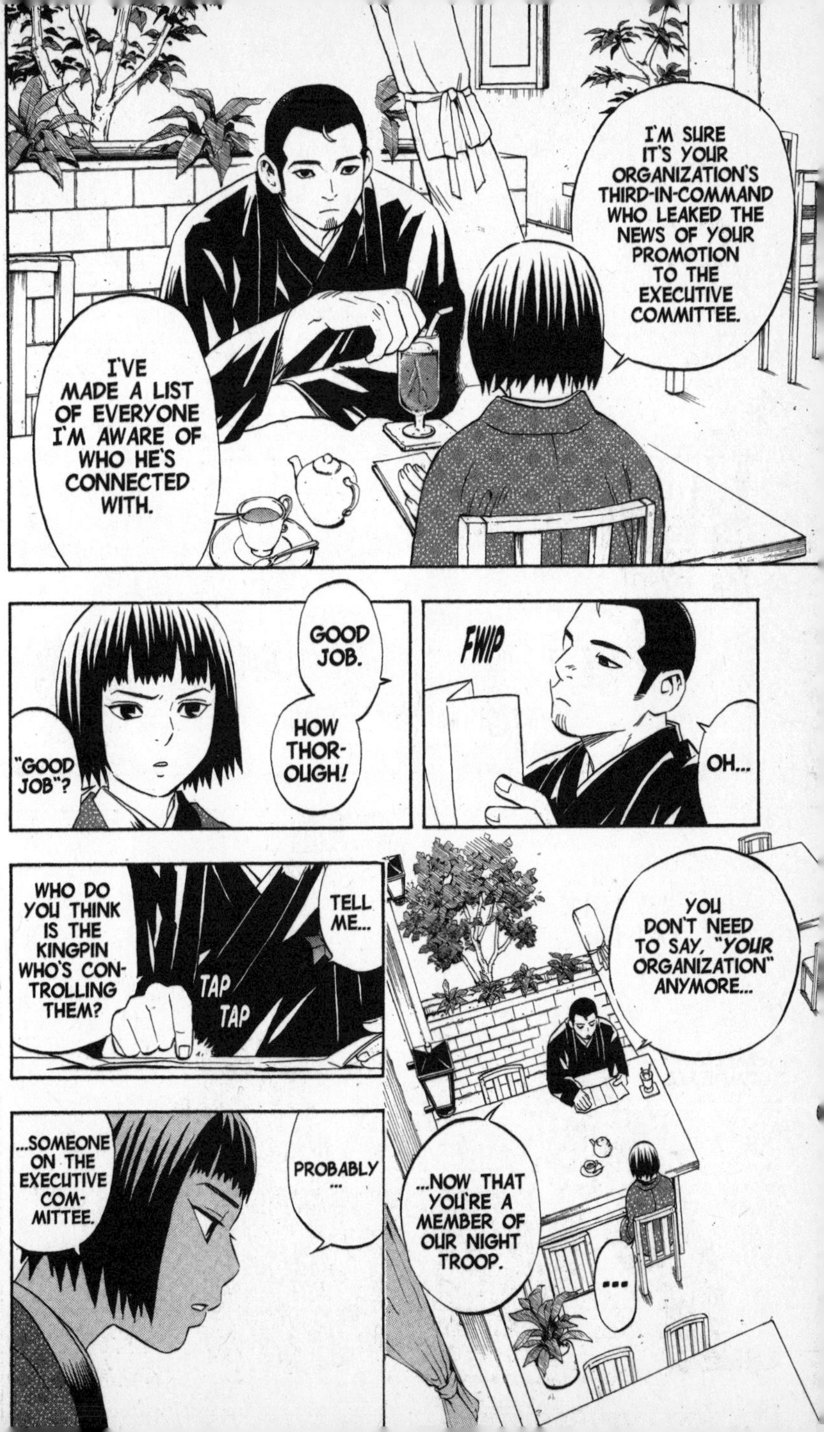
I'M SURE IT'S YOUR ORGANIZATION'S THIRD-IN-COMMAND WHO LEAKED THE NEWS OF YOUR PROMOTION TO THE EXECUTIVE COMMITTEE.
I'VE MADE A LIST OF EVERYONE I'M AWARE OF WHO HE'S CONNECTED WITH.
FWIP
OH...
GOOD JOB.
HOW THOR-OUGH!
"GOOD JOB"?
YOU DON'T NEED TO SAY, "*YOUR* ORGANIZATION" ANYMORE...
...NOW THAT YOU'RE A MEMBER OF OUR NIGHT TROOP.
...
TELL ME...
WHO DO YOU THINK IS THE KINGPIN WHO'S CON-TROLLING THEM?
TAP TAP
PROBABLY...
...SOMEONE ON THE EXECUTIVE COM-MITTEE.

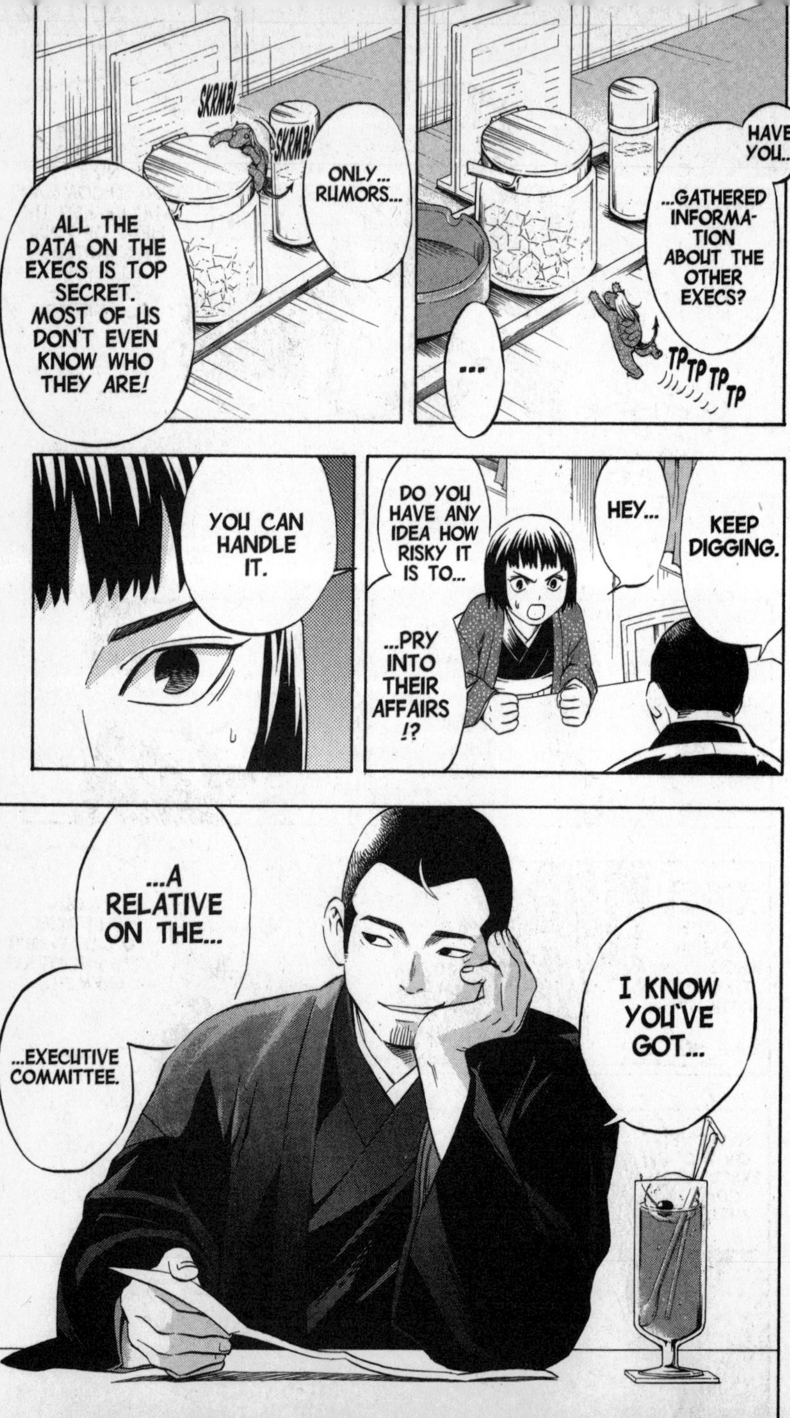
HAVE YOU...
...GATHERED INFORMATION ABOUT THE OTHER EXECS?
TP TP TP TP
...
SKRMBL
SKRMBL
ONLY... RUMORS...
ALL THE DATA ON THE EXECS IS TOP SECRET. MOST OF US DON'T EVEN KNOW WHO THEY ARE!
KEEP DIGGING.
HEY...
DO YOU HAVE ANY IDEA HOW RISKY IT IS TO...
...PRY INTO THEIR AFFAIRS!?
YOU CAN HANDLE IT.
I KNOW YOU'VE GOT...
...A RELATIVE ON THE...
...EXECUTIVE COMMITTEE.

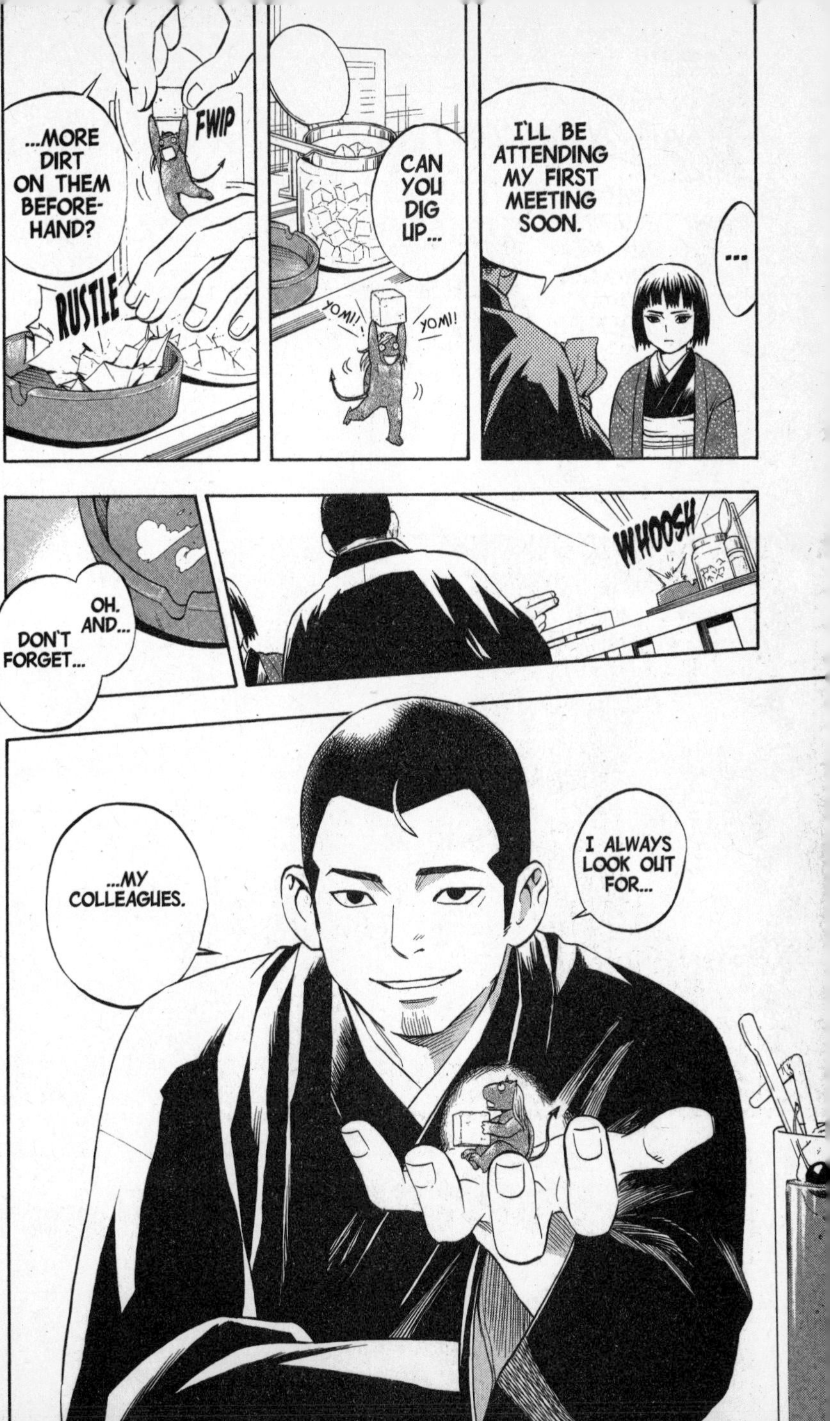
I'LL BE ATTENDING MY FIRST MEETING SOON.
...
CAN YOU DIG UP...
YOMI!
YOMI!
FWIP
...MORE DIRT ON THEM BEFORE-HAND?
RUSTLE
WHOOSH
OH. AND...
DON'T FORGET...
I ALWAYS LOOK OUT FOR...
...MY COLLEAGUES.

Chapter 61: Council of Twelve

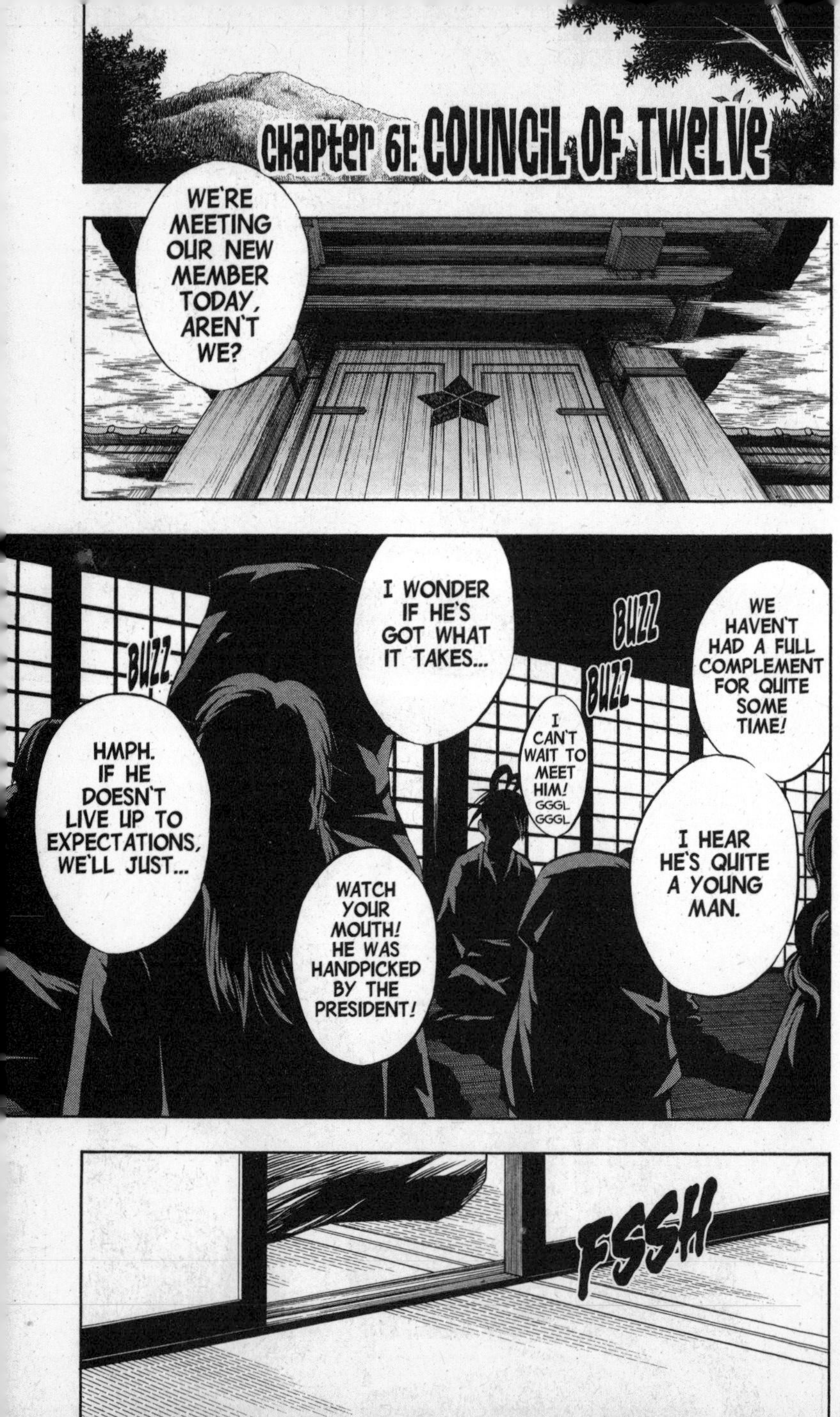
WE'RE MEETING OUR NEW MEMBER TODAY, AREN'T WE?
WE HAVEN'T HAD A FULL COMPLEMENT FOR QUITE SOME TIME!
BUZZ
BUZZ
I HEAR HE'S QUITE A YOUNG MAN.
I CAN'T WAIT TO MEET HIM! GGGL GGGL
I WONDER IF HE'S GOT WHAT IT TAKES...
WATCH YOUR MOUTH! HE WAS HANDPICKED BY THE PRESIDENT!
BUZZ
HMPH. IF HE DOESN'T LIVE UP TO EXPECTATIONS, WE'LL JUST...
FSSH

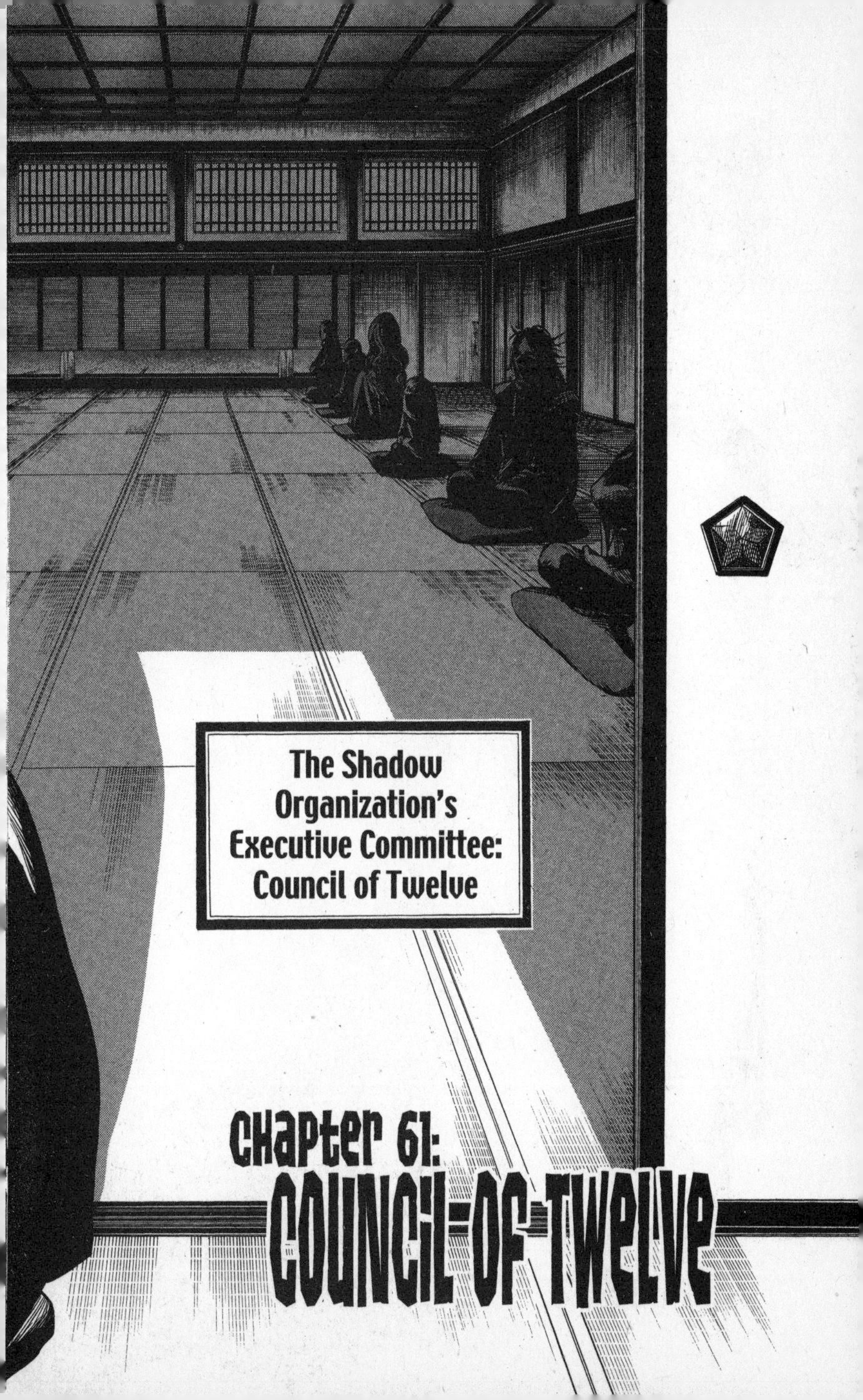
The Shadow Organization's Executive Committee: Council of Twelve
Chapter 61:
Council of Twelve

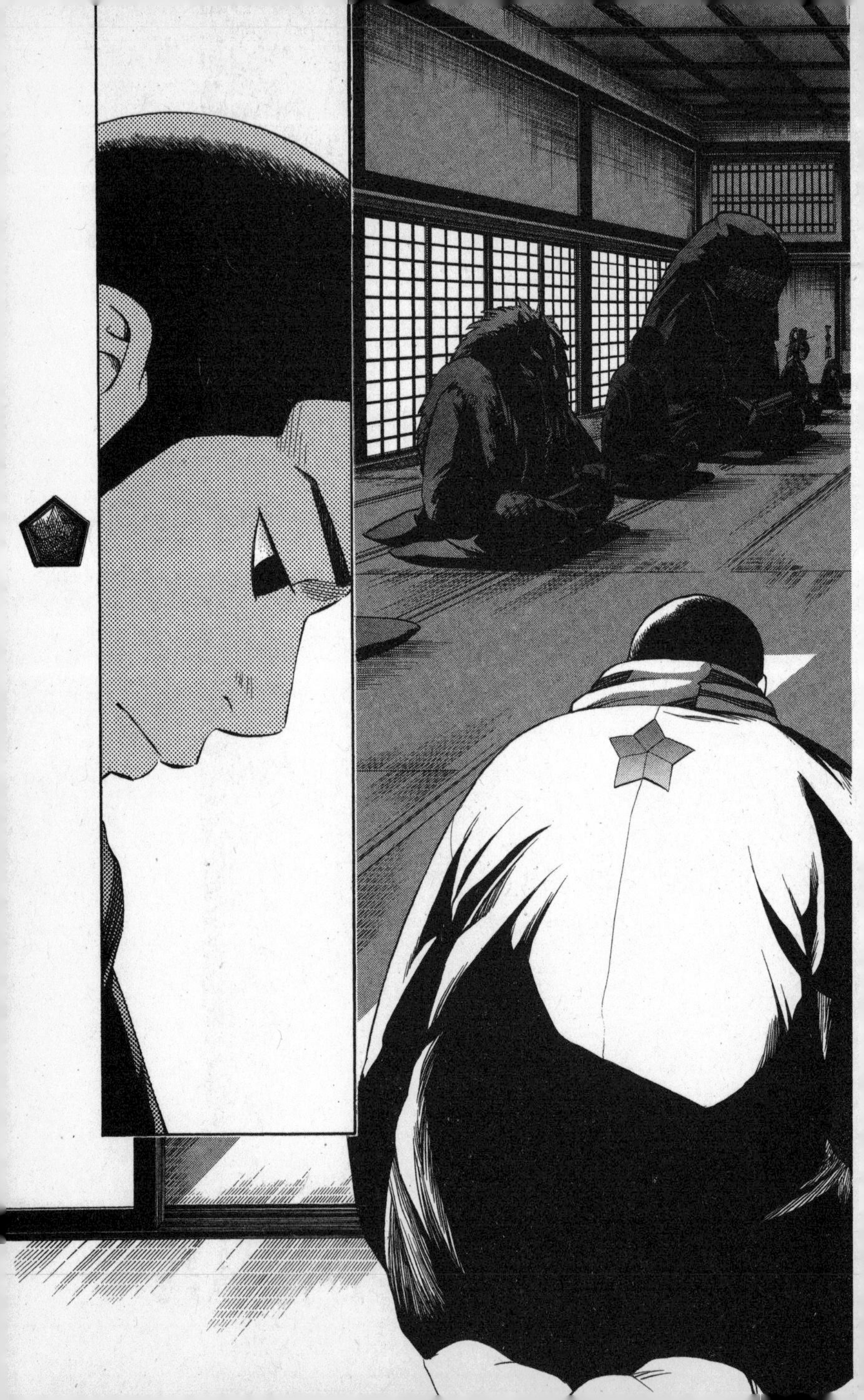

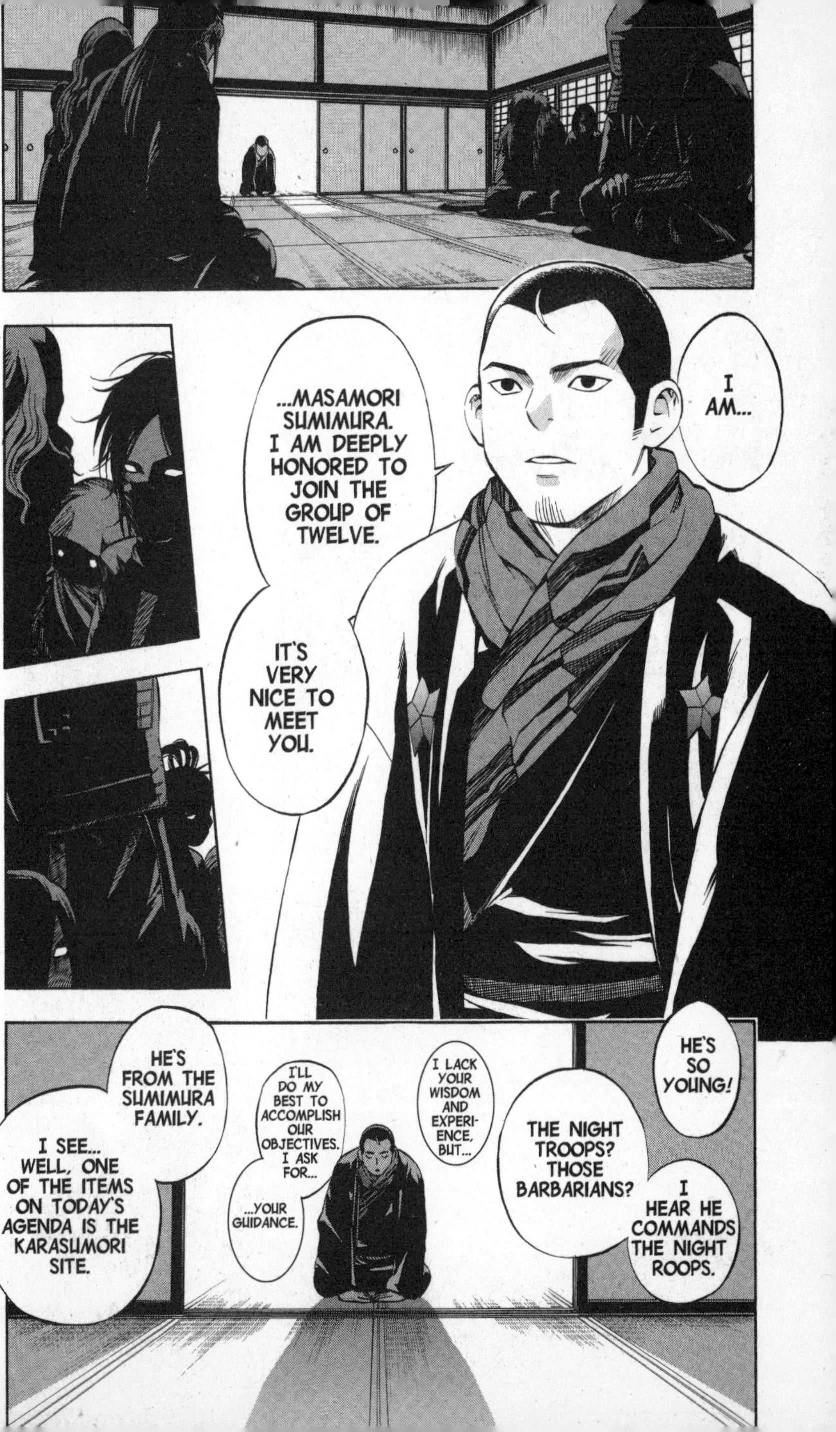
I AM...
...MASAMORI SUMIMURA. I AM DEEPLY HONORED TO JOIN THE GROUP OF TWELVE.
IT'S VERY NICE TO MEET YOU.
HE'S SO YOUNG!
I HEAR HE COMMANDS THE NIGHT ROOPS.
THE NIGHT TROOPS? THOSE BARBARIANS?
I LACK YOUR WISDOM AND EXPERI-ENCE, BUT...
I'LL DO MY BEST TO ACCOMPLISH OUR OBJECTIVES. I ASK FOR...
...YOUR GUIDANCE.
HE'S FROM THE SUMIMURA FAMILY.
I SEE... WELL, ONE OF THE ITEMS ON TODAY'S AGENDA IS THE KARASUMORI SITE.

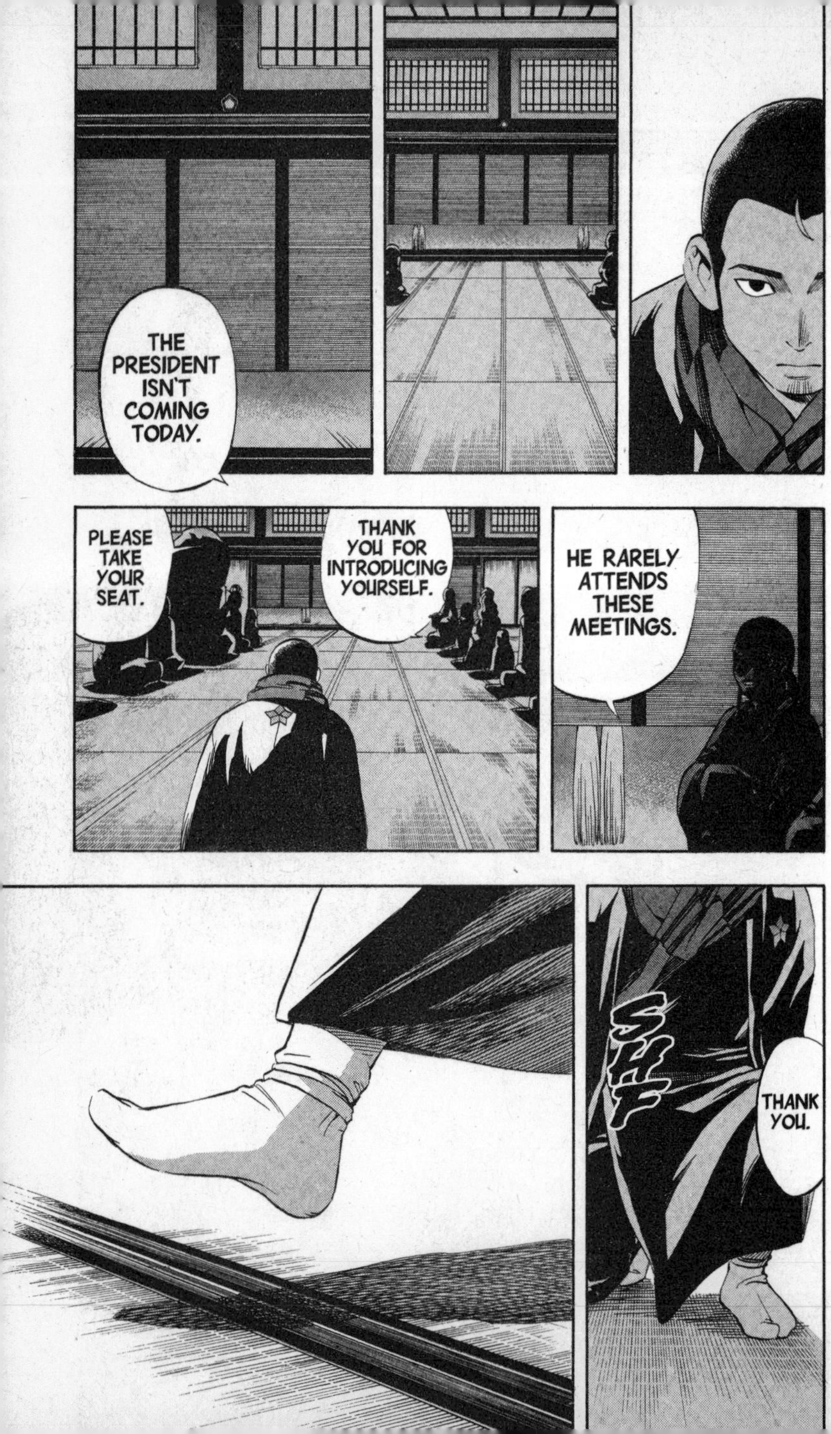
THE PRESIDENT ISN'T COMING TODAY.
HE RARELY ATTENDS THESE MEETINGS.
THANK YOU FOR INTRODUCING YOURSELF.
PLEASE TAKE YOUR SEAT.
THANK YOU.
SHF

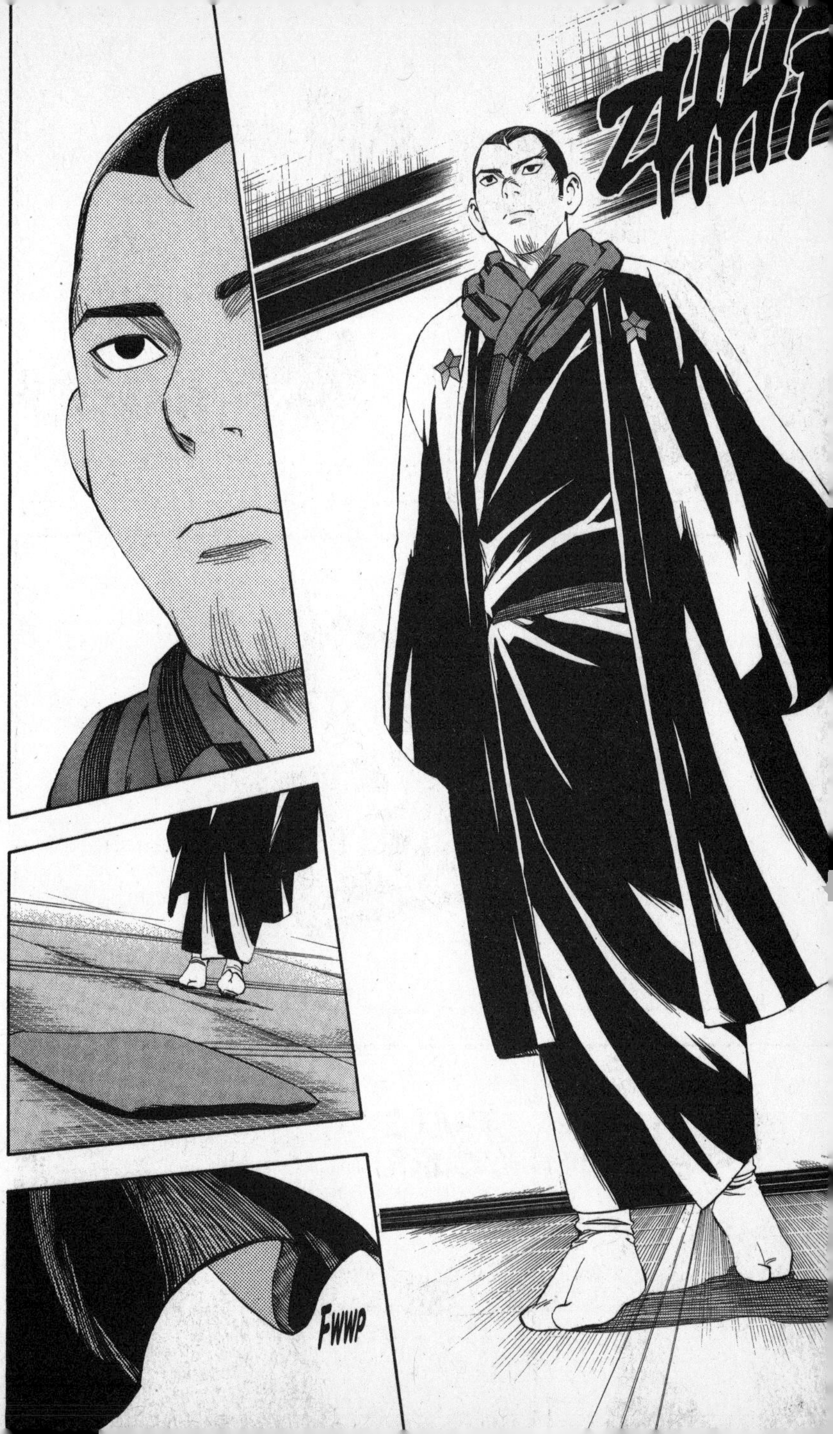
ZHH
FWWP

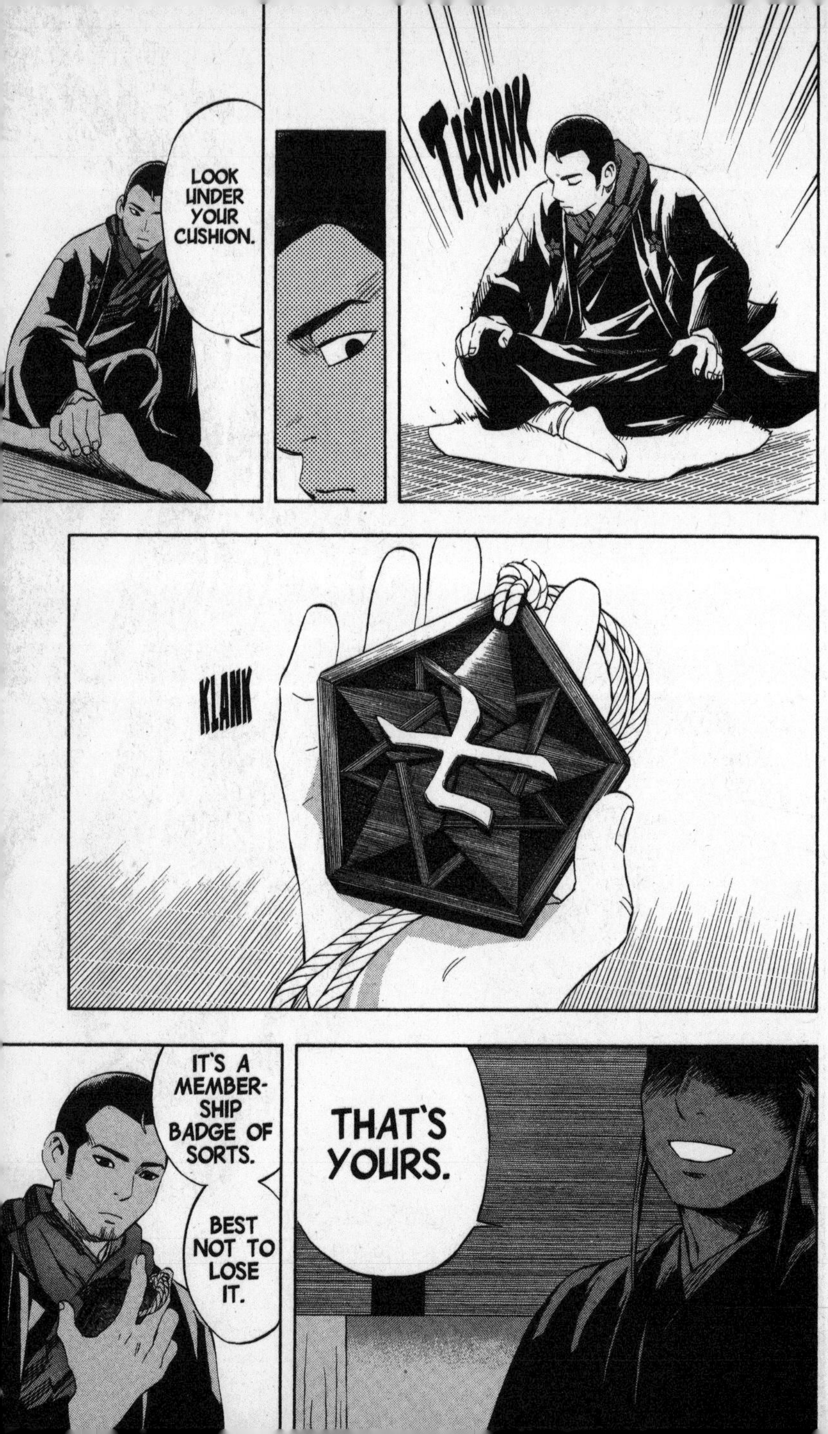
THUNK
LOOK UNDER YOUR CUSHION.
KLANK
THAT'S YOURS.
IT'S A MEMBER-SHIP BADGE OF SORTS.
BEST NOT TO LOSE IT.

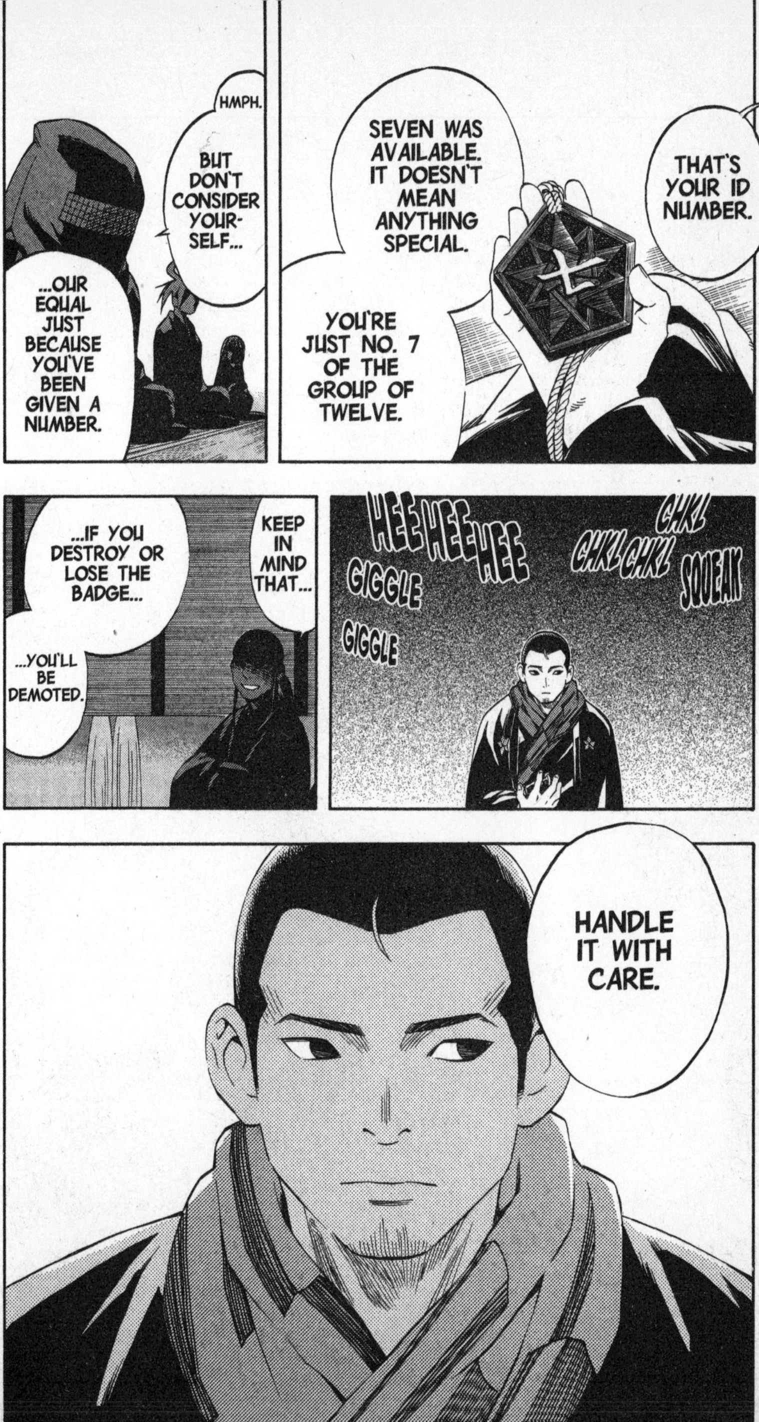
THAT'S YOUR ID NUMBER.
SEVEN WAS AVAILABLE. IT DOESN'T MEAN ANYTHING SPECIAL.
YOU'RE JUST NO. 7 OF THE GROUP OF TWELVE.
HMPH.
BUT DON'T CONSIDER YOUR-SELF...
...OUR EQUAL JUST BECAUSE YOU'VE BEEN GIVEN A NUMBER.
CHKL CHKL CHKL
SQUEAK
HEE HEE HEE
GIGGLE
GIGGLE
KEEP IN MIND THAT...
...IF YOU DESTROY OR LOSE THE BADGE...
...YOU'LL BE DEMOTED.
HANDLE IT WITH CARE.

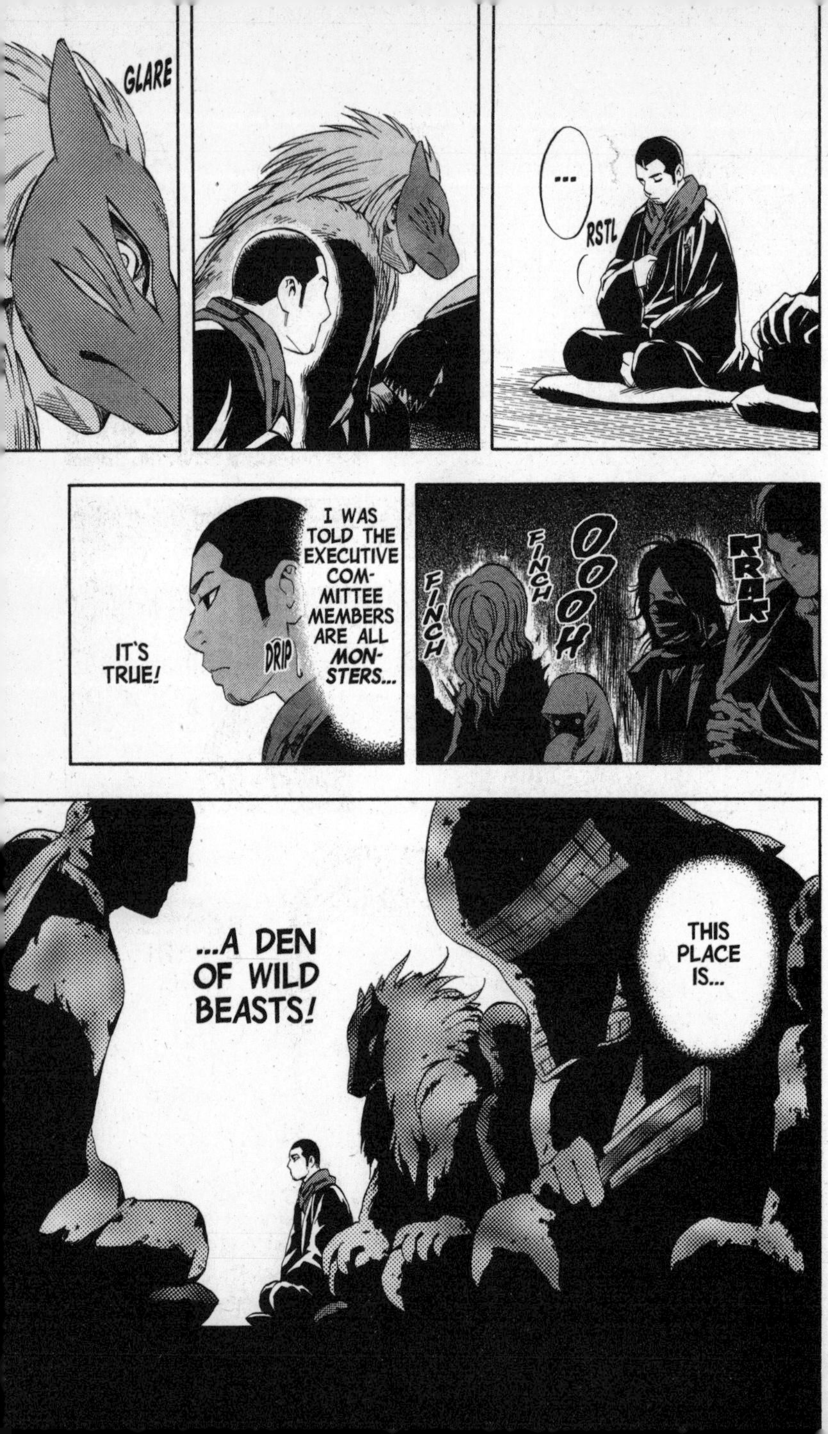
...
RSTL
GLARE
KRAK
OOOOH
FINCH
FINCH
I WAS TOLD THE EXECUTIVE COMMITTEE MEMBERS ARE ALL MONSTERS...
DRIP
IT'S TRUE!
THIS PLACE IS...
...A DEN OF WILD BEASTS!

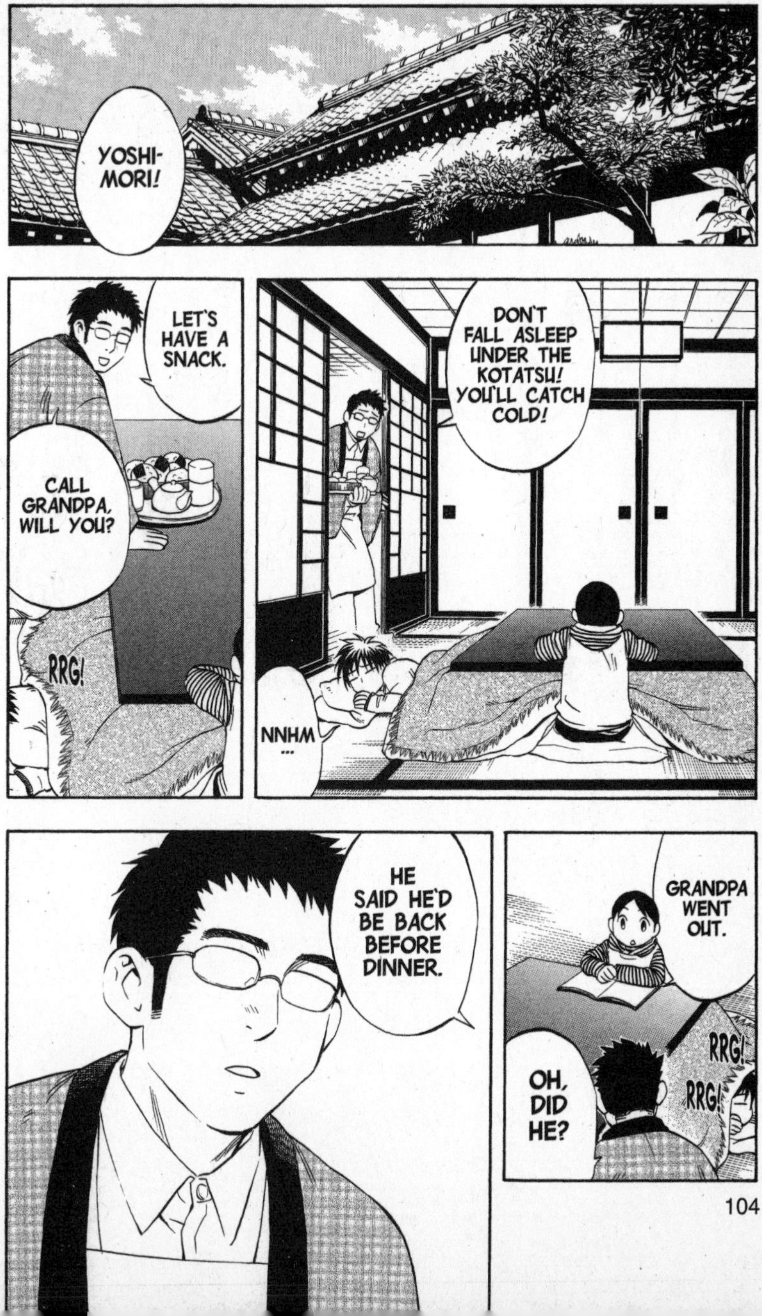
YOSHI-MORI!
DON'T FALL ASLEEP UNDER THE KOTATSU! YOU'LL CATCH COLD!
NNHM...
LET'S HAVE A SNACK.
CALL GRANDPA, WILL YOU?
RRG!
GRANDPA WENT OUT.
RRG!
RRG!
OH, DID HE?
HE SAID HE'D BE BACK BEFORE DINNER.

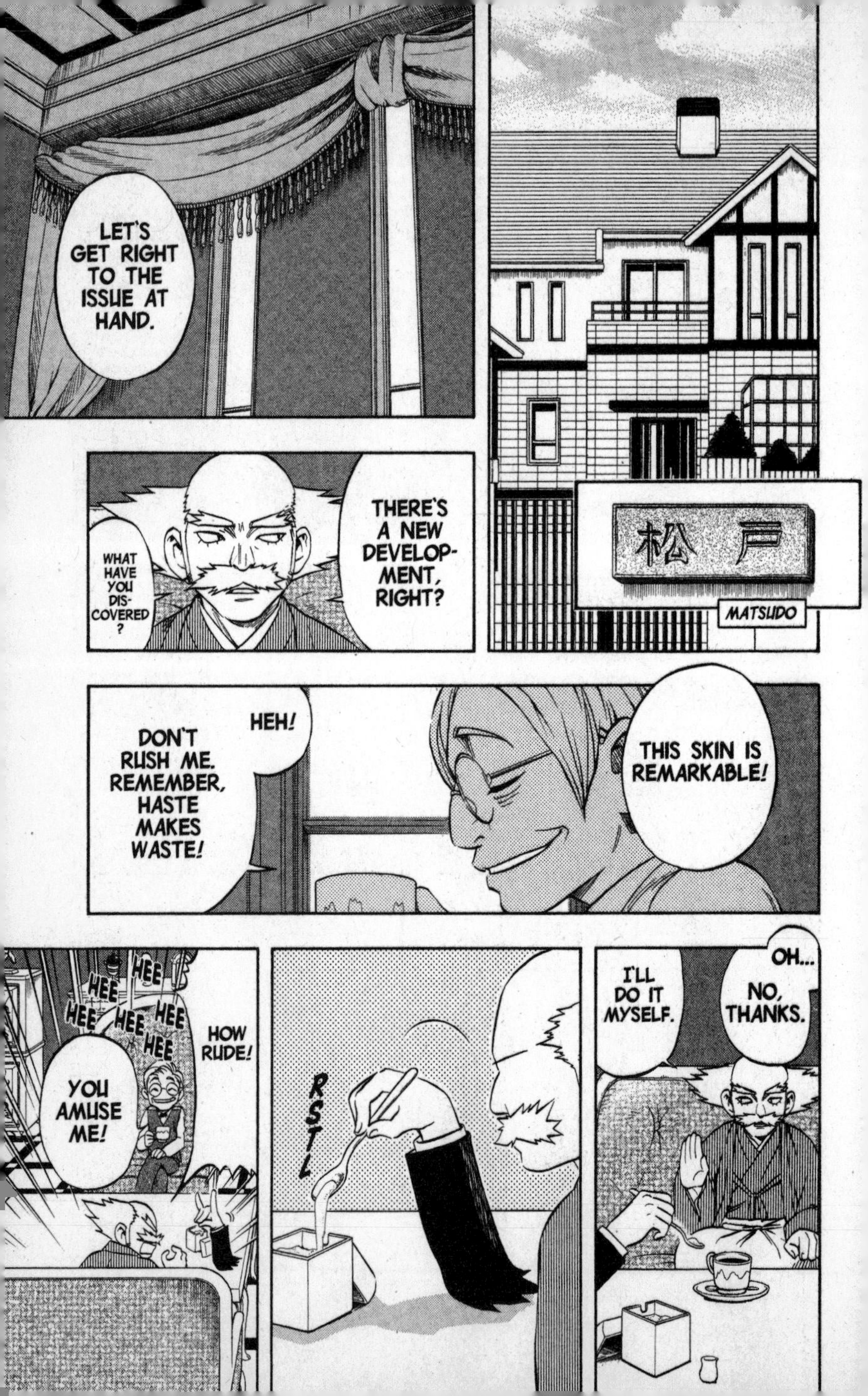
松戸
MATSUDO
LET'S GET RIGHT TO THE ISSUE AT HAND.
THERE'S A NEW DEVELOPMENT, RIGHT?
WHAT HAVE YOU DISCOVERED?
THIS SKIN IS REMARKABLE!
HEH!
DON'T RUSH ME. REMEMBER, HASTE MAKES WASTE!
OH... NO, THANKS.
I'LL DO IT MYSELF.
RSTL
HEE HEE HEE HEE HEE HEE
HOW RUDE!
YOU AMUSE ME!

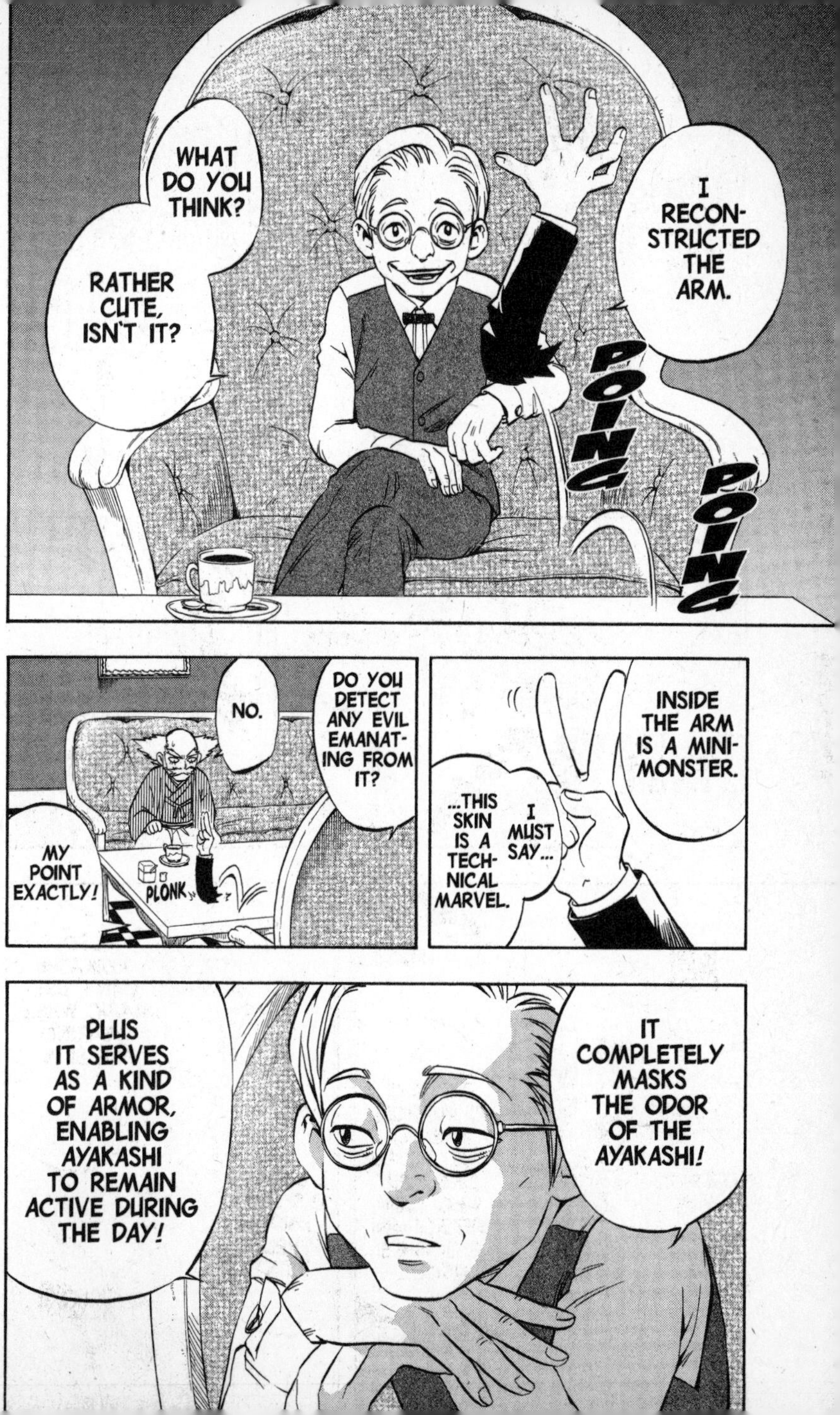
I RECONSTRUCTED THE ARM.
WHAT DO YOU THINK?
RATHER CUTE, ISN'T IT?
POING
POING
INSIDE THE ARM IS A MINI-MONSTER.
I MUST SAY...
...THIS SKIN IS A TECHNICAL MARVEL.
DO YOU DETECT ANY EVIL EMANATING FROM IT?
NO.
MY POINT EXACTLY!
PLONK
IT COMPLETELY MASKS THE ODOR OF THE AYAKASHI!
PLUS IT SERVES AS A KIND OF ARMOR, ENABLING AYAKASHI TO REMAIN ACTIVE DURING THE DAY!

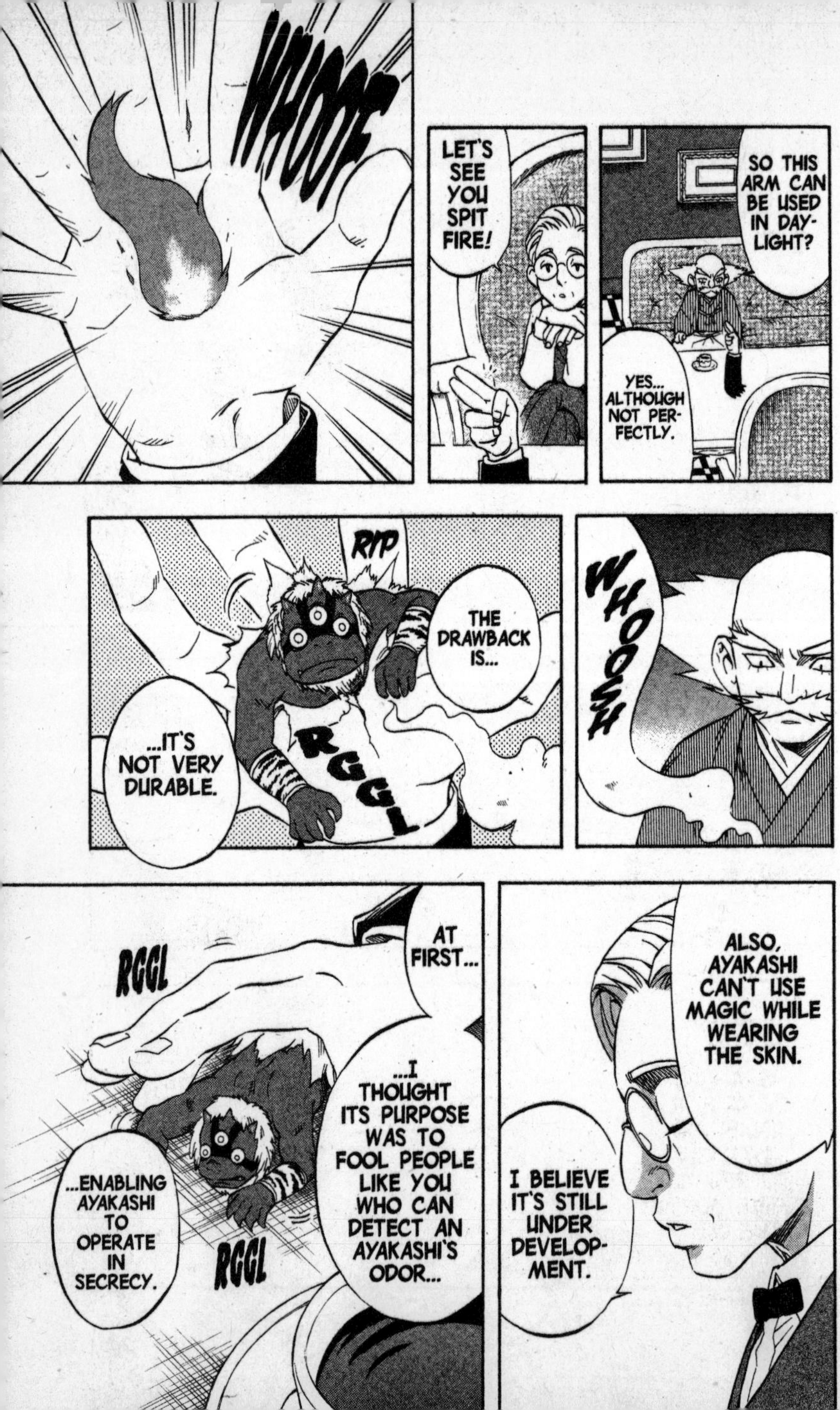
SO THIS ARM CAN BE USED IN DAYLIGHT?
YES... ALTHOUGH NOT PERFECTLY.
LET'S SEE YOU SPIT FIRE!
WHOOF
WHOOOSH
RIP
THE DRAWBACK IS...
RGGL
...IT'S NOT VERY DURABLE.
ALSO, AYAKASHI CAN'T USE MAGIC WHILE WEARING THE SKIN.
I BELIEVE IT'S STILL UNDER DEVELOPMENT.
AT FIRST...
...I THOUGHT ITS PURPOSE WAS TO FOOL PEOPLE LIKE YOU WHO CAN DETECT AN AYAKASHI'S ODOR...
RGGL
...ENABLING AYAKASHI TO OPERATE IN SECRECY.
RGGL

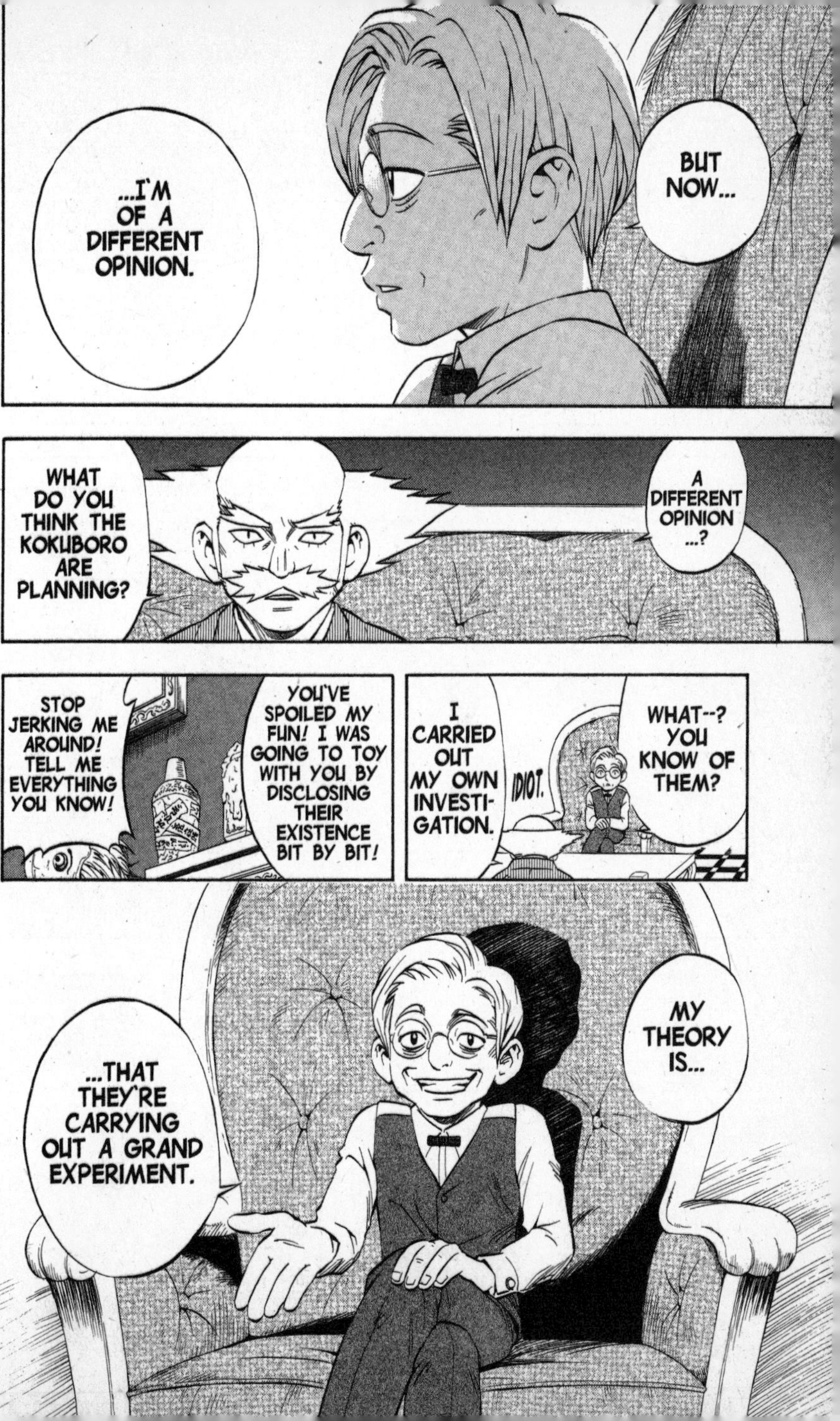
BUT NOW...
...I'M OF A DIFFERENT OPINION.
A DIFFERENT OPINION ...?
WHAT DO YOU THINK THE KOKUBORO ARE PLANNING?
WHAT--? YOU KNOW OF THEM?
IDIOT.
I CARRIED OUT MY OWN INVESTIGATION.
YOU'VE SPOILED MY FUN! I WAS GOING TO TOY WITH YOU BY DISCLOSING THEIR EXISTENCE BIT BY BIT!
STOP JERKING ME AROUND! TELL ME EVERYTHING YOU KNOW!
MY THEORY IS...
...THAT THEY'RE CARRYING OUT A GRAND EXPERIMENT.

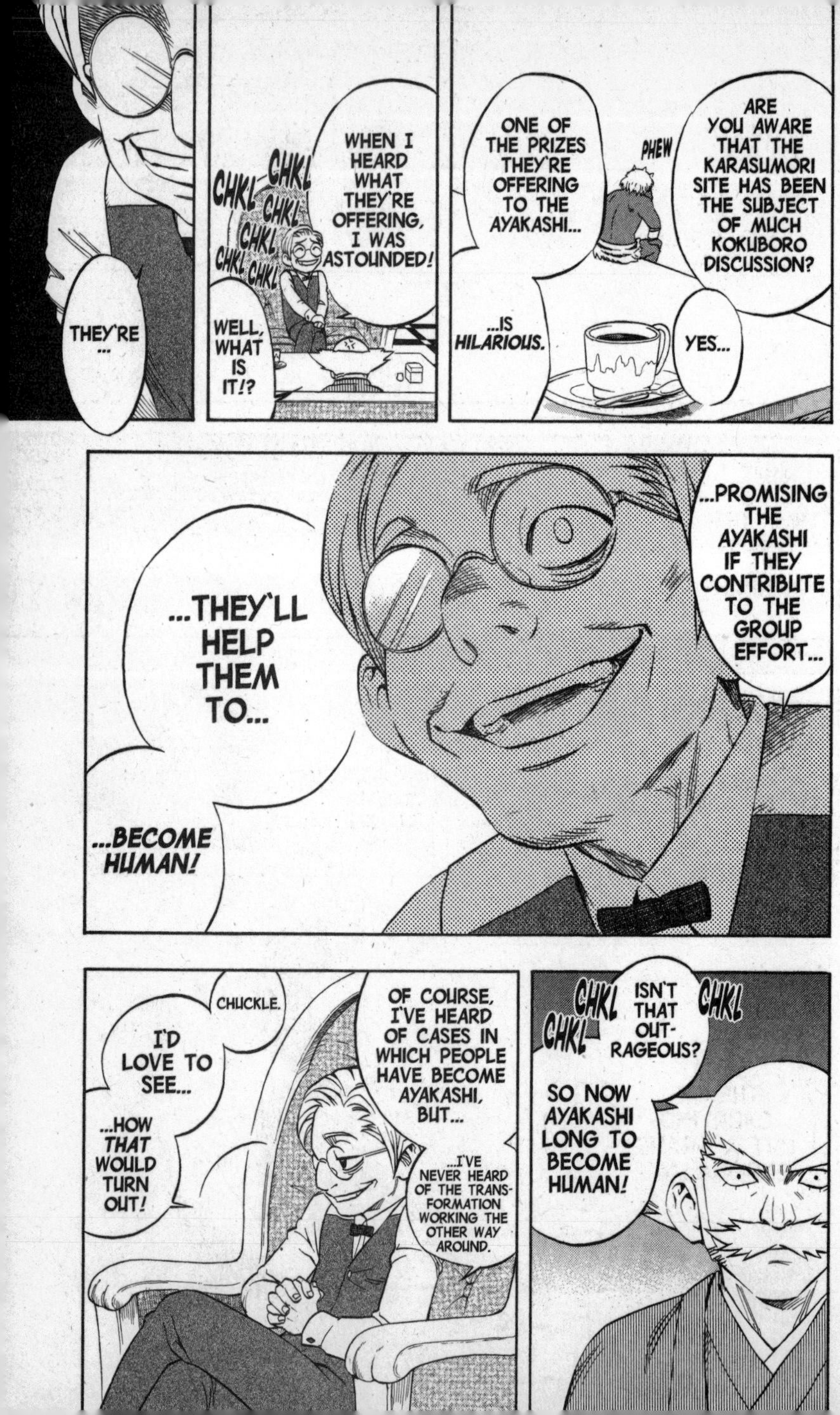
ARE YOU AWARE THAT THE KARASUMORI SITE HAS BEEN THE SUBJECT OF MUCH KOKUBORO DISCUSSION?
PHEW
ONE OF THE PRIZES THEY'RE OFFERING TO THE AYAKASHI...
YES...
...IS *HILARIOUS.*
WHEN I HEARD WHAT THEY'RE OFFERING, I WAS ASTOUNDED!
CHKL CHKL CHKL CHKL CHKL CHKL
WELL, WHAT IS IT!?
THEY'RE ...
...PROMISING THE AYAKASHI IF THEY CONTRIBUTE TO THE GROUP EFFORT...
...THEY'LL HELP THEM TO...
...BECOME HUMAN!
ISN'T THAT OUT-RAGEOUS?
CHKL CHKL CHKL
SO NOW AYAKASHI LONG TO BECOME HUMAN!
OF COURSE, I'VE HEARD OF CASES IN WHICH PEOPLE HAVE BECOME AYAKASHI, BUT...
CHUCKLE.
I'D LOVE TO SEE...
...I'VE NEVER HEARD OF THE TRANS-FORMATION WORKING THE OTHER WAY AROUND.
...HOW *THAT* WOULD TURN OUT!

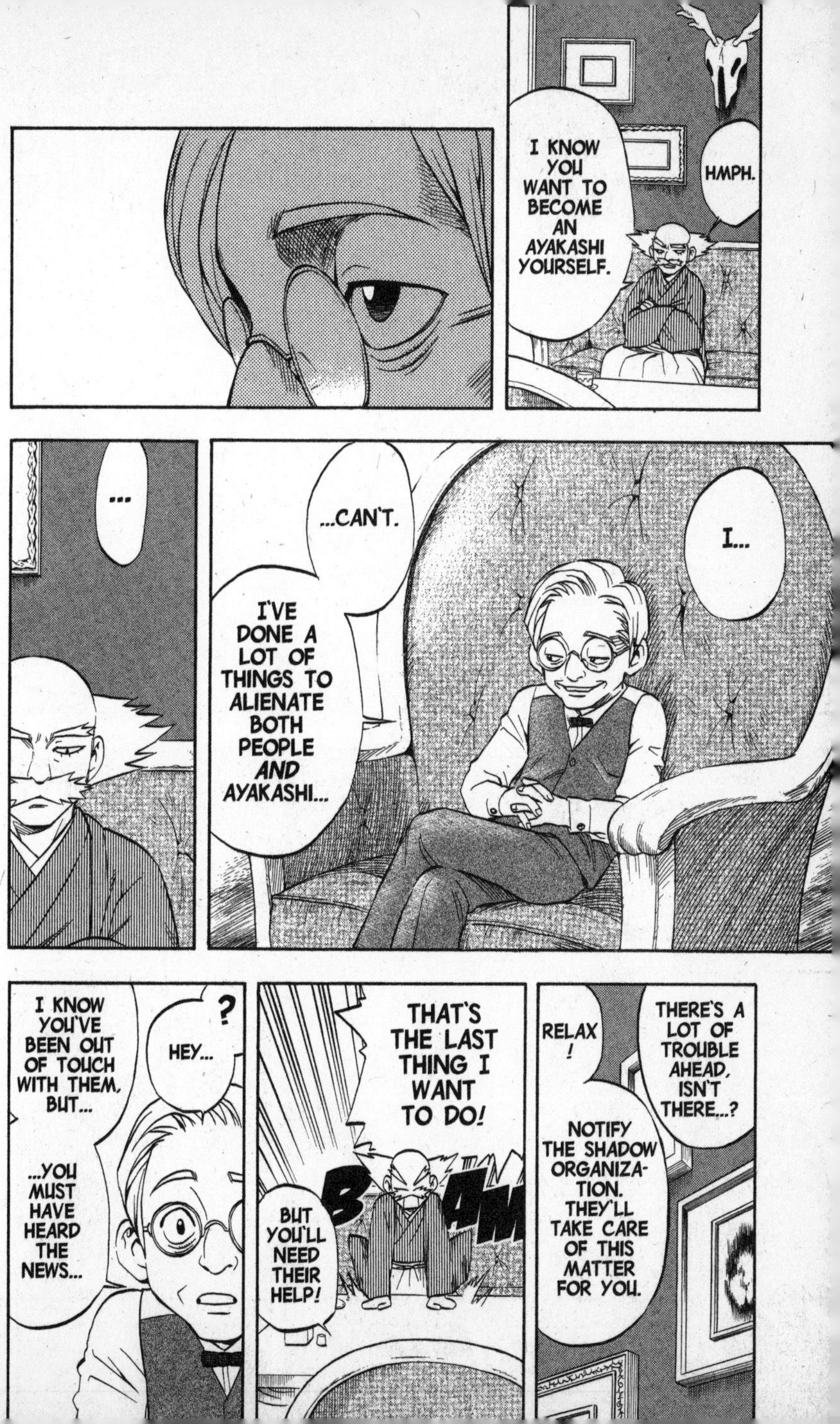
I KNOW YOU WANT TO BECOME AN AYAKASHI YOURSELF.
HMPH.
I...
...CAN'T.
I'VE DONE A LOT OF THINGS TO ALIENATE BOTH PEOPLE *AND* AYAKASHI...
...
THERE'S A LOT OF TROUBLE AHEAD, ISN'T THERE...?
RELAX!
NOTIFY THE SHADOW ORGANIZATION. THEY'LL TAKE CARE OF THIS MATTER FOR YOU.
THAT'S THE LAST THING I WANT TO DO!
BAM
BUT YOU'LL NEED THEIR HELP!
?
HEY...
I KNOW YOU'VE BEEN OUT OF TOUCH WITH THEM, BUT...
...YOU MUST HAVE HEARD THE NEWS...

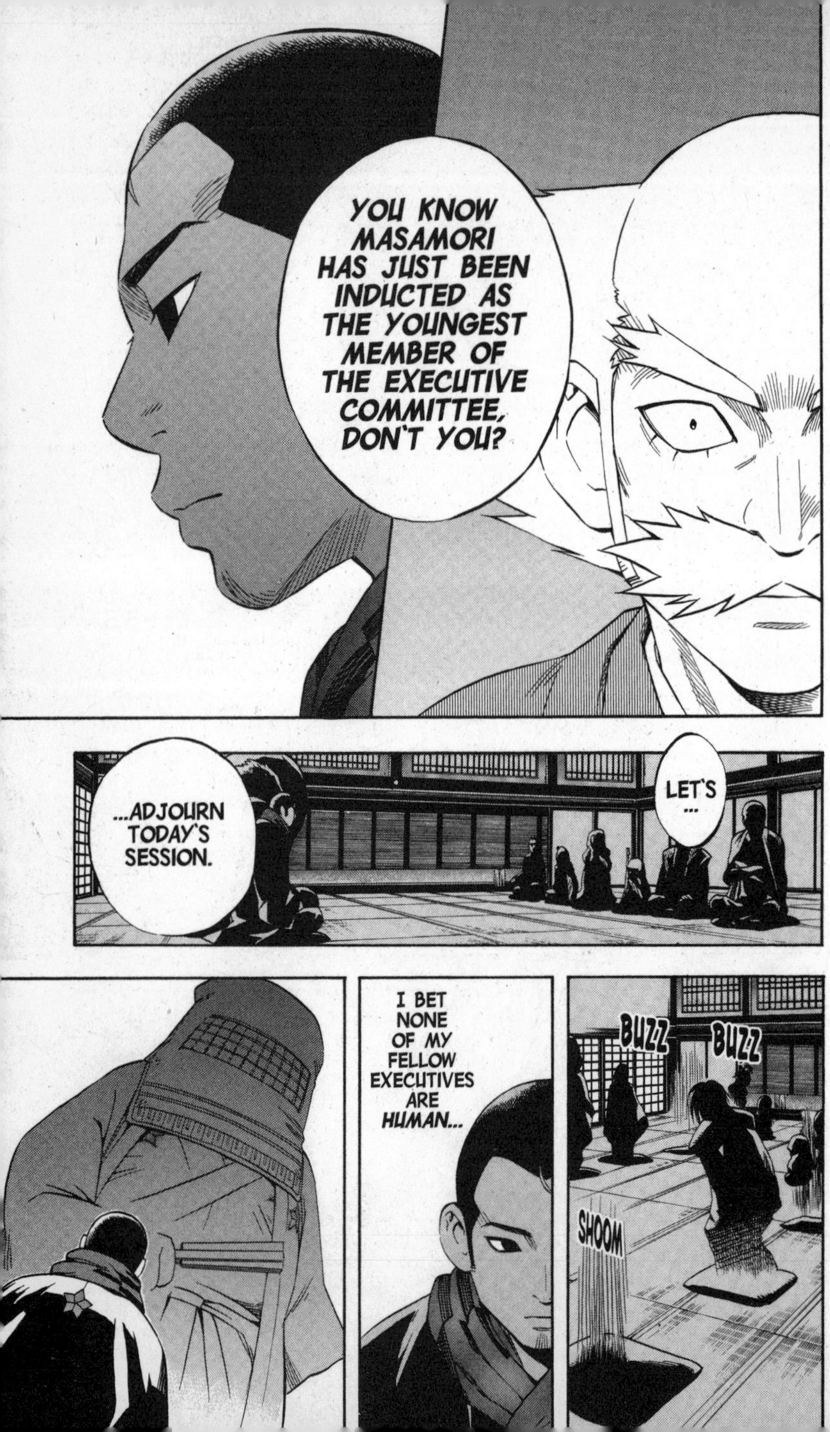
YOU KNOW MASAMORI HAS JUST BEEN INDUCTED AS THE YOUNGEST MEMBER OF THE EXECUTIVE COMMITTEE, DON'T YOU?
LET'S ...
...ADJOURN TODAY'S SESSION.
BUZZ
BUZZ
SHOOM
I BET NONE OF MY FELLOW EXECUTIVES ARE HUMAN...

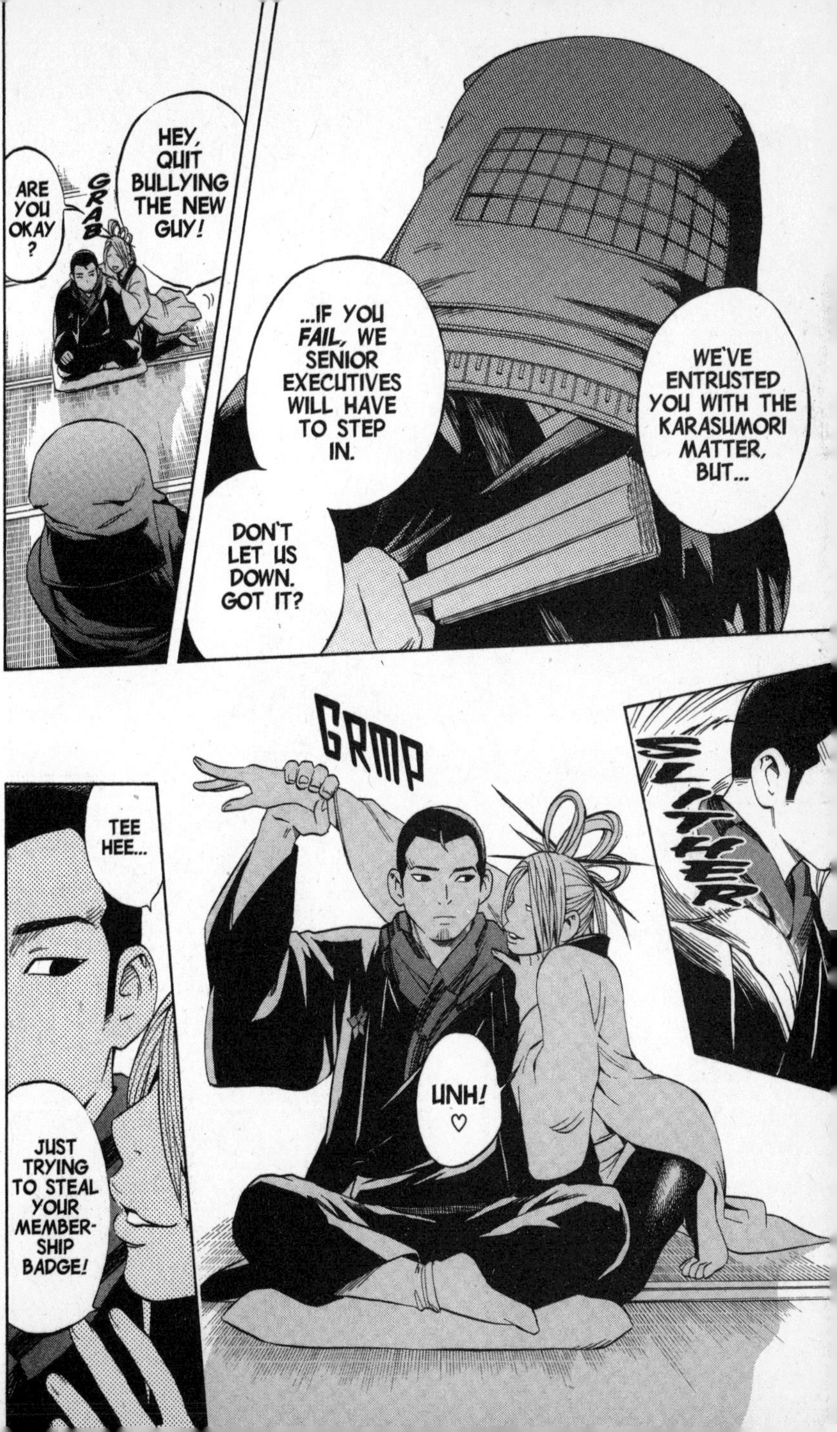
WE'VE ENTRUSTED YOU WITH THE KARASUMORI MATTER, BUT...
...IF YOU *FAIL*, WE SENIOR EXECUTIVES WILL HAVE TO STEP IN.
DON'T LET US DOWN. GOT IT?
HEY, QUIT BULLYING THE NEW GUY!
GRAB
ARE YOU OKAY?
SLITHER
GRMP
UNH! ♡
TEE HEE...
JUST TRYING TO STEAL YOUR MEMBER-SHIP BADGE!

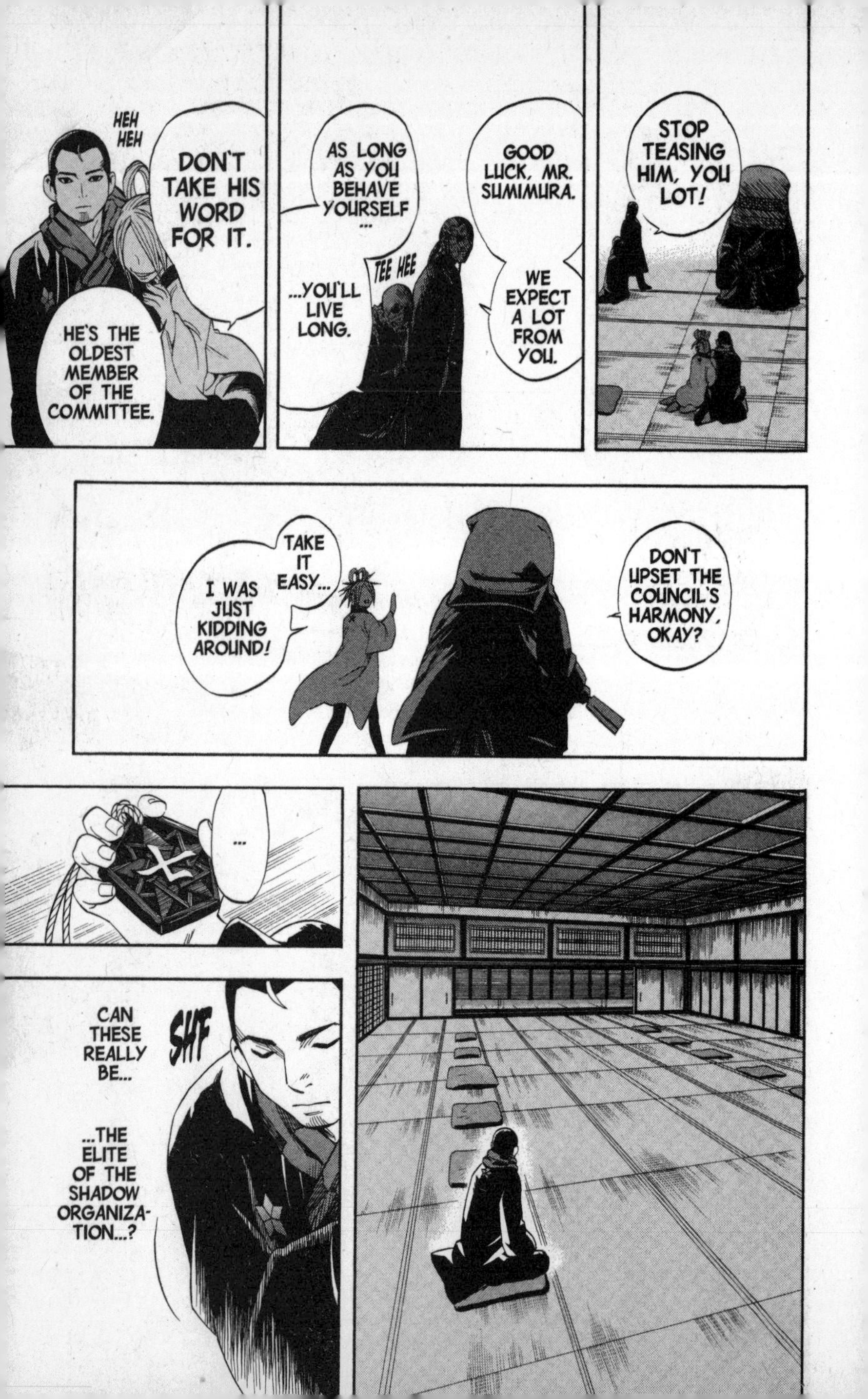
STOP TEASING HIM, YOU LOT!
GOOD LUCK, MR. SUMIMURA.
WE EXPECT A LOT FROM YOU.
AS LONG AS YOU BEHAVE YOURSELF...
TEE HEE
...YOU'LL LIVE LONG.
DON'T TAKE HIS WORD FOR IT.
HEH HEH
HE'S THE OLDEST MEMBER OF THE COMMITTEE.
DON'T UPSET THE COUNCIL'S HARMONY, OKAY?
TAKE IT EASY...
I WAS JUST KIDDING AROUND!
...
CAN THESE REALLY BE...
SHF
...THE ELITE OF THE SHADOW ORGANIZATION...?

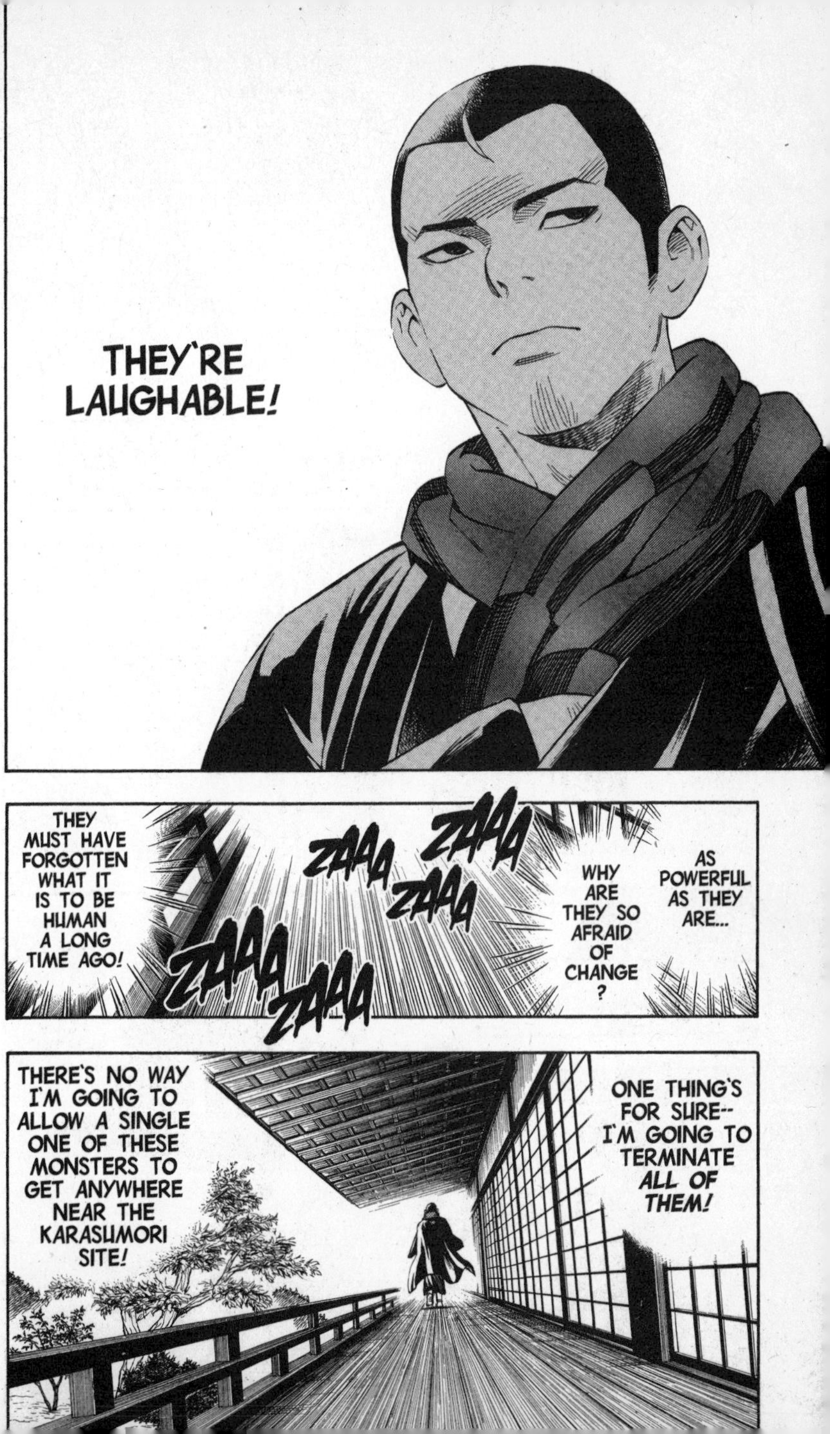
THEY'RE LAUGHABLE!
AS POWERFUL AS THEY ARE...
WHY ARE THEY SO AFRAID OF CHANGE?
ZAAAA ZAAAA ZAAAA ZAAAA ZAAAA ZAAAA
THEY MUST HAVE FORGOTTEN WHAT IT IS TO BE HUMAN A LONG TIME AGO!
ONE THING'S FOR SURE-- I'M GOING TO TERMINATE *ALL OF THEM!*
THERE'S NO WAY I'M GOING TO ALLOW A SINGLE ONE OF THESE MONSTERS TO GET ANYWHERE NEAR THE KARASUMORI SITE!

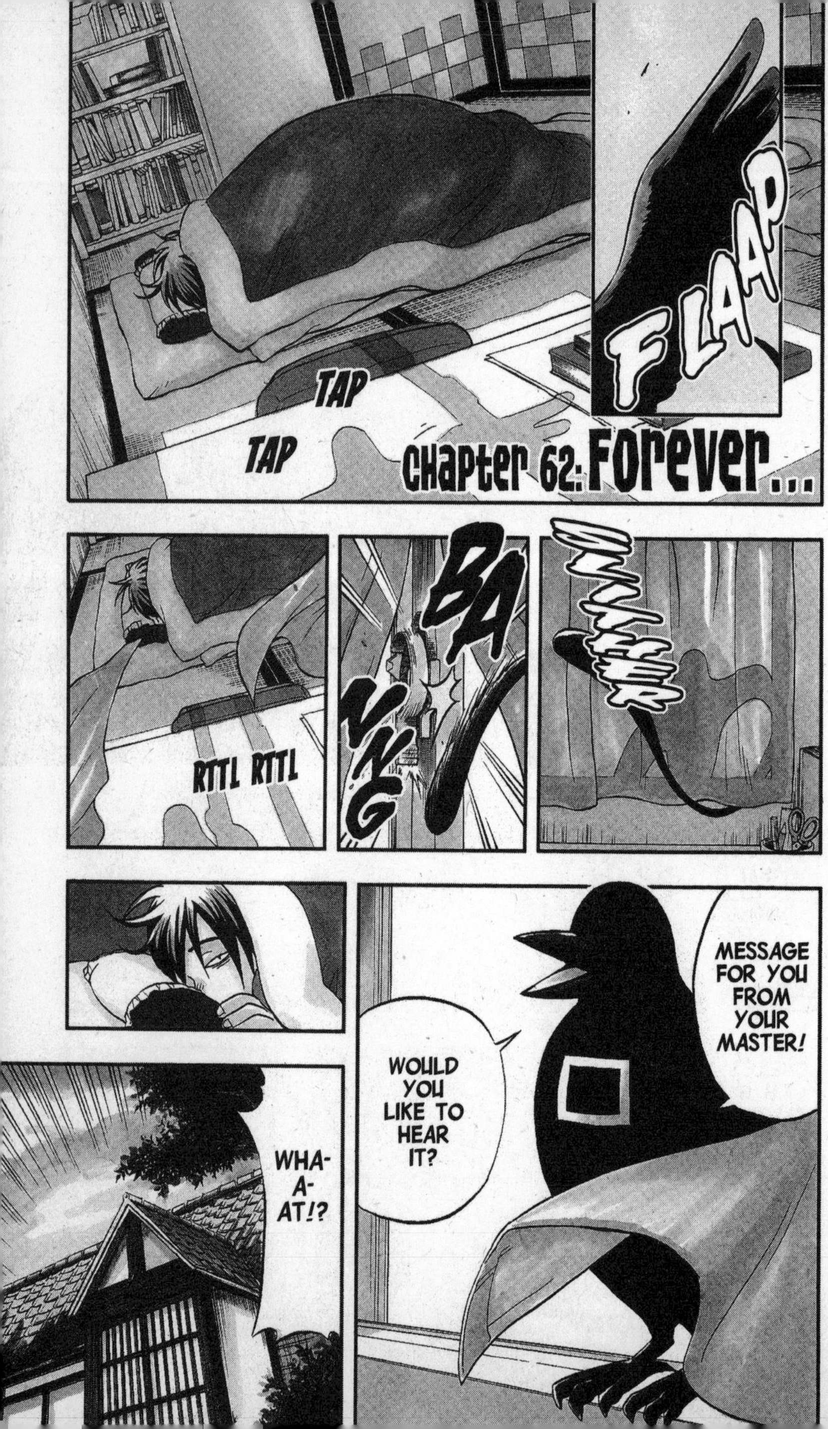
FLAAP
TAP
TAP
Chapter 62: Forever...
BANNG
RTTL RTTL
MESSAGE FOR YOU FROM YOUR MASTER!
WOULD YOU LIKE TO HEAR IT?
WHA-A-AT!?

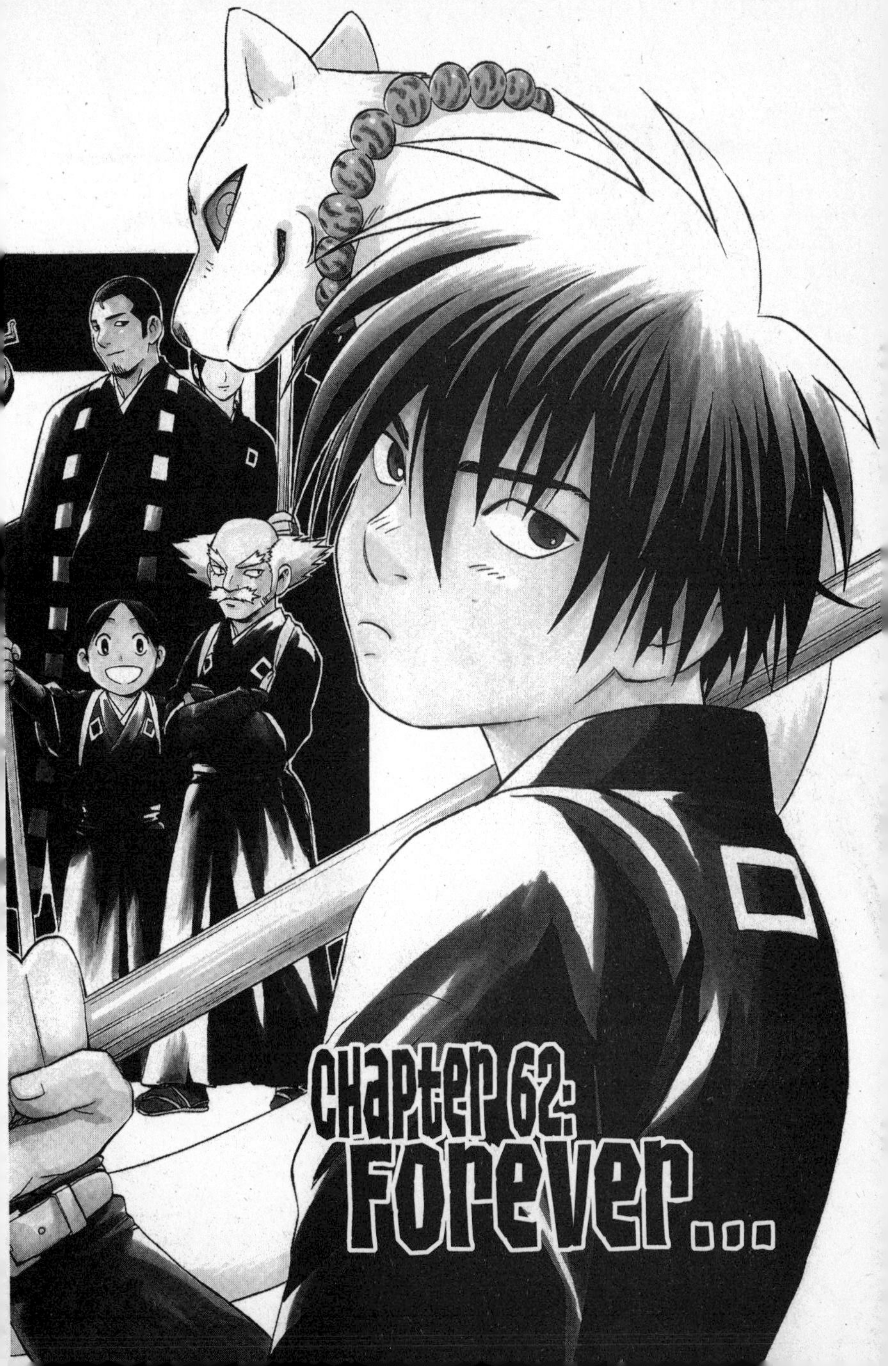

Chapter 62:
Forever...

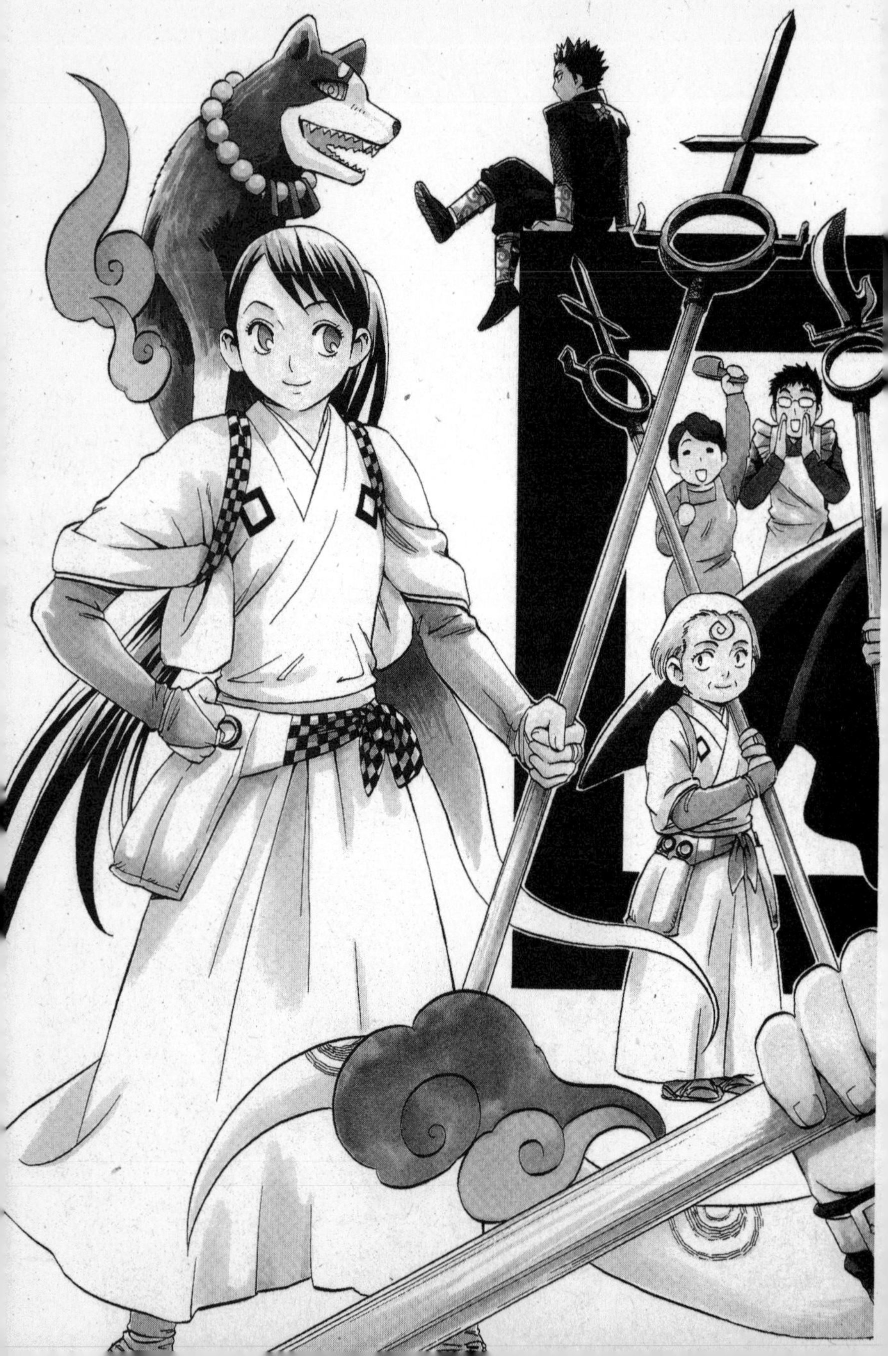

結界師

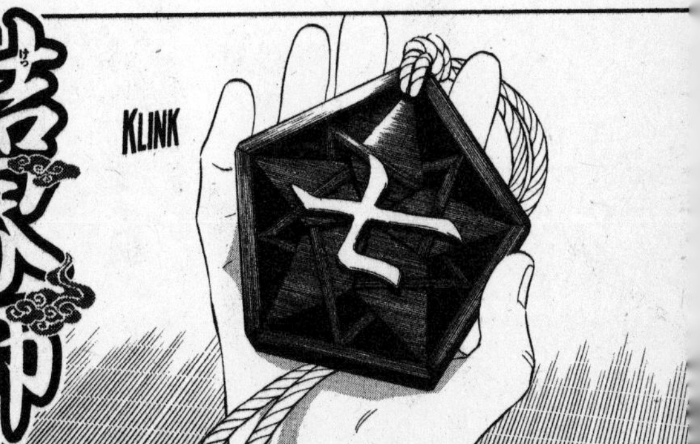
KLINK
七

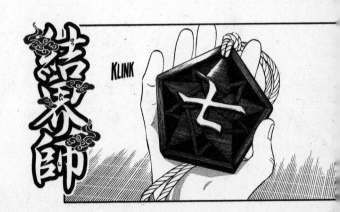

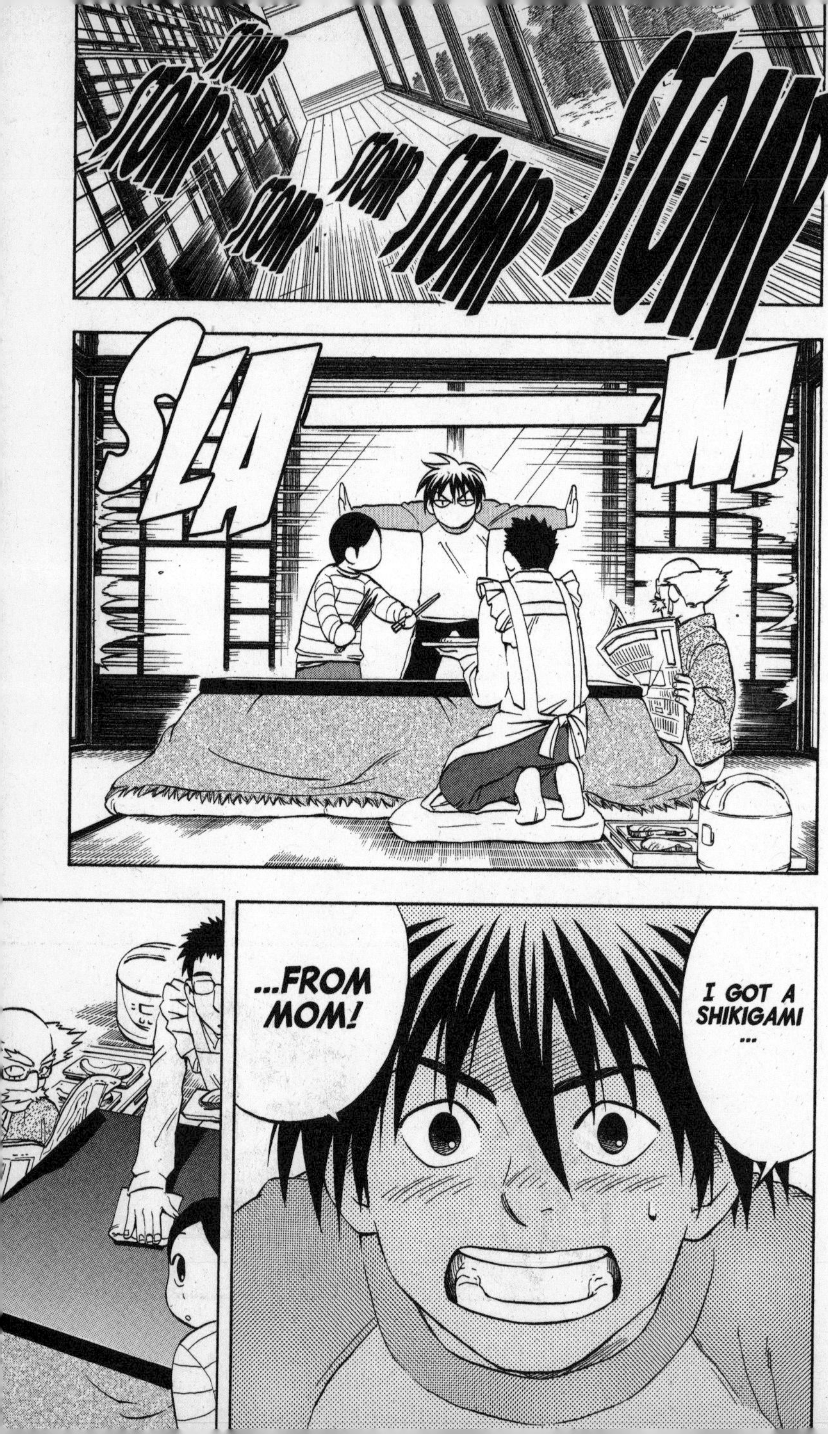
STOMP
STOMP
STOMP
STOMP
STOMP
STOMP
SLAM
I GOT A SHIKIGAMI ...
...FROM MOM!

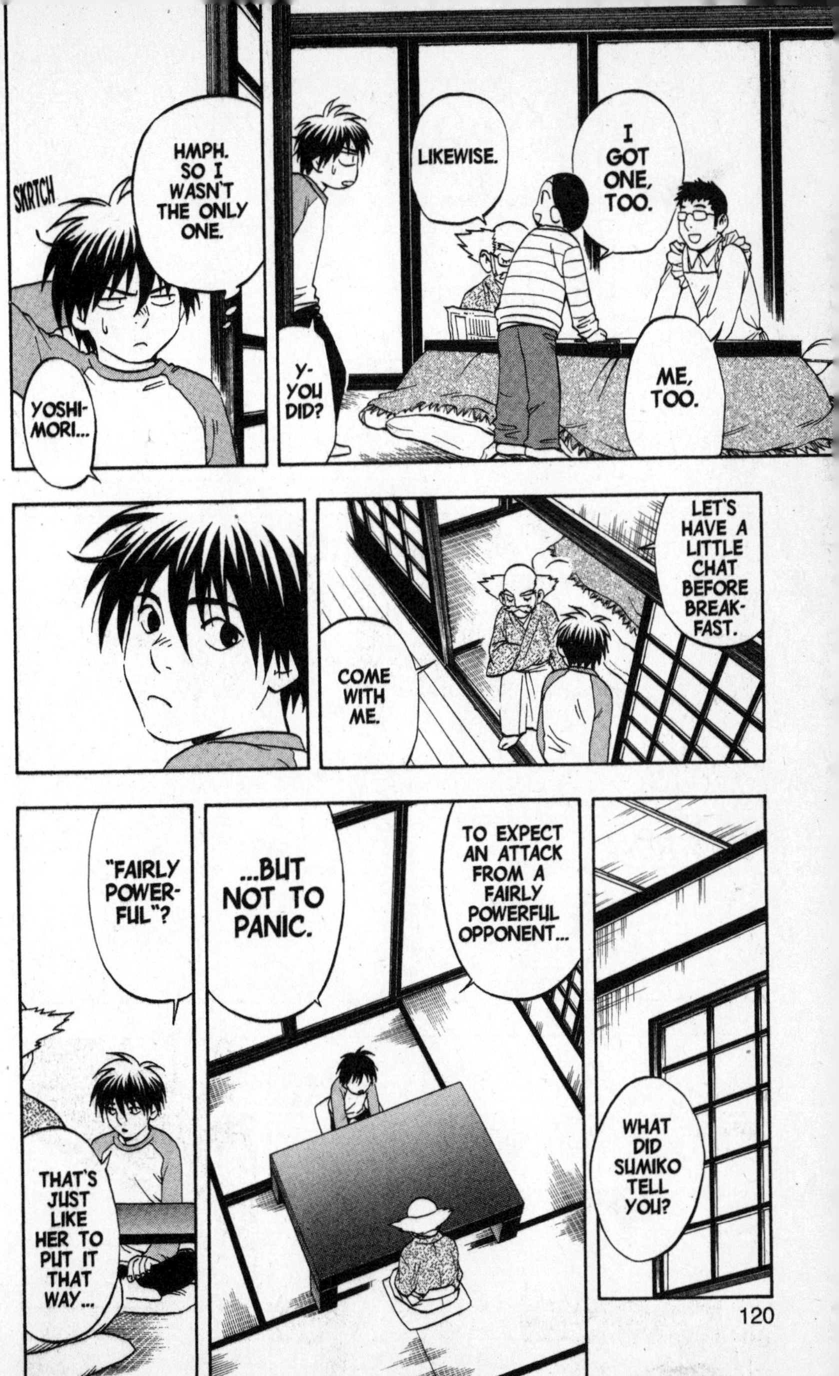
I GOT ONE, TOO.
LIKEWISE.
ME, TOO.
Y-YOU DID?
SKRTCH
HMPH. SO I WASN'T THE ONLY ONE.
YOSHIMORI...
LET'S HAVE A LITTLE CHAT BEFORE BREAKFAST.
COME WITH ME.
WHAT DID SUMIKO TELL YOU?
TO EXPECT AN ATTACK FROM A FAIRLY POWERFUL OPPONENT...
...BUT NOT TO PANIC.
"FAIRLY POWERFUL"?
THAT'S JUST LIKE HER TO PUT IT THAT WAY...

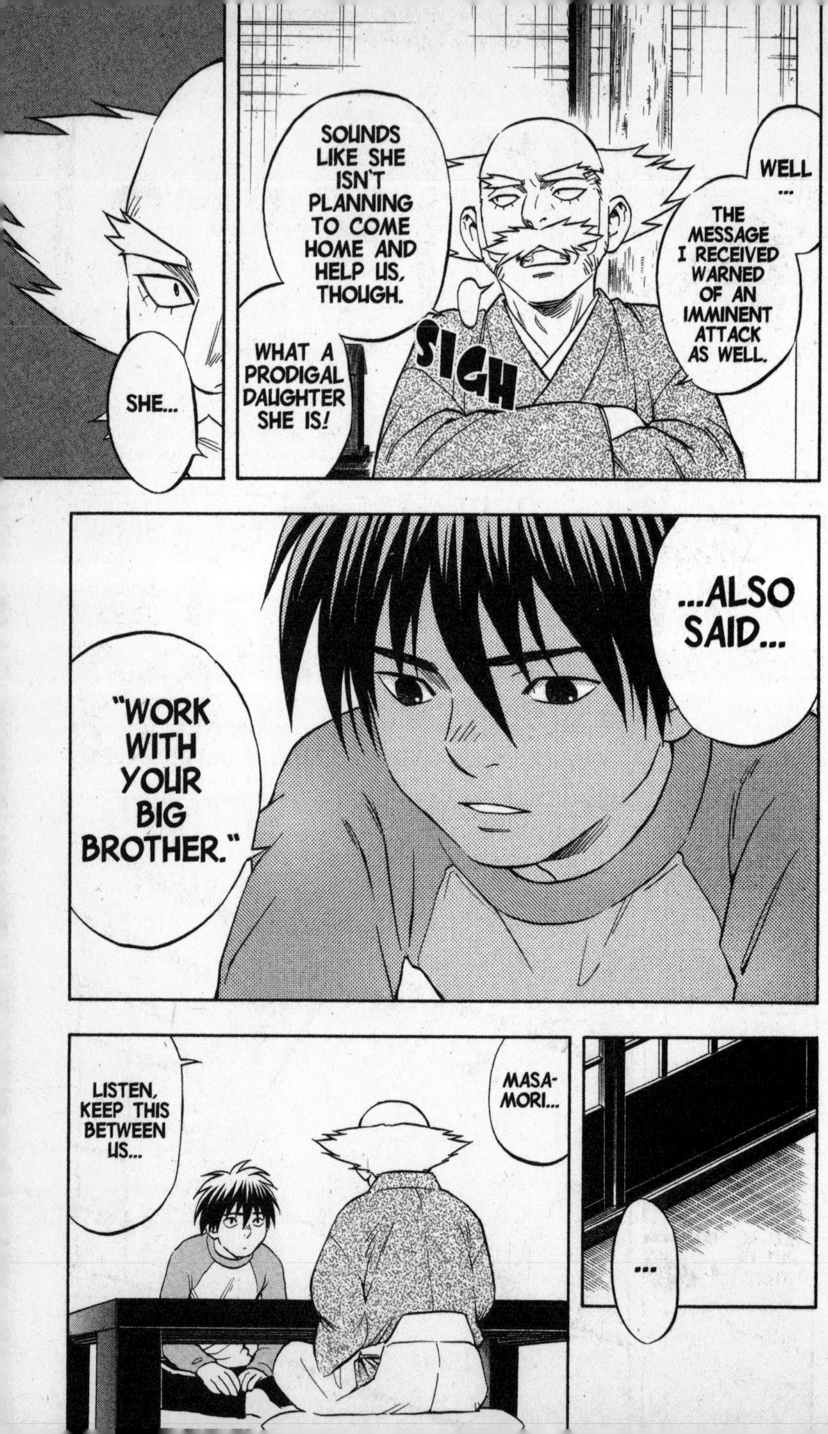
WELL ...
THE MESSAGE I RECEIVED WARNED OF AN IMMINENT ATTACK AS WELL.
SOUNDS LIKE SHE ISN'T PLANNING TO COME HOME AND HELP US, THOUGH.
SIGH
WHAT A PRODIGAL DAUGHTER SHE IS!
SHE...
...ALSO SAID...
"WORK WITH YOUR BIG BROTHER."
...
MASA-MORI...
LISTEN, KEEP THIS BETWEEN US...

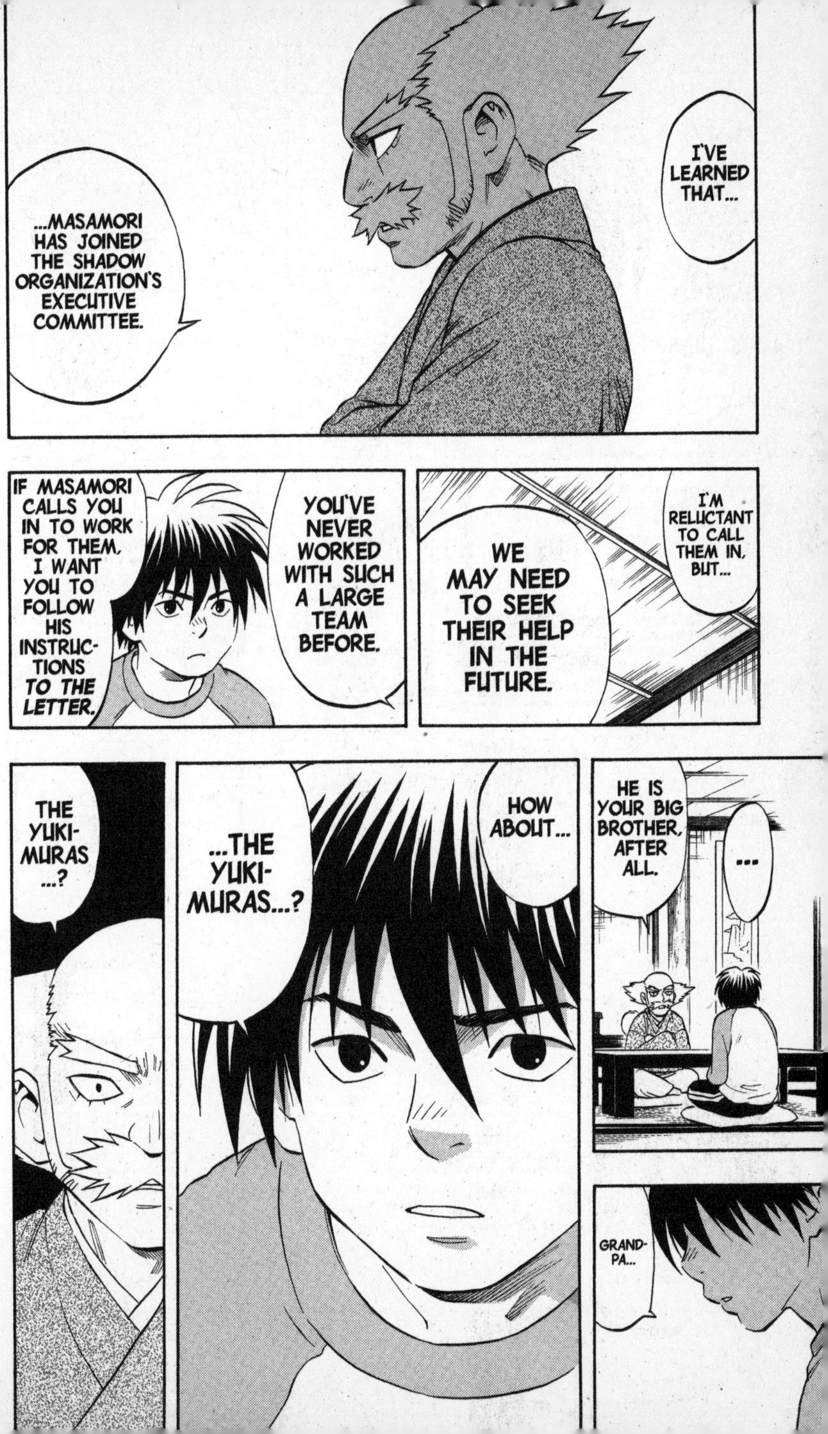
I'VE LEARNED THAT...
...MASAMORI HAS JOINED THE SHADOW ORGANIZATION'S EXECUTIVE COMMITTEE.
I'M RELUCTANT TO CALL THEM IN, BUT...
WE MAY NEED TO SEEK THEIR HELP IN THE FUTURE.
YOU'VE NEVER WORKED WITH SUCH A LARGE TEAM BEFORE.
IF MASAMORI CALLS YOU IN TO WORK FOR THEM, I WANT YOU TO FOLLOW HIS INSTRUC-TIONS TO THE LETTER.
...
HE IS YOUR BIG BROTHER, AFTER ALL.
GRAND-PA...
HOW ABOUT...
...THE YUKI-MURAS...?
THE YUKI-MURAS...?

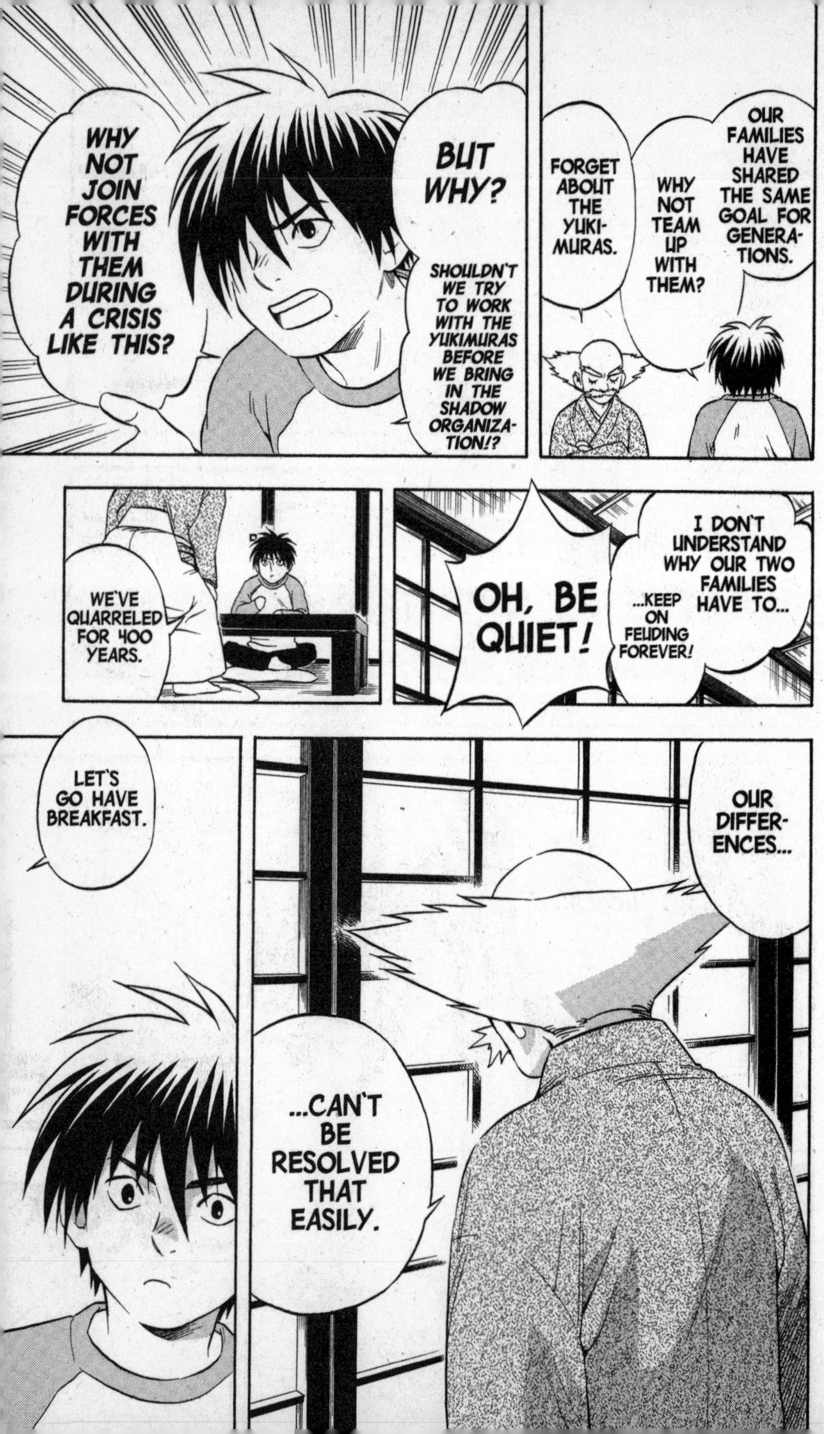
OUR FAMILIES HAVE SHARED THE SAME GOAL FOR GENERATIONS.
WHY NOT TEAM UP WITH THEM?
FORGET ABOUT THE YUKIMURAS.
BUT WHY?
SHOULDN'T WE TRY TO WORK WITH THE YUKIMURAS BEFORE WE BRING IN THE SHADOW ORGANIZATION!?
WHY NOT JOIN FORCES WITH THEM DURING A CRISIS LIKE THIS?
I DON'T UNDERSTAND WHY OUR TWO FAMILIES HAVE TO...
...KEEP ON FEUDING FOREVER!
OH, BE QUIET!
WE'VE QUARRELED FOR 400 YEARS.
OUR DIFFERENCES...
...CAN'T BE RESOLVED THAT EASILY.
LET'S GO HAVE BREAKFAST.

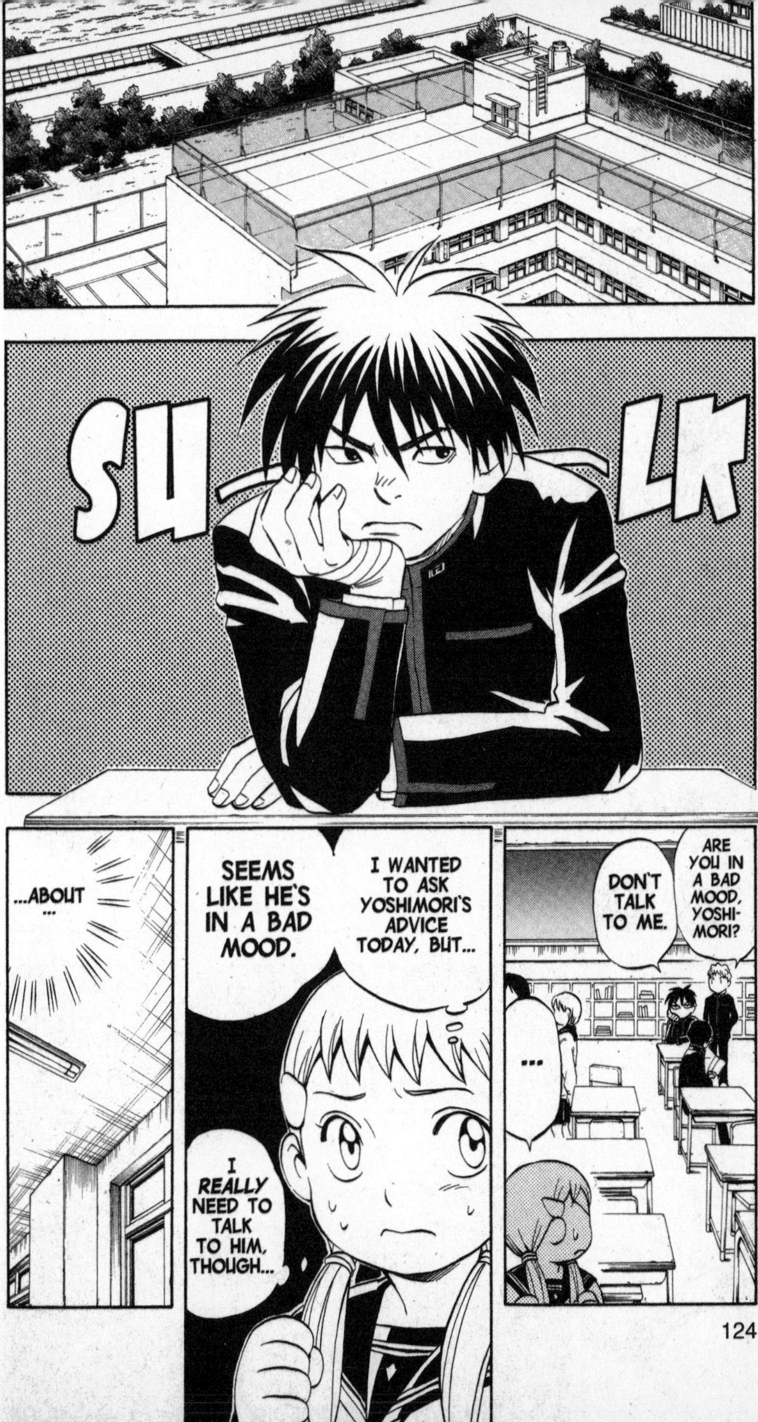
SU
LK
ARE YOU IN A BAD MOOD, YOSHIMORI?
DON'T TALK TO ME.
...
I WANTED TO ASK YOSHIMORI'S ADVICE TODAY, BUT...
SEEMS LIKE HE'S IN A BAD MOOD.
I *REALLY* NEED TO TALK TO HIM, THOUGH...
...ABOUT ...

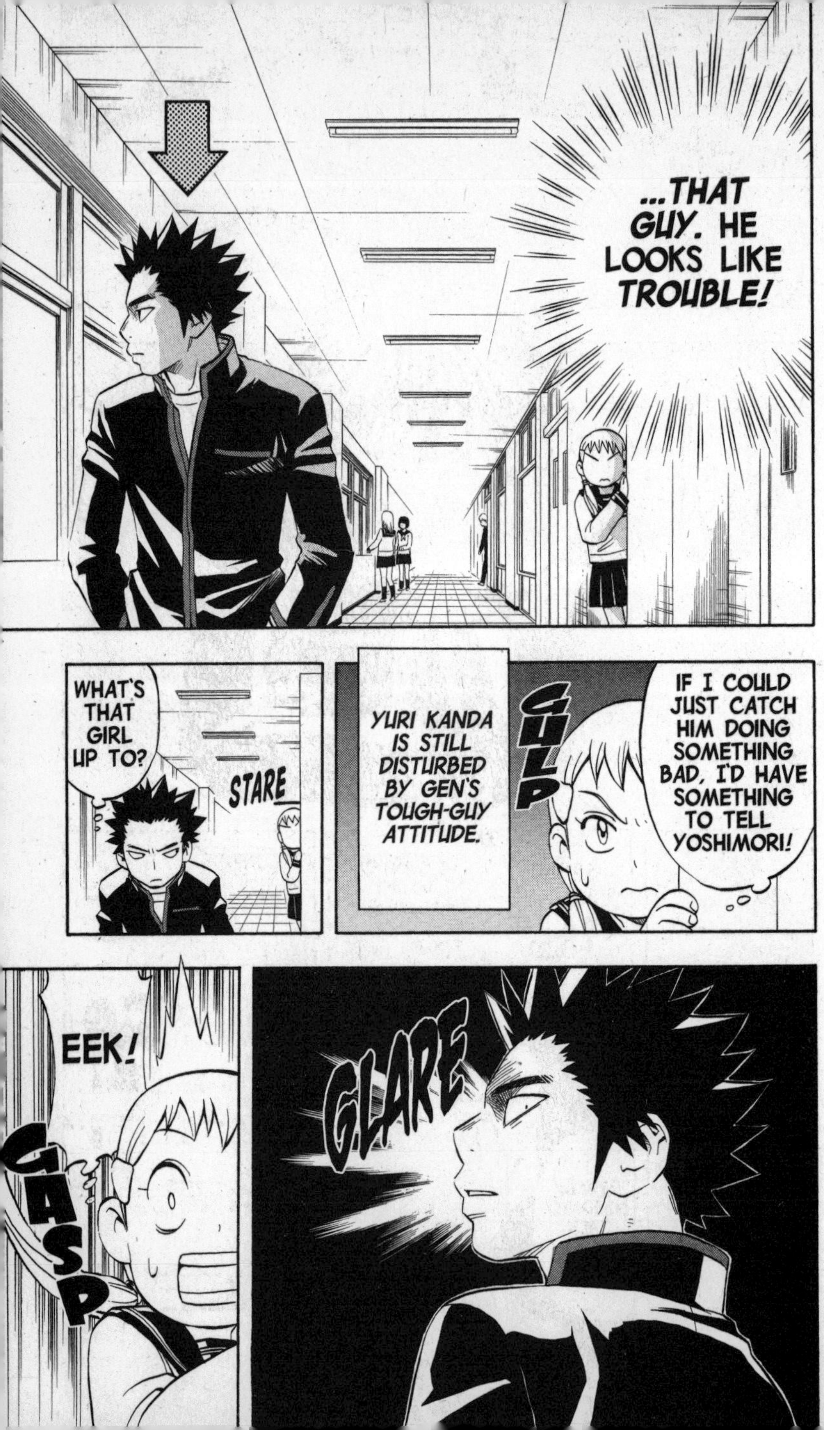
...THAT GUY. HE LOOKS LIKE TROUBLE!
IF I COULD JUST CATCH HIM DOING SOMETHING BAD, I'D HAVE SOMETHING TO TELL YOSHIMORI!
GULP
YURI KANDA IS STILL DISTURBED BY GEN'S TOUGH-GUY ATTITUDE.
WHAT'S THAT GIRL UP TO?
STARE
GLARE
EEK!
GASP

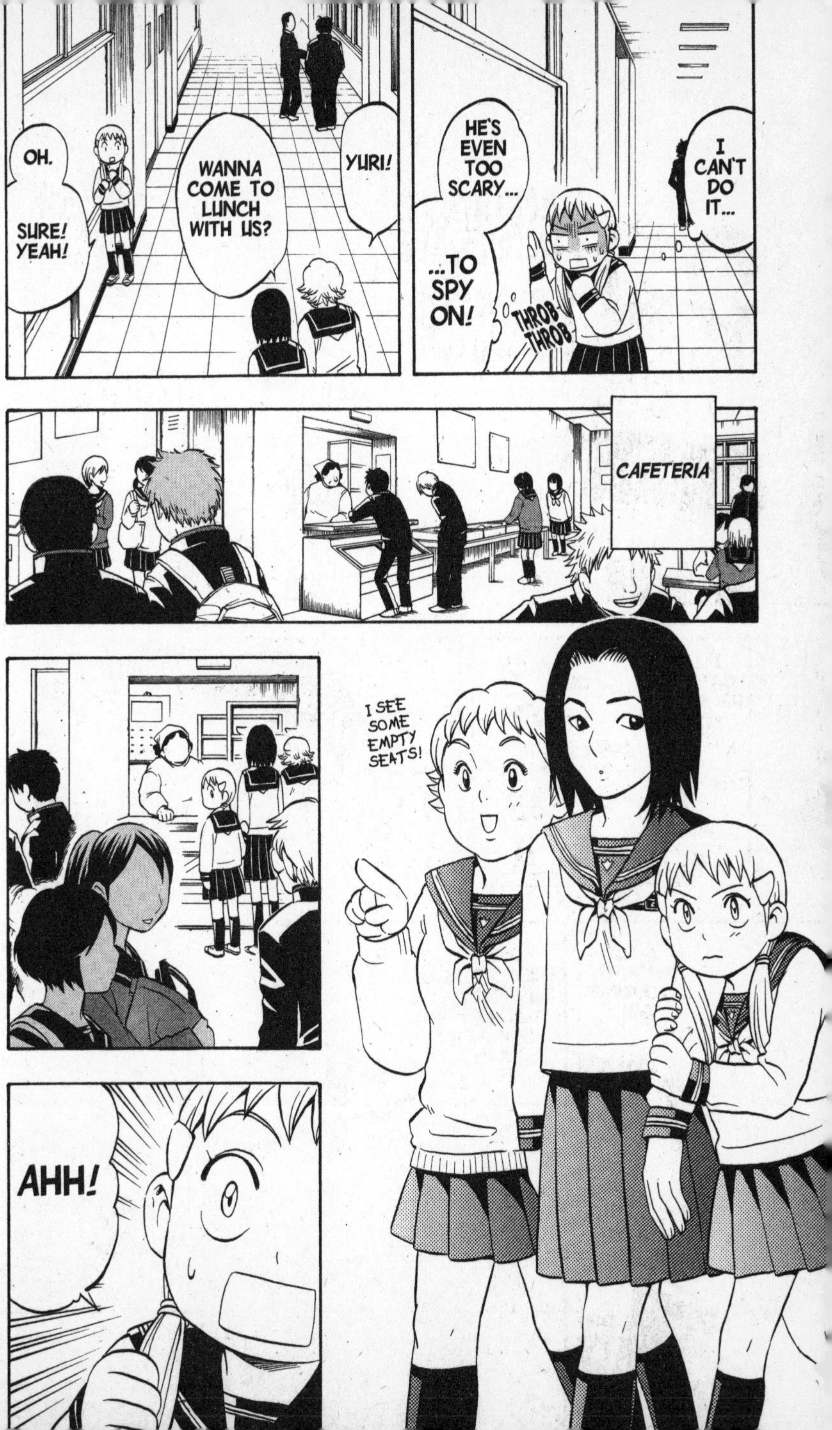
I CAN'T DO IT...
HE'S EVEN TOO SCARY...
...TO SPY ON!
THROB-THROB
YURI!
WANNA COME TO LUNCH WITH US?
OH.
SURE! YEAH!
CAFETERIA
I SEE SOME EMPTY SEATS!
AHH!

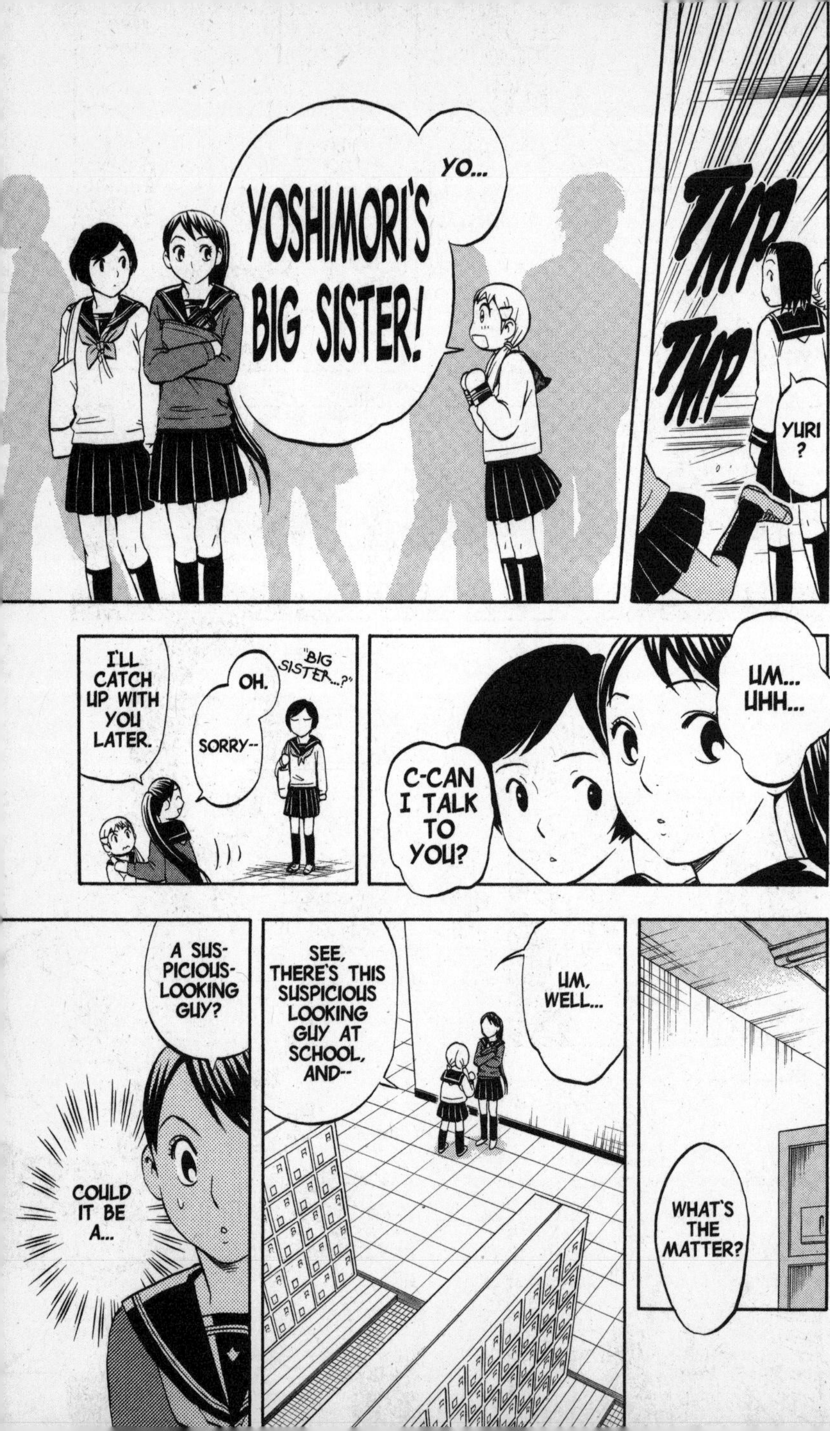
TMP TMP
YURI ?
YO...
YOSHIMORI'S BIG SISTER!
UM... UHH...
C-CAN I TALK TO YOU?
"BIG SISTER...?"
OH.
SORRY--
I'LL CATCH UP WITH YOU LATER.
WHAT'S THE MATTER?
UM, WELL...
SEE, THERE'S THIS SUSPICIOUS LOOKING GUY AT SCHOOL, AND--
A SUS-PICIOUS-LOOKING GUY?
COULD IT BE A...

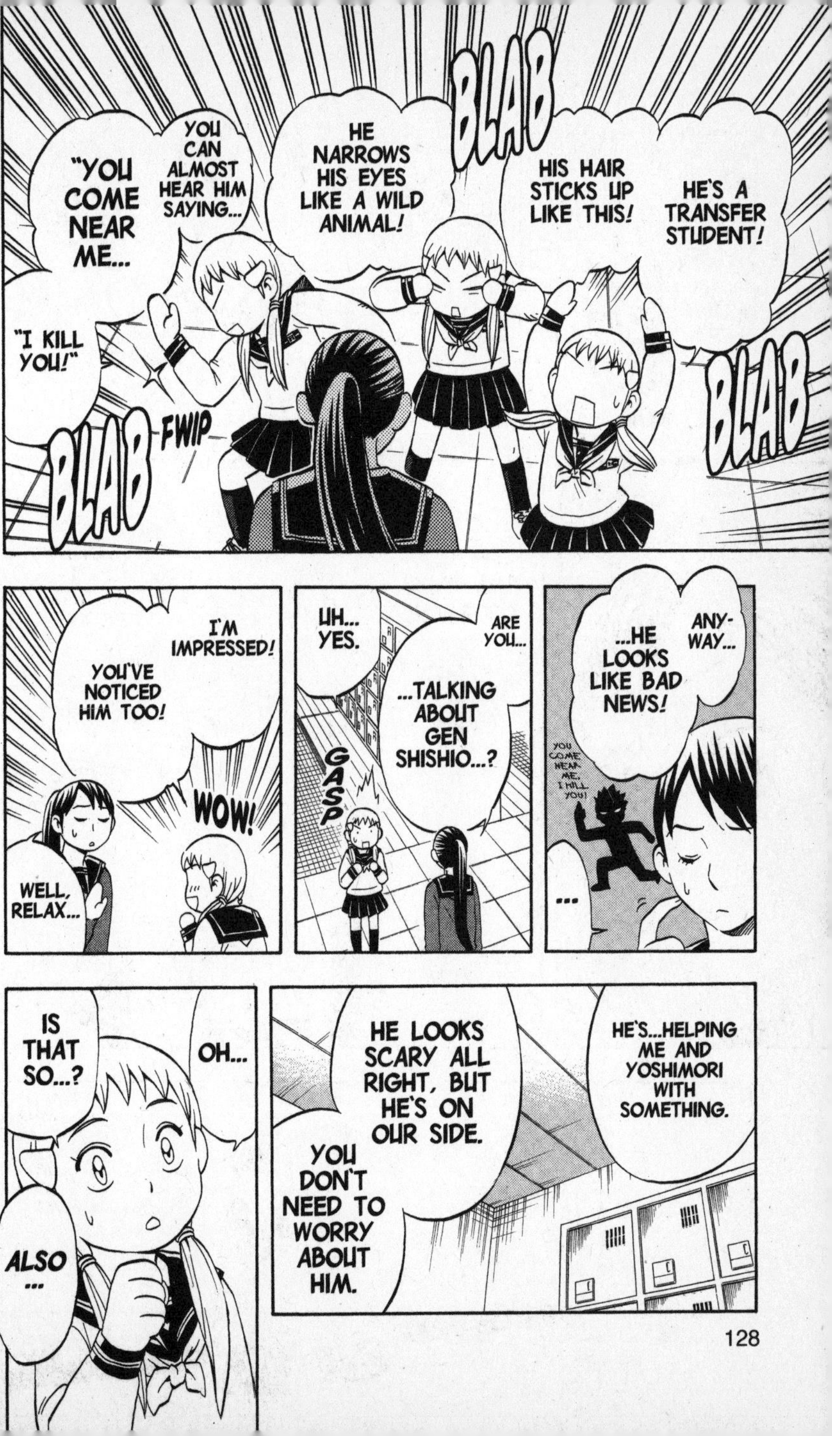
HE'S A TRANSFER STUDENT!
HIS HAIR STICKS UP LIKE THIS!
BLAB
HE NARROWS HIS EYES LIKE A WILD ANIMAL!
YOU CAN ALMOST HEAR HIM SAYING...
"YOU COME NEAR ME...
"I KILL YOU!"
BLAB
FWIP
BLAB
ANY-WAY...
...HE LOOKS LIKE BAD NEWS!
YOU COME NEAR ME, I KILL YOU!
...
ARE YOU...
UH... YES.
...TALKING ABOUT GEN SHISHIO...?
GASP
I'M IMPRESSED!
YOU'VE NOTICED HIM TOO!
WOW!
WELL, RELAX...
HE'S...HELPING ME AND YOSHIMORI WITH SOMETHING.
HE LOOKS SCARY ALL RIGHT, BUT HE'S ON OUR SIDE.
YOU DON'T NEED TO WORRY ABOUT HIM.
OH...
IS THAT SO...?
ALSO ...

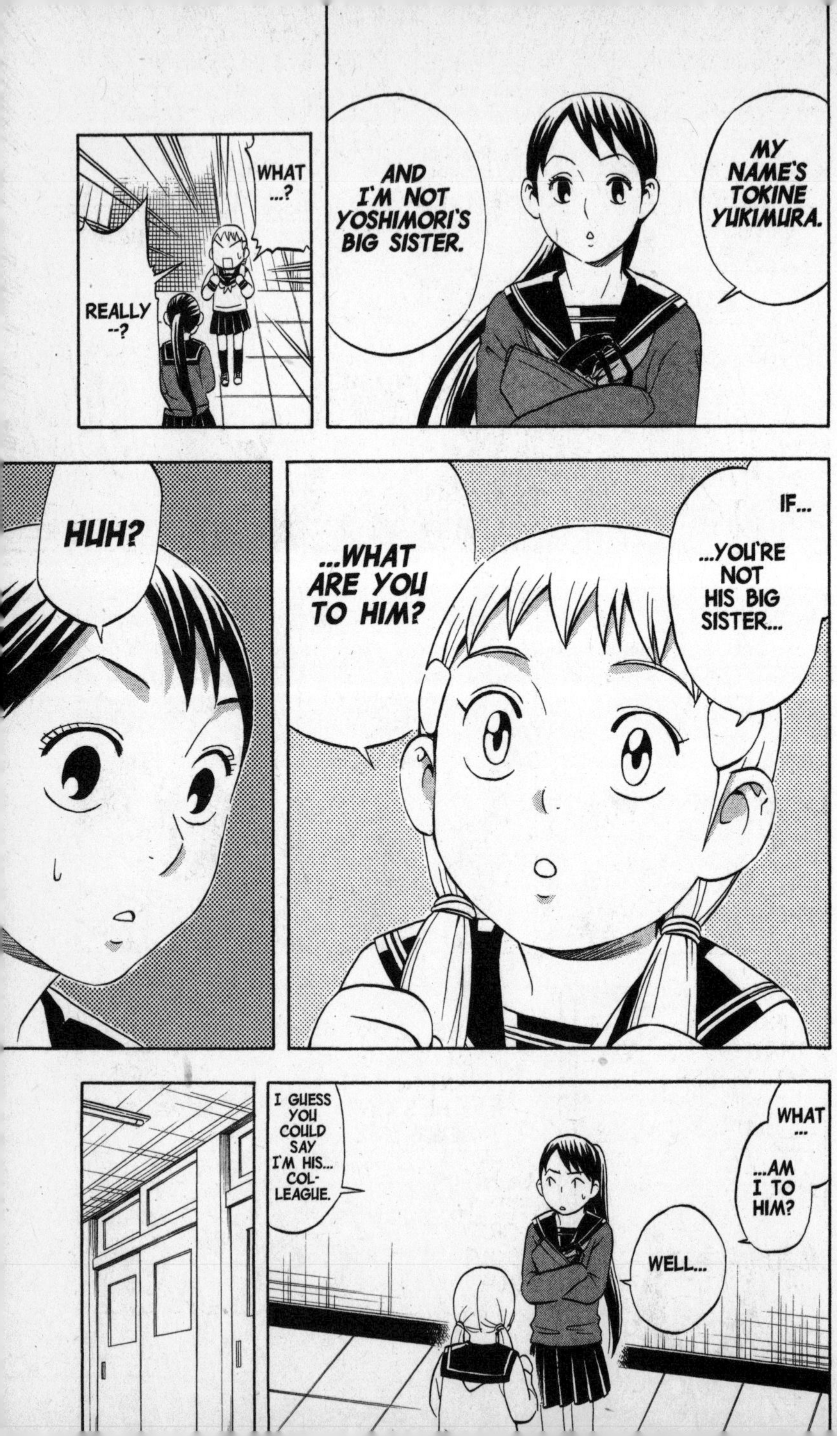
MY NAME'S TOKINE YUKIMURA.
AND I'M NOT YOSHIMORI'S BIG SISTER.
WHAT ...?
REALLY --?
IF...
...YOU'RE NOT HIS BIG SISTER...
...WHAT ARE YOU TO HIM?
HUH?
WHAT ...
...AM I TO HIM?
WELL...
I GUESS YOU COULD SAY I'M HIS... COL-LEAGUE.

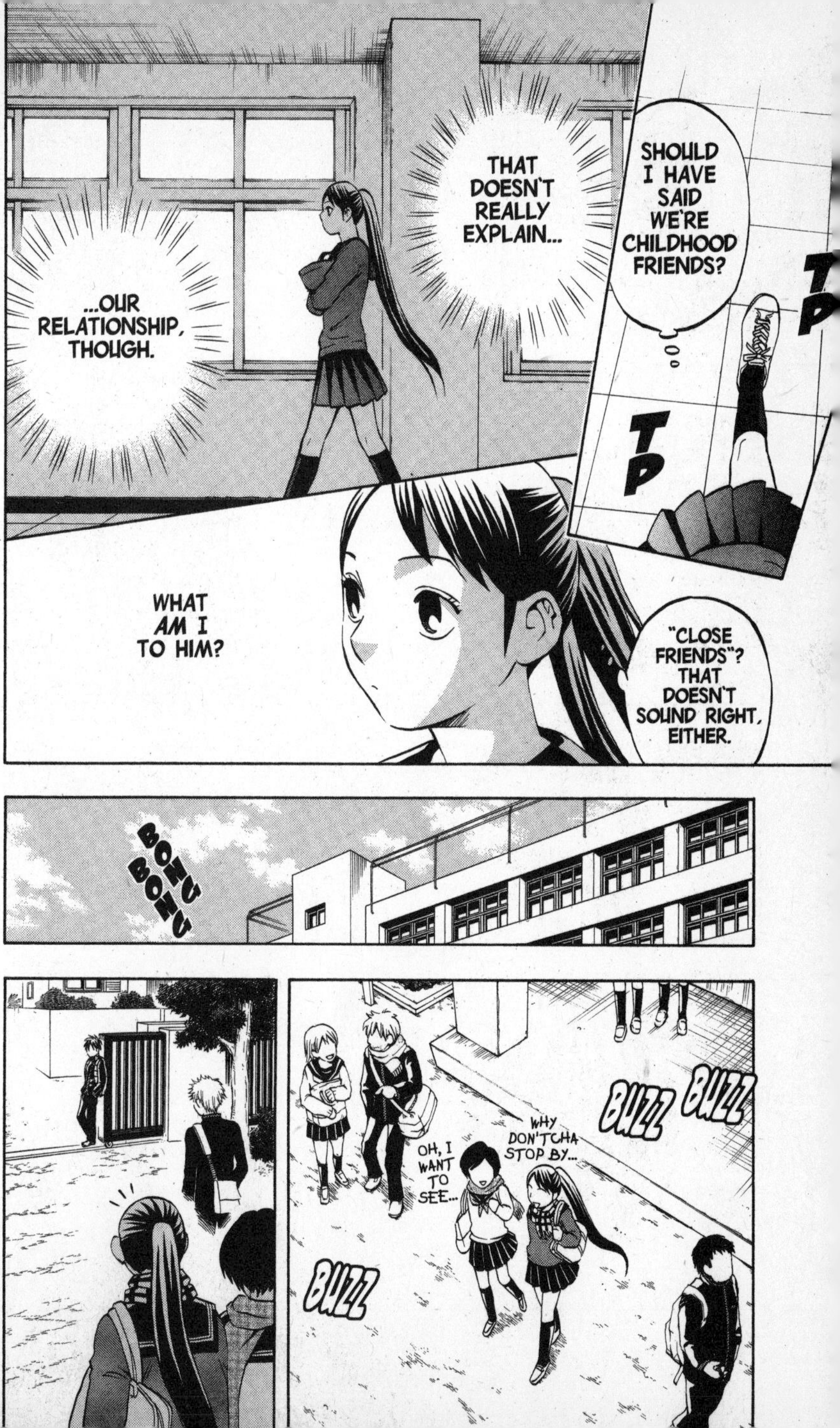
SHOULD I HAVE SAID WE'RE CHILDHOOD FRIENDS?
TP
TP
THAT DOESN'T REALLY EXPLAIN...
...OUR RELATIONSHIP, THOUGH.
"CLOSE FRIENDS"? THAT DOESN'T SOUND RIGHT, EITHER.
WHAT AM I TO HIM?
BONZU BONZU
BUZZ
BUZZ
WHY DON'TCHA STOP BY...
OH, I WANT TO SEE...
BUZZ

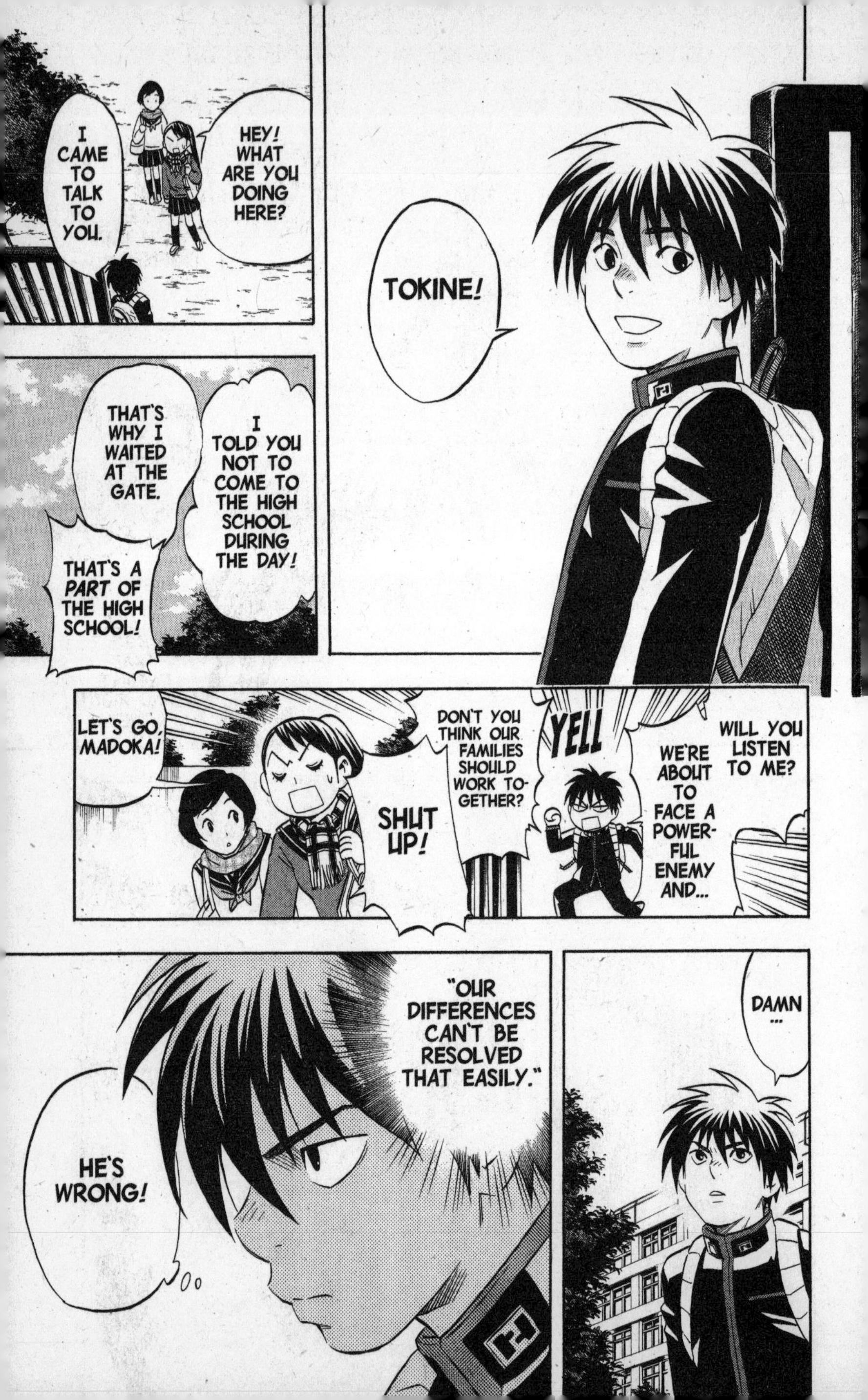
TOKINE!
HEY! WHAT ARE YOU DOING HERE?
I CAME TO TALK TO YOU.
I TOLD YOU NOT TO COME TO THE HIGH SCHOOL DURING THE DAY!
THAT'S WHY I WAITED AT THE GATE.
THAT'S A PART OF THE HIGH SCHOOL!
WILL YOU LISTEN TO ME?
WE'RE ABOUT TO FACE A POWERFUL ENEMY AND...
YELL
DON'T YOU THINK OUR FAMILIES SHOULD WORK TOGETHER?
SHUT UP!
LET'S GO, MADOKA!
DAMN...
"OUR DIFFERENCES CAN'T BE RESOLVED THAT EASILY."
HE'S WRONG!

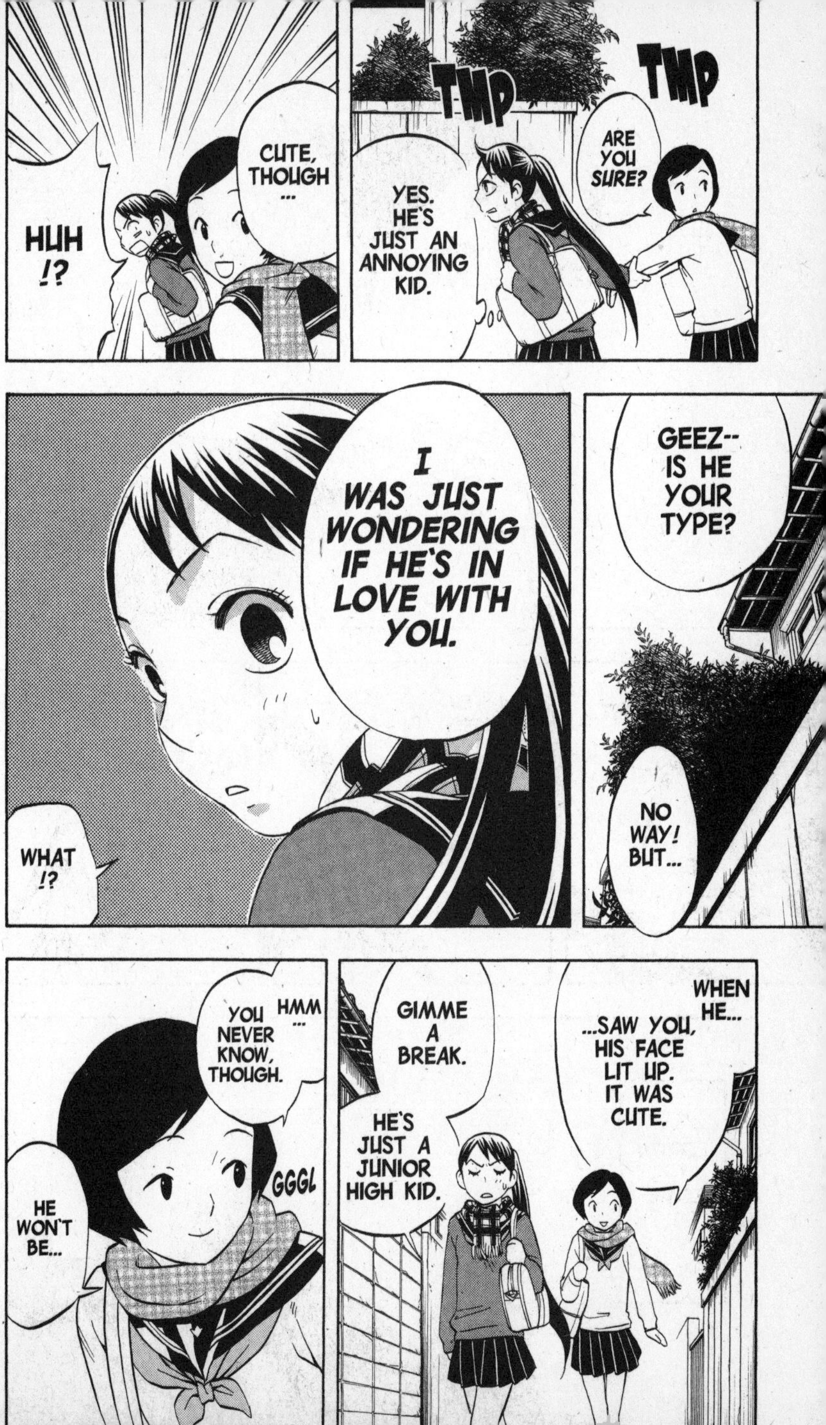
TMP
TMP
ARE YOU SURE?
YES. HE'S JUST AN ANNOYING KID.
CUTE, THOUGH ...
HUH !?
GEEZ-- IS HE YOUR TYPE?
NO WAY! BUT...
I WAS JUST WONDERING IF HE'S IN LOVE WITH YOU.
WHAT !?
WHEN HE...
...SAW YOU, HIS FACE LIT UP. IT WAS CUTE.
GIMME A BREAK.
HE'S JUST A JUNIOR HIGH KID.
HMM ...
YOU NEVER KNOW, THOUGH.
GGGL
HE WON'T BE...

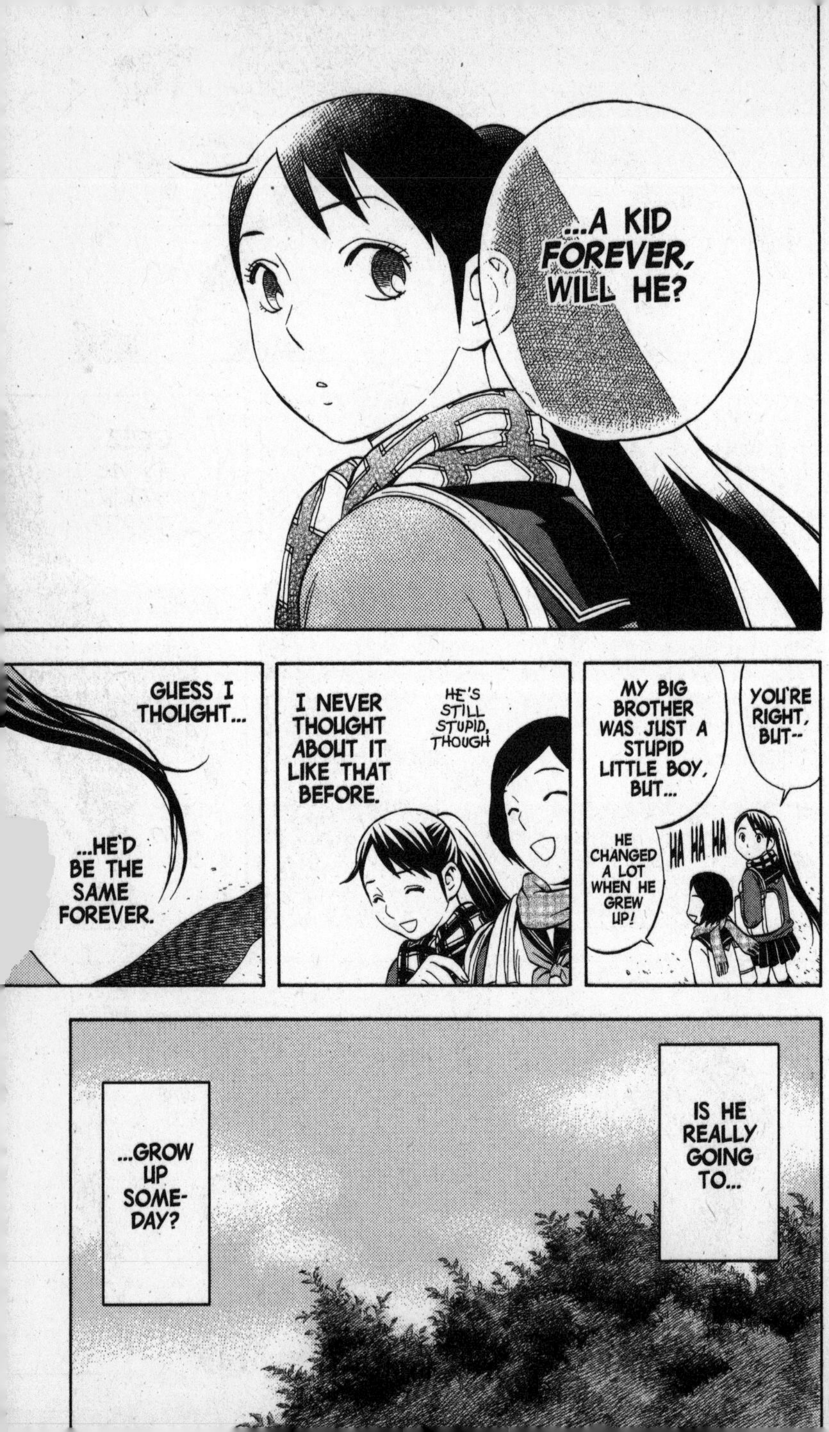
...A KID FOREVER, WILL HE?
YOU'RE RIGHT, BUT--
MY BIG BROTHER WAS JUST A STUPID LITTLE BOY, BUT...
HA HA HA
HE CHANGED A LOT WHEN HE GREW UP!
I NEVER THOUGHT ABOUT IT LIKE THAT BEFORE.
HE'S STILL STUPID, THOUGH
GUESS I THOUGHT...
...HE'D BE THE SAME FOREVER.
IS HE REALLY GOING TO...
...GROW UP SOME-DAY?

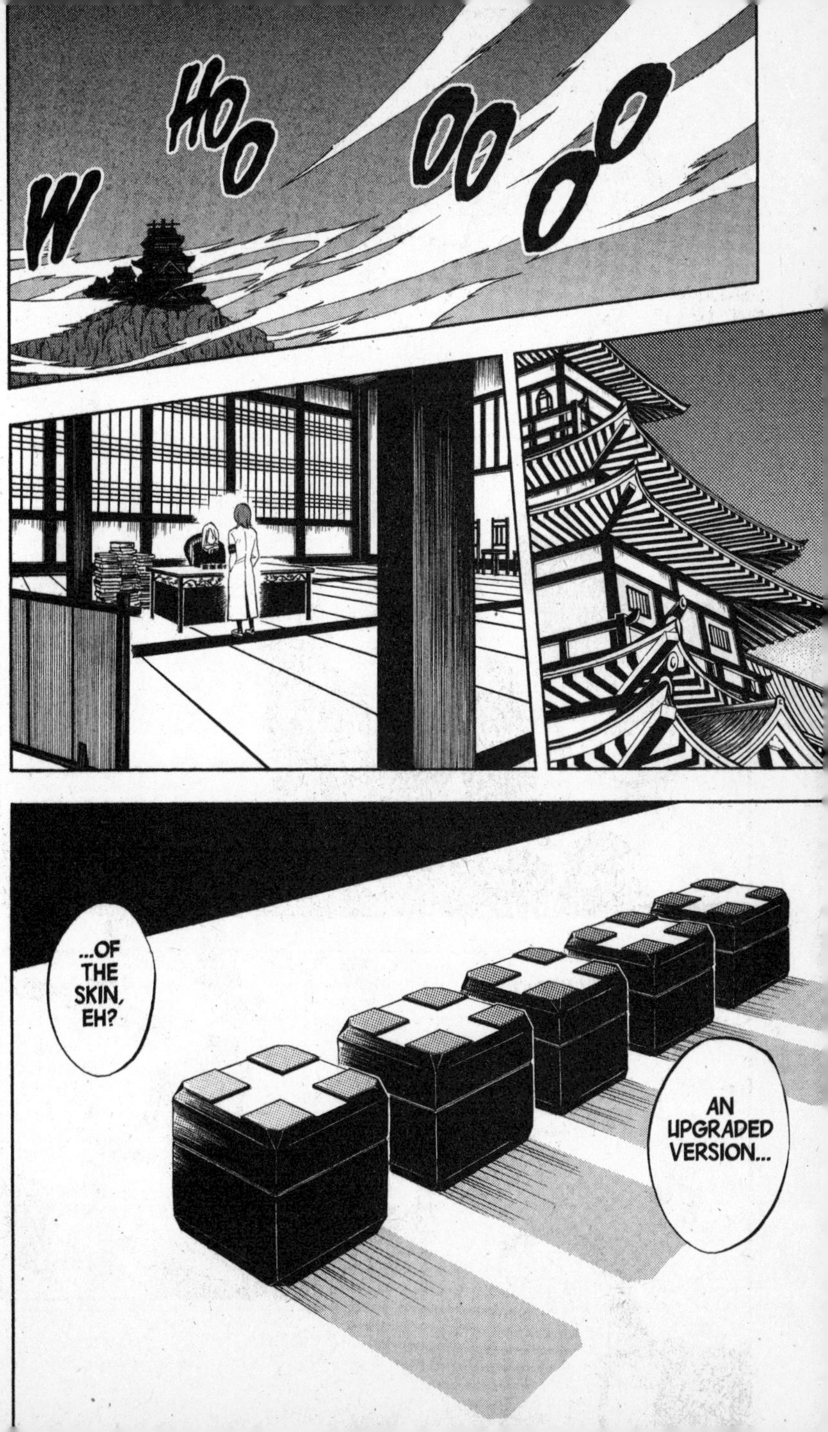
WHOOOOOO
AN UPGRADED VERSION...
...OF THE SKIN, EH?

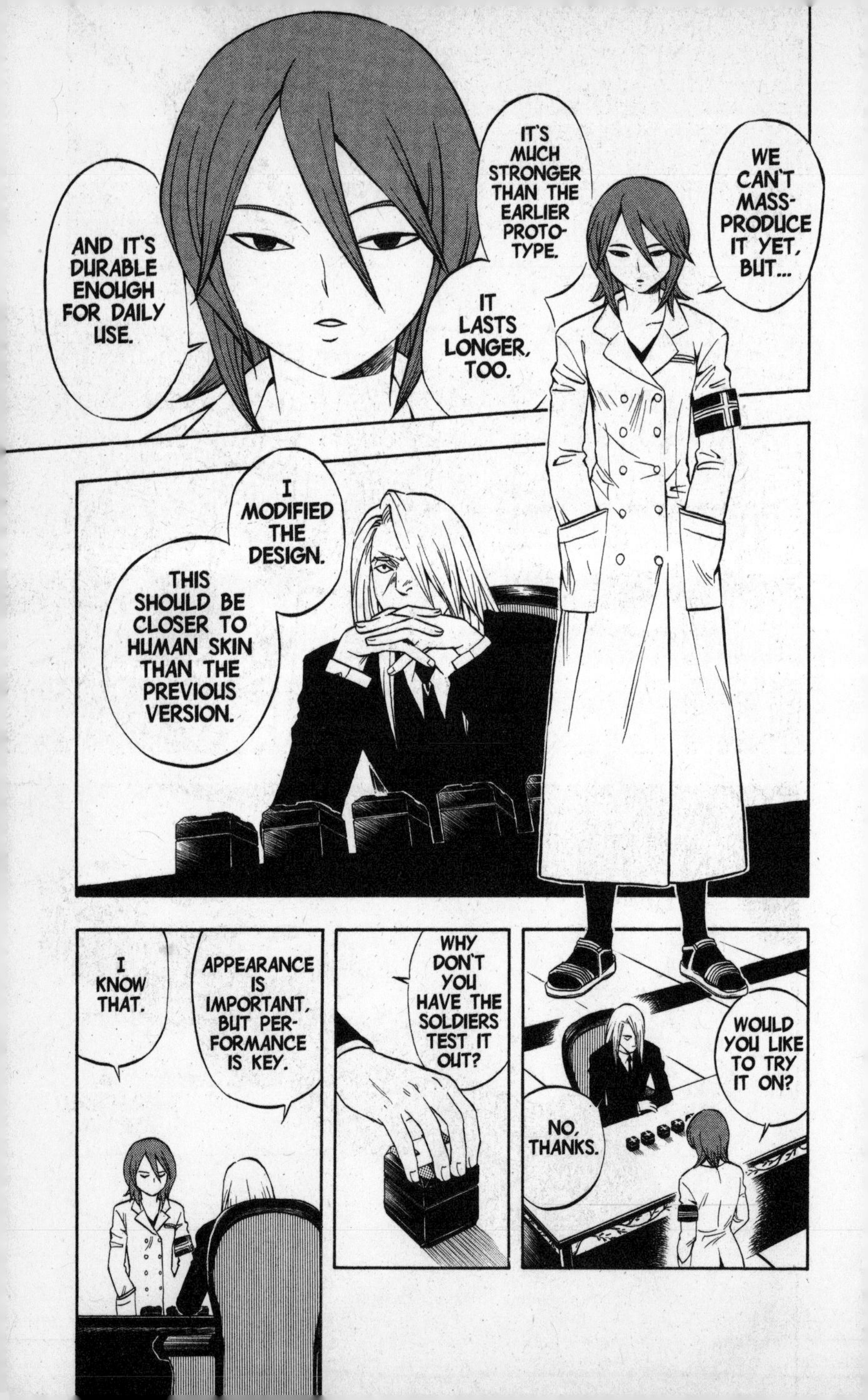
WE CAN'T MASS-PRODUCE IT YET, BUT...
IT'S MUCH STRONGER THAN THE EARLIER PROTOTYPE.
IT LASTS LONGER, TOO.
AND IT'S DURABLE ENOUGH FOR DAILY USE.
I MODIFIED THE DESIGN.
THIS SHOULD BE CLOSER TO HUMAN SKIN THAN THE PREVIOUS VERSION.
WOULD YOU LIKE TO TRY IT ON?
NO, THANKS.
WHY DON'T YOU HAVE THE SOLDIERS TEST IT OUT?
APPEARANCE IS IMPORTANT, BUT PERFORMANCE IS KEY.
I KNOW THAT.

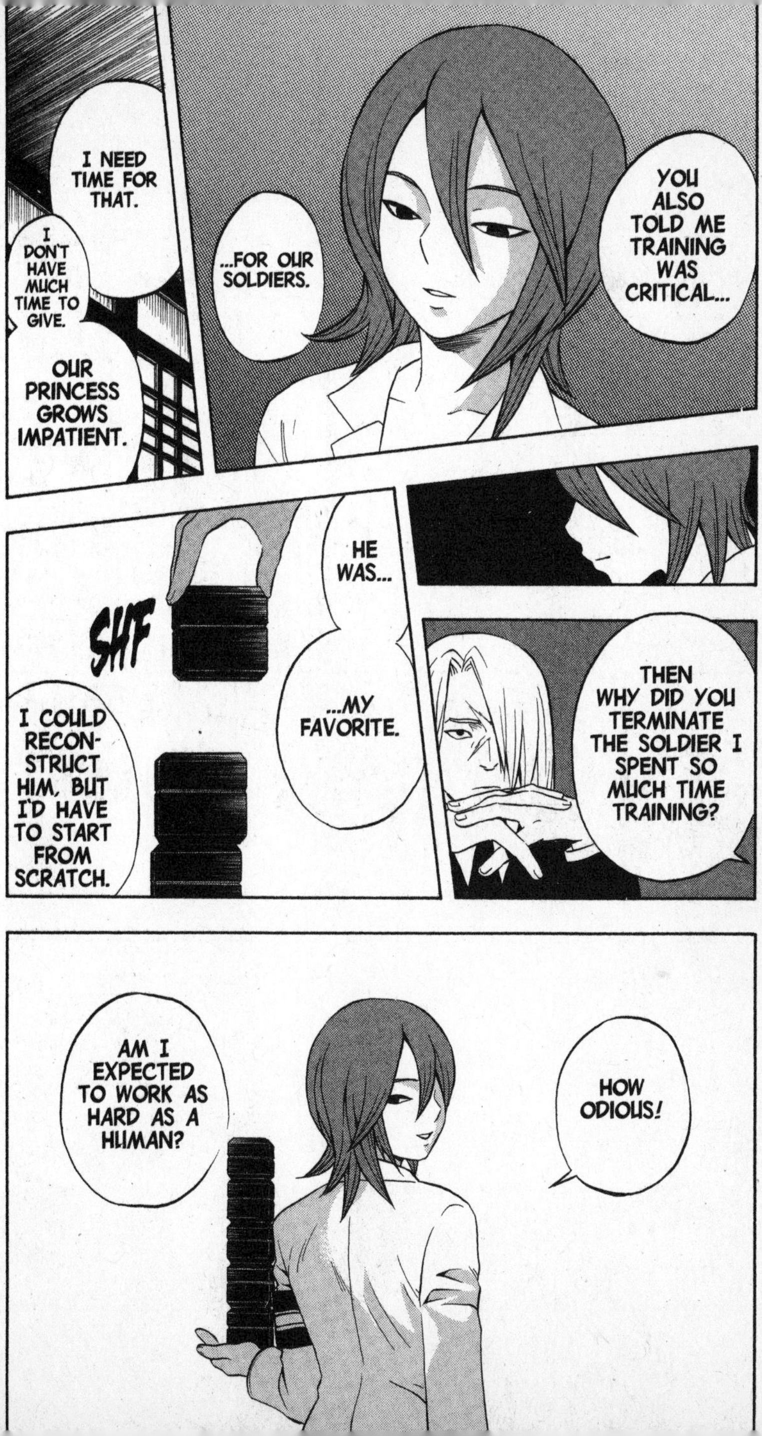
YOU ALSO TOLD ME TRAINING WAS CRITICAL...
...FOR OUR SOLDIERS.
I NEED TIME FOR THAT.
I DON'T HAVE MUCH TIME TO GIVE.
OUR PRINCESS GROWS IMPATIENT.
THEN WHY DID YOU TERMINATE THE SOLDIER I SPENT SO MUCH TIME TRAINING?
HE WAS...
...MY FAVORITE.
SHF
I COULD RECON-STRUCT HIM, BUT I'D HAVE TO START FROM SCRATCH.
HOW ODIOUS!
AM I EXPECTED TO WORK AS HARD AS A HUMAN?

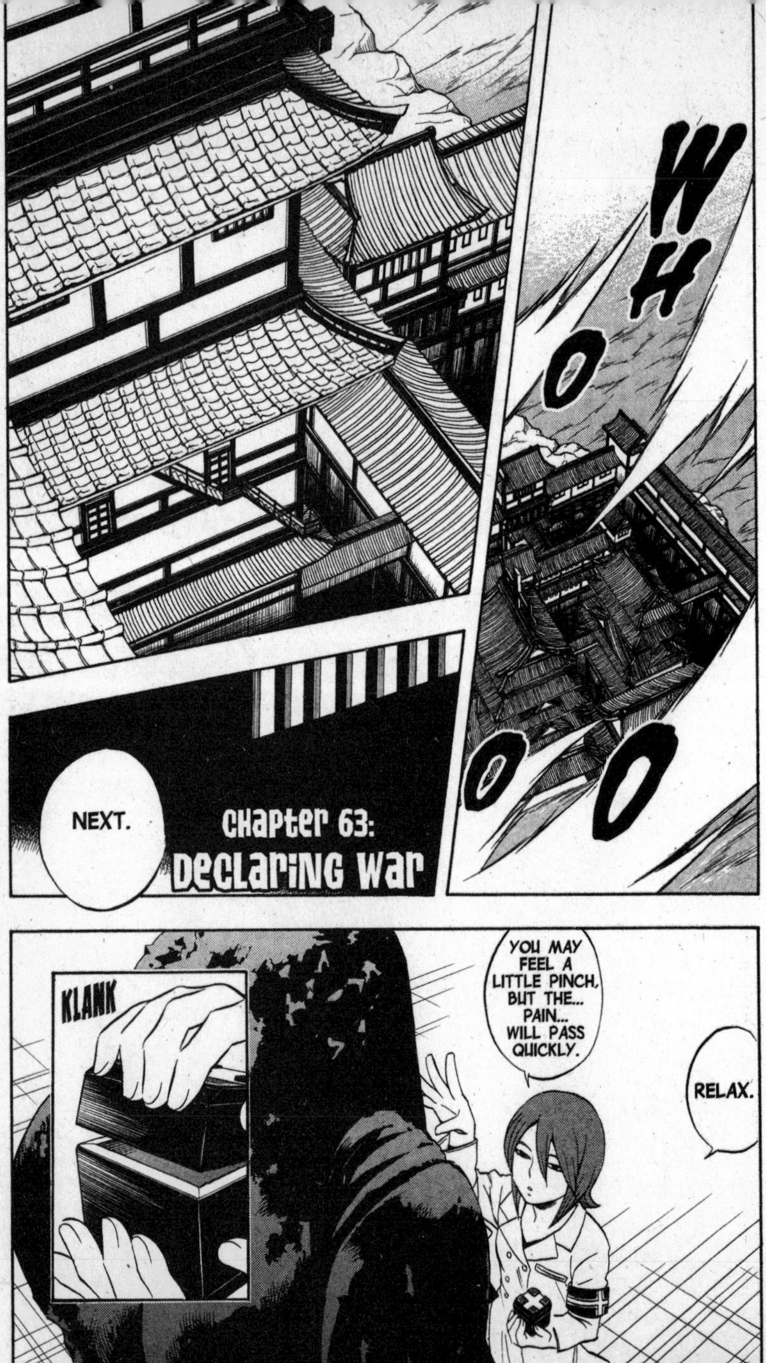
WHOOOO
NEXT.
Chapter 63:
Declaring War
RELAX.
YOU MAY FEEL A LITTLE PINCH, BUT THE... PAIN... WILL PASS QUICKLY.
KLANK

Chapter 63: Declaring War

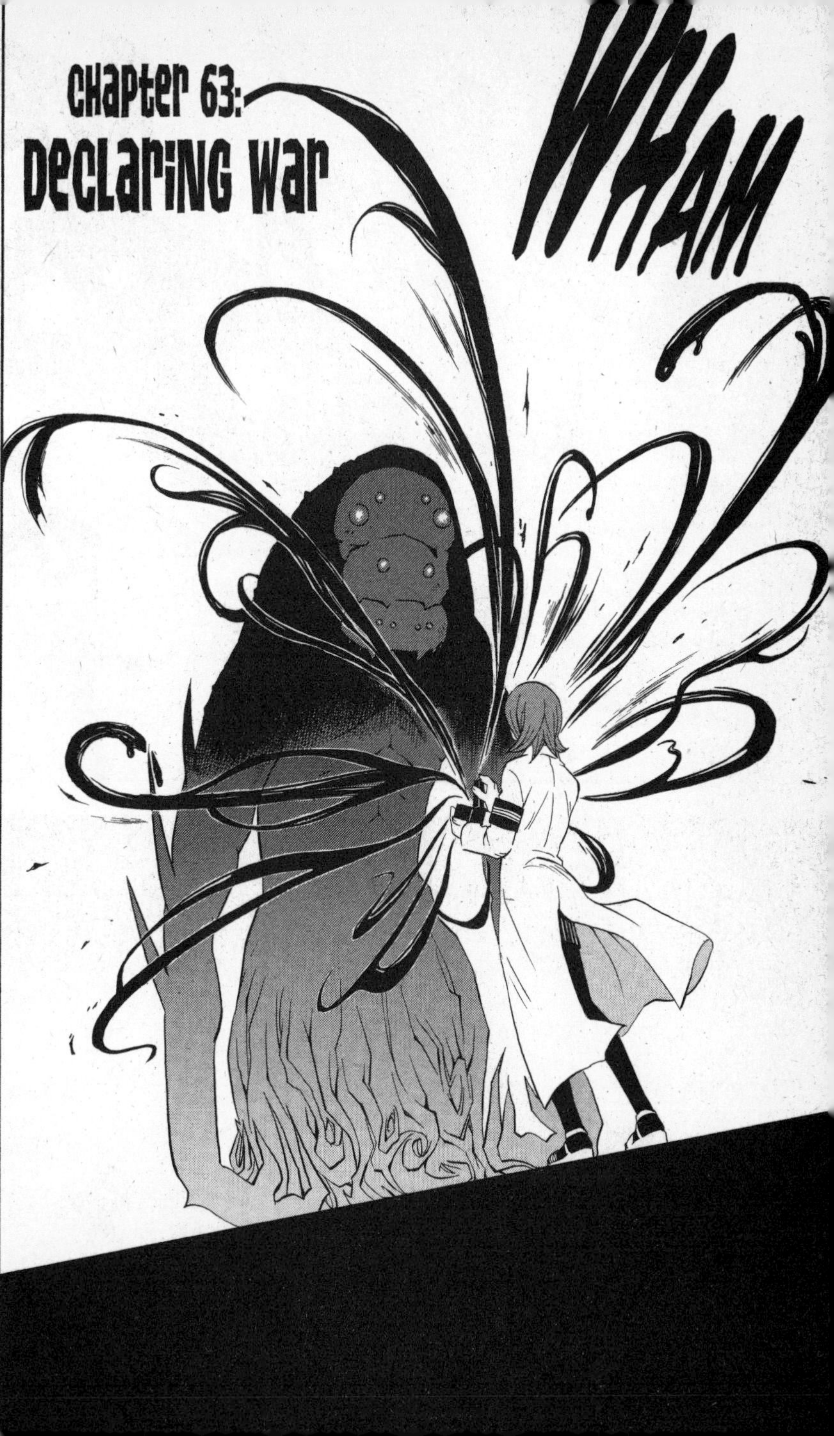
WHAM

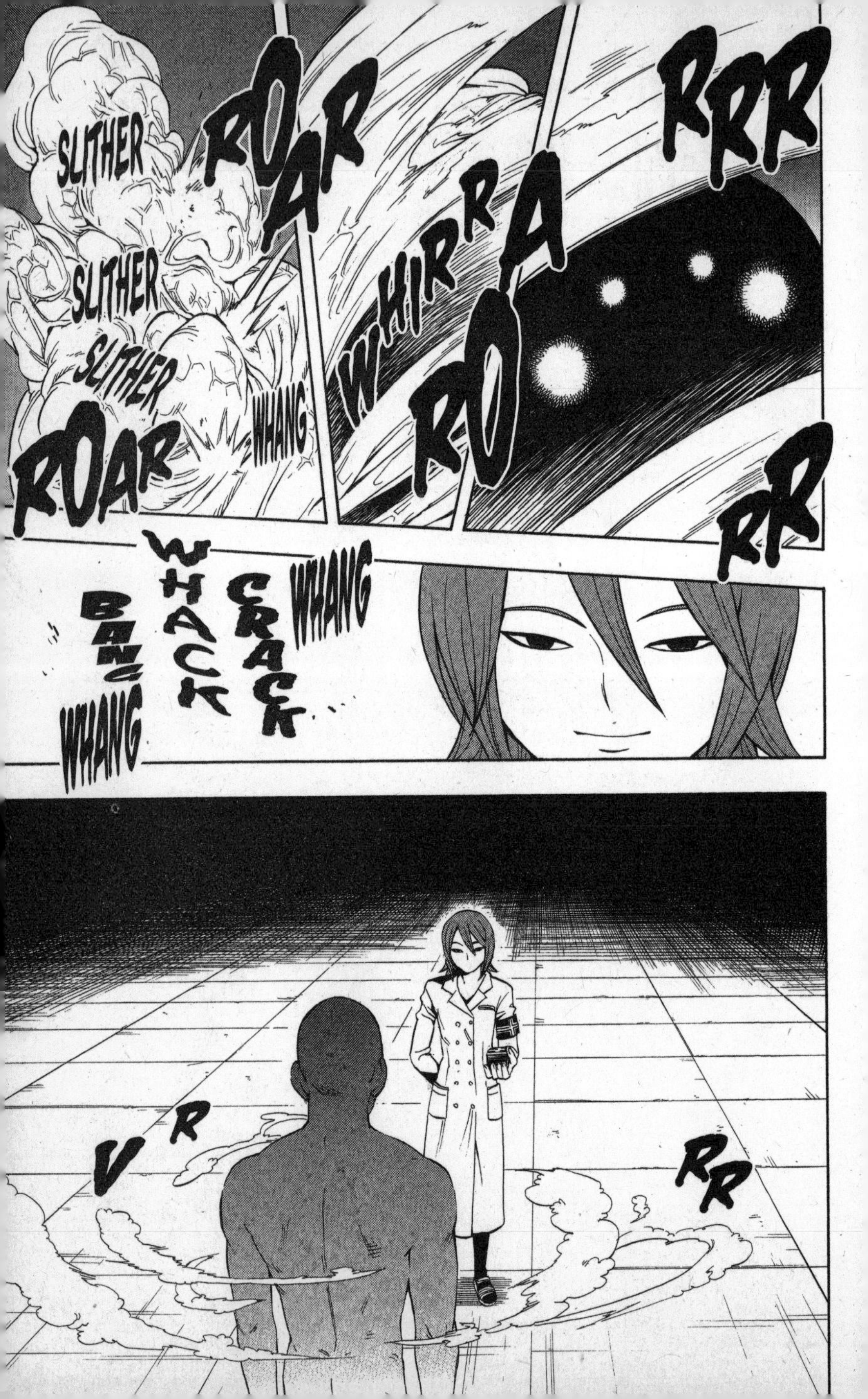
RRR
WHIRRA
ROA
RR
ROAR
SLITHER
SLITHER
SLITHER
ROAR
WHANG
WHANG
CRACK
WHACK
BANG
WHANG
RR
VR

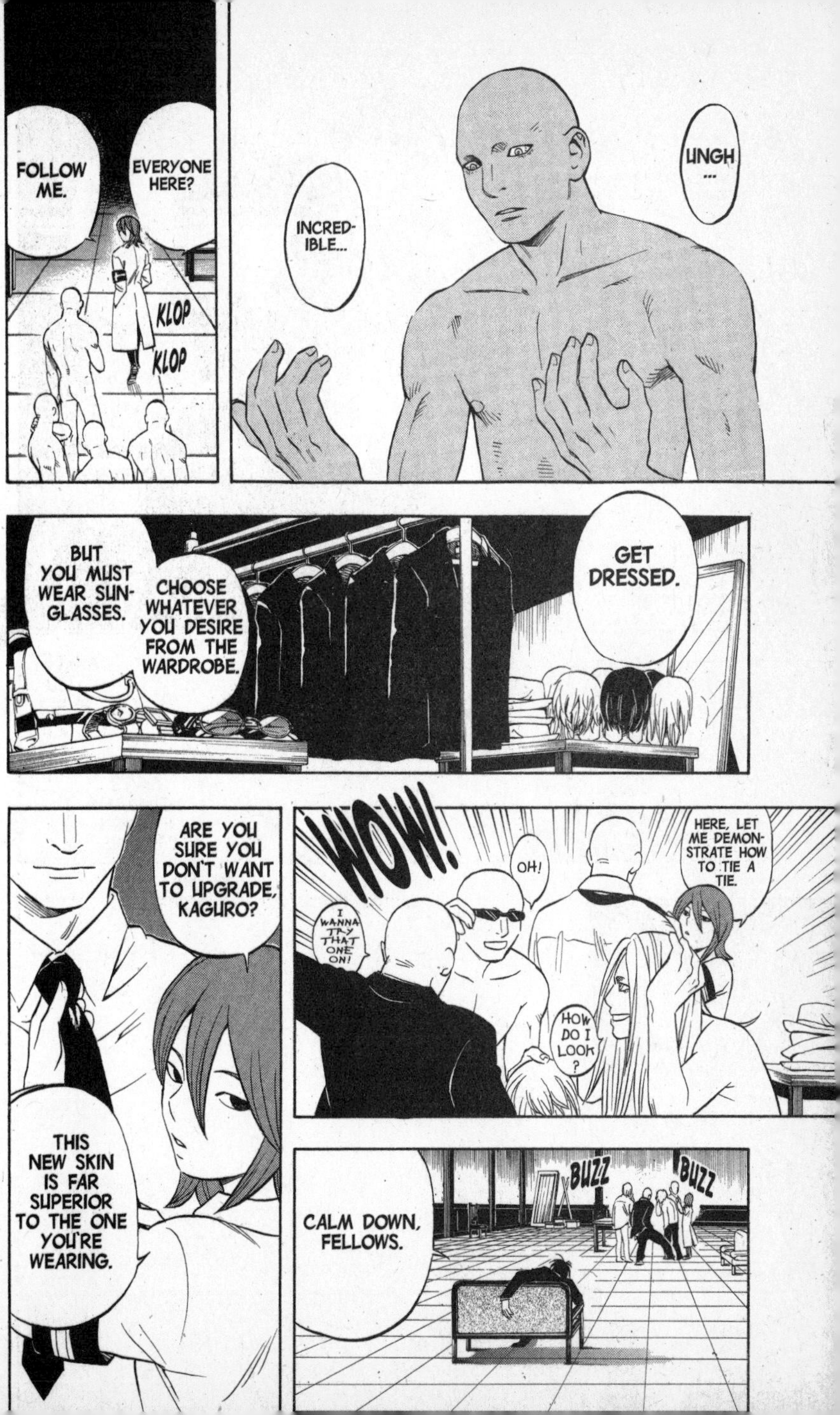
UNGH ...
INCREDIBLE...
EVERYONE HERE?
FOLLOW ME.
KLOP
KLOP
GET DRESSED.
CHOOSE WHATEVER YOU DESIRE FROM THE WARDROBE.
BUT YOU MUST WEAR SUNGLASSES.
WOW!
HERE, LET ME DEMONSTRATE HOW TO TIE A TIE.
OH!
I WANNA TRY THAT ONE ON!
HOW DO I LOOK?
BUZZ
BUZZ
CALM DOWN, FELLOWS.
ARE YOU SURE YOU DON'T WANT TO UPGRADE, KAGURO?
THIS NEW SKIN IS FAR SUPERIOR TO THE ONE YOU'RE WEARING.

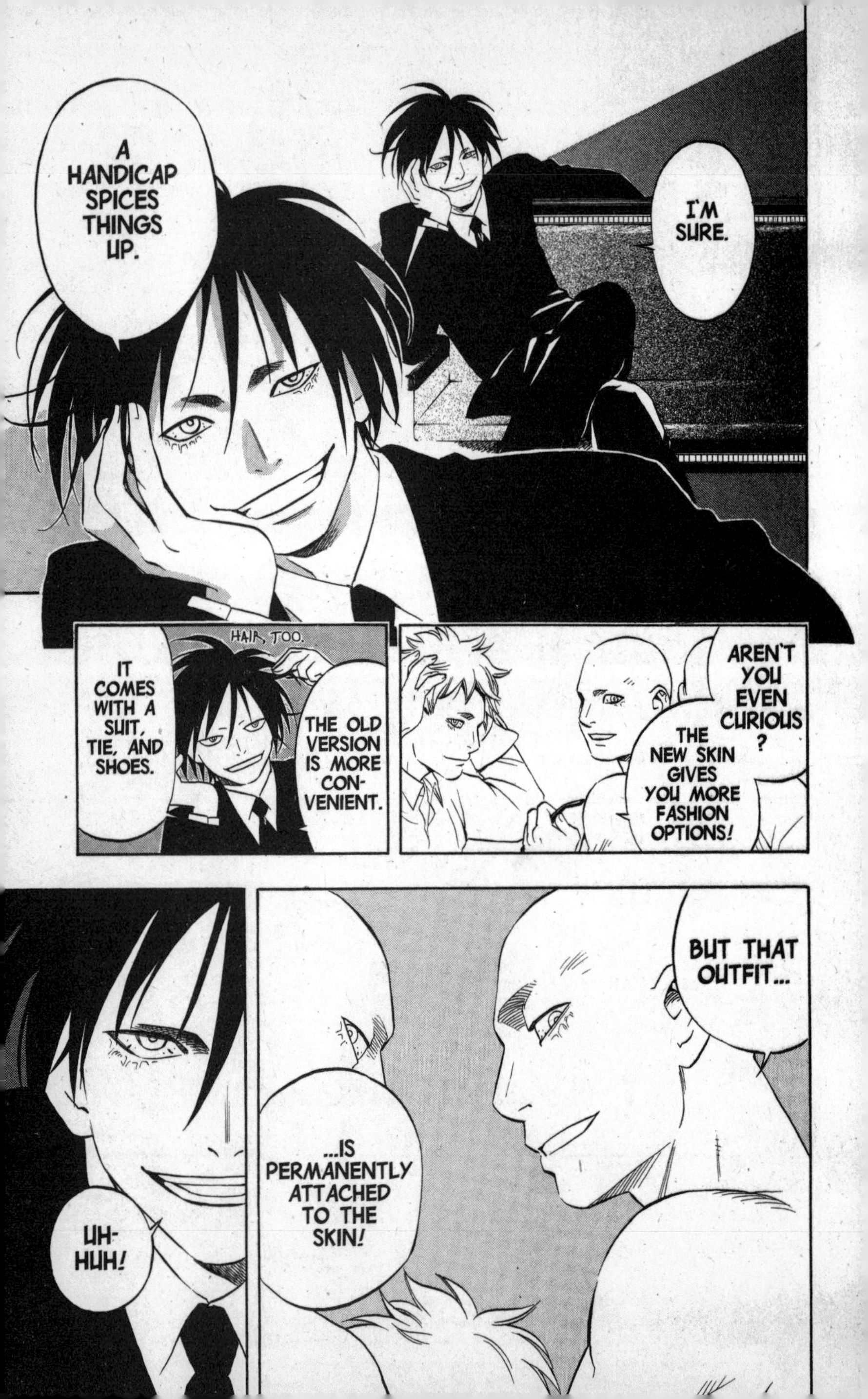
I'M SURE.
A HANDICAP SPICES THINGS UP.
AREN'T YOU EVEN CURIOUS?
THE NEW SKIN GIVES YOU MORE FASHION OPTIONS!
THE OLD VERSION IS MORE CON-VENIENT.
IT COMES WITH A SUIT, TIE, AND SHOES.
HAIR, TOO.
BUT THAT OUTFIT...
...IS PERMANENTLY ATTACHED TO THE SKIN!
UH-HUH!

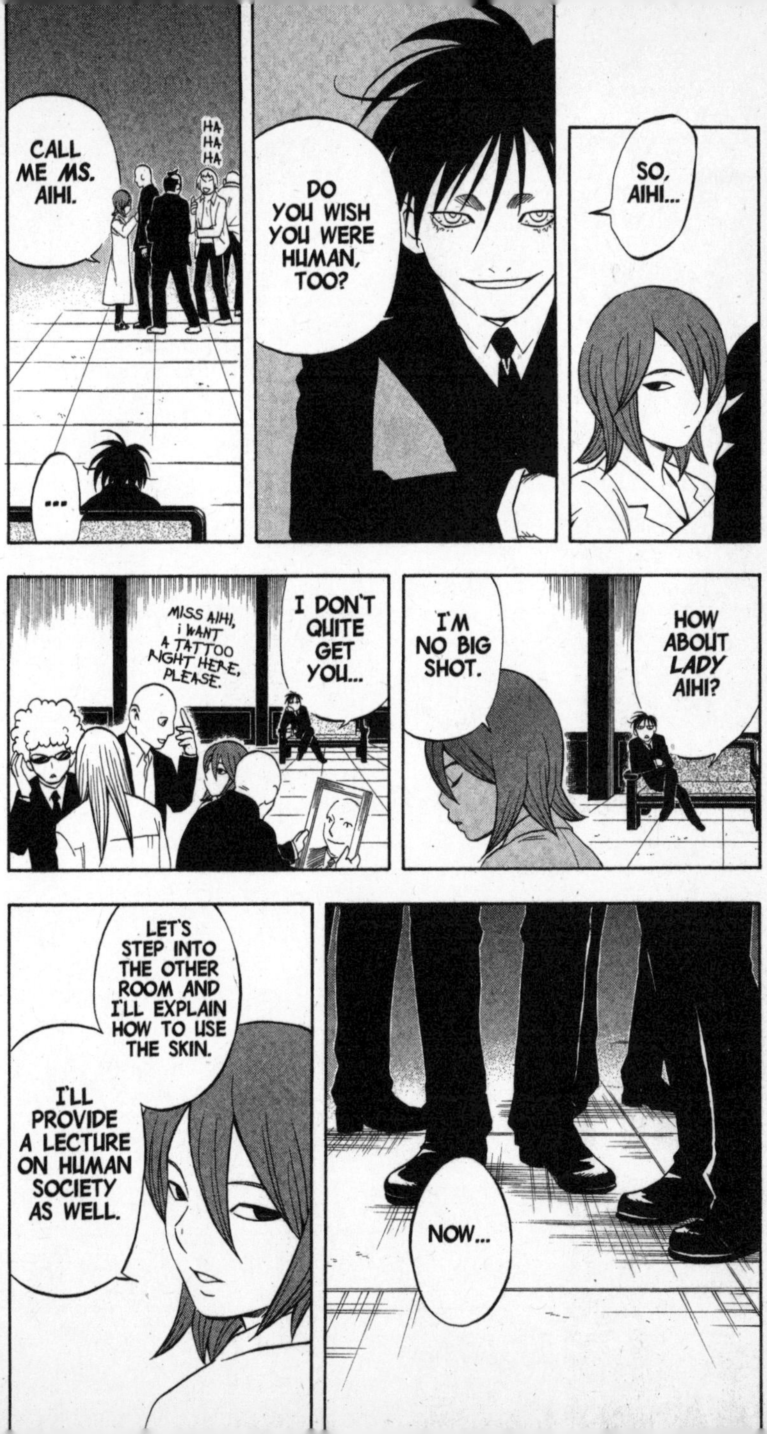
SO, AIHI...
DO YOU WISH YOU WERE HUMAN, TOO?
HA HA HA
CALL ME MS. AIHI.
...
HOW ABOUT LADY AIHI?
I'M NO BIG SHOT.
I DON'T QUITE GET YOU...
MISS AIHI, I WANT A TATTOO RIGHT HERE, PLEASE.
NOW...
LET'S STEP INTO THE OTHER ROOM AND I'LL EXPLAIN HOW TO USE THE SKIN.
I'LL PROVIDE A LECTURE ON HUMAN SOCIETY AS WELL.

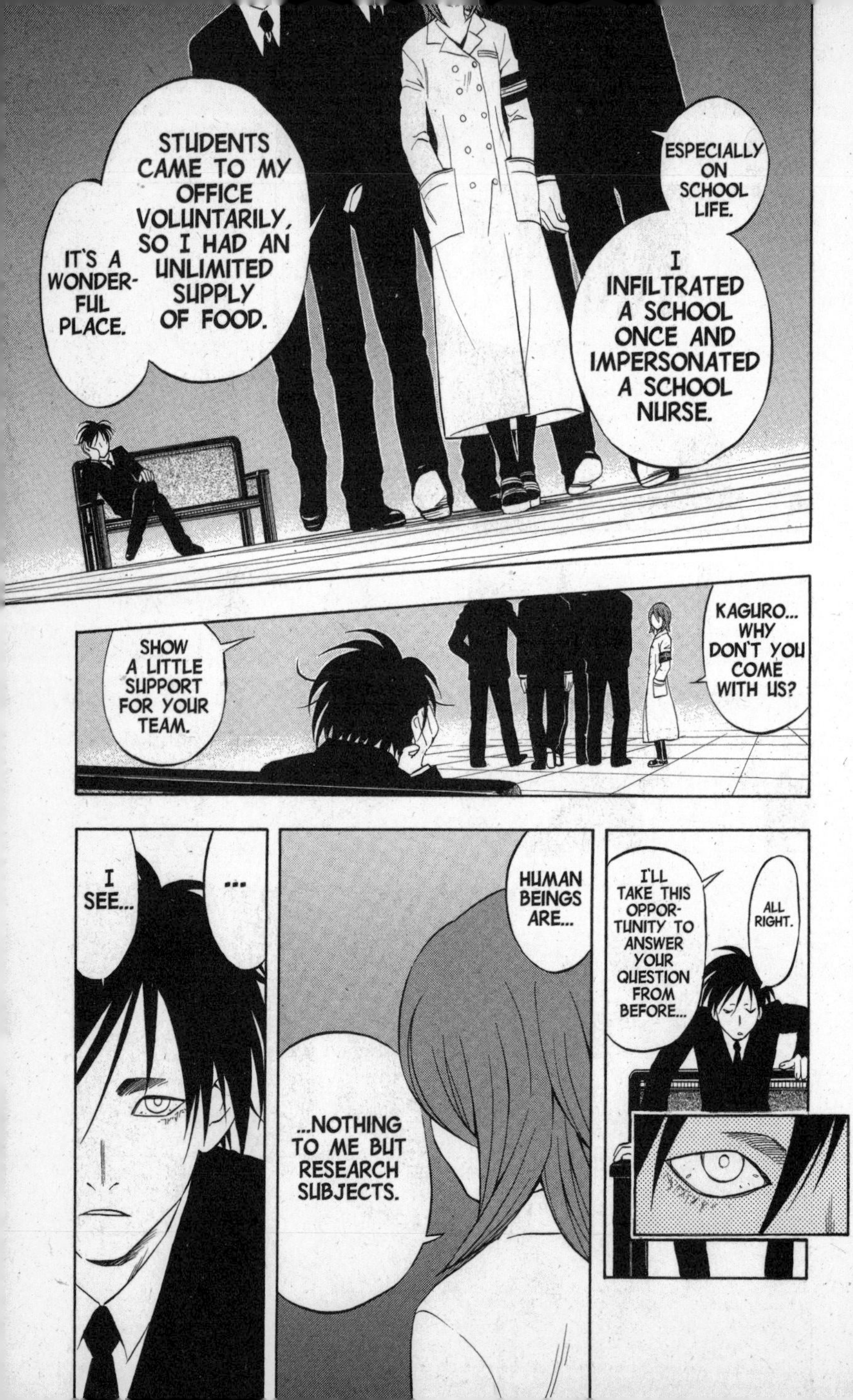
ESPECIALLY ON SCHOOL LIFE.
I INFILTRATED A SCHOOL ONCE AND IMPERSONATED A SCHOOL NURSE.
STUDENTS CAME TO MY OFFICE VOLUNTARILY, SO I HAD AN UNLIMITED SUPPLY OF FOOD.
IT'S A WONDER-FUL PLACE.
KAGURO... WHY DON'T YOU COME WITH US?
SHOW A LITTLE SUPPORT FOR YOUR TEAM.
ALL RIGHT.
I'LL TAKE THIS OPPOR-TUNITY TO ANSWER YOUR QUESTION FROM BEFORE...
HUMAN BEINGS ARE...
...NOTHING TO ME BUT RESEARCH SUBJECTS.
...
I SEE...

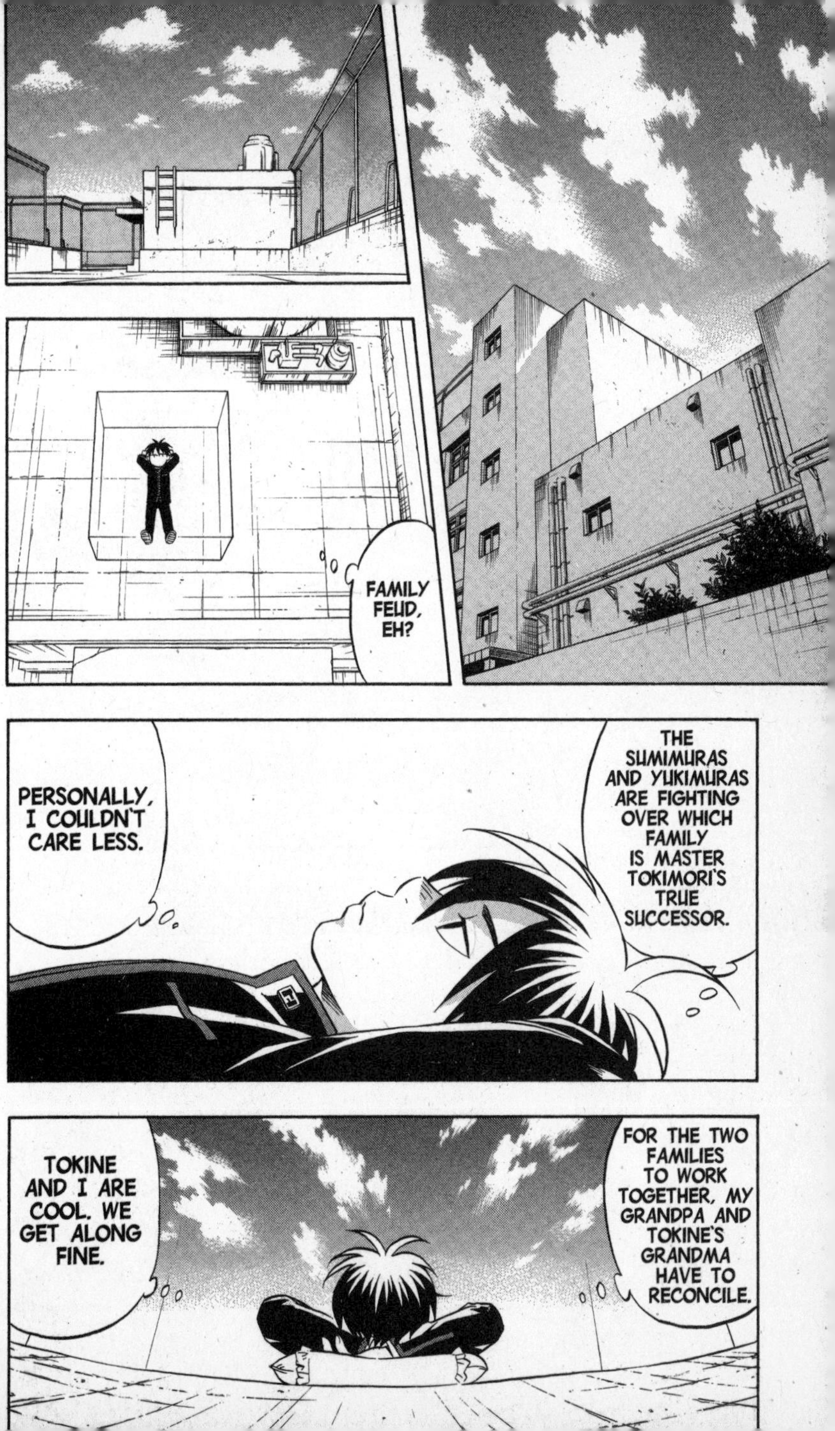
FAMILY FEUD, EH?
THE SUMIMURAS AND YUKIMURAS ARE FIGHTING OVER WHICH FAMILY IS MASTER TOKIMORI'S TRUE SUCCESSOR.
PERSONALLY, I COULDN'T CARE LESS.
FOR THE TWO FAMILIES TO WORK TOGETHER, MY GRANDPA AND TOKINE'S GRANDMA HAVE TO RECONCILE.
TOKINE AND I ARE COOL. WE GET ALONG FINE.

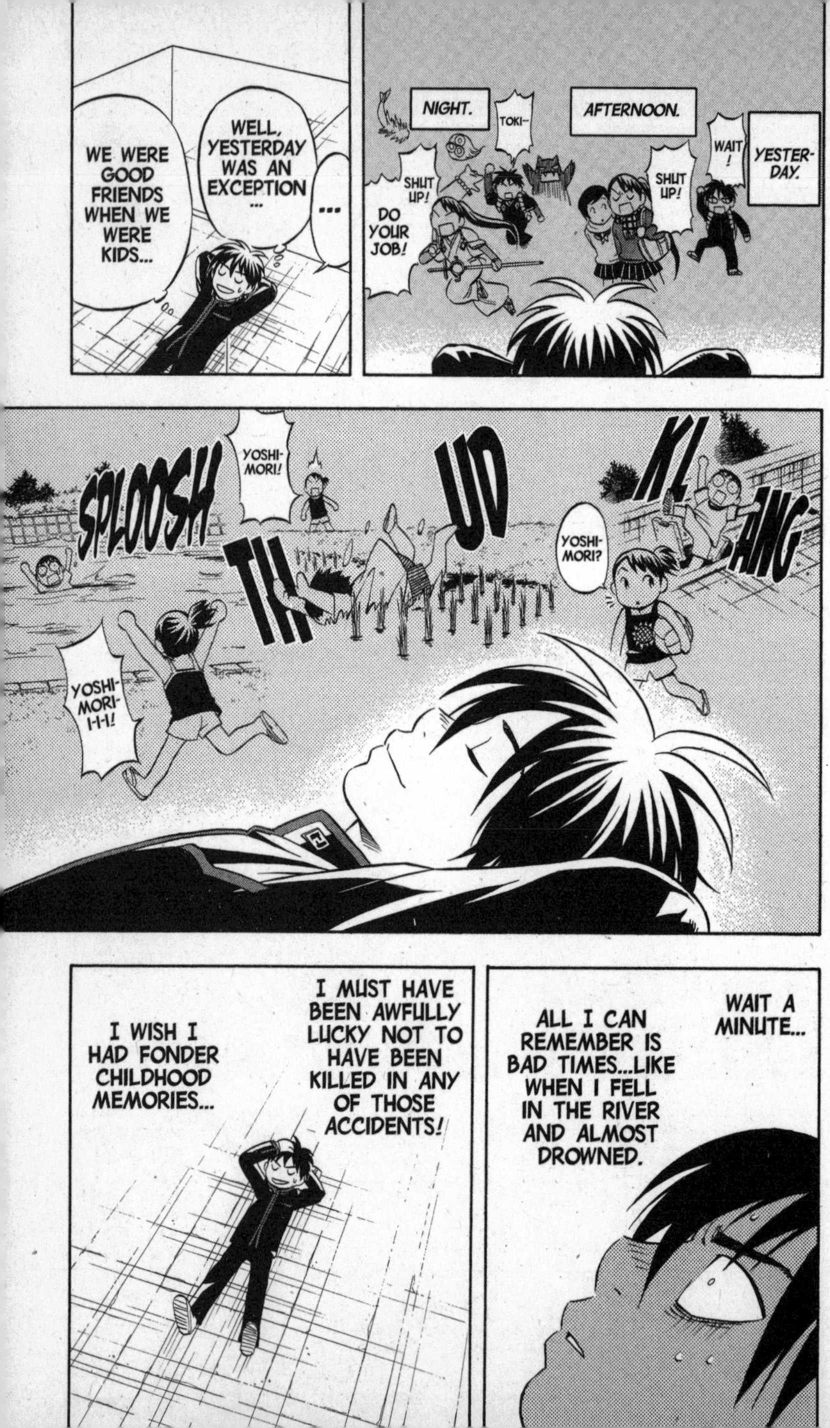
YESTER-DAY.
WAIT!
SHUT UP!
AFTERNOON.
TOKI—
NIGHT.
SHUT UP! DO YOUR JOB!
...
WELL, YESTERDAY WAS AN EXCEPTION...
WE WERE GOOD FRIENDS WHEN WE WERE KIDS...
KL ANG
YOSHI-MORI?
TH UD
YOSHI-MORI!
SPLOOSH
YOSHI-MORI-I-I-I!
WAIT A MINUTE...
ALL I CAN REMEMBER IS BAD TIMES...LIKE WHEN I FELL IN THE RIVER AND ALMOST DROWNED.
I MUST HAVE BEEN AWFULLY LUCKY NOT TO HAVE BEEN KILLED IN ANY OF THOSE ACCIDENTS!
I WISH I HAD FONDER CHILDHOOD MEMORIES...

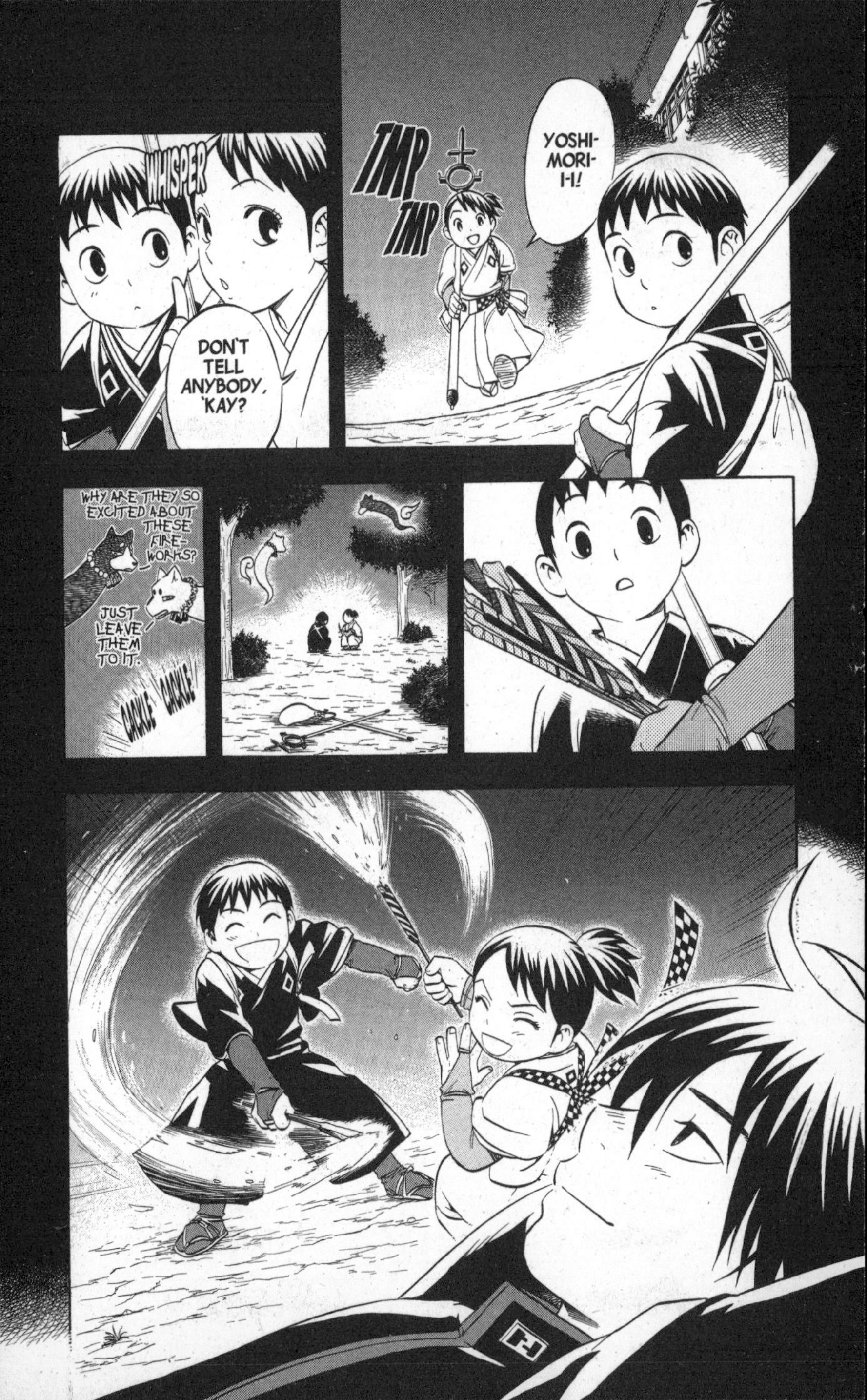
YOSHI-MORI-I-I!
TMP TMP
WHISPER
DON'T TELL ANYBODY, 'KAY?
WHY ARE THEY SO EXCITED ABOUT THESE FIRE-WORKS?
JUST LEAVE THEM TO IT.
CACKLE CACKLE

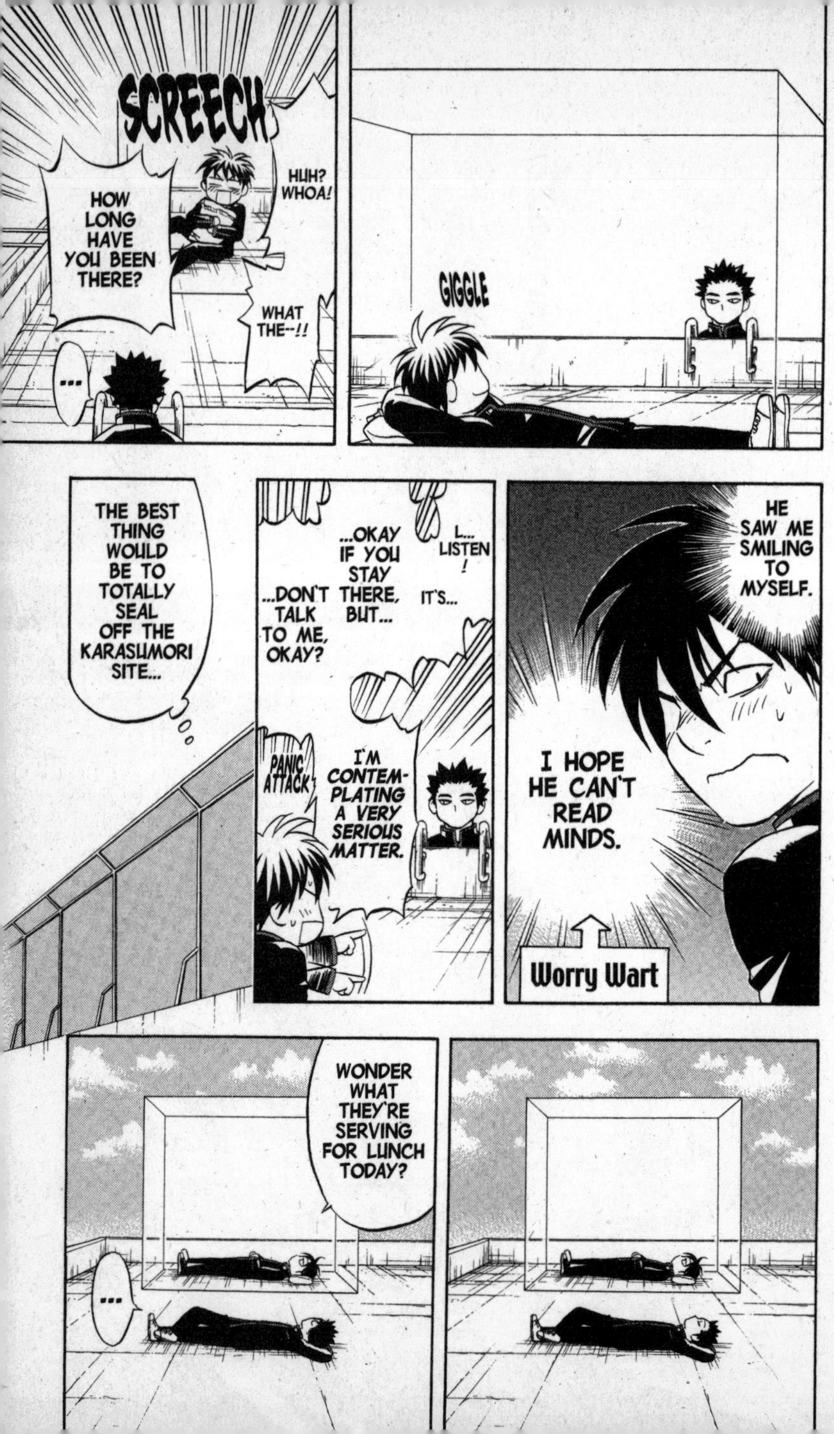
GIGGLE
SCREECH
HUH? WHOA!
HOW LONG HAVE YOU BEEN THERE?
WHAT THE--!!
...
HE SAW ME SMILING TO MYSELF.
I HOPE HE CAN'T READ MINDS.
Worry Wart
L... LISTEN! IT'S...
...OKAY IF YOU STAY THERE, BUT...
...DON'T TALK TO ME, OKAY?
PANIC ATTACK
I'M CONTEMPLATING A VERY SERIOUS MATTER.
THE BEST THING WOULD BE TO TOTALLY SEAL OFF THE KARASUMORI SITE...
WONDER WHAT THEY'RE SERVING FOR LUNCH TODAY?
...

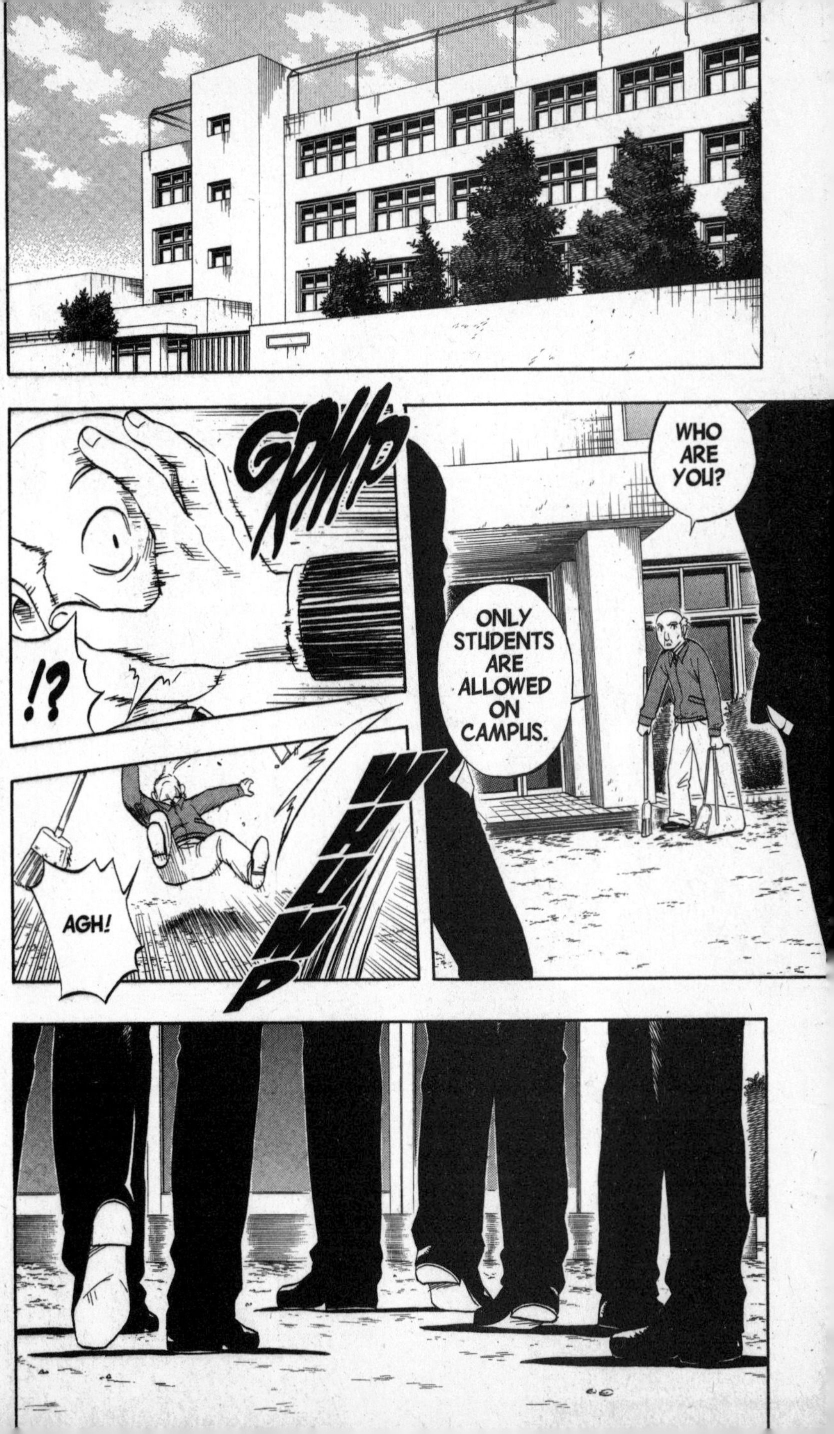
WHO ARE YOU?
ONLY STUDENTS ARE ALLOWED ON CAMPUS.
GRMP
!?
WHUMP
AGH!

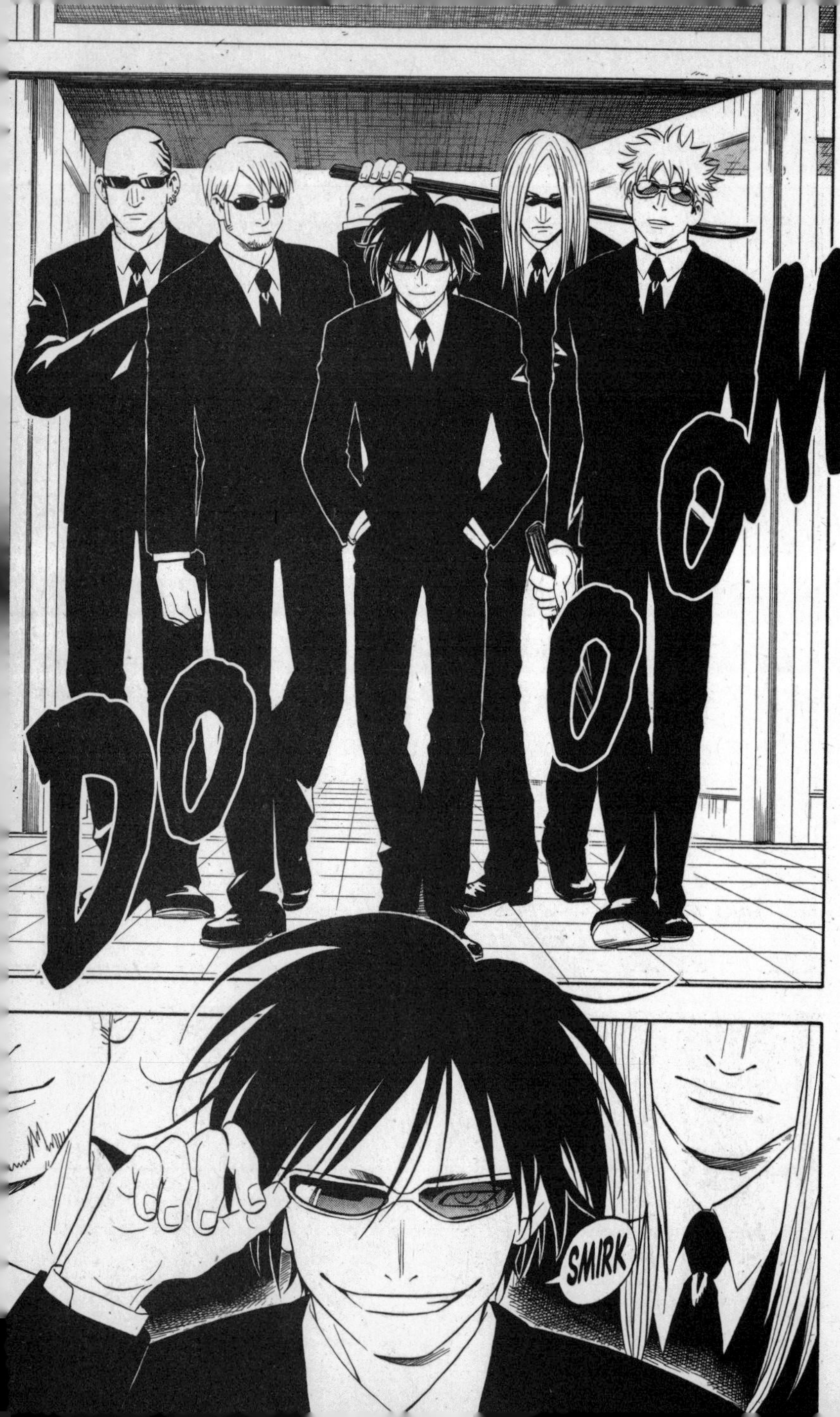
DOOOOM
SMIRK

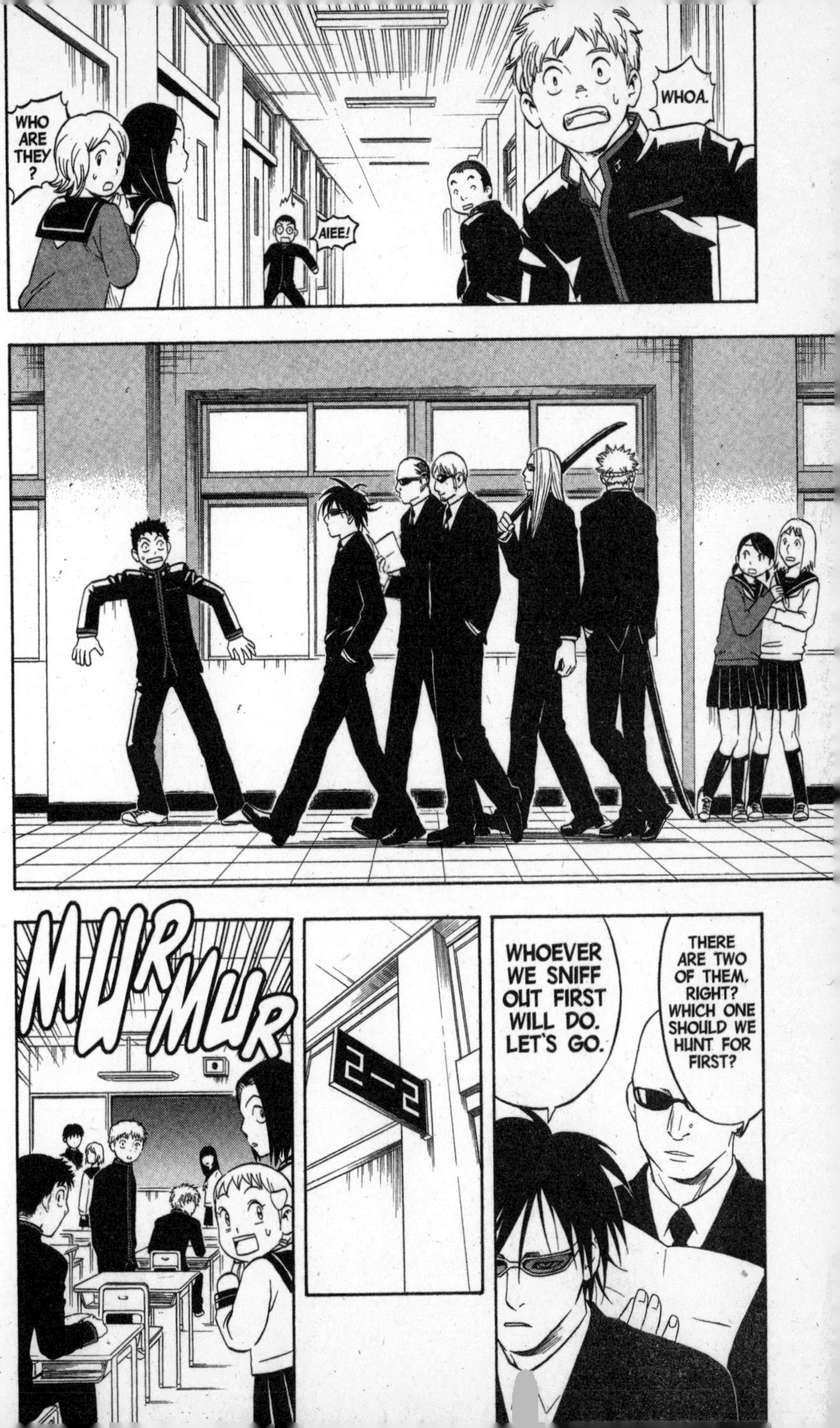
WHOA.
AIEE!
WHO ARE THEY?
THERE ARE TWO OF THEM, RIGHT? WHICH ONE SHOULD WE HUNT FOR FIRST?
WHOEVER WE SNIFF OUT FIRST WILL DO. LET'S GO.
2-2
MUR MUR

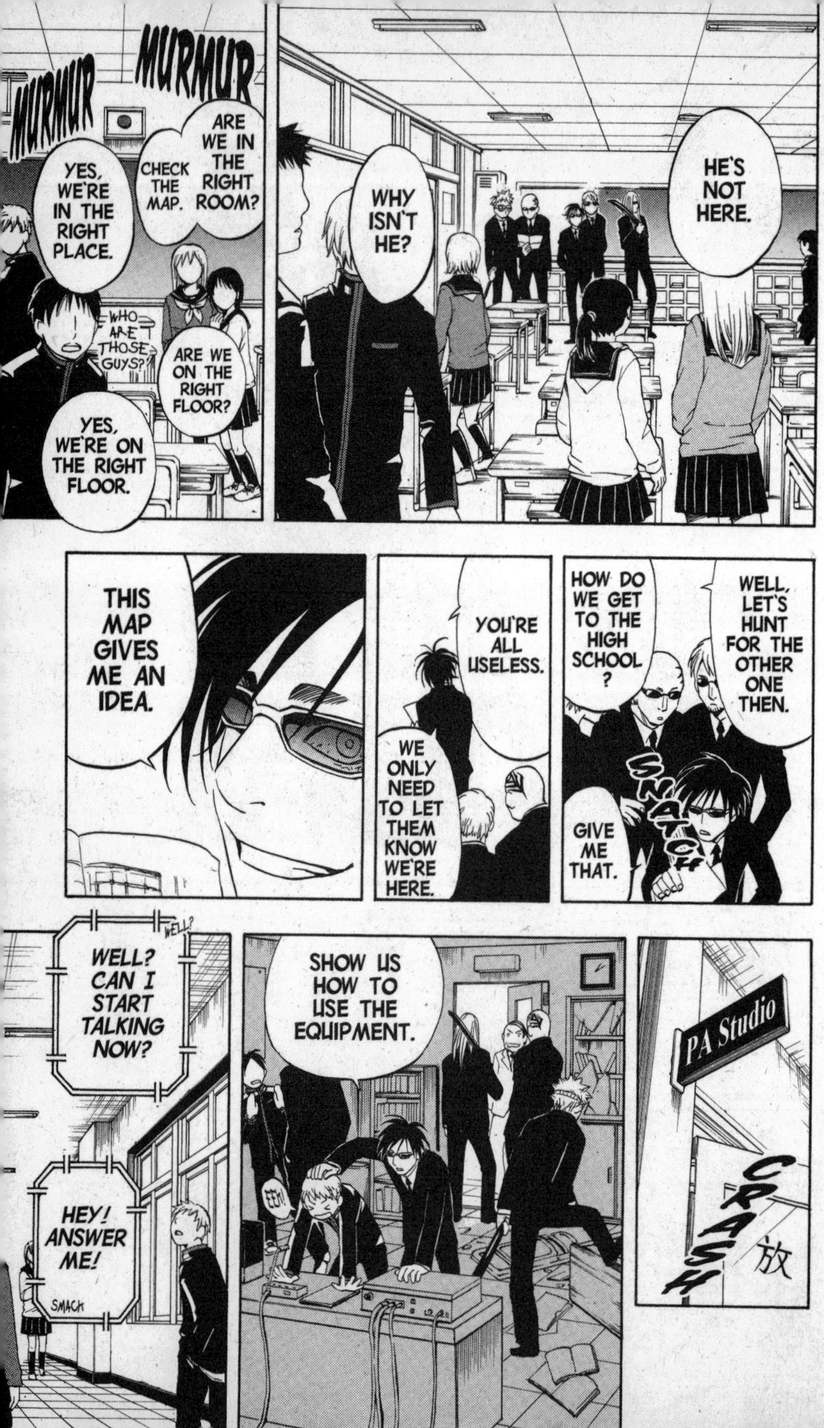
HE'S NOT HERE.
WHY ISN'T HE?
MURMUR
MURMUR
ARE WE IN THE RIGHT ROOM?
CHECK THE MAP.
YES, WE'RE IN THE RIGHT PLACE.
WHO ARE THOSE GUYS?
ARE WE ON THE RIGHT FLOOR?
YES, WE'RE ON THE RIGHT FLOOR.
WELL, LET'S HUNT FOR THE OTHER ONE THEN.
HOW DO WE GET TO THE HIGH SCHOOL?
SNATCH
GIVE ME THAT.
YOU'RE ALL USELESS.
WE ONLY NEED TO LET THEM KNOW WE'RE HERE.
THIS MAP GIVES ME AN IDEA.
PA Studio
CRASH
放
SHOW US HOW TO USE THE EQUIPMENT.
EEK!
WELL?
WELL? CAN I START TALKING NOW?
HEY! ANSWER ME!
SMACK

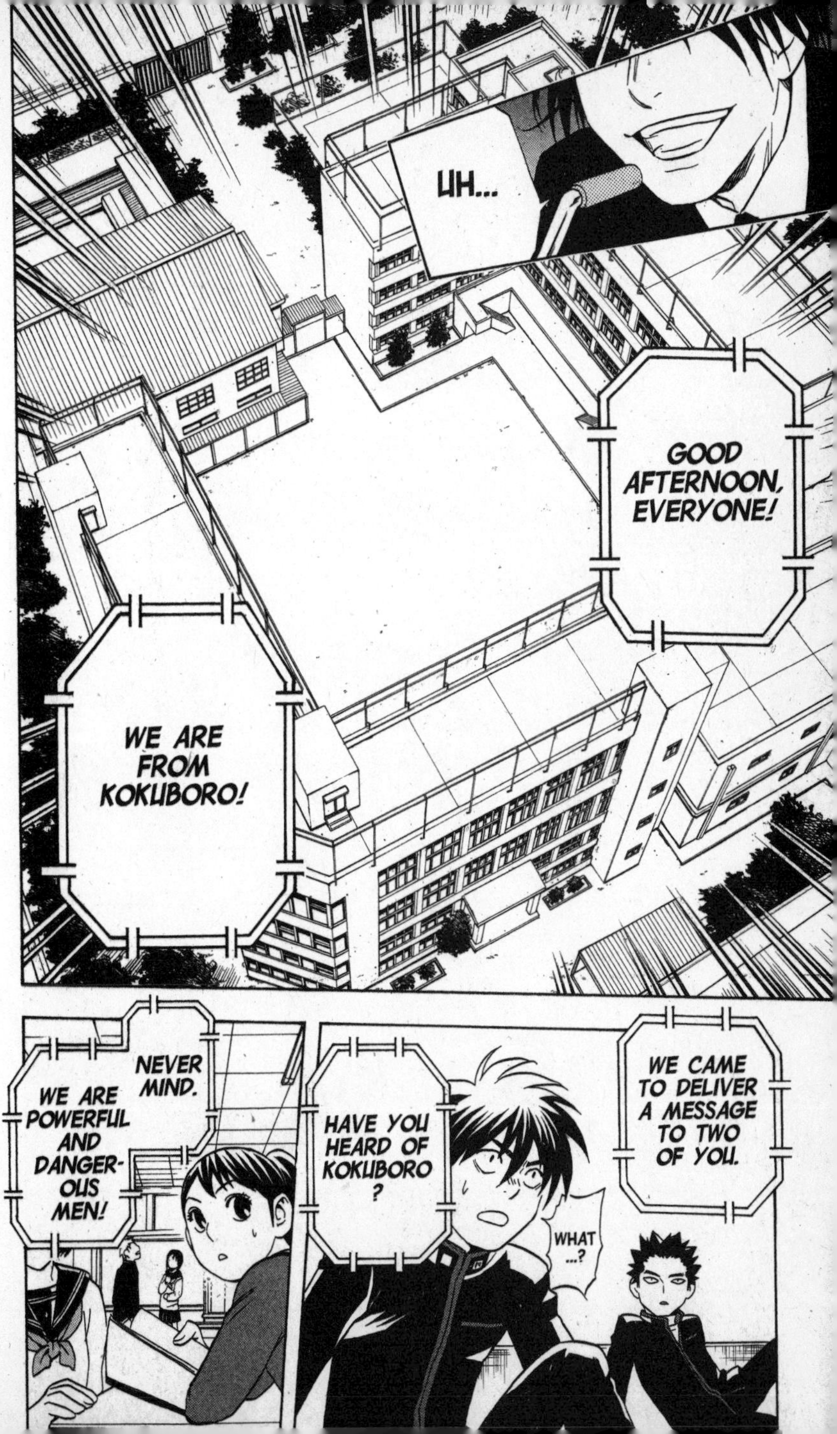
UH...
GOOD AFTERNOON, EVERYONE!
WE ARE FROM KOKUBORO!
WE CAME TO DELIVER A MESSAGE TO TWO OF YOU.
WHAT ...?
HAVE YOU HEARD OF KOKUBORO ?
NEVER MIND.
WE ARE POWERFUL AND DANGER-OUS MEN!

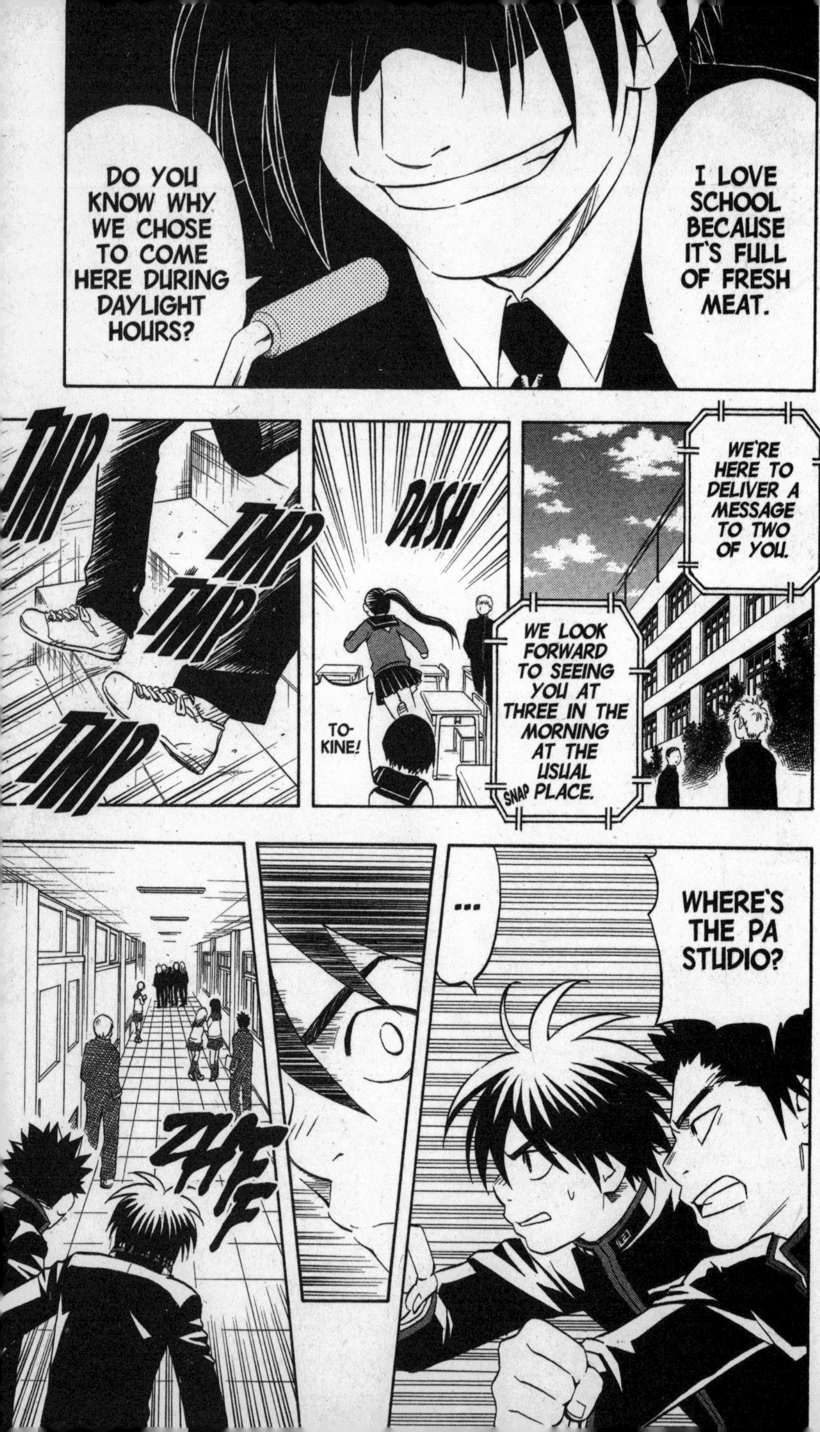
I LOVE SCHOOL BECAUSE IT'S FULL OF FRESH MEAT.
DO YOU KNOW WHY WE CHOSE TO COME HERE DURING DAYLIGHT HOURS?
WE'RE HERE TO DELIVER A MESSAGE TO TWO OF YOU.
WE LOOK FORWARD TO SEEING YOU AT THREE IN THE MORNING AT THE USUAL PLACE.
SNAP
DASH
TO-KINE!
TMP
TMP
TMP
TMP
WHERE'S THE PA STUDIO?
...
ZIP

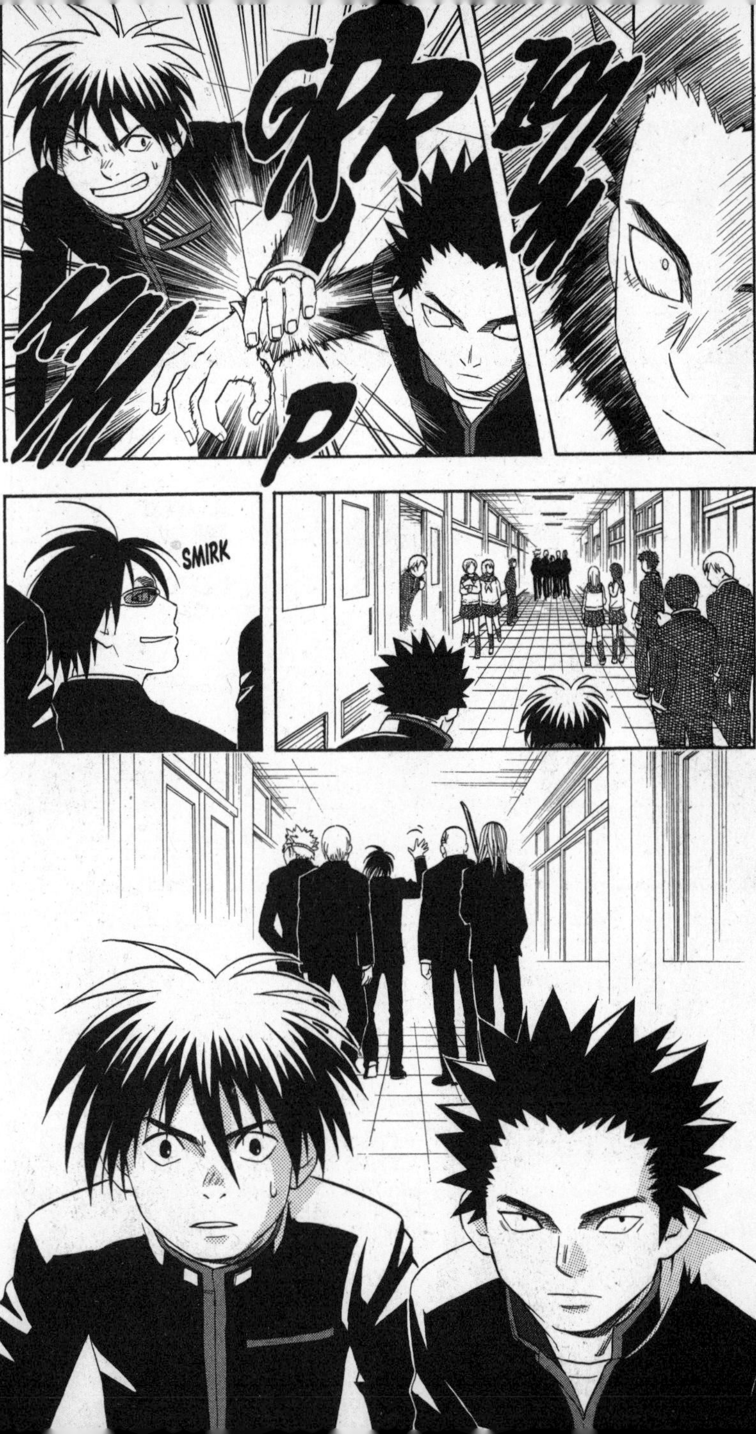
SMIRK

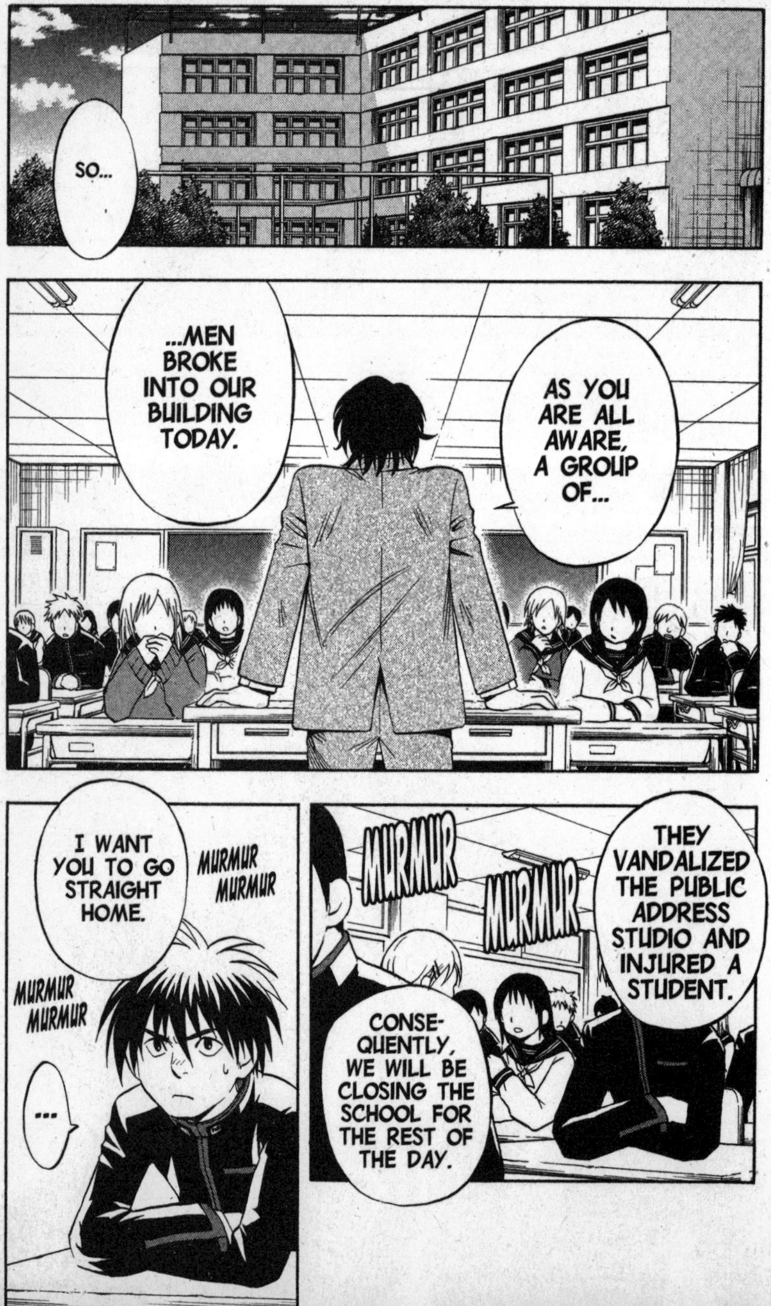
SO...
AS YOU ARE ALL AWARE, A GROUP OF...
...MEN BROKE INTO OUR BUILDING TODAY.
THEY VANDALIZED THE PUBLIC ADDRESS STUDIO AND INJURED A STUDENT.
MURMUR
MURMUR
CONSE-QUENTLY, WE WILL BE CLOSING THE SCHOOL FOR THE REST OF THE DAY.
I WANT YOU TO GO STRAIGHT HOME.
MURMUR MURMUR
MURMUR MURMUR
...

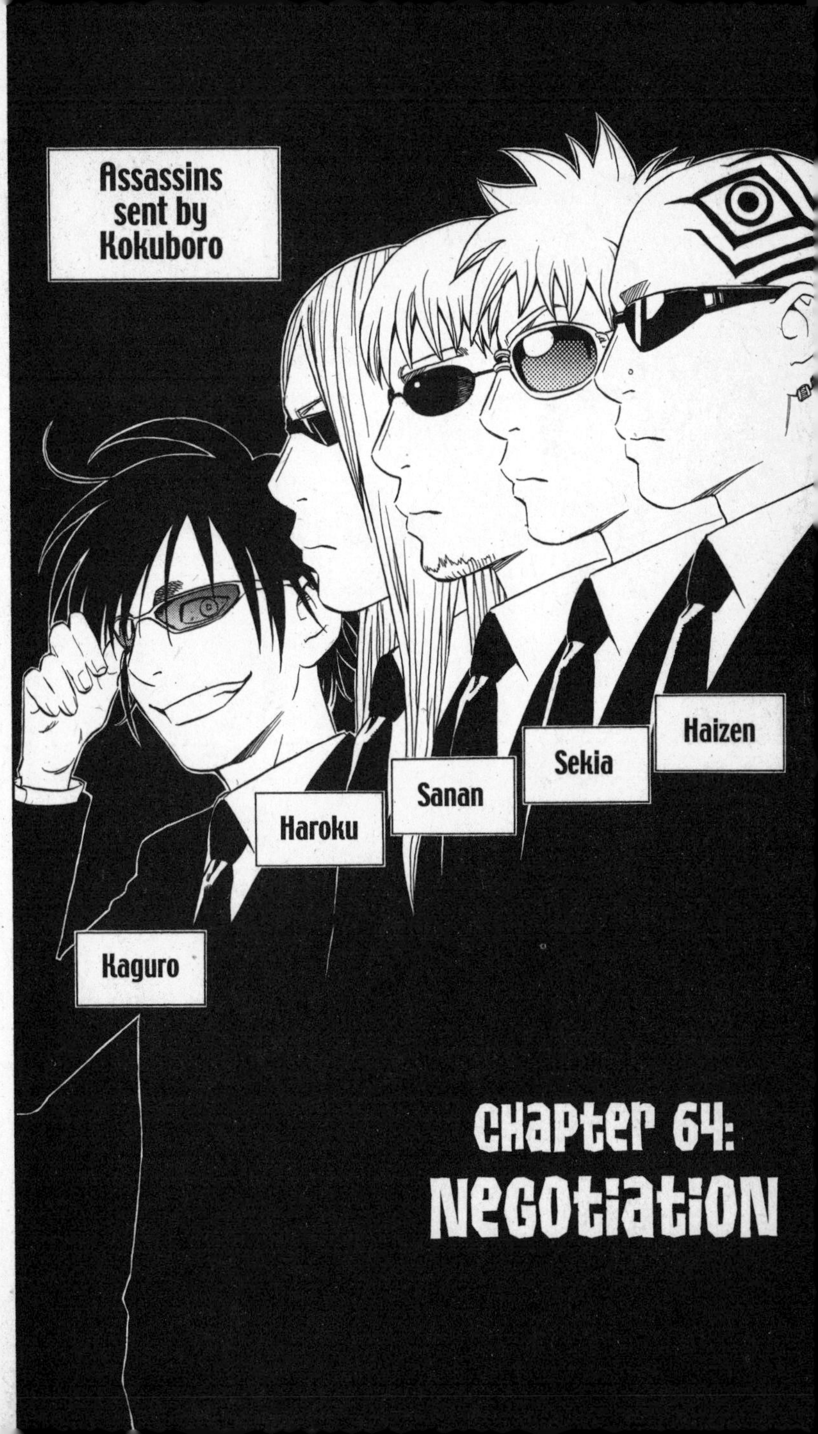
Assassins sent by Kokuboro
Haizen
Sekia
Sanan
Haroku
Kaguro

Chapter 64: Negotiation

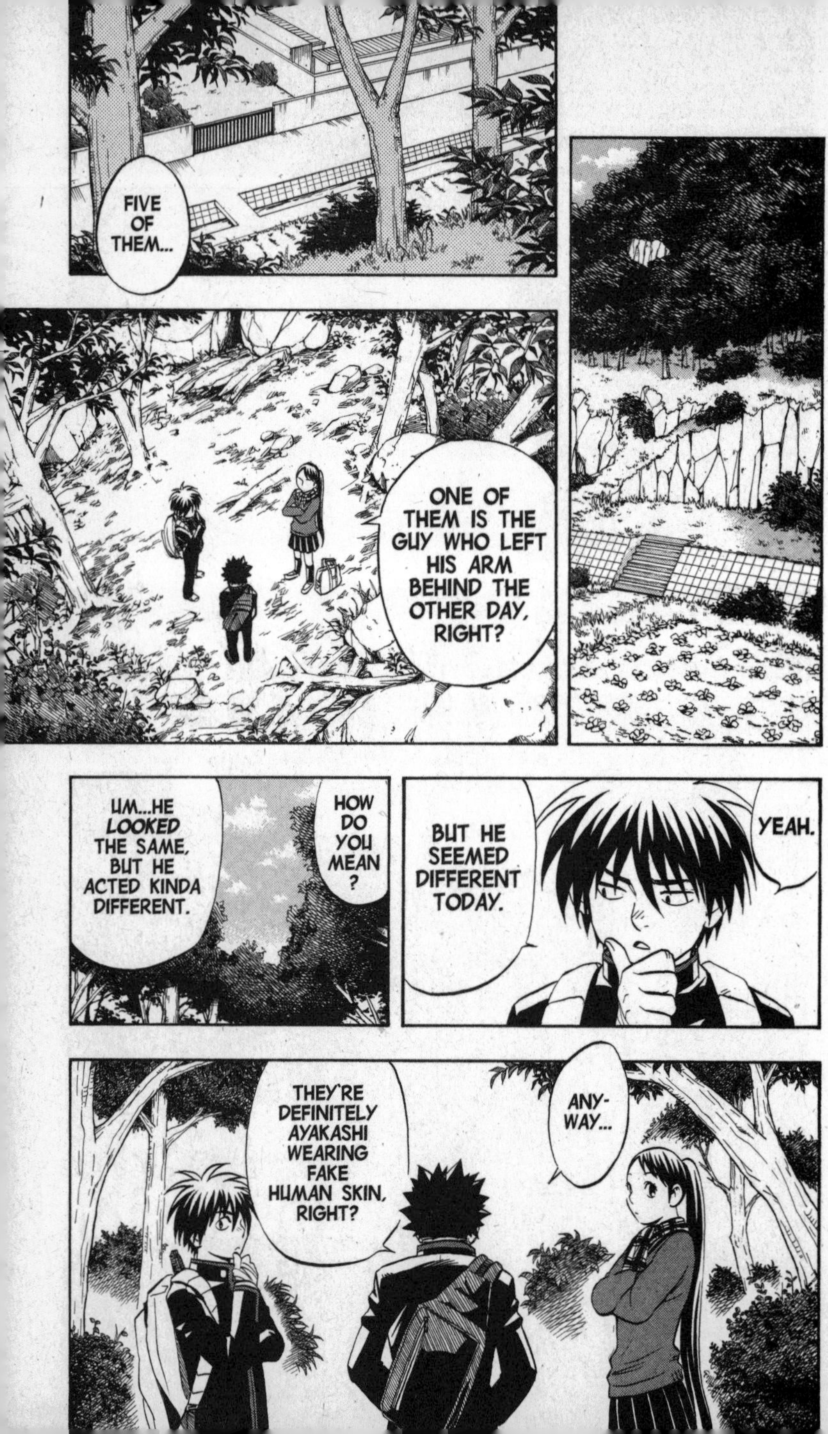
FIVE OF THEM...
ONE OF THEM IS THE GUY WHO LEFT HIS ARM BEHIND THE OTHER DAY, RIGHT?
YEAH.
BUT HE SEEMED DIFFERENT TODAY.
HOW DO YOU MEAN?
UM...HE *LOOKED* THE SAME, BUT HE ACTED KINDA DIFFERENT.
ANY-WAY...
THEY'RE DEFINITELY AYAKASHI WEARING FAKE HUMAN SKIN, RIGHT?

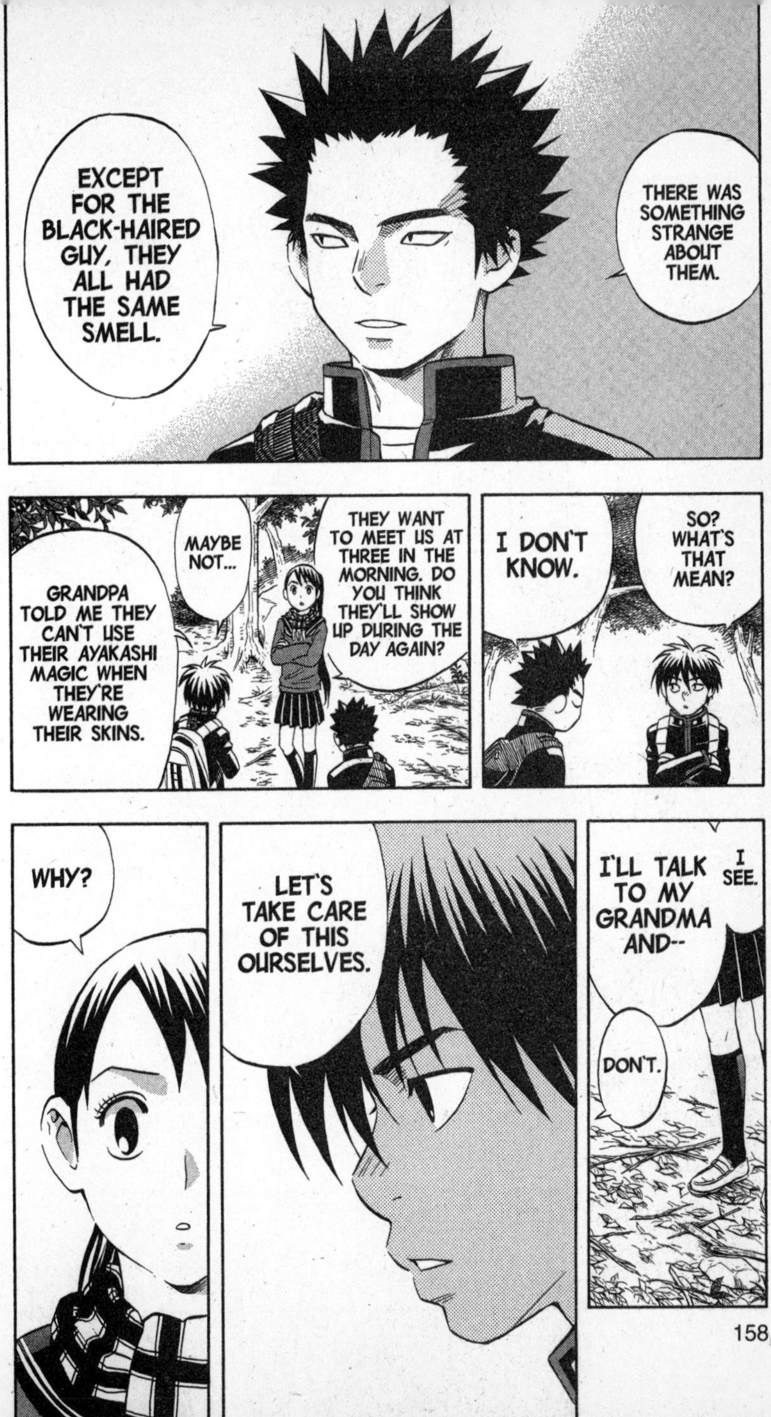
THERE WAS SOMETHING STRANGE ABOUT THEM.
EXCEPT FOR THE BLACK-HAIRED GUY, THEY ALL HAD THE SAME SMELL.
SO? WHAT'S THAT MEAN?
I DON'T KNOW.
THEY WANT TO MEET US AT THREE IN THE MORNING. DO YOU THINK THEY'LL SHOW UP DURING THE DAY AGAIN?
MAYBE NOT...
GRANDPA TOLD ME THEY CAN'T USE THEIR AYAKASHI MAGIC WHEN THEY'RE WEARING THEIR SKINS.
I SEE.
I'LL TALK TO MY GRANDMA AND--
DON'T.
LET'S TAKE CARE OF THIS OURSELVES.
WHY?

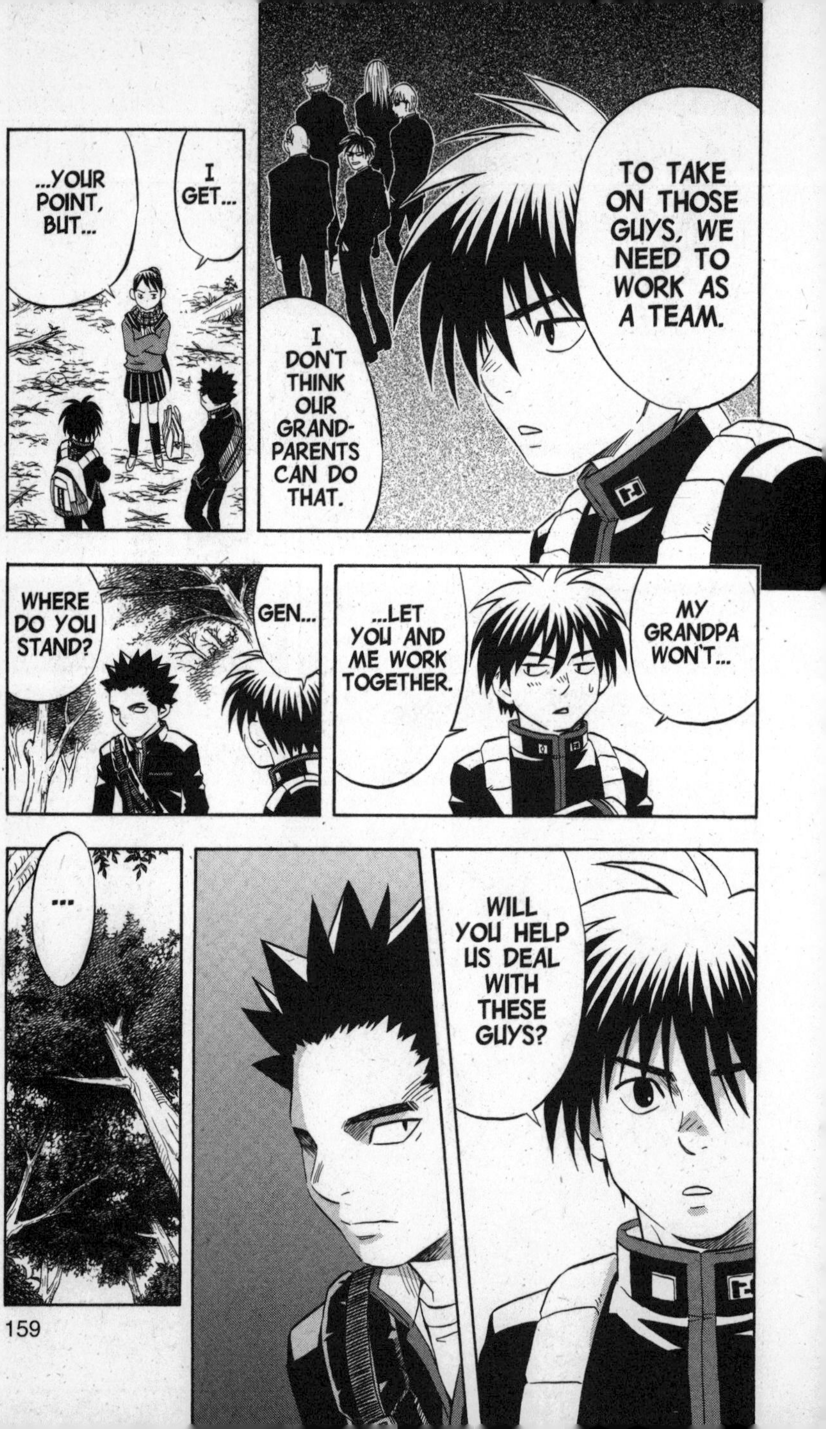
TO TAKE ON THOSE GUYS, WE NEED TO WORK AS A TEAM.
I DON'T THINK OUR GRAND-PARENTS CAN DO THAT.
I GET...
...YOUR POINT, BUT...
MY GRANDPA WON'T...
...LET YOU AND ME WORK TOGETHER.
GEN...
WHERE DO YOU STAND?
WILL YOU HELP US DEAL WITH THESE GUYS?
...

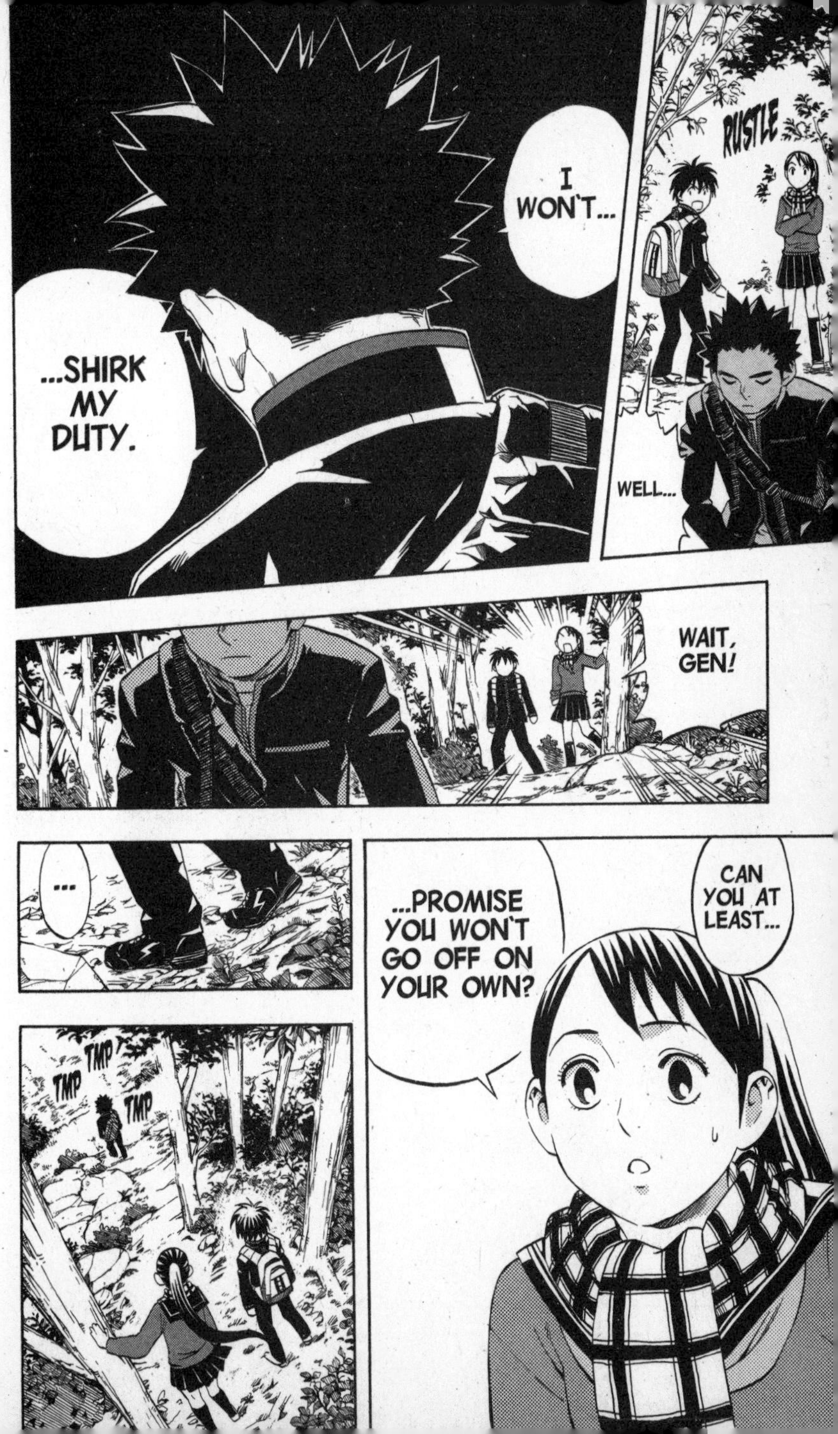
RUSTLE
WELL...
I WON'T...
...SHIRK MY DUTY.
WAIT, GEN!
CAN YOU AT LEAST...
...PROMISE YOU WON'T GO OFF ON YOUR OWN?
...
TMP TMP
TMP TMP

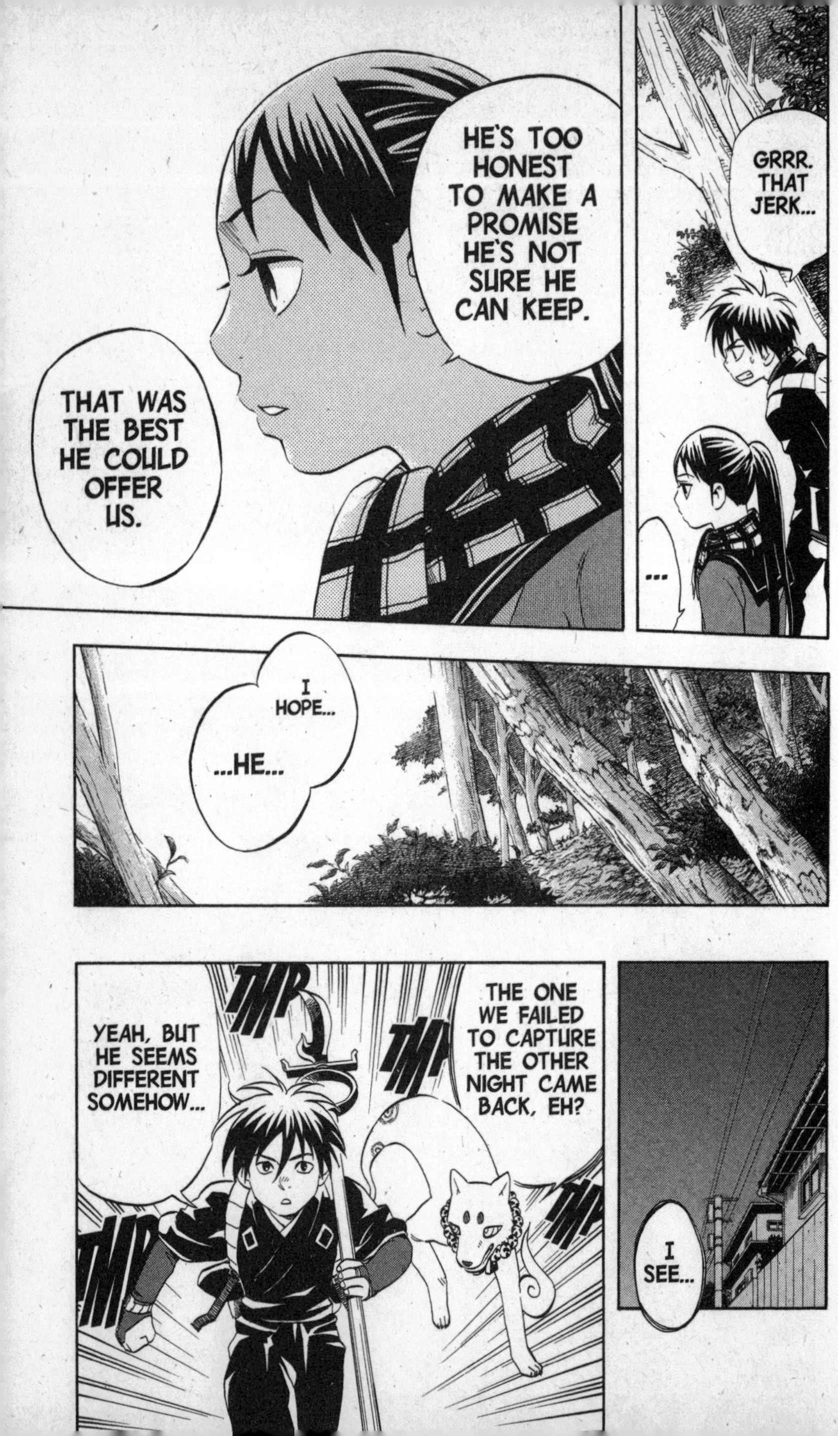
GRRR. THAT JERK...
...
HE'S TOO HONEST TO MAKE A PROMISE HE'S NOT SURE HE CAN KEEP.
THAT WAS THE BEST HE COULD OFFER US.
I HOPE...
...HE...
I SEE...
THE ONE WE FAILED TO CAPTURE THE OTHER NIGHT CAME BACK, EH?
TMP
TMP
YEAH, BUT HE SEEMS DIFFERENT SOMEHOW...
TMP
TMP

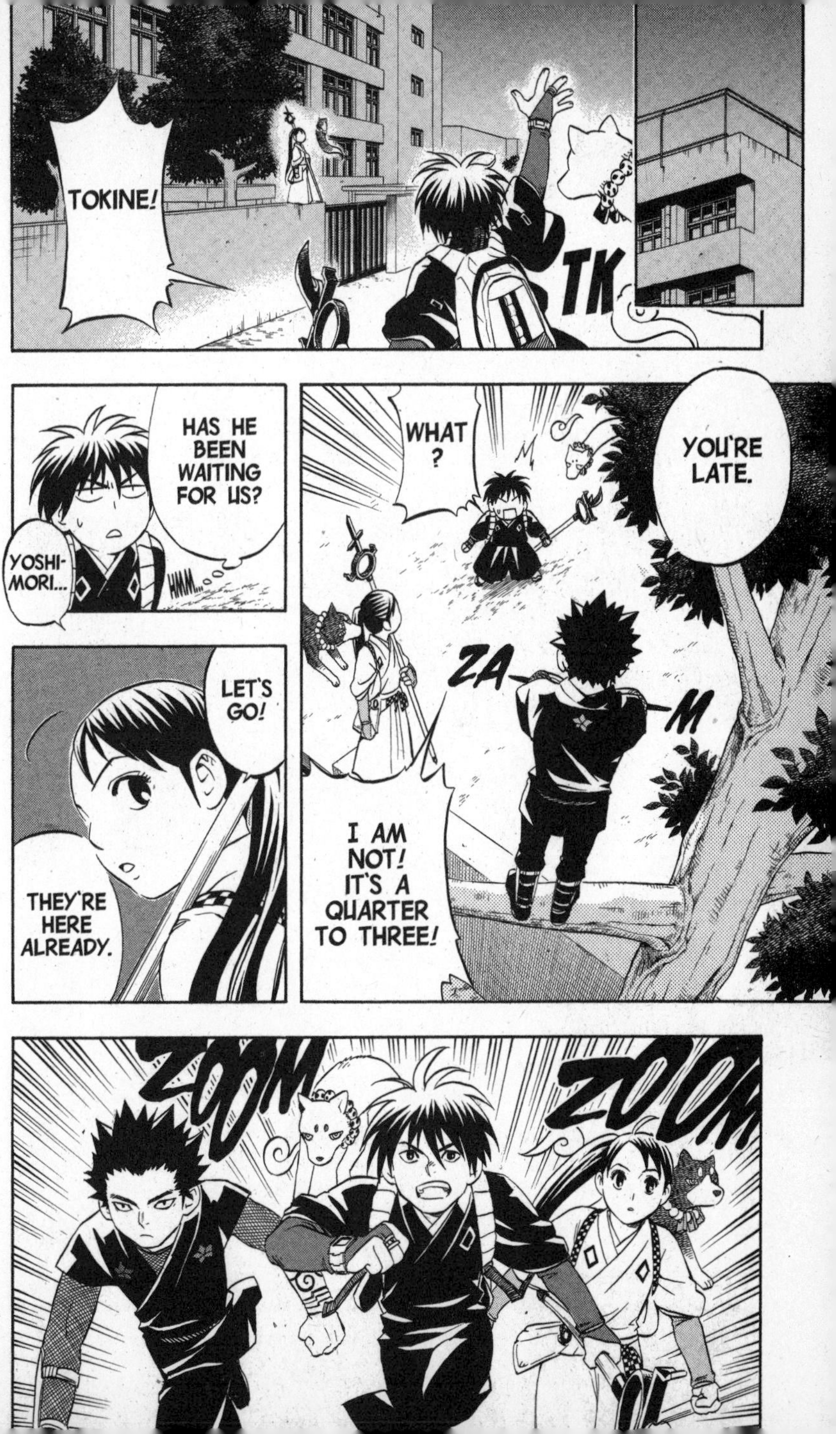
TOKINE!
TK
YOU'RE LATE.
WHAT?
ZA-M
I AM NOT! IT'S A QUARTER TO THREE!
HAS HE BEEN WAITING FOR US?
YOSHIMORI...
HMM...
LET'S GO!
THEY'RE HERE ALREADY.
ZOOM
ZOOM

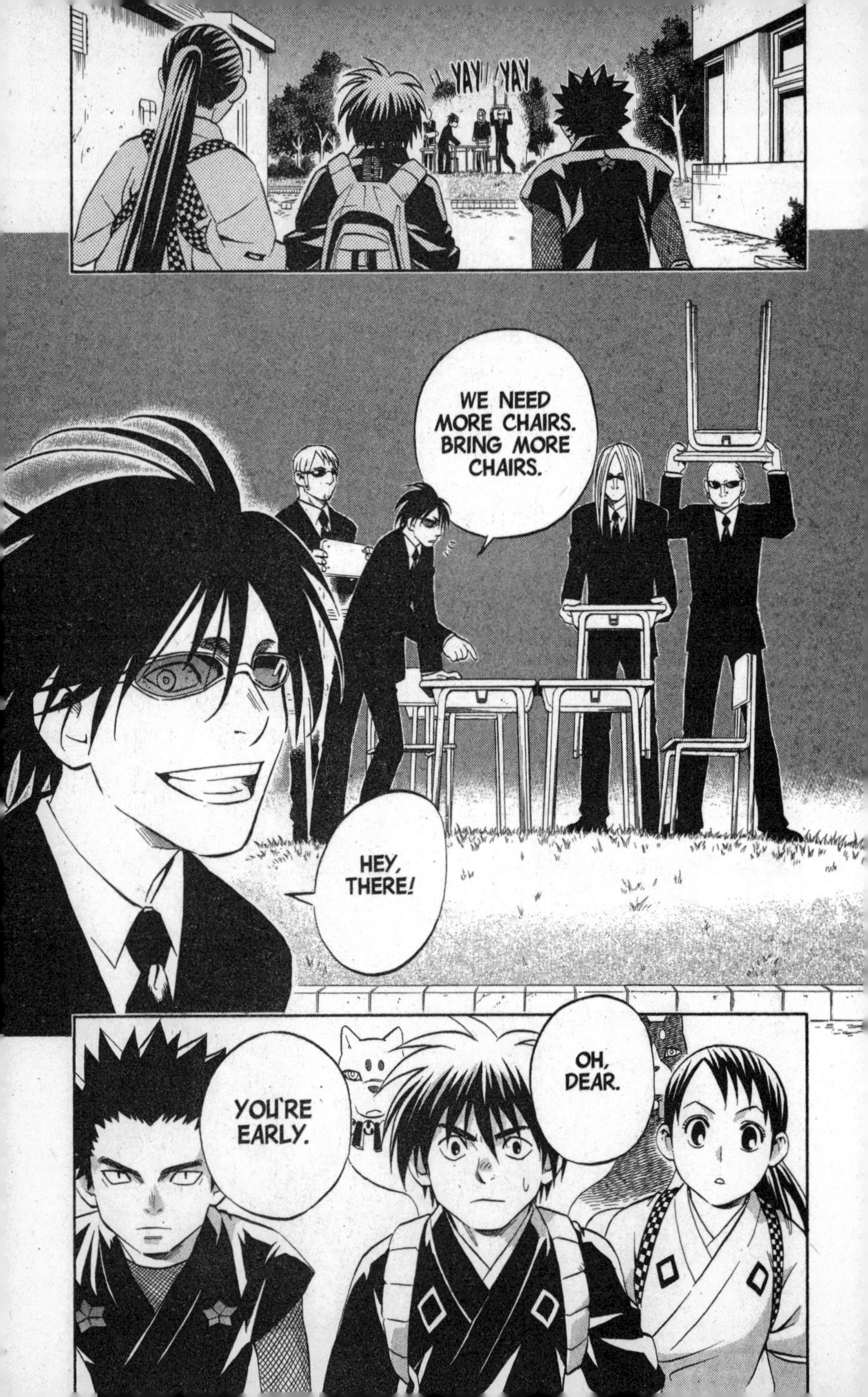
YAY YAY
WE NEED MORE CHAIRS. BRING MORE CHAIRS.
HEY, THERE!
OH, DEAR.
YOU'RE EARLY.

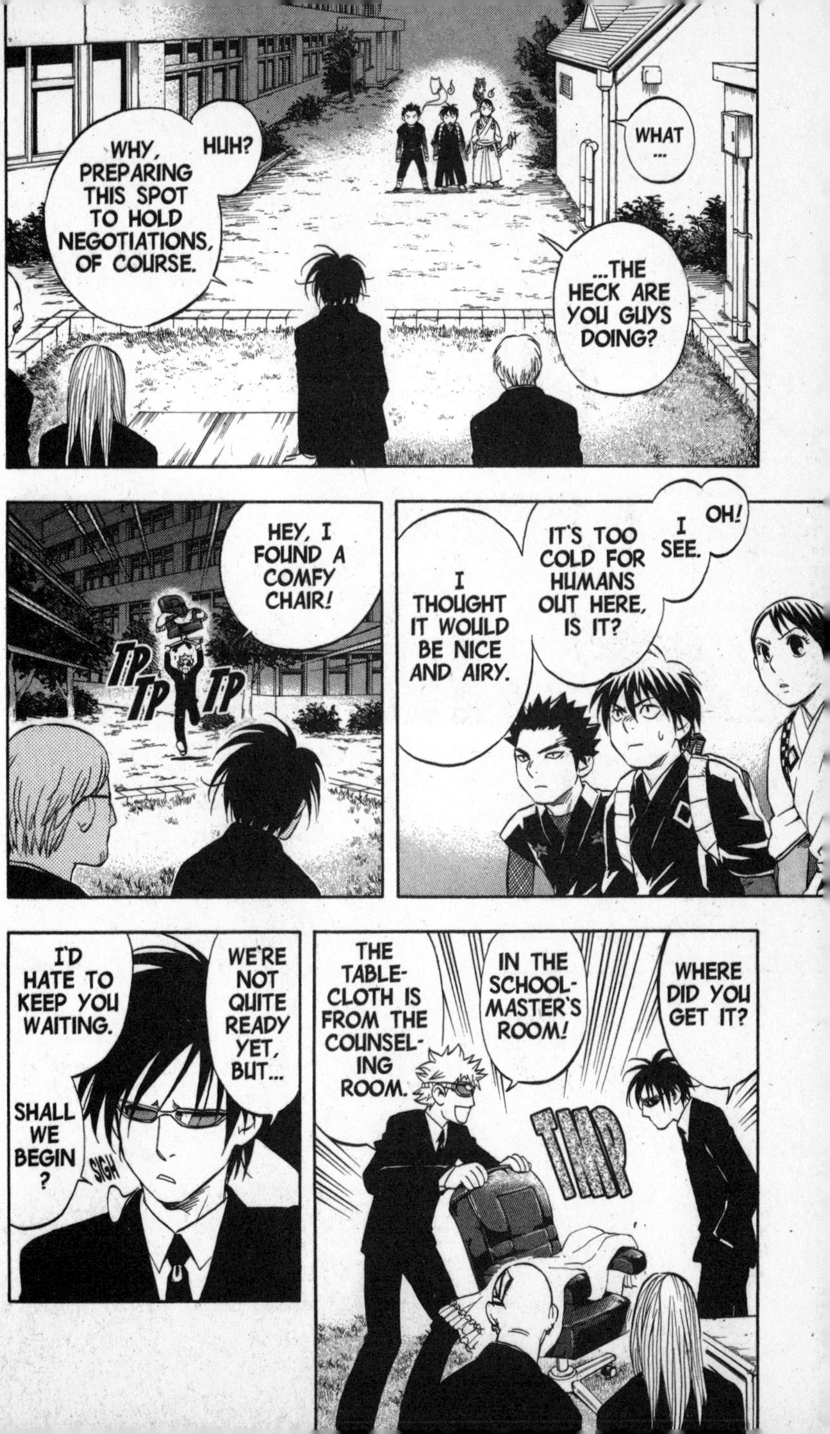
WHAT ...
...THE HECK ARE YOU GUYS DOING?
HUH?
WHY, PREPARING THIS SPOT TO HOLD NEGOTIATIONS, OF COURSE.
OH!
I SEE.
IT'S TOO COLD FOR HUMANS OUT HERE, IS IT?
I THOUGHT IT WOULD BE NICE AND AIRY.
HEY, I FOUND A COMFY CHAIR!
TP TP TP
WHERE DID YOU GET IT?
IN THE SCHOOLMASTER'S ROOM!
THE TABLECLOTH IS FROM THE COUNSELING ROOM.
TMP
WE'RE NOT QUITE READY YET, BUT...
I'D HATE TO KEEP YOU WAITING.
SIGH
SHALL WE BEGIN?

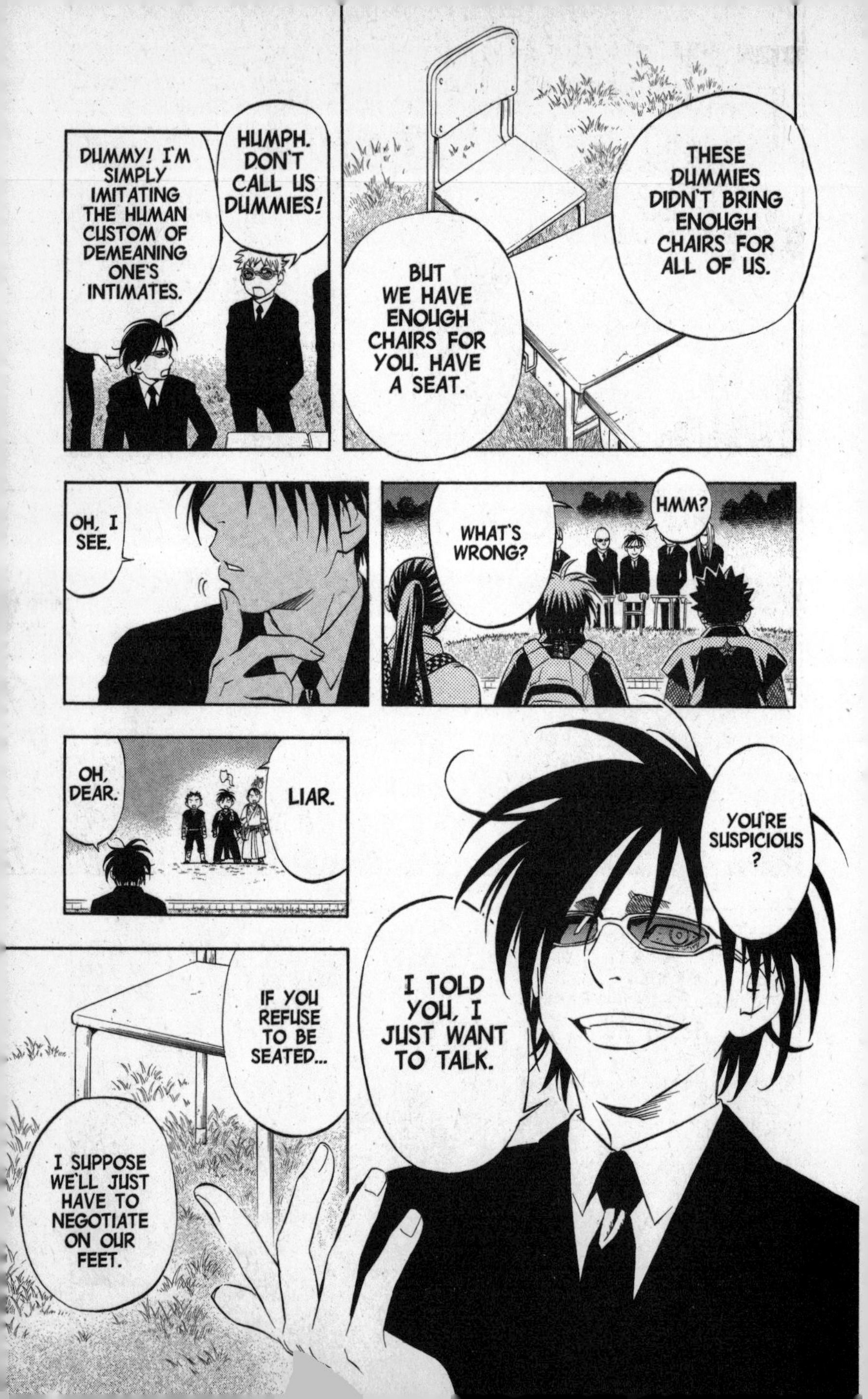
THESE DUMMIES DIDN'T BRING ENOUGH CHAIRS FOR ALL OF US.
BUT WE HAVE ENOUGH CHAIRS FOR YOU. HAVE A SEAT.
HUMPH. DON'T CALL US DUMMIES!
DUMMY! I'M SIMPLY IMITATING THE HUMAN CUSTOM OF DEMEANING ONE'S INTIMATES.
HMM?
WHAT'S WRONG?
OH, I SEE.
YOU'RE SUSPICIOUS?
I TOLD YOU, I JUST WANT TO TALK.
LIAR.
OH, DEAR.
IF YOU REFUSE TO BE SEATED...
I SUPPOSE WE'LL JUST HAVE TO NEGOTIATE ON OUR FEET.

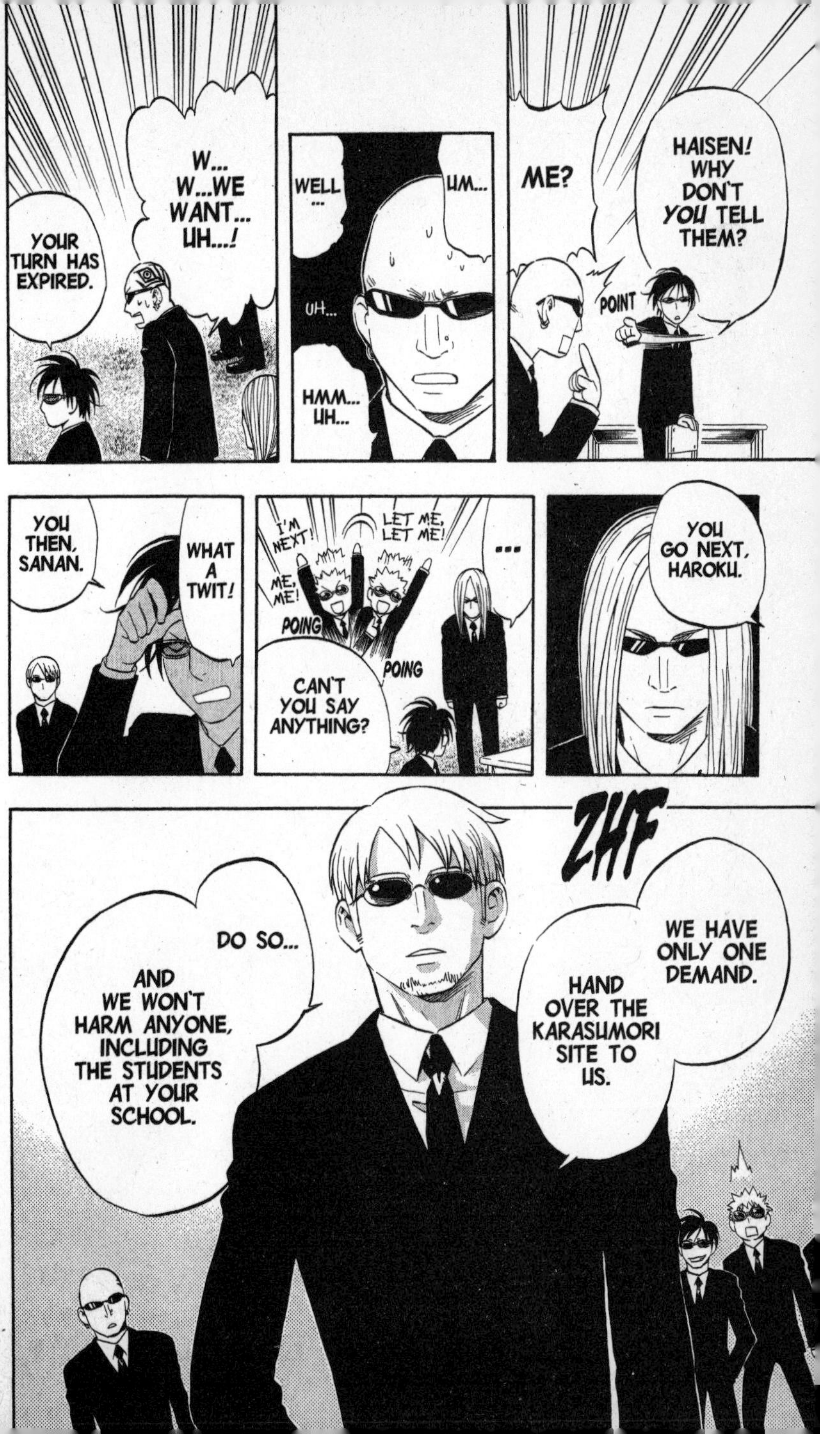
HAISEN! WHY DON'T YOU TELL THEM?
POINT
ME?
UM...
WELL ...
UH...
HMM... UH...
W... W...WE WANT... UH...!
YOUR TURN HAS EXPIRED.
YOU GO NEXT, HAROKU.
...
LET ME, LET ME!
I'M NEXT!
ME, ME!
POING
POING
CAN'T YOU SAY ANYTHING?
WHAT A TWIT!
YOU THEN, SANAN.
ZHF
WE HAVE ONLY ONE DEMAND.
HAND OVER THE KARASUMORI SITE TO US.
DO SO...
AND WE WON'T HARM ANYONE, INCLUDING THE STUDENTS AT YOUR SCHOOL.

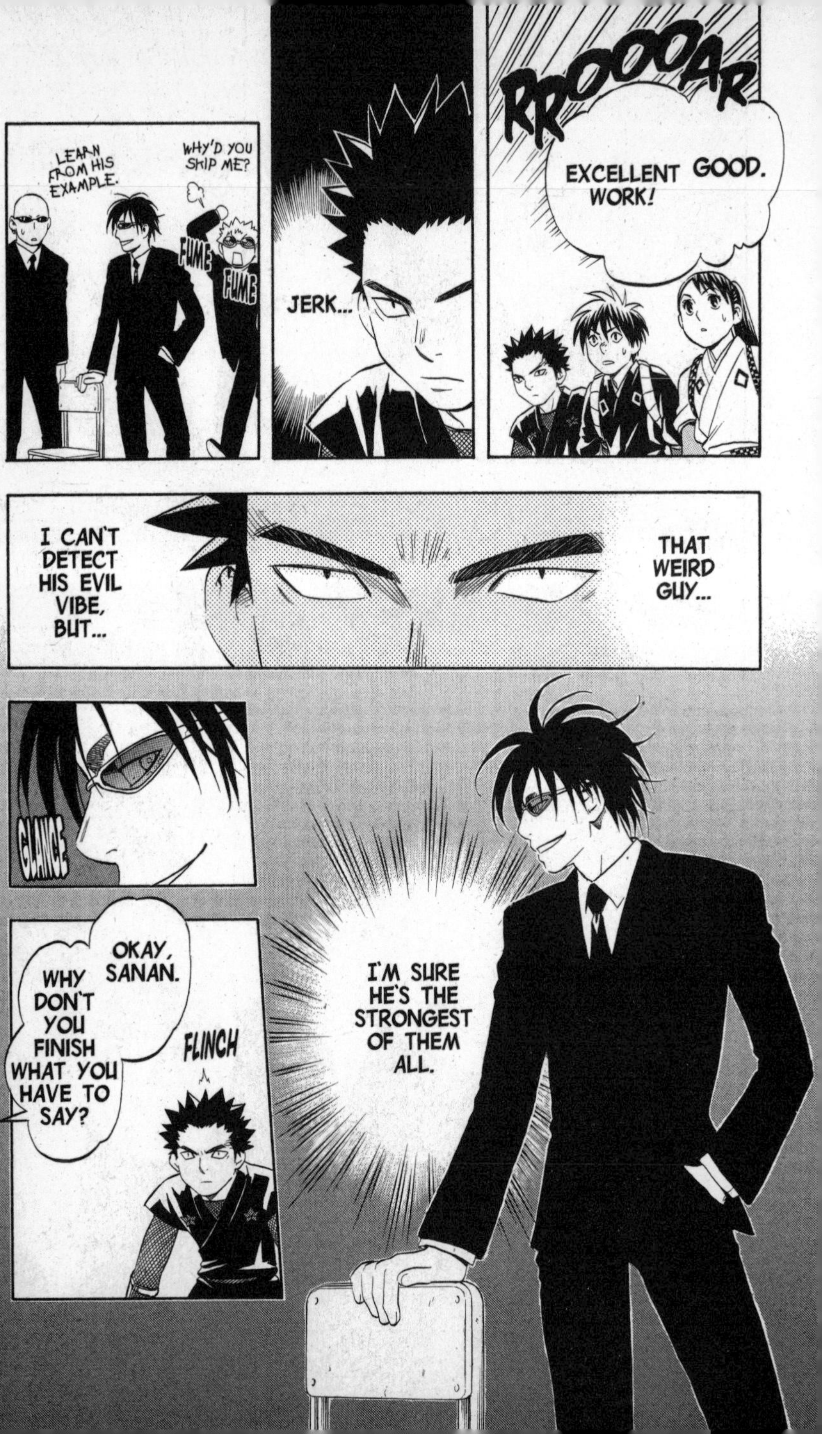
RRROOOAR
GOOD.
EXCELLENT WORK!
JERK...
WHY'D YOU SKIP ME?
LEARN FROM HIS EXAMPLE.
FUME
FUME
THAT WEIRD GUY...
I CAN'T DETECT HIS EVIL VIBE, BUT...
I'M SURE HE'S THE STRONGEST OF THEM ALL.
GLANCE
OKAY, SANAN.
WHY DON'T YOU FINISH WHAT YOU HAVE TO SAY?
FLINCH

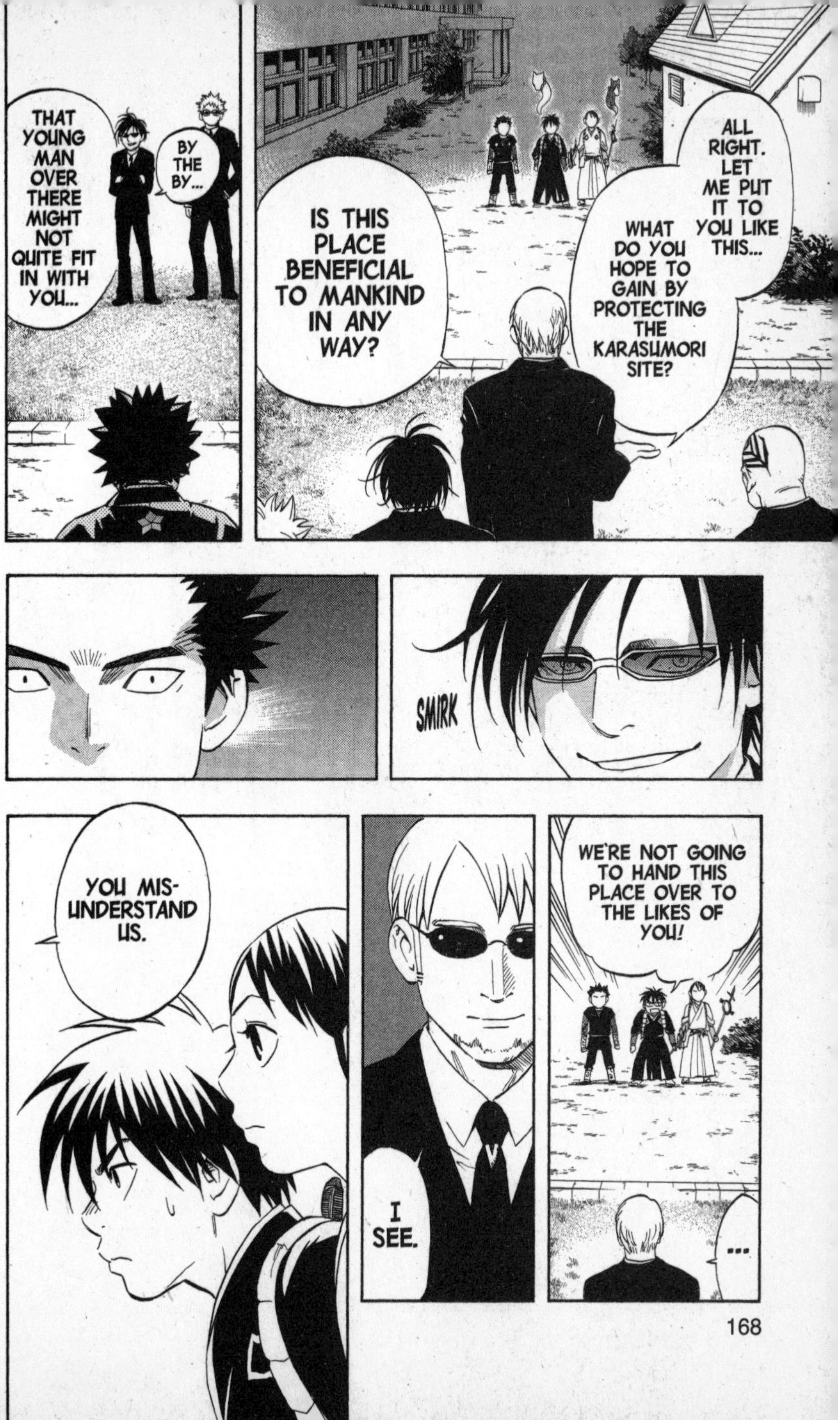
ALL RIGHT. LET ME PUT IT TO YOU LIKE THIS...
WHAT DO YOU HOPE TO GAIN BY PROTECTING THE KARASUMORI SITE?
IS THIS PLACE BENEFICIAL TO MANKIND IN ANY WAY?
BY THE BY...
THAT YOUNG MAN OVER THERE MIGHT NOT QUITE FIT IN WITH YOU...
SMIRK
WE'RE NOT GOING TO HAND THIS PLACE OVER TO THE LIKES OF YOU!
...
I SEE.
YOU MIS-UNDERSTAND US.

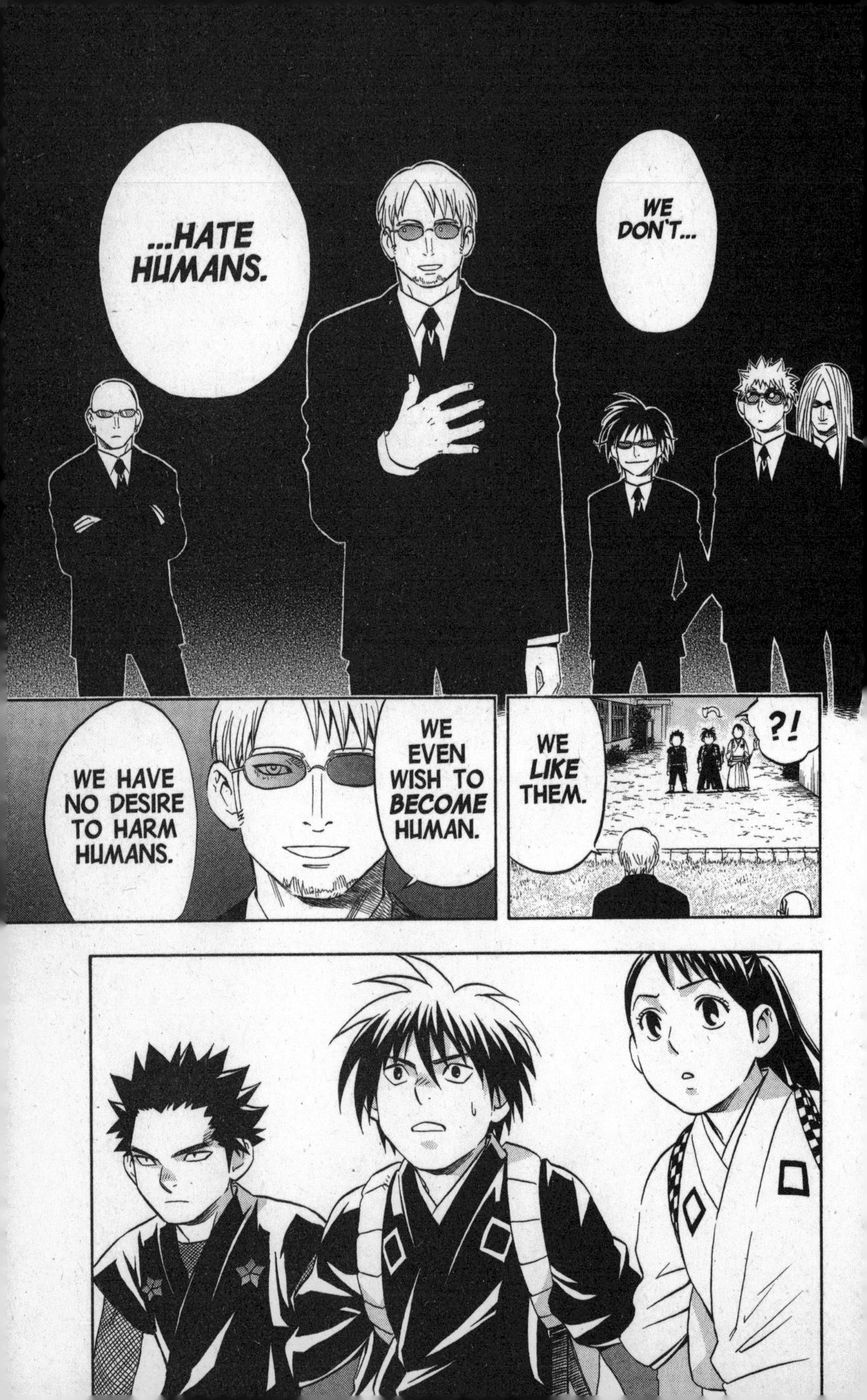
WE DON'T...
...HATE HUMANS.
?!
WE LIKE THEM.
WE EVEN WISH TO BECOME HUMAN.
WE HAVE NO DESIRE TO HARM HUMANS.

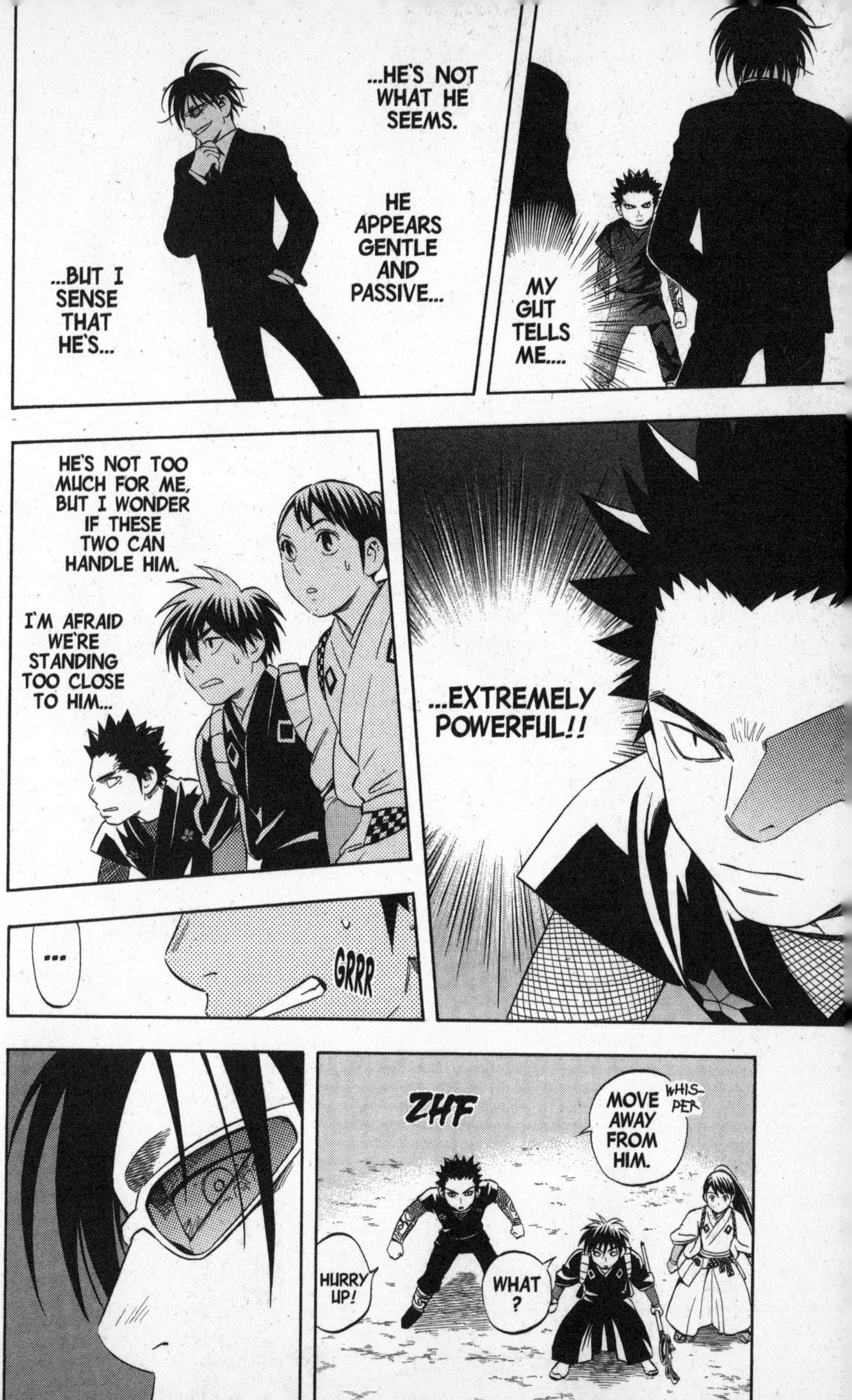
MY GUT TELLS ME....
...HE'S NOT WHAT HE SEEMS.
HE APPEARS GENTLE AND PASSIVE...
...BUT I SENSE THAT HE'S...
...EXTREMELY POWERFUL!!
HE'S NOT TOO MUCH FOR ME, BUT I WONDER IF THESE TWO CAN HANDLE HIM.
I'M AFRAID WE'RE STANDING TOO CLOSE TO HIM...
GRRR
...
WHIS-PER
MOVE AWAY FROM HIM.
ZHF
WHAT?
HURRY UP!

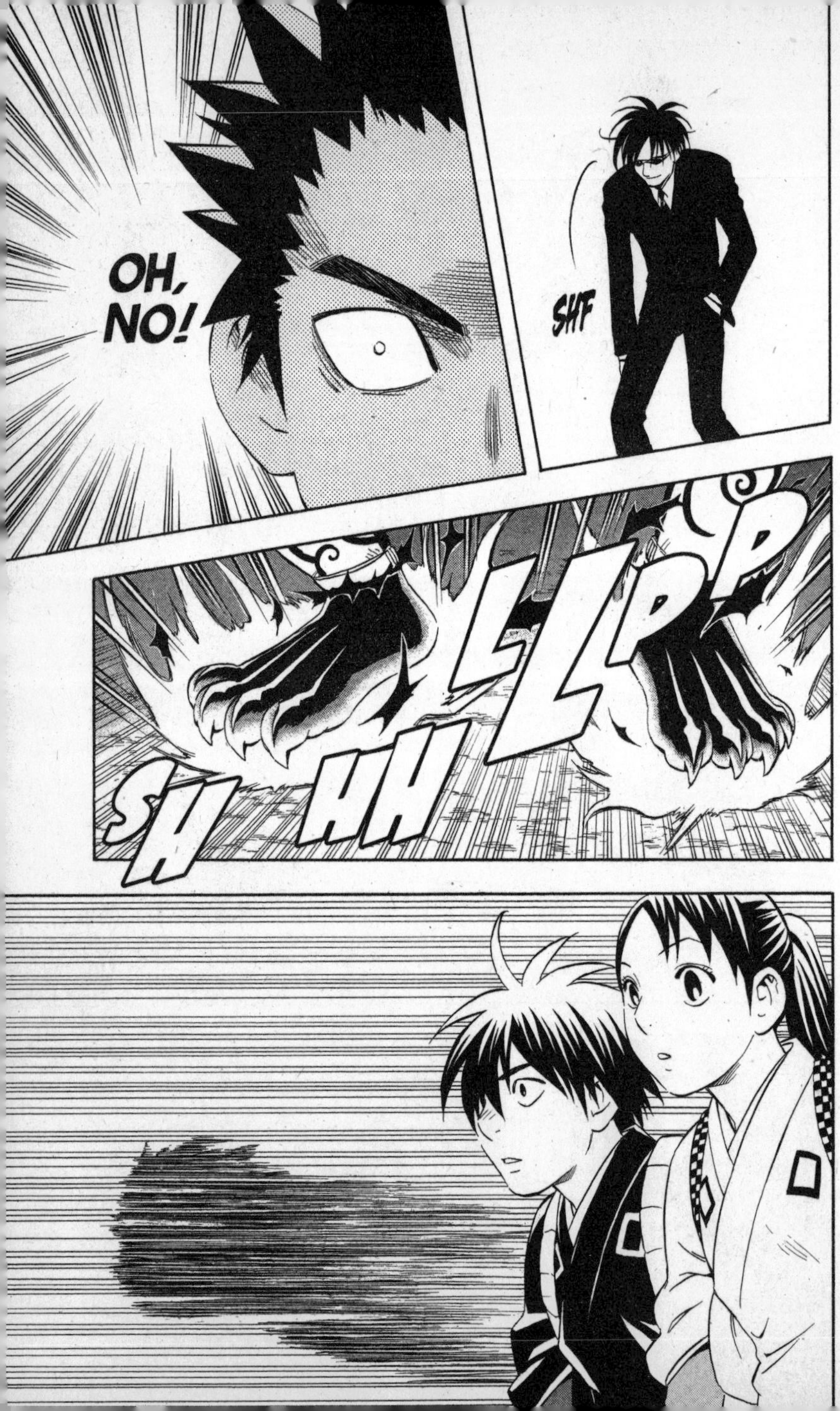
SHF
OH, NO!
SHHHLLP

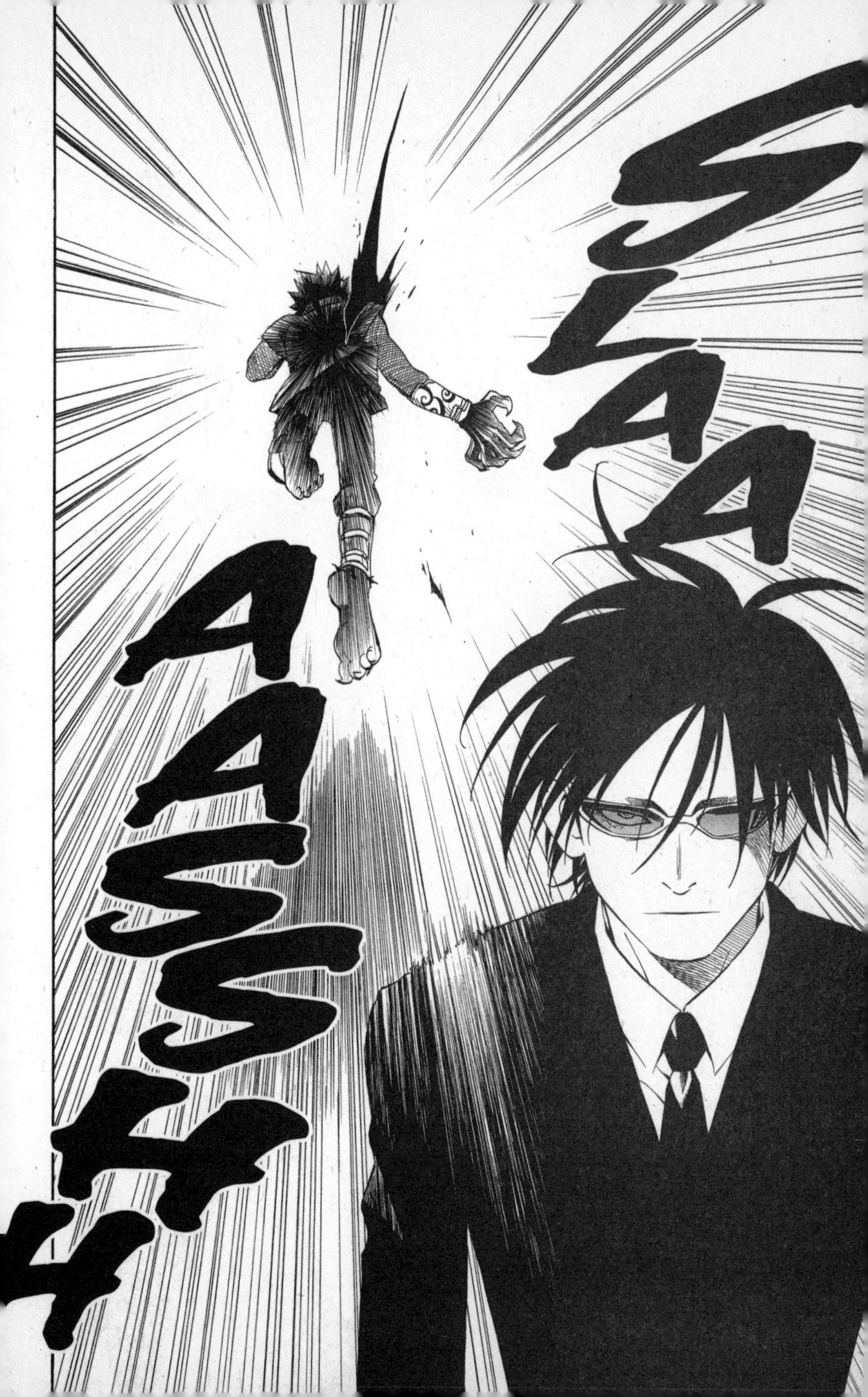
SLAAAAAASSHH

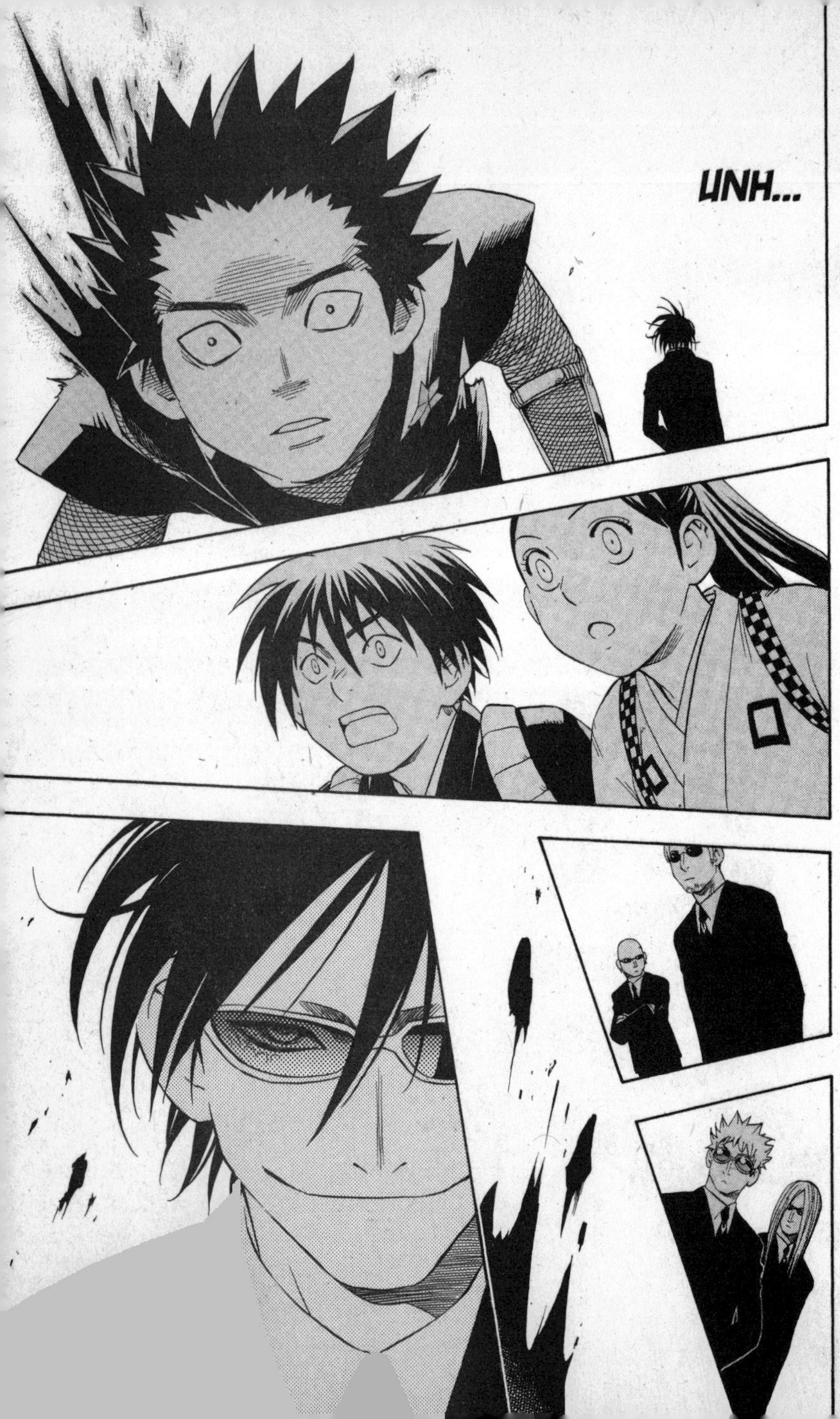
UNH...

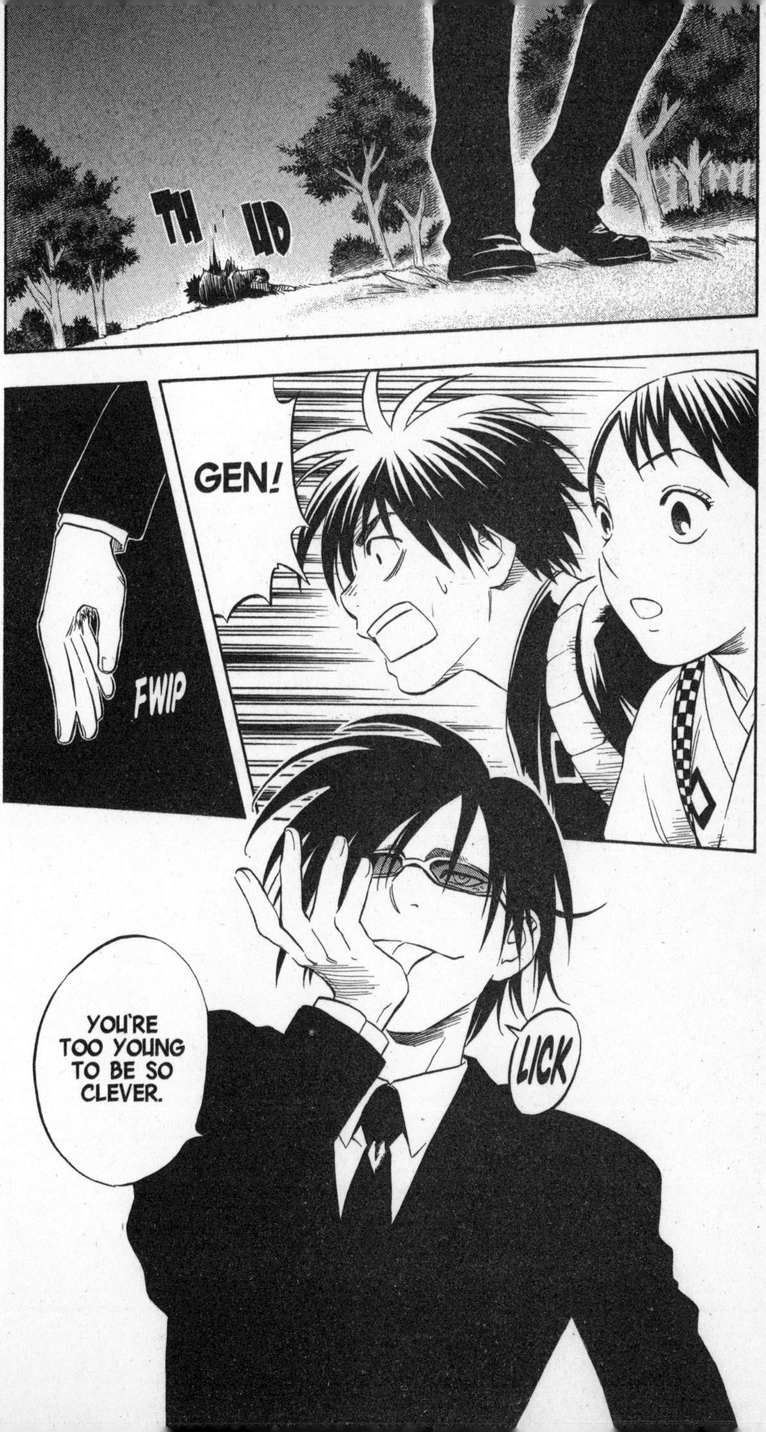
TH UD
GEN!
FWIP
LICK
YOU'RE TOO YOUNG TO BE SO CLEVER.

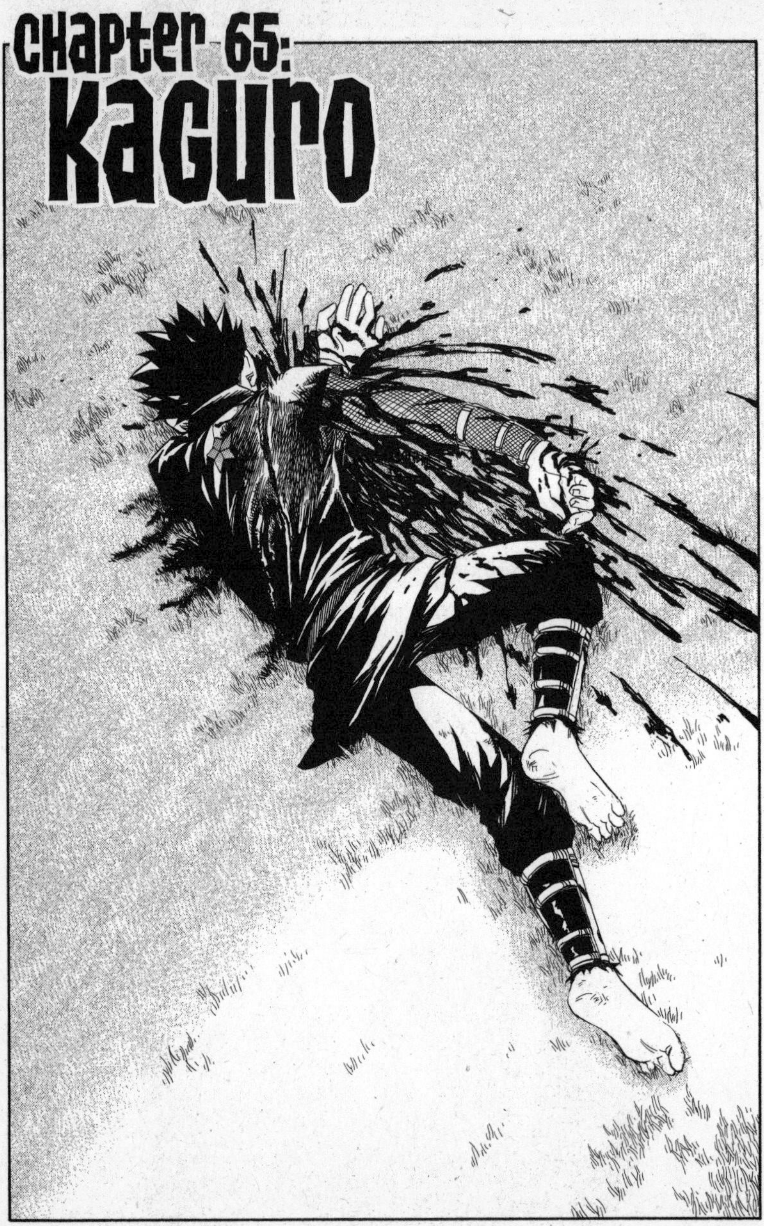
Chapter 65:
Kaguro

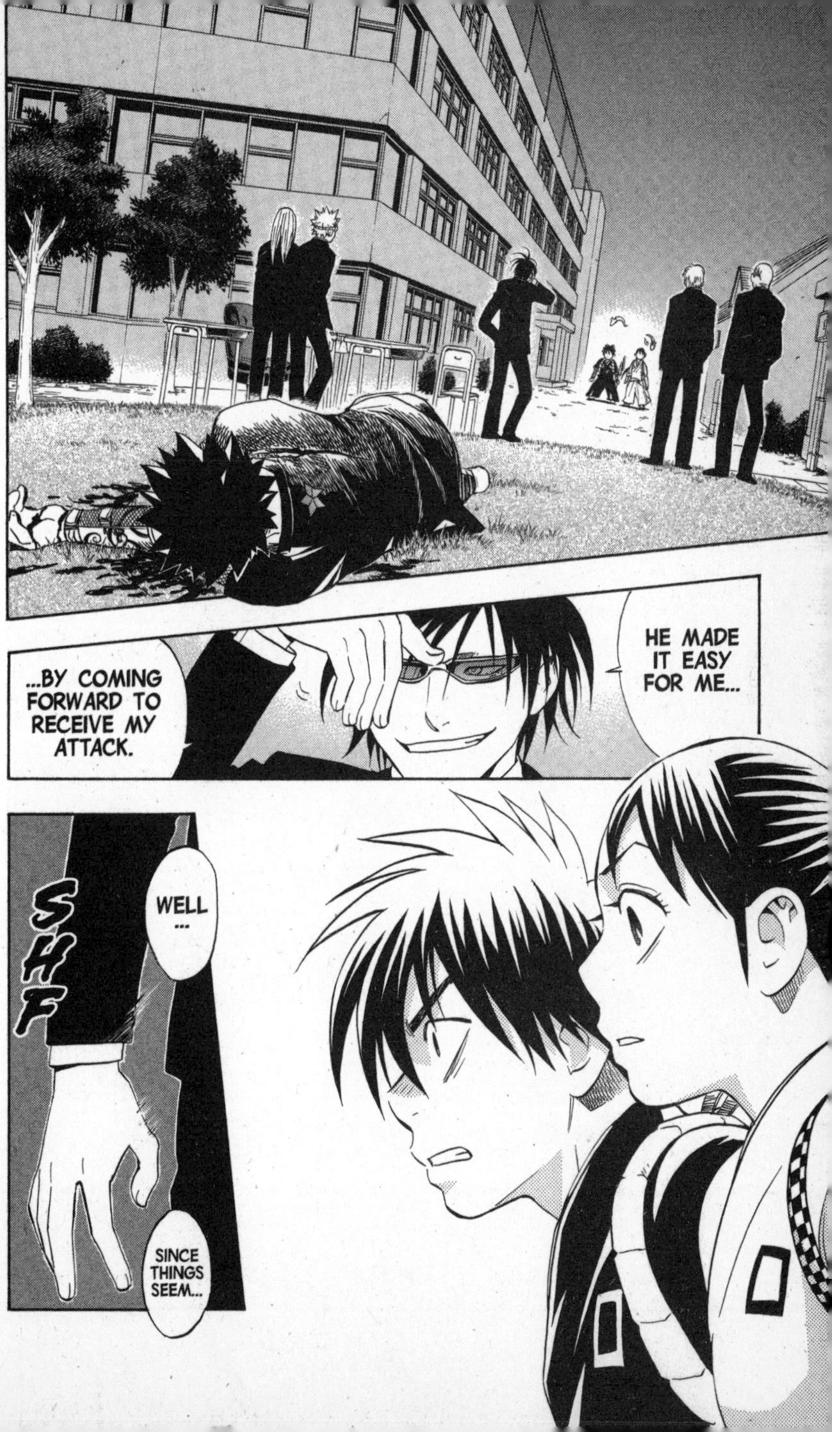
HE MADE IT EASY FOR ME...
...BY COMING FORWARD TO RECEIVE MY ATTACK.
WELL ...
SHF
SINCE THINGS SEEM...

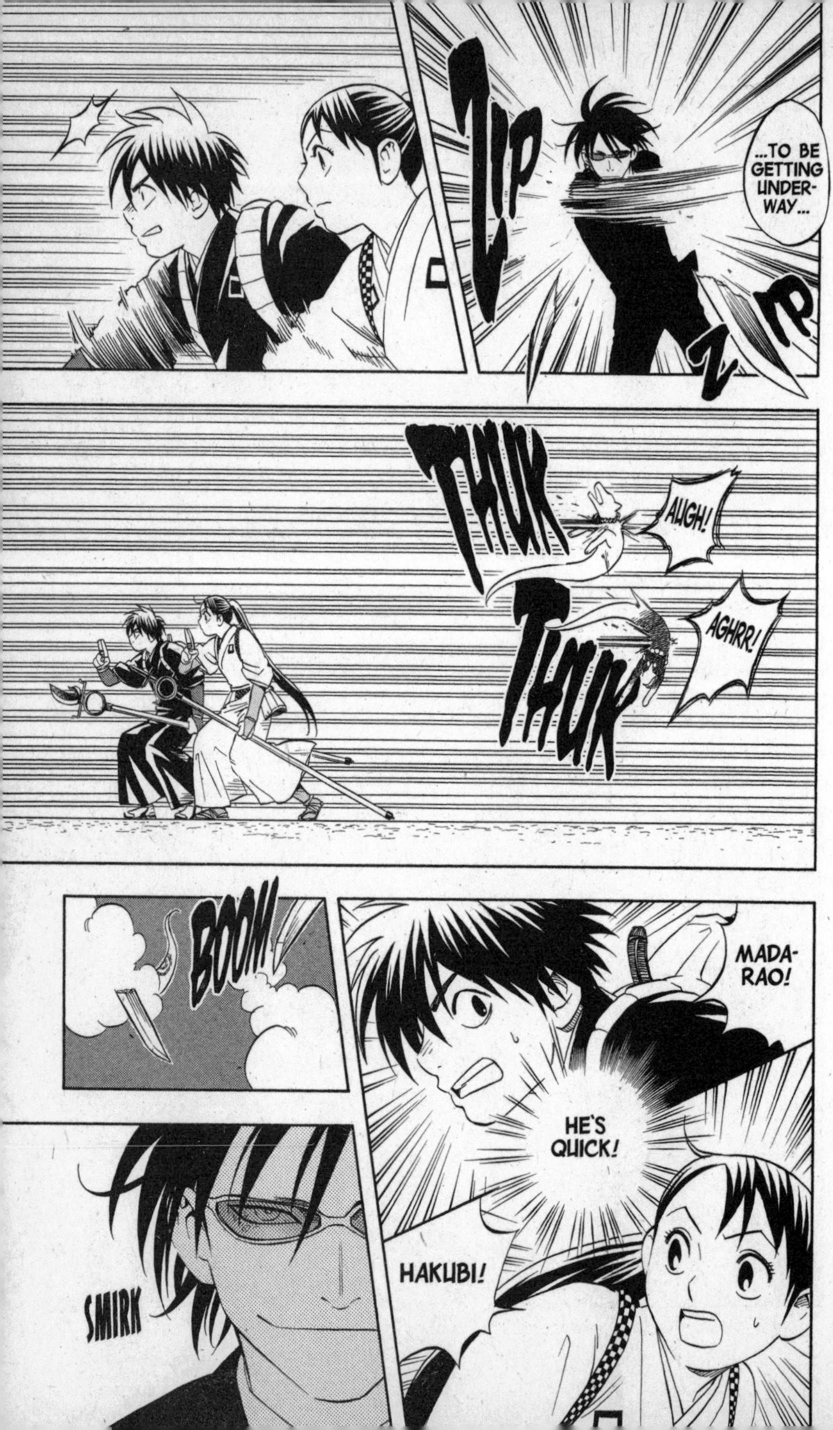
ZIP
...TO BE GETTING UNDER-WAY...
ZIP
THUK
AUGH!
THUK
AGHRR!
MADA-RAO!
HE'S QUICK!
HAKUBI!
BOOM
SMIRK

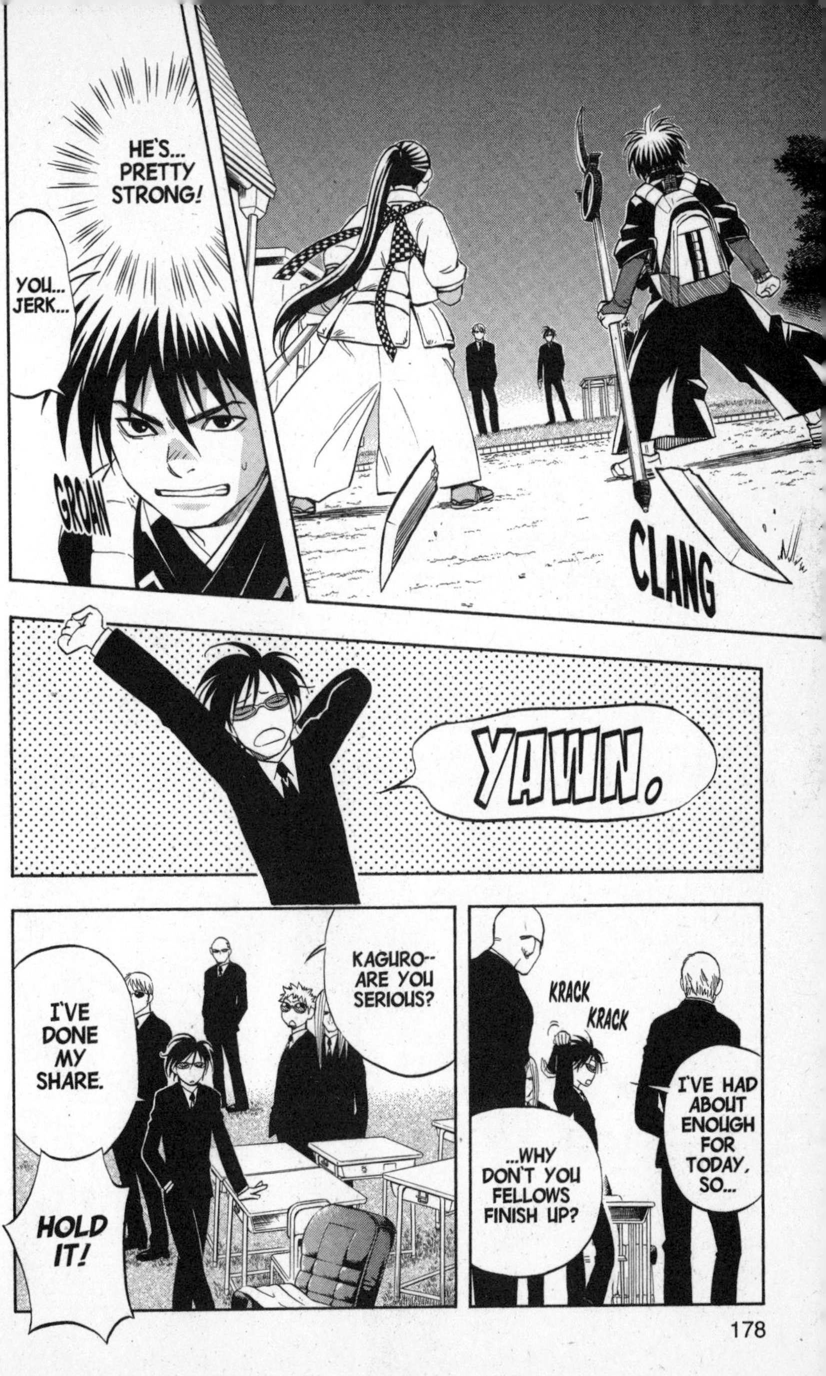
CLANG
HE'S... PRETTY STRONG!
YOU... JERK...
GROAN
YAWN.
KRACK
KRACK
I'VE HAD ABOUT ENOUGH FOR TODAY, SO...
...WHY DON'T YOU FELLOWS FINISH UP?
KAGURO-- ARE YOU SERIOUS?
I'VE DONE MY SHARE.
HOLD IT!

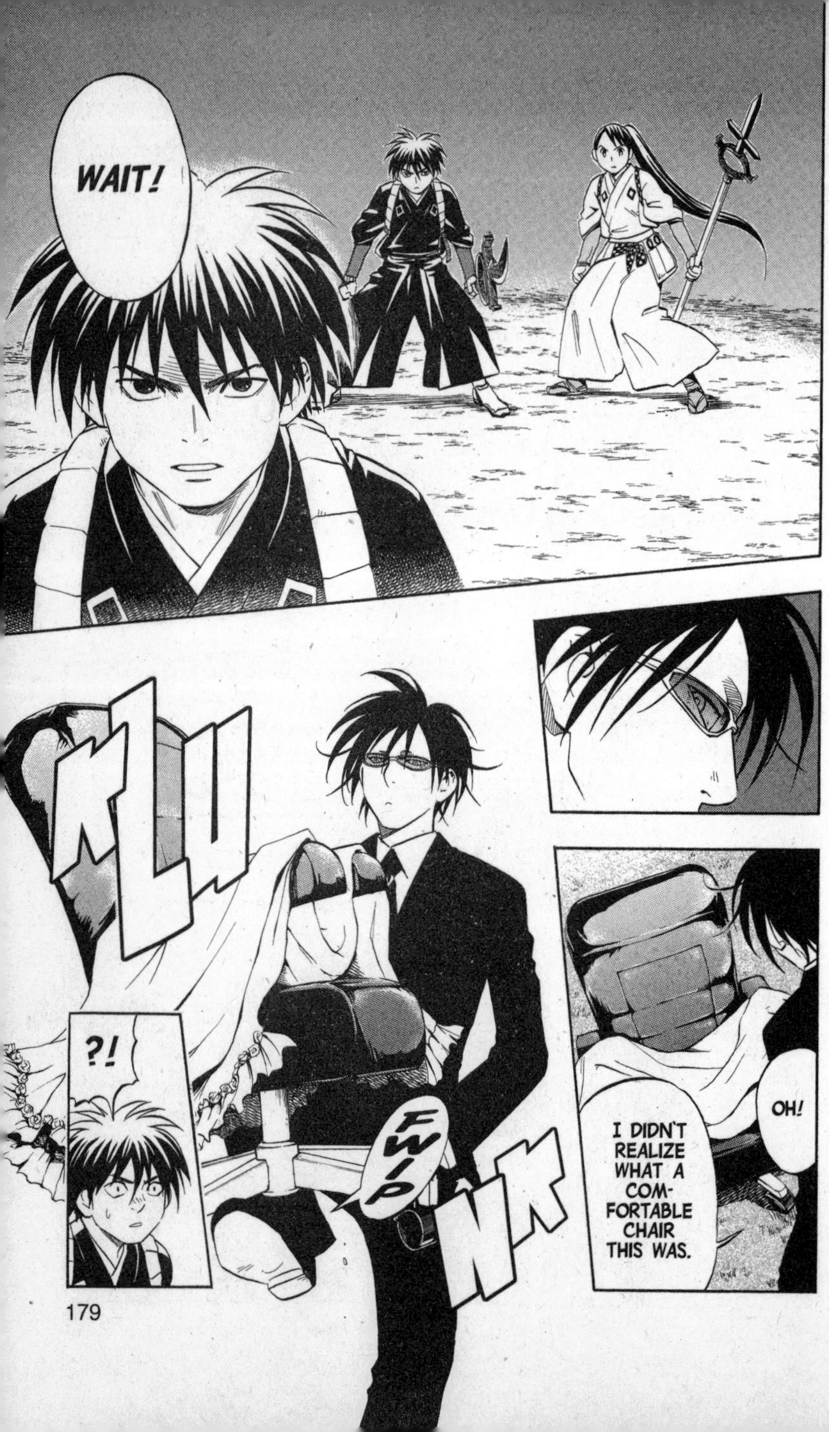
WAIT!
OH!
I DIDN'T REALIZE WHAT A COM-FORTABLE CHAIR THIS WAS.
KLUNK
FWIP
?!

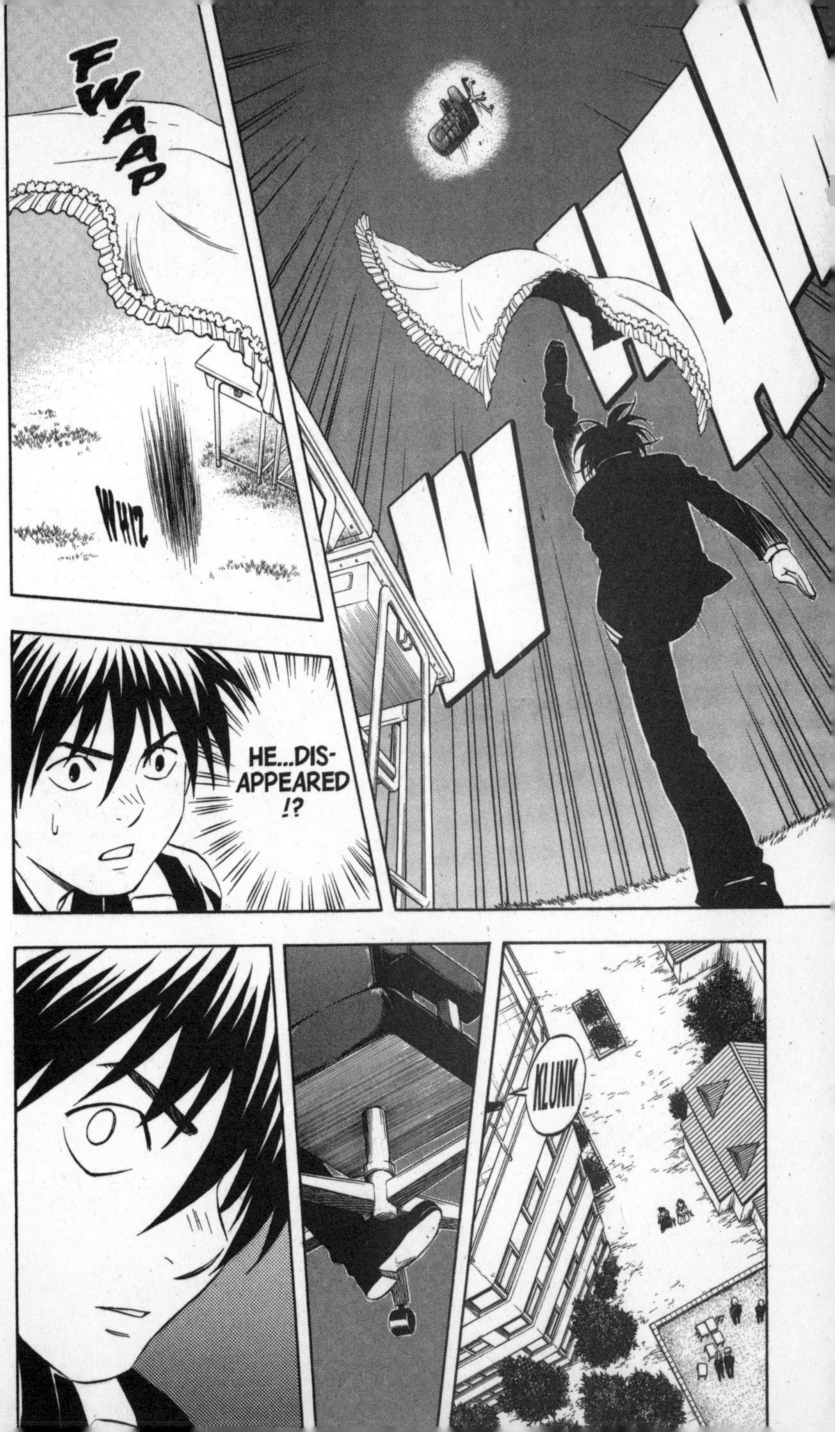
FWAAP
WHIZ
HE...DIS-APPEARED!?
KLUNK

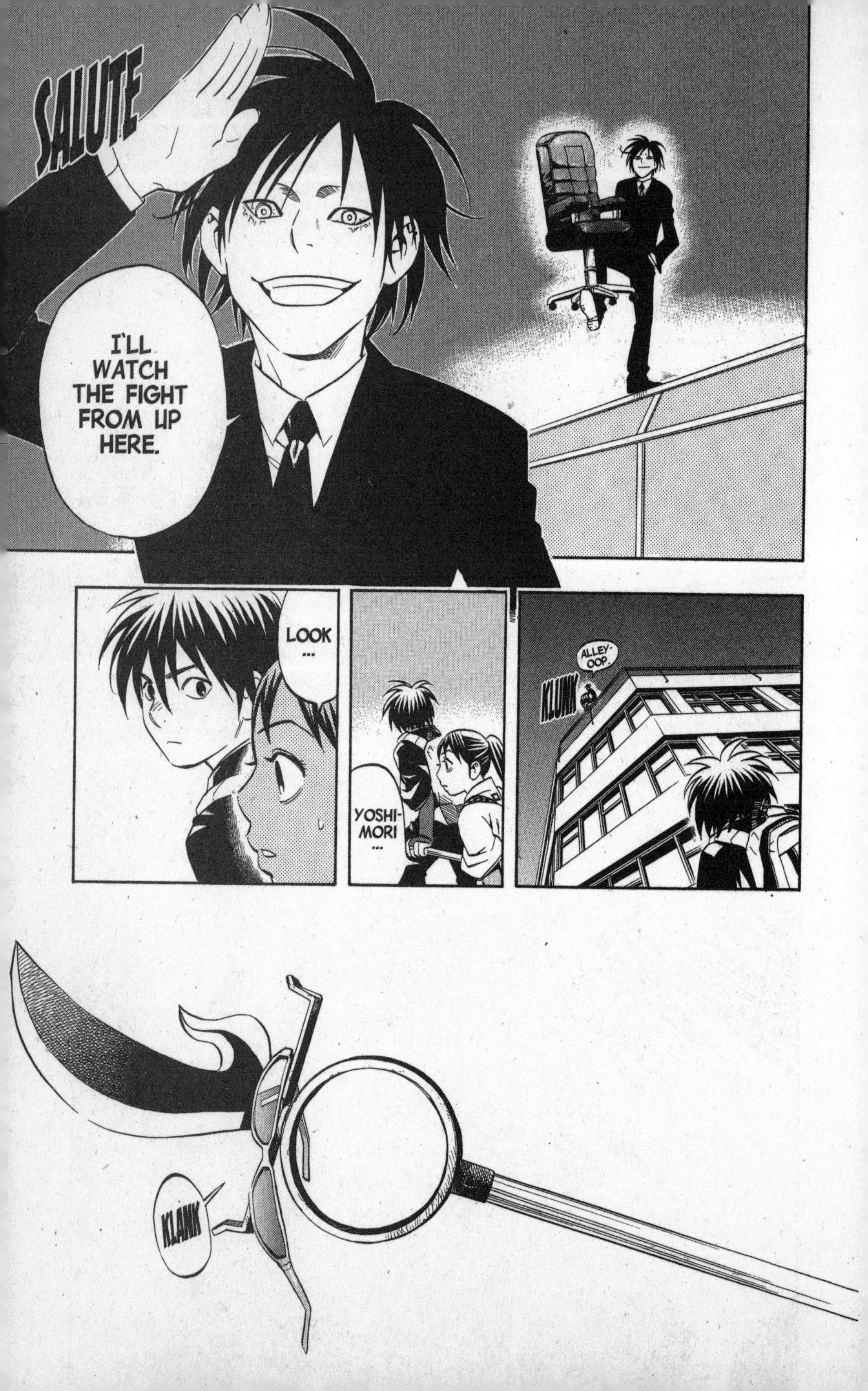
SALUTE
I'LL WATCH THE FIGHT FROM UP HERE.
ALLEY-OOP.
KLUNK
YOSHI-MORI ...
LOOK ...
KLANK

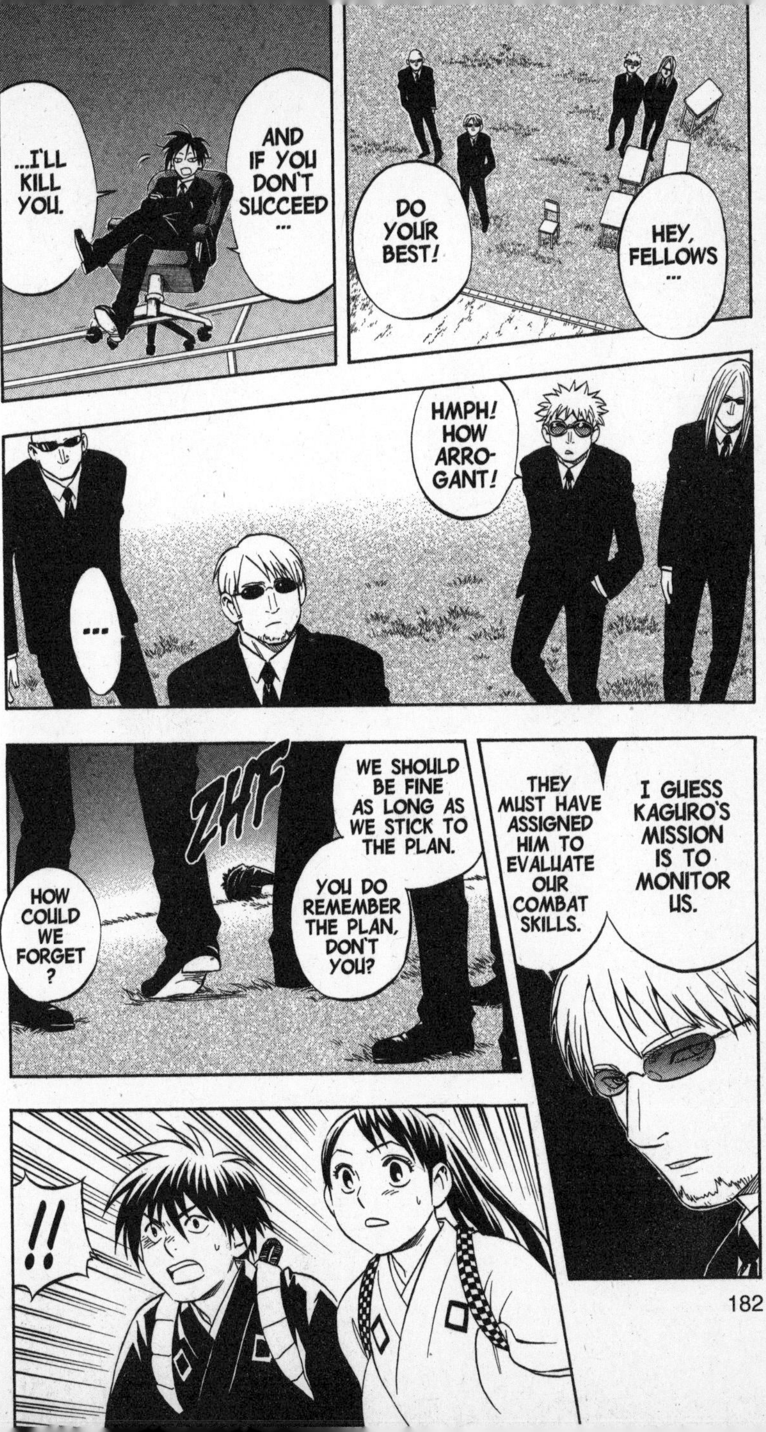
HEY, FELLOWS ...
DO YOUR BEST!
AND IF YOU DON'T SUCCEED ...
...I'LL KILL YOU.
HMPH! HOW ARRO-GANT!
...
I GUESS KAGURO'S MISSION IS TO MONITOR US.
THEY MUST HAVE ASSIGNED HIM TO EVALUATE OUR COMBAT SKILLS.
WE SHOULD BE FINE AS LONG AS WE STICK TO THE PLAN.
YOU DO REMEMBER THE PLAN, DON'T YOU?
ZHF
HOW COULD WE FORGET ?
!!

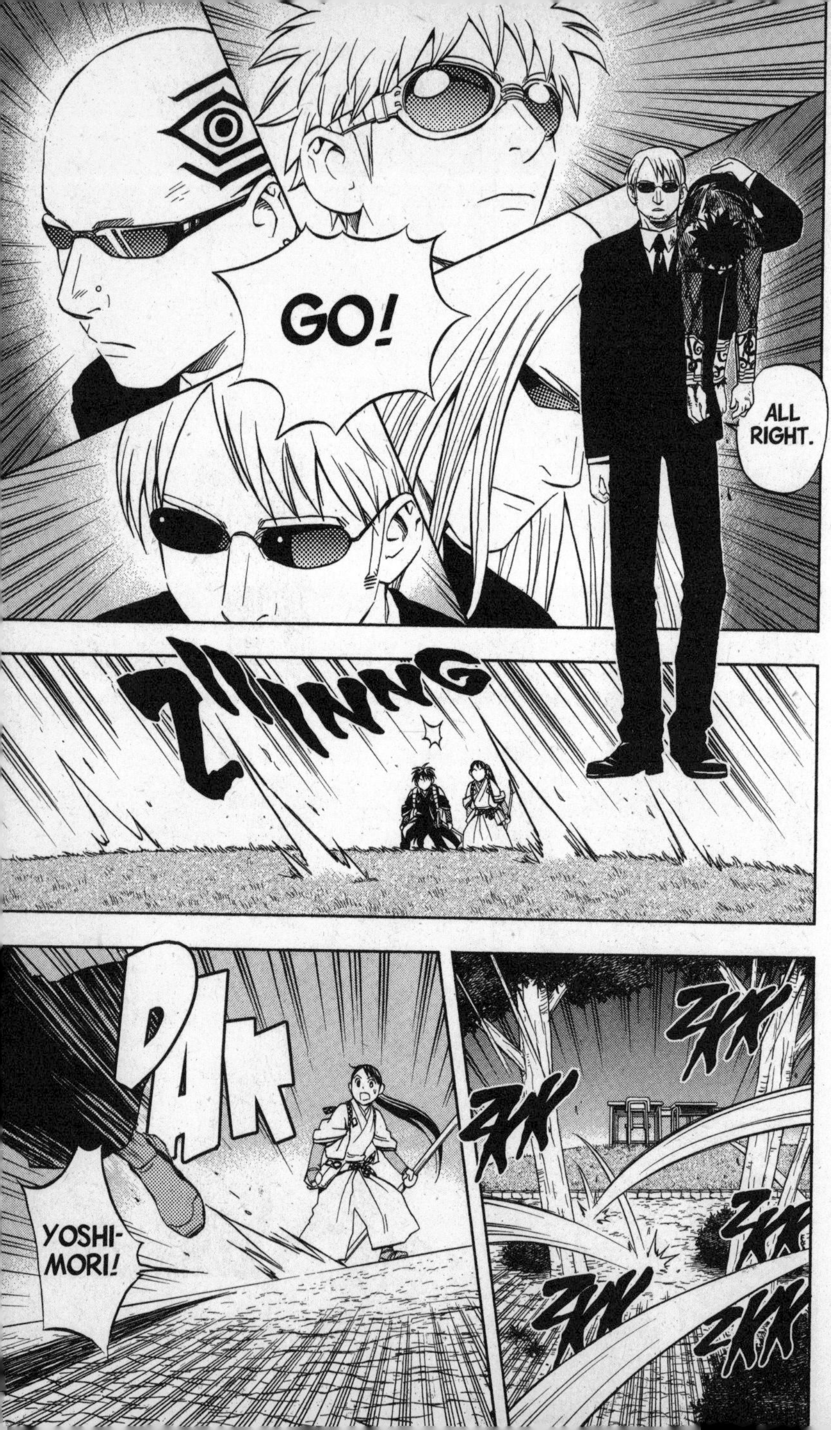
ALL RIGHT.
GO!
ZIIIINNG
ZAK
ZAK
ZAK
ZAK
ZAK
ZAK
DAK
YOSHI-
MORI!

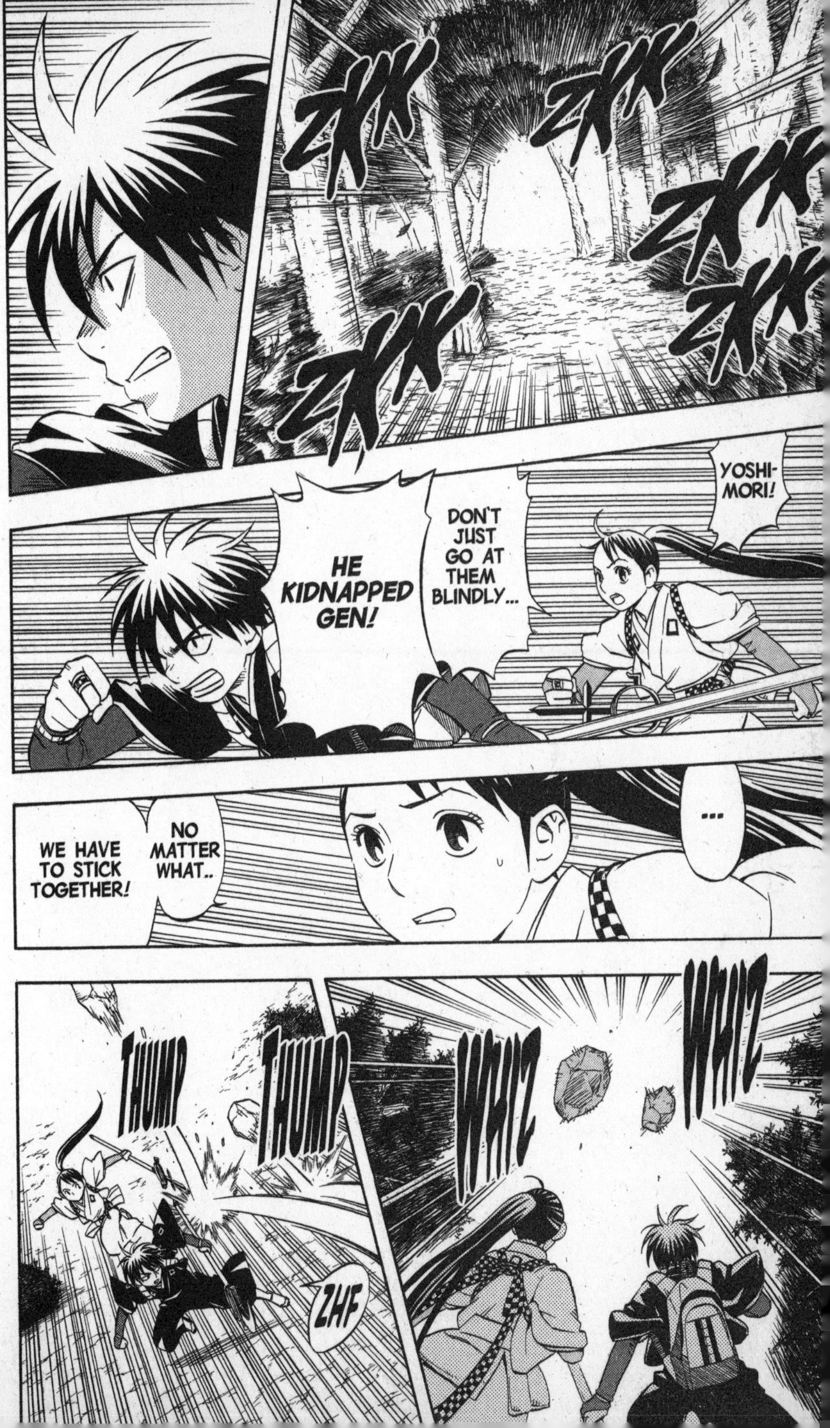
YOSHI-
MORI!
DON'T JUST GO AT THEM BLINDLY...
HE KIDNAPPED GEN!
...
NO MATTER WHAT..
WE HAVE TO STICK TOGETHER!
WHIZ
WHIZ
THUMP
THUMP
ZHF

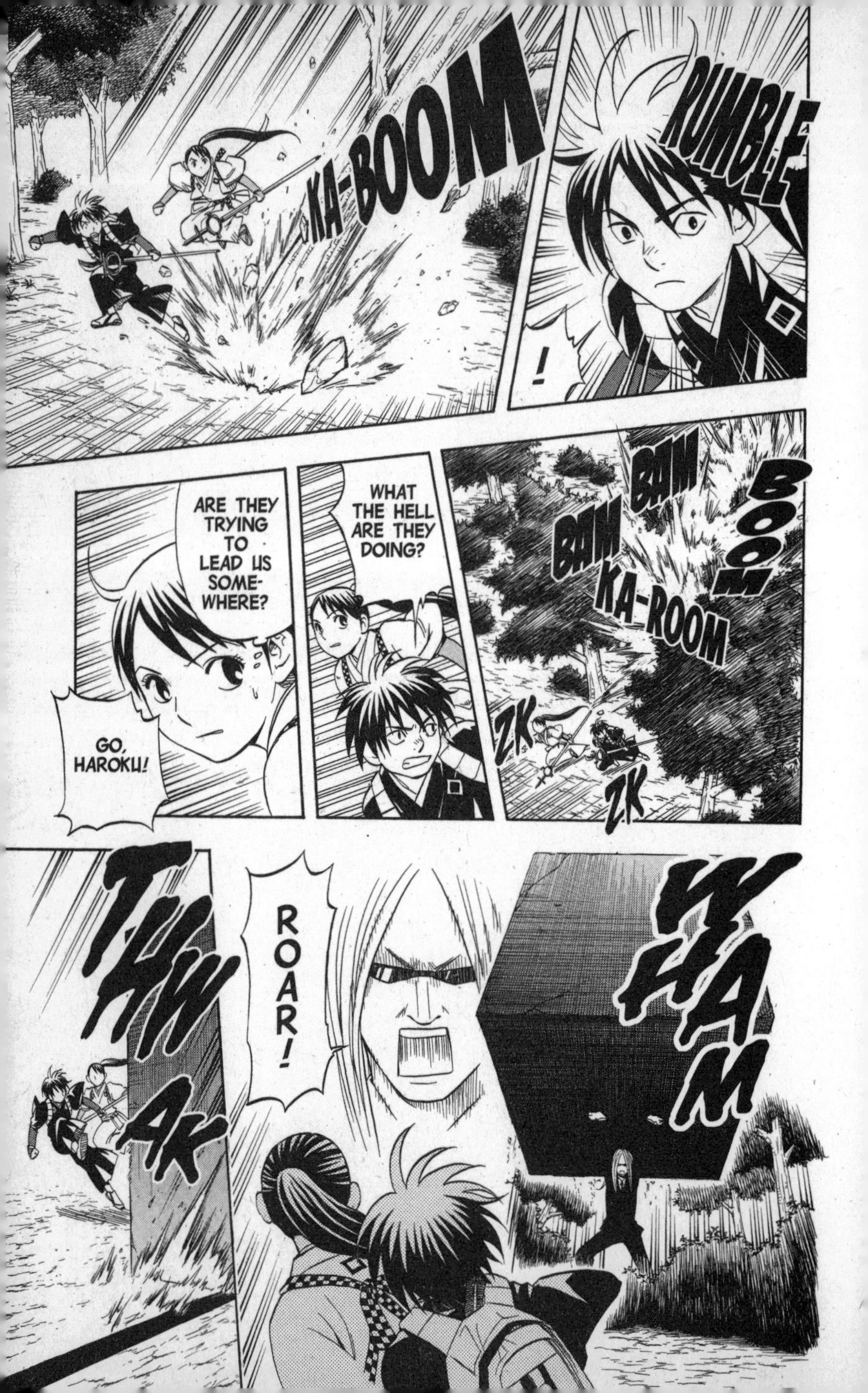
RUMBLE
!
KA-BOOM
BOOM
BAM
BAM
BAM
KA-ROOM
ZK
ZK
WHAT THE HELL ARE THEY DOING?
ARE THEY TRYING TO LEAD US SOME-WHERE?
GO, HAROKU!
WHAM
ROAR!
THWAK

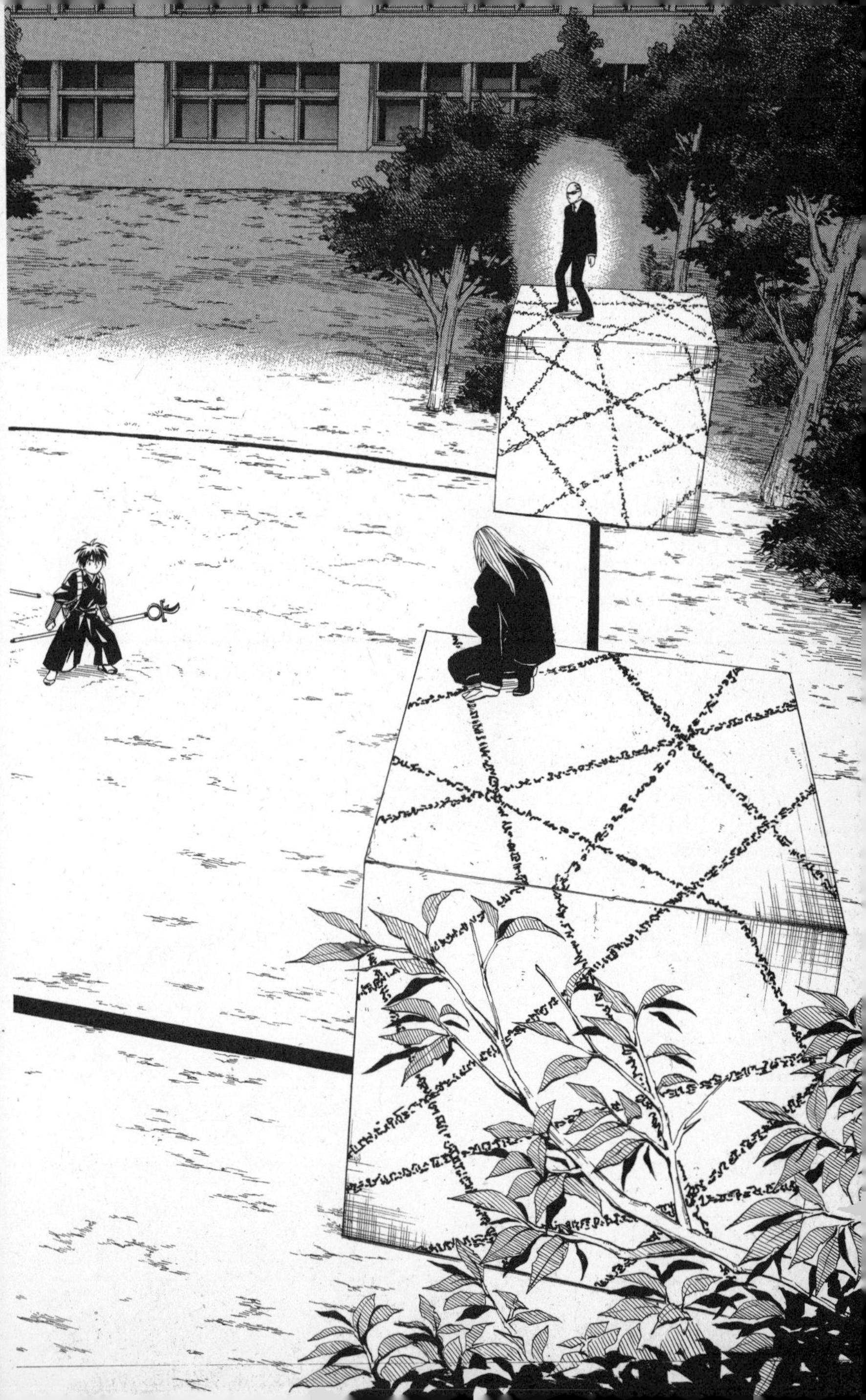

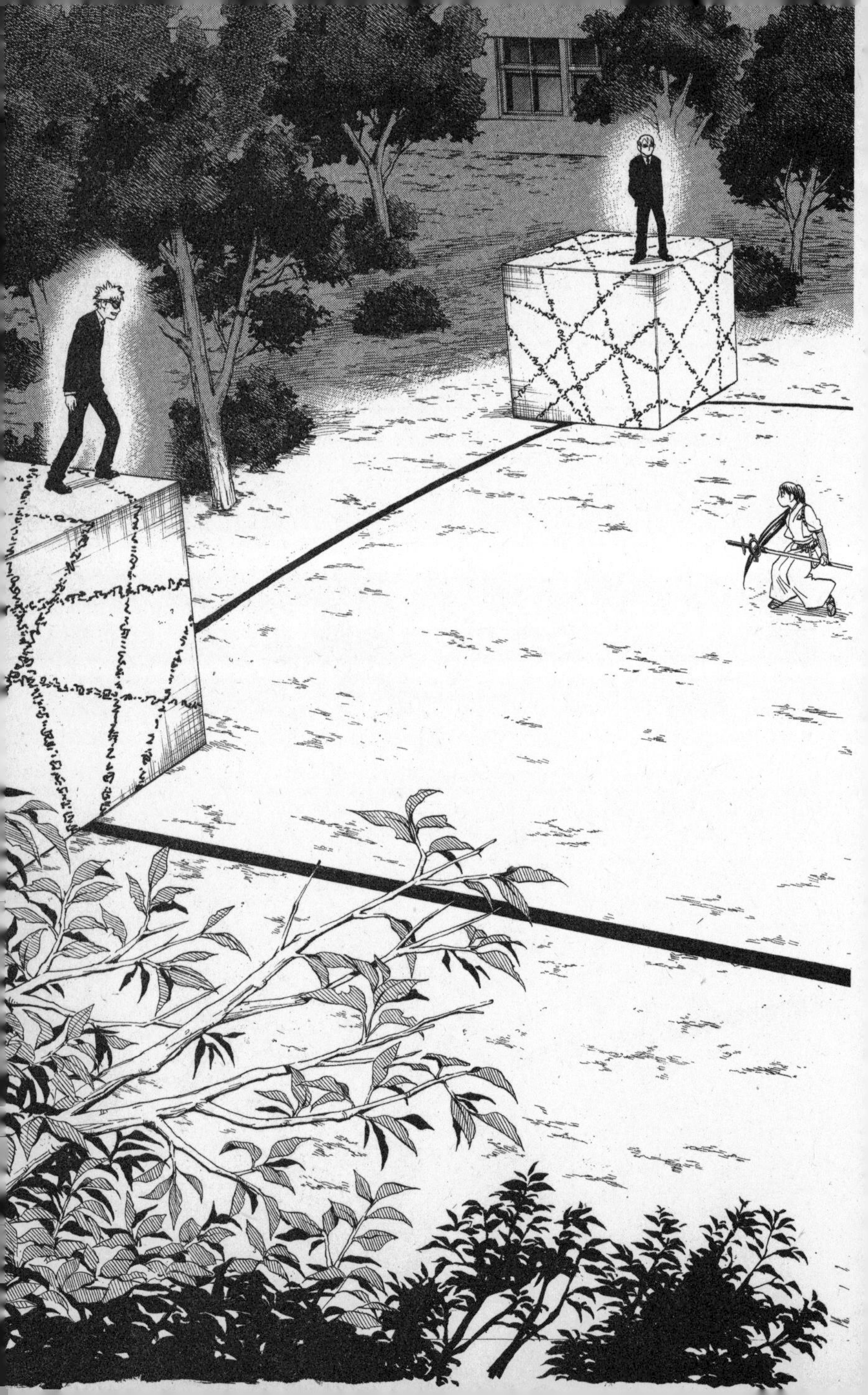

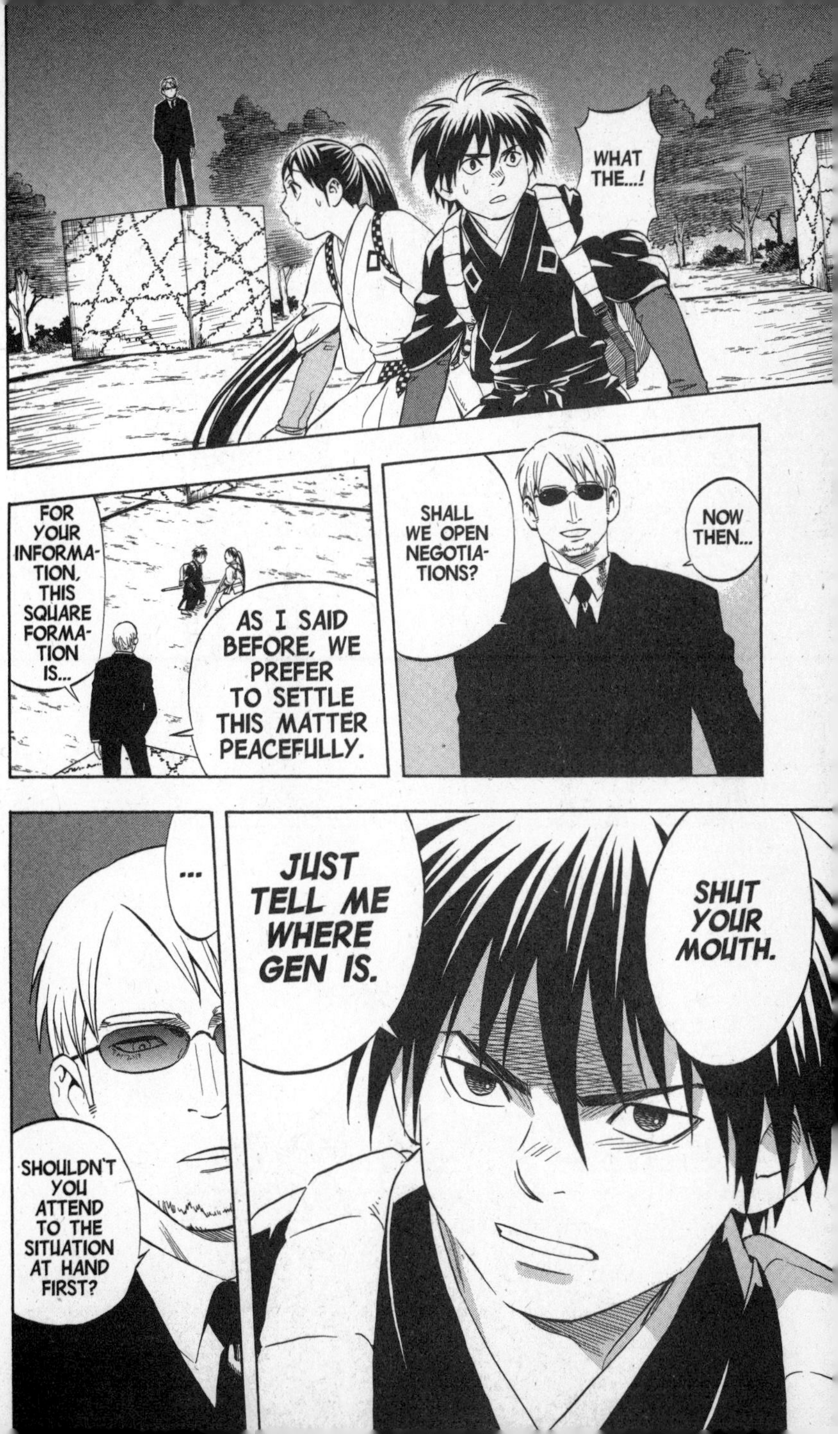
WHAT THE...!
NOW THEN...
SHALL WE OPEN NEGOTIATIONS?
AS I SAID BEFORE, WE PREFER TO SETTLE THIS MATTER PEACEFULLY.
FOR YOUR INFORMATION, THIS SQUARE FORMATION IS...
SHUT YOUR MOUTH.
JUST TELL ME WHERE GEN IS.
...
SHOULDN'T YOU ATTEND TO THE SITUATION AT HAND FIRST?

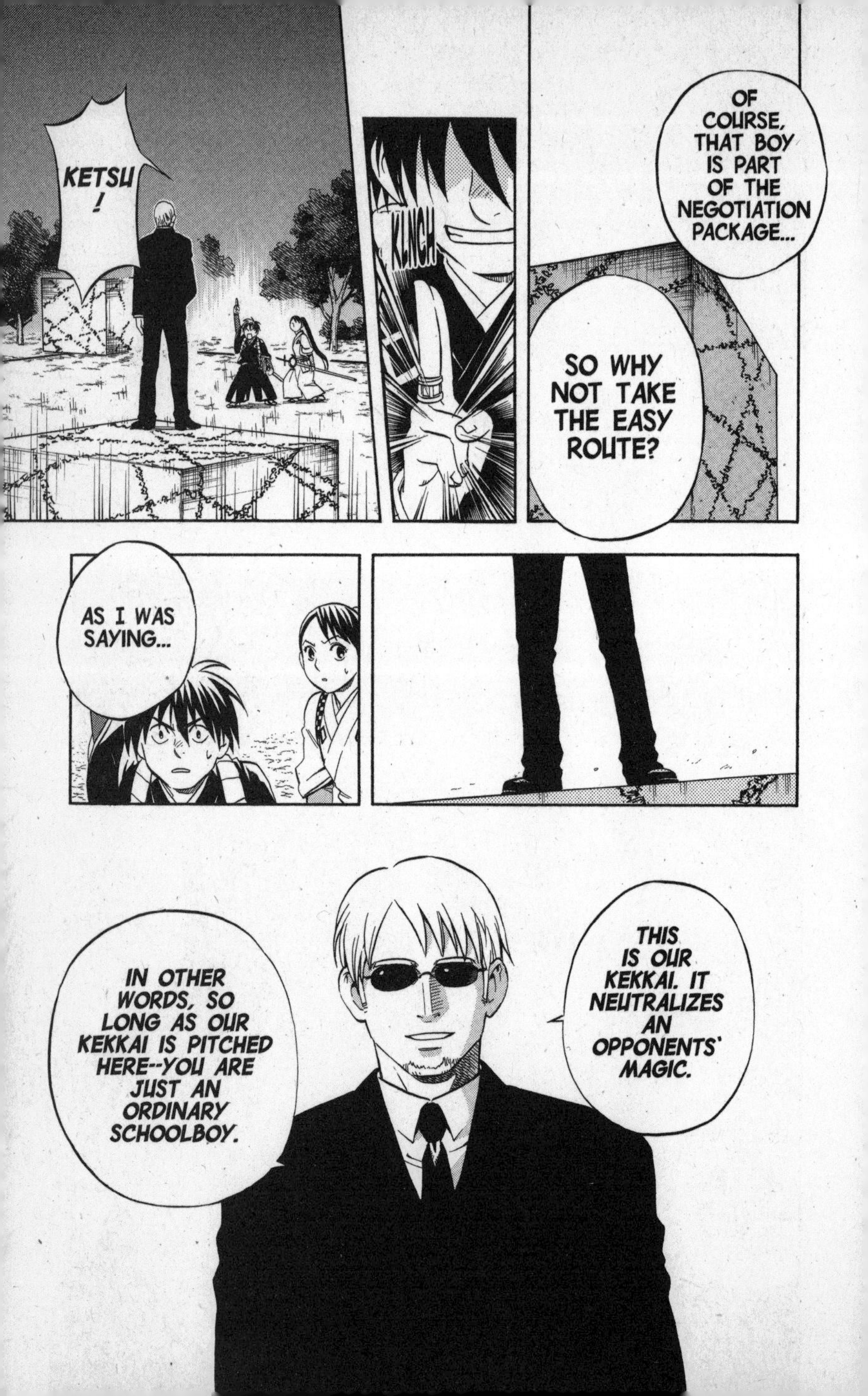
OF COURSE, THAT BOY IS PART OF THE NEGOTIATION PACKAGE...
SO WHY NOT TAKE THE EASY ROUTE?
KLINCH
KETSU!
AS I WAS SAYING...
THIS IS OUR KEKKAI. IT NEUTRALIZES AN OPPONENTS' MAGIC.
IN OTHER WORDS, SO LONG AS OUR KEKKAI IS PITCHED HERE--YOU ARE JUST AN ORDINARY SCHOOLBOY.

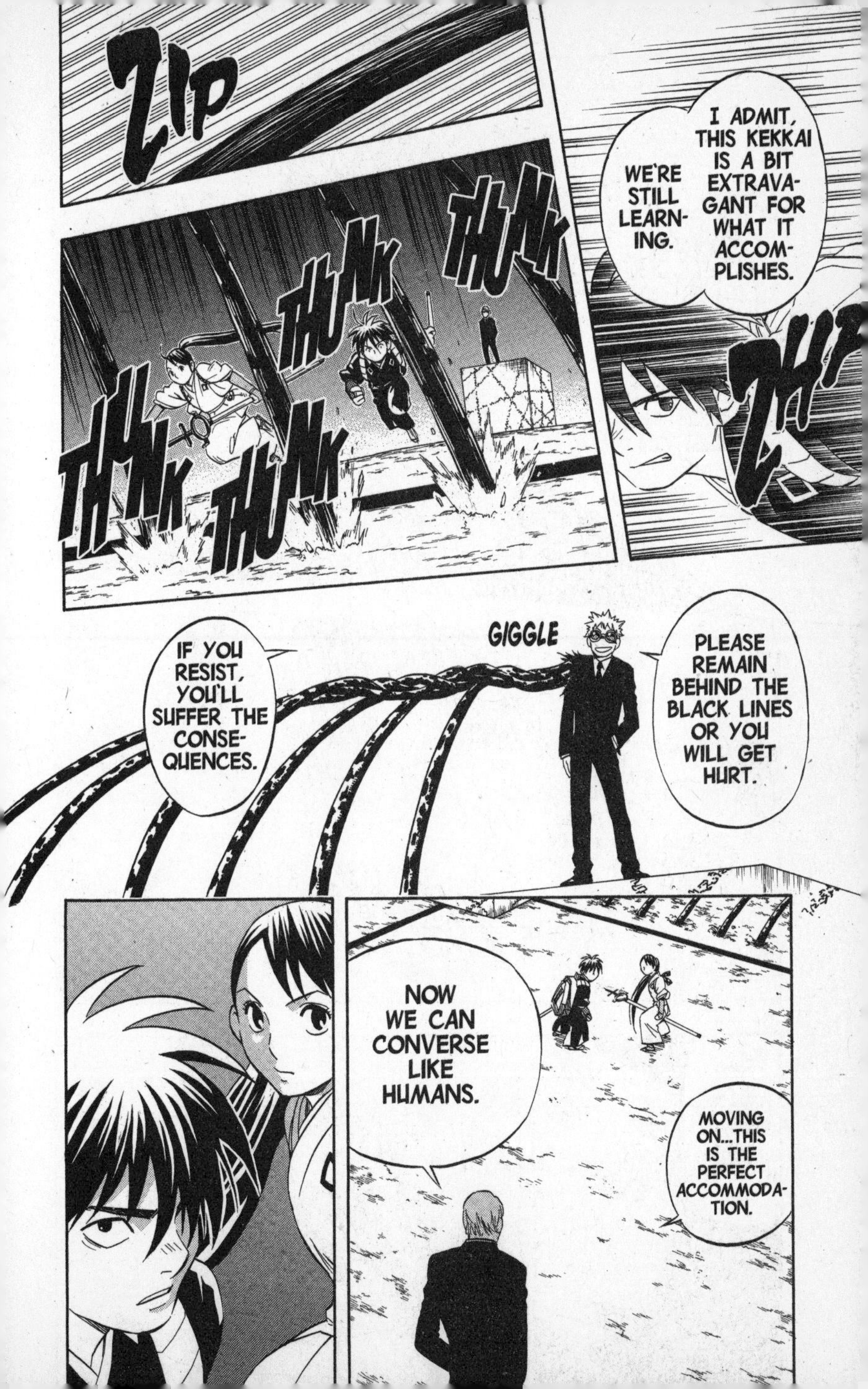
I ADMIT, THIS KEKKAI IS A BIT EXTRAVAGANT FOR WHAT IT ACCOMPLISHES.
WE'RE STILL LEARNING.
ZIP
THUNK
THUNK
THUNK
THUNK
PLEASE REMAIN BEHIND THE BLACK LINES OR YOU WILL GET HURT.
GIGGLE
IF YOU RESIST, YOU'LL SUFFER THE CONSEQUENCES.
MOVING ON...THIS IS THE PERFECT ACCOMMODATION.
NOW WE CAN CONVERSE LIKE HUMANS.

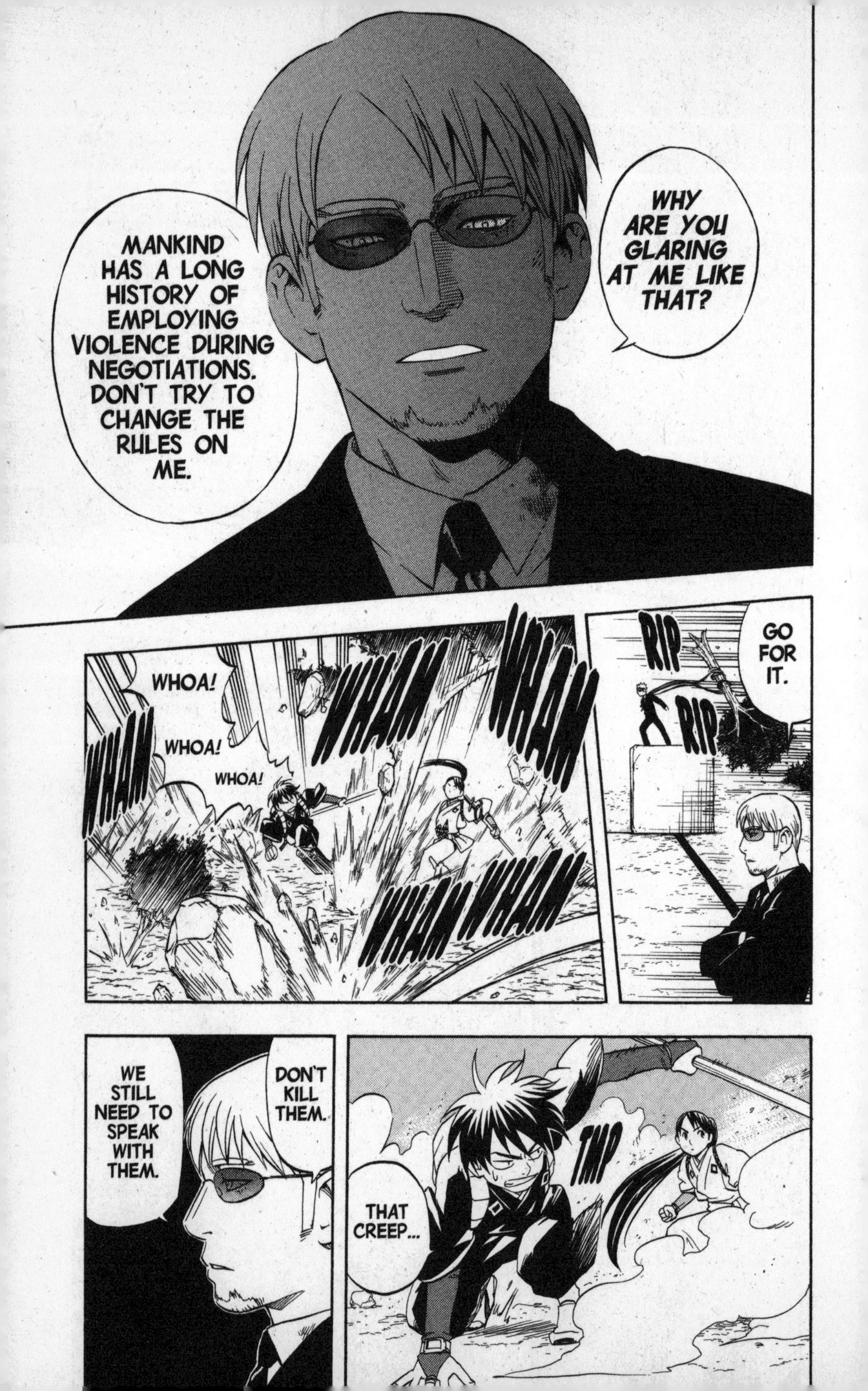
WHY ARE YOU GLARING AT ME LIKE THAT?
MANKIND HAS A LONG HISTORY OF EMPLOYING VIOLENCE DURING NEGOTIATIONS. DON'T TRY TO CHANGE THE RULES ON ME.
GO FOR IT.
RIP
RIP
WHAM
WHAM
WHOA!
WHOA!
WHOA!
WHAM WHAM
WHAM
THP
THAT CREEP...
DON'T KILL THEM.
WE STILL NEED TO SPEAK WITH THEM.

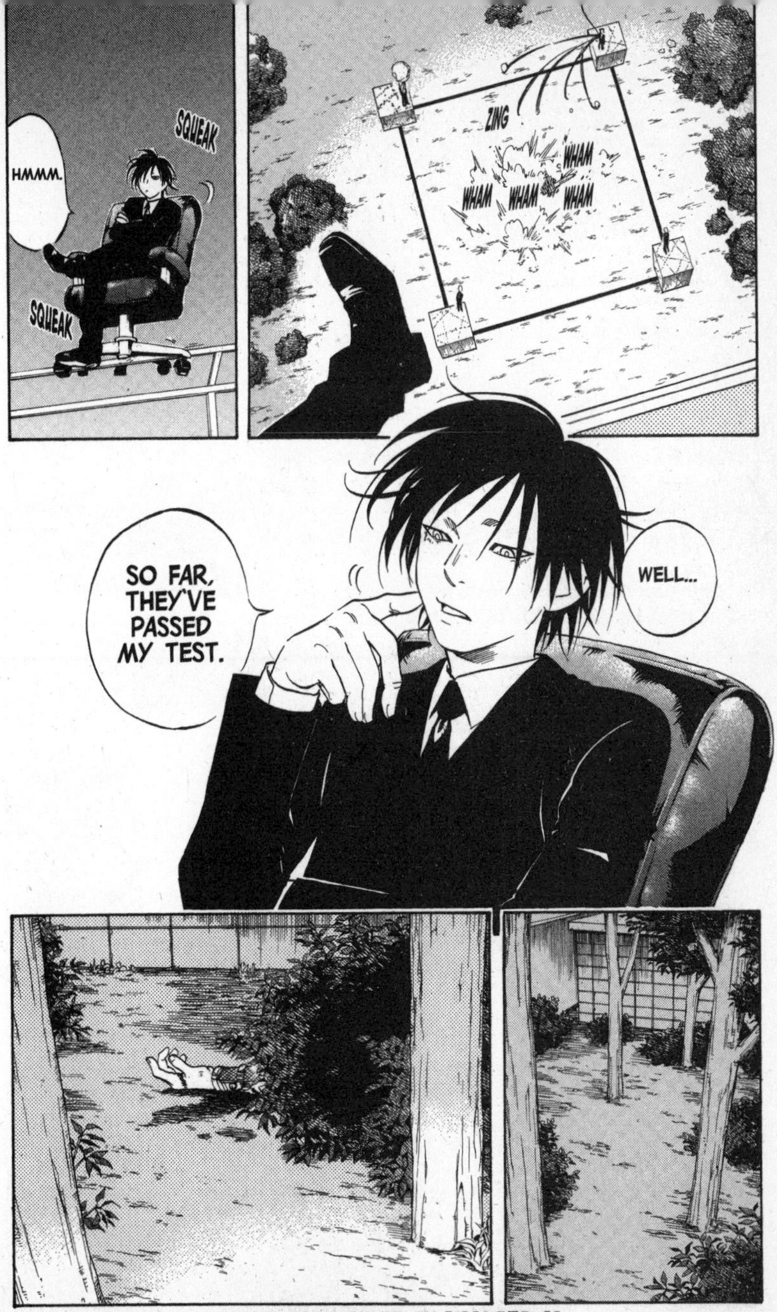
ZING
WHAM
WHAM
WHAM
WHAM
SQUEAK
HMMM.
SQUEAK
WELL...
SO FAR, THEY'VE PASSED MY TEST.

TO BE CONTINUED IN VOLUME 8!

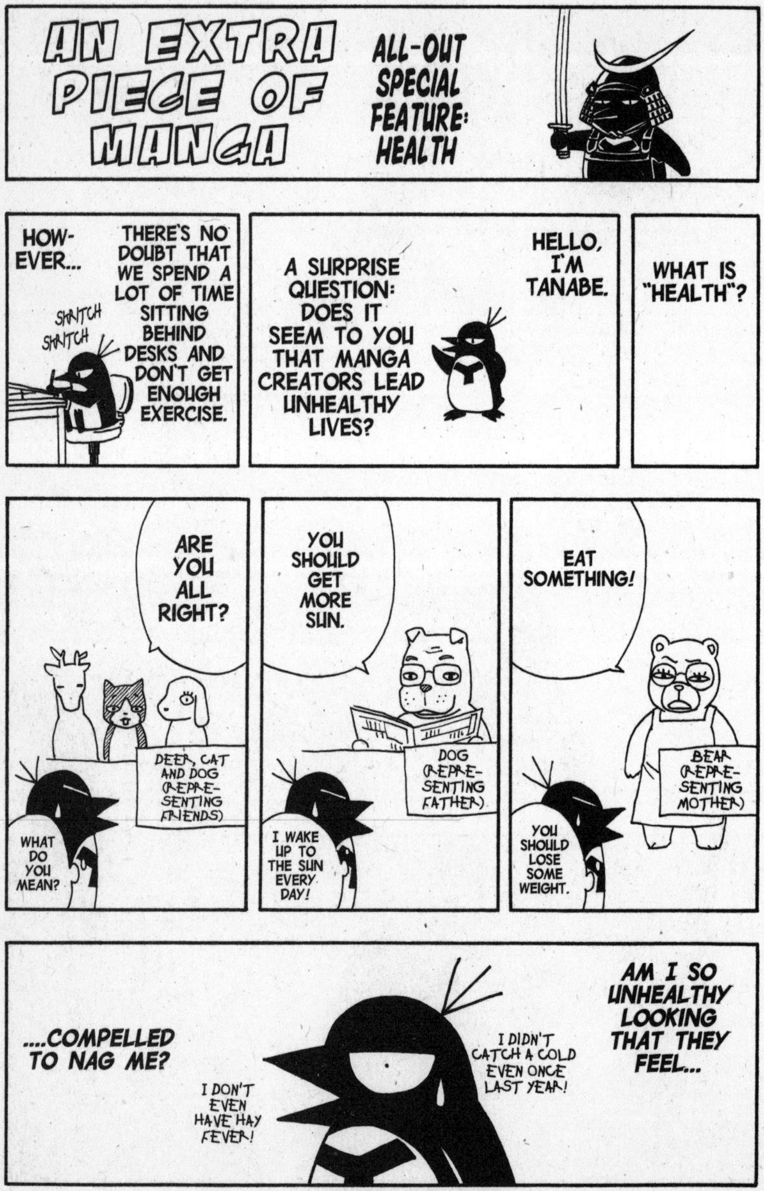
ALL-OUT SPECIAL FEATURE: HEALTH
AN EXTRA PIECE OF MANGA
WHAT IS "HEALTH"?
HELLO, I'M TANABE.
A SURPRISE QUESTION: DOES IT SEEM TO YOU THAT MANGA CREATORS LEAD UNHEALTHY LIVES?
HOW-EVER...
THERE'S NO DOUBT THAT WE SPEND A LOT OF TIME SITTING BEHIND DESKS AND DON'T GET ENOUGH EXERCISE.
SKRITCH SKRITCH
EAT SOMETHING!
BEAR (REPRE-SENTING MOTHER)
YOU SHOULD LOSE SOME WEIGHT.
YOU SHOULD GET MORE SUN.
DOG (REPRE-SENTING FATHER)
I WAKE UP TO THE SUN EVERY DAY!
ARE YOU ALL RIGHT?
DEER, CAT AND DOG (REPRE-SENTING FRIENDS)
WHAT DO YOU MEAN?
AM I SO UNHEALTHY LOOKING THAT THEY FEEL...
I DIDN'T CATCH A COLD EVEN ONCE LAST YEAR!
I DON'T EVEN HAVE HAY FEVER!
....COMPELLED TO NAG ME?

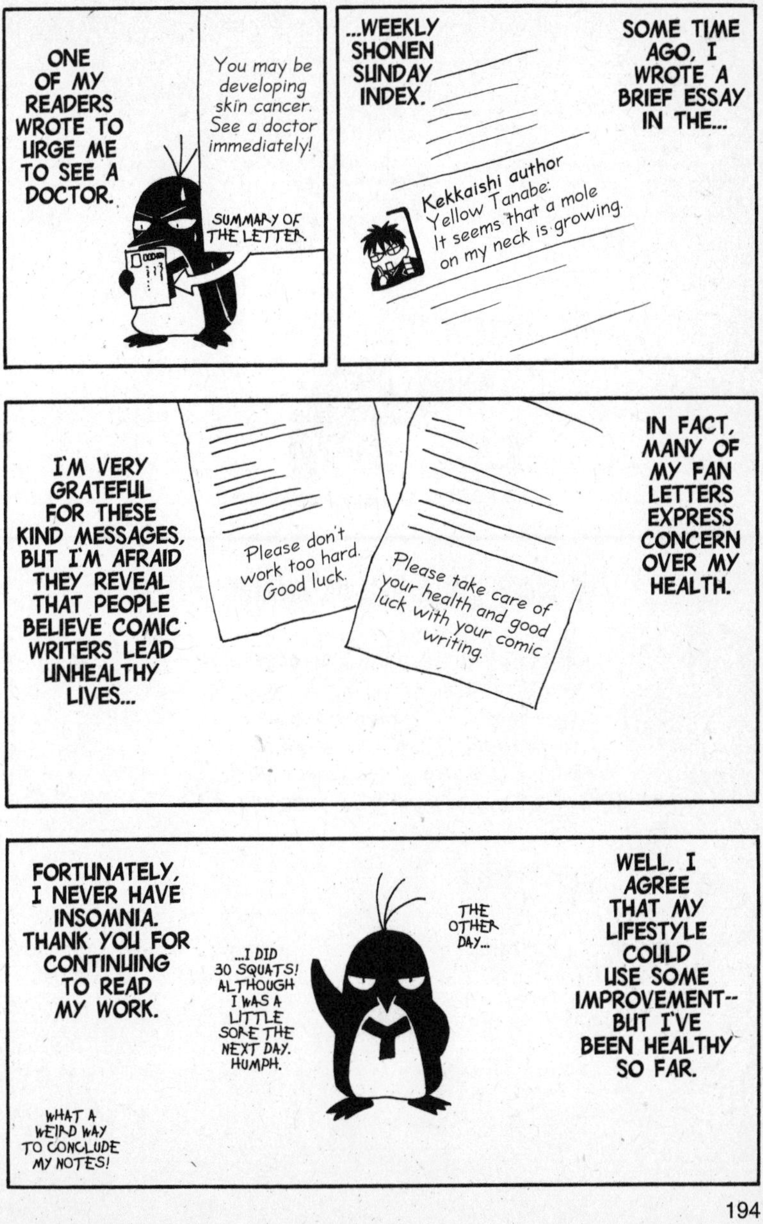
SOME TIME AGO, I WROTE A BRIEF ESSAY IN THE...
...WEEKLY SHONEN SUNDAY INDEX.
Kekkaishi author Yellow Tanabe: It seems that a mole on my neck is growing.
ONE OF MY READERS WROTE TO URGE ME TO SEE A DOCTOR.
You may be developing skin cancer. See a doctor immediately!
SUMMARY OF THE LETTER.
IN FACT, MANY OF MY FAN LETTERS EXPRESS CONCERN OVER MY HEALTH.
Please take care of your health and good luck with your comic writing.
Please don't work too hard. Good luck.
I'M VERY GRATEFUL FOR THESE KIND MESSAGES, BUT I'M AFRAID THEY REVEAL THAT PEOPLE BELIEVE COMIC WRITERS LEAD UNHEALTHY LIVES...
WELL, I AGREE THAT MY LIFESTYLE COULD USE SOME IMPROVEMENT-- BUT I'VE BEEN HEALTHY SO FAR.
THE OTHER DAY...
...I DID 30 SQUATS! ALTHOUGH I WAS A LITTLE SORE THE NEXT DAY. HUMPH.
FORTUNATELY, I NEVER HAVE INSOMNIA. THANK YOU FOR CONTINUING TO READ MY WORK.
WHAT A WEIRD WAY TO CONCLUDE MY NOTES!

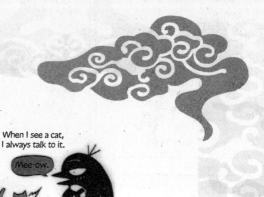

When I see a cat,
I always talk to it.

Mee-ow.

MESSAGE FROM YELLOW TANABE

I definitely like cats more than dogs. I love
how self-centered cats are. But I've never
had a cat as a pet. Although I've had
parakeets and goldfish—the kinds of
creatures cats love to eat. What I really
want to have as a pet is...a penguin.

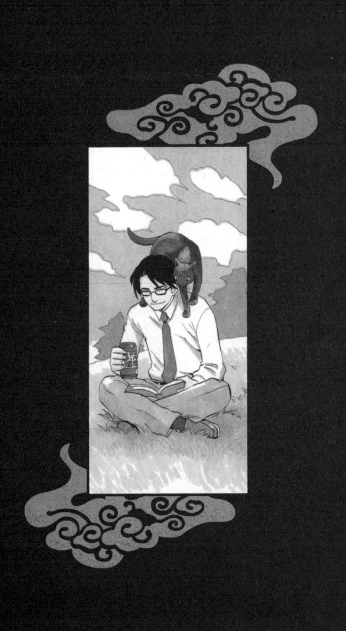

Fullmetal Alchemist Profiles

Get the background story and world history of the manga, plus:

- Character bios
- New, original artwork
- Interview with creator Hiromu Arakawa
- Bonus manga episode only available in this book

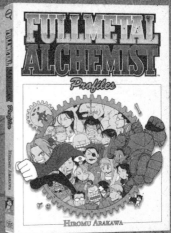

Fullmetal Alchemist Anime Profiles

Stay on top of your favorite episodes and characters with:

- Actual cel artwork from the TV series
- Summaries of all 51 TV episodes
- Definitive cast biographies
- Exclusive poster for your wall

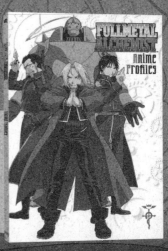

KEKKAISHI

VOLUME 7
VIZ MEDIA EDITION
STORY AND ART BY YELLOW TANABE

Translation/Yuko Sawada
Touch-up Art & Lettering/Stephen Dutro
Cover Design & Graphic Layout/Amy Martin
Editor/Annette Roman

Managing Editor/Annette Roman
Editorial Director/Elizabeth Kawasaki
Editor in Chief/Alvin Lu
Sr. Director of Acquisitions/Rika Inouye
Senior VP of Marketing/Liza Coppola
Exec. VP of Sales & Marketing/John Easum
Publisher/Hyoe Narita

Published by VIZ Media, LLC
P.O. Box 77010
San Francisco, CA 94107

10 9 8 7 6 5 4 3 2 1
First printing, November 2006

www.viz.com

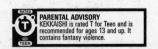

PARENTAL ADVISORY
KEKKAISHI is rated T for Teen and is
recommended for ages 13 and up. It
contains fantasy violence.

store.viz.com